D0212889

A
Bibliography
of
Theatre Technology

A
Bibliography
of
Theatre Technology

Acoustics and Sound, Lighting, Properties, and Scenery

John T. Howard, Jr.

Greenwood Press
Westport, Connecticut ● London, England

0 16.792
H 84 f

Library of Congress Cataloging in Publication Data

Howard, John T.
  A bibliography of theatre technology.

  Includes indexes.
    1. Theaters—Stage-setting and scenery—Bibliography.
2. Stage lighting—Bibliography. 3. Architectural
acoustics—Bibliography. 4. Theaters—Construction—
Bibliography. I. Title.
Z5784.S8H68   [PN2091.S8]   016.792'025   81-7204
ISBN 0-313-22839-6 (lib. bdg.)   AACR2

Library of Congress Catalog Card Number: 81-7204
ISBN: 0-313-22839-6

First published in 1982

Greenwood Press
A division of Congressional Information Service, Inc.
88 Post Road West, Westport, Connecticut 06881

Printed in the United States of America

10 9 8 7 6 5 4 3 2 1

DEDICATED TO
ELEANOR, JACK,
MARGO, and SUSAN

Contents

Preface

This bibliography of publications and other print materials on four main aspects of theatre technology is intended for researchers of theatre history and theatre production. The present work lists and indexes 5,718 references, part of a data base built up over a period of three years at the University of Massachusetts Computing Center. References are entered alphabetically by title under the broad categories of Acoustics and Sound, Lighting, Properties, and Scenery, and in an opening section on Research Materials and Collections. Detailed topical access is provided in a subject index organized according to the same five main divisions. An integrated author index completes the work.

The ongoing computer project also includes thousands of works on theatre architecture, which have been excluded from this volume because of their accessibility through other bibliographic tools. Each week the data bank is updated with new entries and information, and it is hoped that periodic revision of the printed volume will be possible as well. As I have many requests for searches, I have attempted to interest my co-workers in computer use of the data base. However, computer literacy in the arts is at least ten years away, and these efforts often prove unsuccessful: thus, my interest in publishing this work so that I may get back to my drafting table.

In compiling the data bank and bibliography, I searched all volumes of twenty-five periodicals page by page, consulted existing bibliographies (listed here under Research Materials and Collections), and explored forty libraries and collections. Much theatre technology comes from non-theatre sources, so I have included many non-theatrical works. The bibliography contains M.A., M.F.A., and PhD. theses, though production theses are not included. I have also cited original sketches and renderings of scene designs. I would greatly appreciate suggestions, emendations, and new entries, which should be sent to me at Mount Holyoke College, South Hadley, Massachusetts, 01075.

Main Listing Description

1. The components of each entry include, where relevant and available, the title,, author, publisher, date, Library of Congress number (LOCN), and International Standard Book Number (ISBN); volume and page information is given for journal articles.

2. Abbreviations:

JA	January	S	September
F	February	O	October
M	March	N	November
AP	April	D	December
MY	May	WI	Winter
JE	June	SP	Spring
JL	July	SUM	Summer
AG	August	FALL	Autumn

ABTT	Association of British Theatre Technicians
ARCH.	Architectural
BROADSIDE	Newsletter of American Theatre Library
IES	Illuminating Engineering Society
OISTT	International Organization of Sceneographers and Theatre Technicians
SMPTE	Society of Motion Picture and Television Employees
TABS	Publication of Rank Strand Ltd., England
USA	United Scenic Artists
USITT	United States Institute for Theatre Technology

3. Leading articles in titles appear in parentheses at the end of the title. Example: History of Scenery (The).

4. Because the entries were compiled over three years from many sources

and by many typists, there is some variation in the form of the information on the publisher.

5. Authors' names were entered in the main listing as found while searching periodicals, bibliographies, and card catalogs, hence, there are some variations. However, I chose one form of the name for the author index, so that all of his or her work could be found through one entry.

Subject Index Description

1. Names of individuals are given last name first. Example: Jones, Bob.

2. Key words from titles and theatre names are indexed as well as general subjects. Example: "Calculations of Candle-Power and Color Temperature of Tungsten Lamps" is indexed under "candle power" and "color temperature."

3. To ease the search for a particular subject, index items are entered as narrowly and specifically as possible. Example: An item on fluorescent lamps will be found under "fluorescent" rather than "lamps."

4. In cases where subject headings were broken up chronologically and a date fell into two time periods, it was placed in the earlier period. Example: Material for 1960 will be found within 1950-1960, not 1960-1970.

5. Play titles are given in quotation marks. Example: "Hello Dolly."

From Computer to Print

Because a computer was used to store and format the text, a few adjustments of the English language became necessary.

1. In an alphabetized list the sequence is:
   special characters
   letters a-z
   numbers 0-9
   blank
Example: "Roman Theatre"
                    color
                    color and light
                    6 theatres

2. The data was entered in upper case and later transposed to upper and lower case. In a few places, the computer refused to change lower case letters to upper case. Example: Xvlcm.

3. For the few entries that are without dates, the computer inserted "no date."

Acknowledgments

I would like to thank the following institutions for their financial assistance: Mount Holyoke College, the University of Massachusetts Computing Center, Theatre Techniques Incorporated, and Five Colleges, Incorporated.

Conrad A. Wogrin, director of the University of Massachusetts Computing Center, Robert H. Gonter, associate director, and Ruth Berggren, advisor, facilitated my introduction to the computer with their patient help and instruction. Professors Joseph Donohue and James Ellis have shown the way for this and future computer-based theatrical compilations through their work on the mammoth London Stage Project.

The present compiler is additionally indebted to the Mount Holyoke Computer Center and to Professors Howard Nicholson, John Durso, and Paul Dobosh for making facilities available to him. Typists Leslie Case and Donna Ridgeway have done heroic service in learning how to deal with the computer (as well as with the compiler) and typing multitudinous entries. Barbara Jones, Susan Snively, and Jack Erwin, all of the Mount Holyoke College faculty, have proved to be more than close friends by proofreading the text.

Libraries have come to be havens of sanity and peace in my theatrical production-oriented world. Particular thanks go to Anne C. Edmonds and her staff at the Mount Holyoke library, and Jeanne T. Newlin, curator, and Martha R. Mahara, assistant curator of the Harvard Theatre Collection.

The United States Institute of Theatre Technology and especially Herb Greggs and Arnold Aronson have greatly assisted in publicizing the project. Finally, I would like to thank Nancy Enggass and Oliver Allyn of Mount Holyoke College, William Allison of Pennsylvania State Univeristy, and Marilyn Brownstein of Greenwood Press for their support and encouragement.

I
Research Materials and Collections

1   Administrative Intern
Programs in Professional
Resident Theatres. Hardy,
Michael C. Theatre News,
S/o 1978, Vol. XI, No.
1, P. 17-20.

2   American Dissertations
on Drama and the Theatre, a
Bibliography. Litto,
Fredric M. Kent State
Press, 1969, Kent, Ohio.

3   American Theatrical Arts
a Guide to Manuscripts &
Special Collections in
United States & Canada.
Young, William C.
American Library
Association, 1971. LOCN:
26935 Y68 Ref

4   American Theatrical
Periodicals, 1798-1967.
Stratman, Carl J. Duke
Univ. Press, 1970, Durham,
N.C. LOCN: Z 6935 S75
ISBN: 0-8223-0228-4

5   Annals of the New York
Stage. Odell, G.C.D.
Columbia University Press,
1927-49, New York, 15
Vols.

6   Annotated Bibliography
of Scene and Costume Design
in the Past Hundred Years.
Pevitts, Robert. Ph.D.
Thesis, Southern Illinois
University, 1977.

7   Architectural Graphic
Standards, Fifth Edition.
Ramsey, Charles George and
Sleeper, Harold Reeve.
John Wiley, 1956, New York.

8   Are You Going to Build a
Theatre? a Bibliography.
National Theatre
Conference, 1946,
Cleveland.

9   Basic Technical
References. Miller, James
H. and Rubin, Joel E.
Educational Theatre
Journal, D 1952, Vol. 4,
P. 4.

10   Bibliographical
Procedures and Style, a
Manual For Bibliographers
in the Library of
Congress. G.P.O.
030-001-00013-3. No Date.

11   Bibliographic History of
Electricity and Magnetism,
Chronologically Arranged.
Mottelay, Paul F. London,
1922.

12   Bibliography for Arena
Theatre, (A). Williams,
Dallas S. Educational
Theatre Journal, O 1958,
Vol. 10, P. 259-267.

13   Bibliography of
Acoustics of Buildings.
Watson, F. R. National
Research Council, No. 99,
Reprinted from the Journal
of the American Society
of Acoustical Engineers,
Jl 1931, P. 14.

14   Bibliography of
Bibliographies in
Electrical Engineering
1918-1929 (A). Maymard,
Kathrine. Special
Libraries Association,
1931, Providence, Rhode
Island.

15   Bibliography of Books
Related to Stage Lighting
(A). Harris, Judy. M.F.A.
Thesis, Carnegie-Melon
University, 1961.

16   Bibliography of
Dissertations on Theatrical
Lighting, Architecture, and
Technical Work (A).
Howard, John T. Jr.
Theatre Design &
Technology, Su 1980 Vol.
XVI, No. 2, P. 21-24.

17   Bibliography of Medieval
Drama. Stratman, Carl J.
University of California
Press, 1954, Berkeley, Ca.
LOCN: Z 5782 A2 S8

18   Bibliography of

Stagelighting. Nelson, Richard E. Class Paper, Penn State Univ. No Date.

19   Bibliography of Theatre & Stage Design: a Select List of Books and Articles. Cheshire, David F. British Theatre institute, 1960-1970, (Roger Hudson), 30 Clareville St. London SW 7 Saw England ABTT. ISBN: 0-904512-01-0

20   Bibliography of Theatre and Stage Design. Cheshire, David F. Commission for a British Theatre Institute, 1974, London. LOCN: 25784.S8 C45 /   Na6821 ISBN: 0904512010

21   Bibliography of the History of Technology. Ferguson, Eugene S. MIT Press, 1968, Cambridge. LOCN: Z 7914 F4 Ref

22   Biographical Dictionary of Actors, Actresses, Musicians, Dancers, Managers, & Other Stage Personnel in London 1660-1800, (A). Highfill, Philip H. Jr. Southern Illinois University Press, 1973-75.

23   Biographical Dictionary of American Architects (Deceased). Withey Henry F. and Withey, Elsie Rathburn. New Age Publishing Co., 1956, Los Angeles.

24   Black Theatre: a Resource Directory. Primus, Mark (Ed). Black Theatre Alliance, 1973, (1546 Broadway, NY, NY 10036.).

25   Brander Matthews Dramatic Museum (Columbia). Broadside, Fall, 1974, Vol. 2, No. 2, P. 2.

26   Brander Matthews

Dramatic Museum at Columbia University. Theatre Magazine, F 1925, P. 11.

27   Bristol University Theatre Collection. Theatre Notebook Sp 1958, Vol. XII, No. 3, P. 91.

28   Britain's Theatrical Periodicals. Stratman, Carl J. New York Public Library, 1972, New York. LOCN: Z 6935 S76 1972 ISBN: 0-87104-034-4

29   British Theatre Directory 1979. Drama Book Specialists, 1979, New York.

30   British Theatre Museum, The. Stone, George Winchester. Theatre Notebook, Wi 1963, Vol. XVIII, No. 2, P. 49.

31   Catalogue of the Allen A. Brown Collection of Books Relating To the Stage. Boston Public Library, 1919, Boston, Ma.

32   Catalog of the Norman Bel Geddes Theatre Collection. Hunter, Frederick J. G. K. Hall, 1973, Boston. LOCN: Pn2096 G37t4 ISBN: 0-8161-0137-9

33   Catalog of the Theatre and Drama Collections. Part 2: Theatre Collection: Books on the Theatre. G. K. Hall, 1967, Boston.

34   Check List (A). McPharlin, Paul. Players Magazine, O 1940, Vol. 17, No. 1, P. 7.

35   Check List of Books and Periodicals Written, Designed and Edited by Edward Gordon Craig. Fletcher, Ifan Kyrle. Theatre Notebook, 1955, Vol. 10, P. 50.

36   Classification for the
Performing Arts (A).
Trussler, Simon. London
Commission for a British
Theatre Institute, 1974,
London. ISBN: 904512 00 2

37   Cleveland Museum's
Theatre Models.
Architecture and Building,
Ag, 1942, P. 4.

38   Complete New Glossary of
Technical Theatrical Terms.
The Strand Electric
Company, 1947, London.

39   Contemporary Theatre
Architecture; An
Illustrated Survey.
Silverman, Maxwell and
Bowman, Ned A. New York
Public Library, 1965, New
York. LOCN: Na 6821 S55

40   Covent Garden Archives
(The). Rosenthal, Harold.
Theatre Notebook, 1951,
Vol. 6, P. 42.

41   Cumulated Dramatic Index
1909-1949: a Cumulation of
f. W. Fazon Company's
Dramatic Index. G. K.
Hall, 1965, Boston.

42   Description and Analysis
of Four Monthly American
Theatre Magazines
1900-1950. Rude, John A.
Ph.D. Thesis, University
of Missouri, 1973.

43   Development of Scenic
Art and Stage Machinery: A
List of References in the
New York Public Library
(The). Gamble, William
Burt. New York Public
Library, 1928, New York.

44   Digest and Appraisal of
Research in Stage Lighting.
Watson, Lee. M.F.A.
Thesis, Yale University,
1951.

45   Directory for the Arts.
Center for Arts

Information, 152 West 42nd
St., New York, N.Y. 10036.
No Date.

46   Directory of American
College Theatre (1976).
White, Allen S. American
Theatre Association
Publication, 1976.

47   Directory of Forthcoming
Publications. Theatre
Crafts, F 1978, Vol. 12,
No. 2, P. 106.

48   Directory of Graduate
Programs in Theatre Design
and Technology. Smith,
R.L. USITT Education
Commission, 1978, 443 P.

49   Directory of Technical
Literature. Lucier, Mary.
Theatre Crafts, F 1978,
Vol. 12, No. 2, P. 4.

50   Directory of Technical
Literature. Theatre Crafts
Ja 1977.

51   Directory of Theatre
Research Resources in
Greater London. Howard,
Diana. Commission for a
British Theatre Institute,
1974, London.

52   Documenting Performance:
the Theatre on Film and
Tape Collection. Lucier,
Mary. Theatre Crafts, N/D
1978, Vol. 12, No. 7, P.
12.

53   Drama Museum (A).
Theatre Magazine (The), S
1912, Vol. XVI, No. 139,
P. 92.

54   Edward Gordon Craig: a
Bibliography. Fletcher,
Ifan Kyrle and Rood,
Arnold. Society for
Theatre Research, 1967,
London.

55   Edward Gordon Craig: a
Check-List. Fletcher, Ifan
Kyrle. Theatre Arts

Monthly, Ap 1935, Vol.
XIX, No. 4, P. 293.

56   Encyclopedia of
Scenographers 534bc-1900
(An). Lacy, Robin. Ph.D.
Thesis, University of
Denver, 1959.

57   English Theatrical
Literature 1559-1900: a
Bibliography. Arnott,
James Fullarton. Society
for Theatre Research, 1970,
London.

58   Exhibition of Theatrical
Designs and Historical
Materials from the
Suny-Binghamton Theater
Collections. University
Art Gallery, 1970,
Binghamton, New York.

59   Glossary of Assorted
Stage Terms. Tabs, S 1938,
Vol. 2, No. 1, P. 11,
01938, Vol. 2, No. 2, P.
11.

60   Glossary of Stage
Lighting. McCandless,
Stanley. Theatre Arts
Monthly, 1926, P.627-642,
Vol. 10.

61   Glossary of Technical
Stage Terms. Loundsbury,
Warren C. M.A. Thesis,
University of Washington,
1952.

62   Glossary of the Theatre
in English, French, Italian
and German. Band-Kuzmany,
Karin. Elsevier, C. 1950,
New York.

63   Graduate Theses
Completed at the OSU
Theatre Research Institute
1954-1974. Cooperman, Gail
and Sesak, Mary M.
Theatre Studies, 1975, Vol.
20, P. 59.

64   Guide to Doctoral
Dissertations in
Communication Studies and

Theatre (A). Enos, Richard
Leo and Mcclaran, Jeanne
L. University Mocrofilms
International. No Date.

65   Guide to Subject
Collections. Ash, Lee.
R.R. Bowker Co., 1978.
ISBN: 0-8352-0924-5

66   Guide to the Special
Collections of Prints and
Photographs in the Library
of Congress. Banderbilt,
Paul. Library of Congress,
1955, Washington, D.C..

67   Guide to the Theatre and
Drama Collections at the
University of Texas (A).
Hunter, Frederick J.
University of Texas Press,
1967, Austin.

68   Handlist of Dictionaries
on Technical Theatre (A).
Trapido, Joel. Theatre
Design and Technology, My
1968 & O 1968, No. 13,
&14,.

69   Index-Theatre Crafts,
Volumes 12 & 13. Theatre
Crafts, N/d 1979, Vol.
13, No. 6, P. 94.

70   Index of Articles and
Book Reviews Appearing in
Theatre Design and
Technology. USITT
Publication. No Date.

71   Index of Illustrations:
Theatre Buildings. World
Theatre, Wi 1964:5, Vol.
13, No. 4, P. 319-320.

72   Index of Theatre Crafts
1967-1977. Theatre Crafts,
N/D 1977, Vol. 11, No. 6,
P. 41.

73   Index To: Photographs of
Scene Designs Theatre Arts
1916-1964 (An). Hammack,
Alan. Theatre
Documentation, Fall 1970,
Sp 1971, Vol. 3, No. 1 &
2, P. 29.

74   Index to Handicrafts, Modelmaking, and Workshop Practices. Turner, Harriet P. and Winslow, Amy. F. W. Faxon, 1965, Boston, Massachusetts.

75   Index to Plays in Periodicals. Keller, Dean H. Scarecrow Press, 1971, Metuchen, J.J. Supplement 1973. Suppliment Same Title. ISBN: 0-8108-0335-6

76   Index to the Journal of the OSU Research Institute. Cooperman, Gail. Theatre Studies, 1975, Vol. 20, P. 64.

77   Industry Organizations. Watson, Lee. Lighting Dimensions, O 1977, P. 15.

78   International Theatre Directory. Pride, Leo B. Editor. World Trade Academy, 1971, New York.

79   International Vocabulary of Technical Theatre Terms. Rae, Kenneth and Southern, Richard (Editors). Max Reinhardt Publisher, 1959, Belgium.

80   Journals for the Designer and Technician. Theatre Design & Technology F 1966.

81   Libraries' Point of View in Theatre Research. Myers, K. A.L.A. Bulletin, Ag 1940, Vol. 34, P. 232.

82   Lighting Archive at Pennsylvania State University (The). Tabs Sp 1976.

83   Lighting for the Arena Stage; an Annoted Bibliography. Averyt, B. Theatre Design & Technology D 1970.

84   List of References on Outdoor Theatres, Compiled in the Departments of Landscape Architecture and Regional Planning, Harvard University. McNamara, Katherine. Harvard University. No Date.

85   List of Works on Electricity in the New York Public Library. Bulletin, New York Public Library, N 1902 - Ja 1093, Vol. 6-7.

86   Literature on Theatres. Gerhard, William P. Building News, Je 27, 1896, Vol. 52, P. 125-126.

87   London Theatres and Music Halls 1850-1950. Howard, Diana. Library Association (The), 1970, London. LOCN: Pn 2596 L6 H595 Ref ISBN: 85365 4719

88   Lytton's Theatre Seating Plans; London England. Stubs Publns., 1967, New York.

89   Manufacturers and Suppliers. Theatre Crafts, F 1978, Vol. 12, No. 2, P. 112.

90   Manufacturer Profiles, Part I. Lighting Dimensions, Je 1979, Vol. 3, No. 6, P. 18.

91   Motion Picture Theatre Architecture: a Film Research Bibliography. Chamberlain, Stephen C. M.A. Thesis, Columbia University, 1976.

92   Museum in the Making (A). Irving, Laurence. Theatre Notebook, Ja 1966, Vol. XXI, No. 1, P. 38.

93   Museum of Broadcasting. Broadside, Sp, 1977, Vol. 4, No. 4, P. 1.

94   National Directory for the Performing Arts/

Educational. Handel, Beatrice (Editor). John Wiley & Sons, 1978, New York. LOCN: Pn 1s77 N3rff 1978 ISBN: 0-471-03304-9

95   National Directory for the Performing Arts and Civic Centers. Handel, Beatrice (Editor). John Wiley & Sons, 1978, New York. LOCN: Pn 2289 N38 1978 Ref ISBN: 0-471-03303-0

96   National Theatre Memory Bank. Meyers, Paul. Theatre Crafts, N 1969.

97   New York Times Directory of the Theater (The). Arno Press (Quadrangle/New York Times Book Co.) 1972. LOCN: 73-3054 ISBN: 0-8129-0364-1

98   Open Stage and the Modern Theatre in Research and Practice (The). Southern, Richard. Faber and Faber, 1953, London.

99   Oxford Companion to the Theatre (The). Hartnoll, Phyllis (Editor). Oxford University Press, 1957, London.

100   Partial Index to the Russian Journal Scenic Techniques & Technology, 1965 to 1968. Theatre Design & Technology, F 1970.

101   Partial List of Theatres Constructed Since 1946. Theatre Design & Technology, My 1965 & O 1965.

102   Pennsylvania State University Theatre Lighting Archives. Pennsylvania State University, 1975, College Park, Pa.

103   Performing Arts Books in Print. Schoolcraft, Ralph

Newman. Drama Book Specialists, 1973, New York.

104   Performing Arts Libraries and Museums of the World. Theatre Arts Books, 1969, 336 Sixth Avenue, New York, 10014.

105   Performing Arts Resources. Perry, Ted (Ed). Drama Book Specialists, 1974, Vol. 1.

106   Performing Arts Resources. Theatre Library Association. Drama Book Specialists, 1975, New York.

107   Performing Arts Resources. Henderson, Mary C. (Editor). Theatre Library Association, 1978, New York.

108   Planning for the Theatre; a Detailed Check List and Bibliography of Theatre Building Design for Users, Architects, and Consultants. Bowman, Ned A. Scenographic Media, Norwalk, Ct. 1965.

109   Plays in Periodicals: an Index to English Language Scripts In Twentieth Century Journals. Patterson, Charlotte A. G. K. Hall, 1970, Boston. LOCN: Z5781p3

110   Polish Theatrical Audiences in Figures. Huasbrandt, Andrzej. Theatre in Poland (The), 1970, Warsaw, P. 64.

111   Preservation of Theatre Material (The). Freedley, George. A.L.A Bulletin, S 1941, Vol. 35, P. 174.

112   Product Listings, Part II. Lighting Dimensions, Je 1979, Vol. 3, No. 6, P. 25.

113   Recent Patents. Theatre
Design & Technology, 1965
and after.

114   Recent Publications on
Theatre Architecture.
Theatre Design & Technology
Continuing Item, 1965 and
After.

115   Recent Publications on
Theatre Architecture
1960-1971. Bowman, Ned A.
Scenographic Media,
Norwalk, Conn., Or USITT
Journal. No Date.

116   Research Center for the
Federal Theatre Project
(The). Walsh, Elizabeth D.
and Greene, Brenda Z.
Theatre Design &
Technology, Fall, 1978,
Vol. XIV, No. 3, P.
23-24.

117   Save That Theatre:
Ninteenth Century Opera
Houses, Halls and Academies
from the National List of
Historic Theatre Buildings.
Chesley, G. Theatre
Crafts Ja 1976.

118   Scenery for the Theatre.
Burris-Meyer, Harold and
Cole, Edward C. Little,
Brown and Company, 1971,
Boston Toronto. LOCN:
Pn2091. S8b8 1971

119   Scientific American and
Its Supplement As Sources
for Information About
Theatre Technology.
Hubbell, Douglas Kent.
Ph.D. Thesis, Indiana
University, 1978.

120   Selected and Annotated
Bibliography, and Other
Sources Of Information for
Architects and Other
Members of Theatre Planning
Teams. Wolff, Robert W.
US Institute for Theatre
Technology, New York. No
Date.

121   Selected Bibliography of
Hand Books and Text Books
on Procedure, Materials,
and Maintenance in the
Theatre Shop (A). Van
Brunt, Thomas. Theatre
Documentation, 1970, Vol.
3, No. 1 & 2, P. 61.

122   Selected Bibliography on
Design and Construction;
Auditorium and Stage.
American School &
University, 1947, 19th
Yearbook, 236-237.

123   Selected Sources and a
Bibliography for a History
of Scenery to 1660.
Nacarow, David A.
M.F.A.Thesis, 1963, Yale
University.

124   Selective Bibliography
of Handbooks and Textbooks
on Metal Working and
Plastic Working for the
Theatre Scene Shop. Brunt,
T.V. Theatre Design and
Technology, S 1975.

125   Settings for
Shakespearean Productions.
Hammack, Alan. Players, J
1956, Vol. 41, P. 96.

126   Shubert Archive (The): a
Future Dream for Scholars.
Ndini, William. Theatre
Design and Technology, Fall
1978, Vol. XIV, No. 3, P.
23.

127   Simon's Directory of
Theatrical Materials,
Services & Information.
Simon, Bernard (Editor).
Package Publicity Service,
1972, New York. LOCN:
74-31545 ISBN:
0-911100-02-4

128   Sources of Information
on 18th and 19th Century
Theatres in Sussex. Steer,
Francis W. Theatre
Notebook, Wi 1958, Vol.
XII, No. 2, P. 58.

129   Source Book in Theatrical History (A). Nagler, A.M. Dover Publications, Inc. 1952 New York.

130   Special Collections: Theatre. Rachow, Louis A. Haworth Press, Will Be Forthcoming in Fall 1980, New York.

131   Special Effects Cinematography: a Bibliography. Fielding, Raymond E. Journal of the Society of Motion Picture and Television Engineers, Je, 1960, Vol. 69, P. 421.

132   Stage Scenery: a List of References to Illustrations Since 1900. Gamble, William Burt. Bulletin of the New York Public Library, 21 Ap 1917, P. 239, My 1917 25.

133   Stage Scenery, Machinery, and Lighting: a Guide to Information Sources. Stoddard, Richard. Gale Research Co., 1977, Detroit. LOCN: 25784.S8 S79 / Pn2091.S8 ISBN: 081031374x

134   Stubs: the Seating Plan Guide. Schattner, Meyer. Citadel Press, 1969, New York.

135   TAG Technical Library and Information Sheets. Tag Foundation, Ltd., (Technical Assistance Group), 463 West St., Ny,ny 10014. No Date.

136   TCG Survey 1979. Theatre Communications Group, Inc. Theatre Communication Group Inc., 1980,new York.

137   Theatre and Allied Arts. Baker, Blanch M. B. Blom, 1967, New York. LOCN: 25781. B18 1967

138   Theatre Architecture: a Brief Bibliography. Pawley, Frederic Ardmn. Theatre Atrs, 1932, New York.

139   Theatre Architecture and Cinemea Architecture: a Guide To Information Sources. Stoddard, Richard. Gale Research, 1978, Detroit. ISBN: 0-8103-1426-6

140   Theatre Arts Prints. John Day, 1929, New York.

141   Theatre Backstage from a to Z. Loundsbury, Warren C. University of Washington Press, 1967, Seattle.

142   Theatre Bibliography. Moorehead, Singleton P. American Association of Architectural Bibliographers (The) Publication No. 2. No Date.

143   Theatre Collection of the New York Public Library. Freedley, George. Players Magazine, Jl/Ag 1946, Vol. 22, No. 6, P. 5.

144   Theatre Crafts Index 67-77. Theatre Crafts, N 1977.

145   Theatre Design & Technology in Dance. A Selected Annotated Bibliography. Teitelbaum, R. Theatre Design & Technology, My 1970.

146   Theatre Design. Izenour, George C. McGraw-Hill Book Company, 1977, New York. LOCN: Na6821 I94 Folio ISBN: 0070320861

147   Theatre Glossary. Tabs, Ap 1947, Vol. 5, No. 1.

148   Theatre Language; a
Dictionary of Terms in
English of the Dramas &
Stage from Medieval to
Modern Times. Bowman,
Walter Parker. Theatre
Arts Books, 1961, New York.
located at the Harvard
Theatre Collection.

149   Theatre Lighting: an
Illustrated Glossary.
Wehlburg, Albert F. C.
Drama Book Specialists,
1975, New York. LOCN:
Pn2091.E4 W4 ISBN:
0910482691

150   Theatre Management,
Economics, and Producing in
America: a Selected
Bibliography. Langley,
Stephen. Theatre Design &
Technology, My 1971, No.
25, P. 28.

151   Theatre Museums of
Europe. Raines, Lester.
Players Magazine, Ja/F
1936, Vol. 12, No. 3, P.
9.

152   Theatre Pictorial: a
History of World Theater As
Recorded In Drawings,
Paintings, Engravings, and
Photographs. Alman,
George. University of
California Press, 1953, Los
Angeles.

153   Theatre Terminology - on
the Clarification of Names.
Southern, Richard and
Smith, Ray C., Editor.
United States Institute of
Theatre Technicians, S
1961, New York.

154   Theatrical Designs from
the Baroque through
Neoclassicism: Unpublished
Material from American
Private Collections.
Freedley, George. Bittner,
1940, New York.

155   Thesaurus of Technical
Stage Terms. Thorton,

Helen. Ph.D. Thesis,
University of Denver, 1951.

156   Title Index to Acta
Scaenographica. Bowlick,
L. Theatre Design &
Technology F 1967.

157   Traps, Flaps and
Transformations. Walker,
Donald. ABTT News, O 1979,
P. 19.

158   Treatise on the
Decorative Part of Civil
Architecture (A).
Chambers, William. Blom,
1968, New York.

159   USITT Theatre Survey.
Theatre Design &
Technology, D 1965, No. 3,
P. 28.

160   W. J. Lawrence: a
Handlist. Shuttleworth,
Bertram. Theatre Notebook,
Ap/Je 1954, Vol. 8, P.
12.

161   Who's in Lighting
Directory Issue. Lighting
Dimensions, Vol. 3, No.
5, My 1979.

162   York's National Theatre
List. Lindner Corp. N
1933, New York.

II
Acoustics and Sound

163   Absorption of Sound by Materials, the. Watson, F. R. Illinois University Engineering Experiment Station Bulletin, N 1927, No. 172, P. 27.

164   Acoustical Defects Visualized by Light Rays; Correction of Acoustics in the Ziegfeld Theatre. Rosenblatt, M.C. American Architect, Ap. 1930, Vol. 137, P. 40.

165   Acoustical Design; School of Music, Montana State University. Progressive Architecture, Ap 1954,vol. XXXV, P. 118-120.

166   Acoustical Designing in Architecture. Knudsen, V. O. and Harris, C. M. John Wiley and Sons, 1950, New York.

167   Acoustical Design for Performing Arts Spaces. Kirkegaard, R.L. Theatre Design & Technology, Fall 1979, Vol. XV, No. 3, P. 4-7.

168   Acoustical Design in the Hill Memorial Auditorium, University Of Michigan. Tallant, Hugh. T Brickbuilder (The), 1913, Vol. 22, No. 8.

169   Acoustical Design of Auditoria. Parkin, P. H. and Allen, W. A. Nature, Jl 18, 1953, Vol. CLXXII, P. 98-99.

170   Acoustical Design of Multi-Purpose College Auditorium. Johnson, Russell. American School & University, 1962-1963, P. 139-140.

171   Acoustical Design of the Theatre. Knudsen, V. O. and Harris, C. M. Architectural Record, N 1948, Vol. CIV, P. 139-144.

172   Acoustical Foundations of Music (The). Backus, John. Norton, 1969, New York.

173   Acoustical Holography. Metherell. Scientific American, O 1969, P. 36.

174   Acoustical Study of the Auditorium. Willimon, Edward L. M.A. Thesis, Columbia University, 1948.

175   Acoustics, Architecture and Music. Roy. Arch Inst Can J, O 1955, P.398-399.

176   Acoustics, Noise and Buildings. Parkin, P. H. F. A. Praeger, 1958, New York.

177   Acoustics, Noise and Buildings. Parkin, P. H. Faber & Faber, 1963, London.

178   Acoustics and Acting in the Theatre of Dionysus Eleothereus. Hunningher, Benjamin. Noord-Hollandsche Uitg.Mij. 1956, Amsterdam.

179   Acoustics and Architecture. Sabine, Paul E. McGraw-Hill, 1932, New York.

180   Acoustics and Reverberation. Costa, David D. Progressive Architecture, S 1960, P. 180.

181   Acoustics and Sound Exclusion; Royal Festival Hall. Arch. Review, Je 1951, Vol. CIX, No. 4207, P. 377.

182   Acoustics Considerations, Junior High School. Progressive Architecture, D 1952, Vol. XXXIII, P. 77.

183   Acoustics for Architects. Richardson, E.

G. Longman's Green and Co.
1946, New York.

184   Acoustics for the
Architect. Burris-Meyer,
Harold. Reinhold, 1957, New
York.

185   Acoustics In-The-Round
at the Berlin Philharmonic.
Lanier, R.S. Architectural
Forum, My 1964.

186   Acoustics in Modern
Building Practice.
Ingerslev, Fritz.
Architectural Press, 1952,
London.

187   Acoustics in Relation to
Architecture and Building;
the Laws Of Sound As
Applied to the Arrangement
of Buildings. Smith, Thomas
Roger. Crosby Lockwood &
Sons, 1895, London.

188   Acoustics in Theatre
Design. Sabine, Paul E.
Arch. forum, S 1932, P.
261-265.

189   Acoustics in the New
Concert Hall: Colston Hall,
Bristol and Royal Festival
Hall, London. Allen, W.A.
Et Al. Roy Inst Brit Arch
J, D 1951, P.30-46, Vol.
LIX.

190   Acoustics in the Royal
Festival Hall. Bolt, R. H.
Architectural Forum, Ag
1951, Vol. XCV, No. 2, P.
180-181.

191   Acoustics of Auditoria
(The). Building Digest,
1952, P.88-97, Vol. XII,
No. 3.

192   Acoustics of
Auditoriums. Watson, F. R.
Scientific American
Supplement, D 1914, Vol.
78, P. 358-359; 380-382.

193   Acoustics of Buildings;
Including Acoustics of

Auditoriums and Sound-
Proofing of Rooms. Watson,
F. R. John Wiley & Sons,
3rd Ed., 1941, New York.

194   Acoustics of Greek
Theaters. Shankland, R.S.
Physics Today, O 1973.

195   Acoustics of Kastner's
Design, for Kharkov.
Theatre Management, S 1931,
P. 4.

196   Acoustics of Modern
Auditoriums. Watson, F. R.
Arch Rec, Je 1946, Vol. IC,
P. 119-123.

197   Acoustics of Music
Shells (The). Kamphoefer,
Henry L. Pencil Points
Progressive Architecture S,
1945, P. 93 & O, 1945, P.
98.

198   Acoustics of Music.
Bartholomew, Wilmer T.
Prentice Hall, 1950, 2d
Ed., New York.

199   Acoustics of
Philharmonic Hall, New
York, During Its First
Season. Beranek, Leo L.
Acoustical Society of
America Journal, Jl 1964,
P. 1247-62.

200   Acoustics of
Philharmonic Hall. Beranek,
Leo L. Architectural
Record, S 1962, P. 197-204.

201   Acoustics of Picture
Theatres. Swan, C.M.
Architectural Forum, N,
1929, Vol. 51, P. 545.

202   Acoustics of St. Peter's
and Patriarchal Basilicas
in Rome. Shankland, R.S.
and Shankland, H.S.
Brickbuilder (The), 1913,
Vol. 22, No. 8.

203   Acoustics of Theatres.
Watson, F. R. Play-Book,
The, Ag 1914, Vol. 2, No.
3, P. 19-23.

204   Acoustics of the Chicago Civic Opera House. Sabine, Paul E. Architectural Forum, Ap, 1930, Vol. 52, P. 599.

205   Acoustics of the Italian Opera House and the Wagner Theatre Compared. Bagenal, Hope. Journal of the Royal Institute of British Architects, D 1920, Vol. 38, P. 98.

206   Acoustics of the Jesse Jones Performing Arts Hall, Houston, Texas. Klepper, D.L. and Newman, R.B. and Watters, B.G. Unpublished Paper, 75th Acoustical Society of America Meeting, My 1968, Ottawa, Canada.

207   Acoustics of the Royal Festival Hall, London. Parkin, P. H. and Allen, W. A. Acoustical Society of America, Mr 1953, Vol. XXV, P. 246-259.

208   Acoustics: Theatre's Neglected Stepchild. Jaffe, C. Theatre Crafts Ja 1968.

209   Acoustics. Projection Engineering, S 1929, P. 14, 19, D 1929, P. 15.

210   Acoustics. Better Theatre, Ap 11, 1931, P. 87.

211   Acoustics. Theatre Engineering, My 1930, P. 69, Je 1930, P. 29, Ag 1930, P. 17; S 1930, P. 30; Mr 1931, P. 23.

212   Acoustics. Sabine, Wallace Clement. American Institute of Architects. Journal of Proceedings, 32d Annual Convention, 1898, P.32-49.

213   Acoustics. Wood, Alexander. Dover, 1966, New York.

214   Acoustics. Beranek, Leo L. McGraw-Hill, 1954, New York.

215   Acoustic Considerations in the Film Board Studios. Curtis, R. W. Society of Motion Picture and Television Engineers Journal, D 1957, Vol. LXVI, P. 731-734.

216   Acoustic Design (The). Bagenal, Hope. Architect and Building News, 1951, Vol. CIC, No. 4300, P. 581.

217   Acoustic Diagram of the Saville Theatre Prepared By H. Bagal. Bagal, H. Architectural Record, O. 1931, Vol. 70, P. 106.

218   Acoustic Surface Waves. Keno. Scientific American, O 1972, P. 50.

219   Acousto-Electronic Auditorium. Olsen, Harry F. Progressive Architecture, N 1959, P. 165.

220   Actor and Architect. Joseph, Stephen. University of Toronto Press, 1964, Toronto, Also, Manchester Univ. Press, 1964, Manchester, England. LOCN: Na 6821 J6

221   All Trivial Fond Record on the Users of Early Recordings of British Hall Performers. Senelick, Laurence. Theatre Survey, N 1975.

222   Also a Gala Opening in Pittsburgh. Vecsey, George. New York Times (The), S 12, 1971, P.82.

223   Analysis of Reflection Patters in Auditoria. Lochner, J. P. A. and Meffert, P. Acoustical Society of America, Journal, S 1963, Vol. XXXV, No. 9, P. 1429-1431.

224   Analyzing the
Architecture of Sound
Motion Picture Theatres.
Friend, W. K. Western
Architect, My 1930, Vol.
39, P. 79-82.

225   Appliances for
Noise-Making. Popular
Mechanics F 1929, Vol. 51,
P. 270.

226   Applications of the
Ca3080 & Ca3080a
High-Performance
Operational
Transconductance
Amplifiers. Wittlinger,
H.A. RCA ICAN 6668, S
1971.

227   Application of Rating
Scales to Quantify
Subjective Evaluations for
a Group of Concert Halls.
Watters, B.G. and Johnson,
F.R. and Kirkegaard, R.L.
Unpublished Paper: Audio
Engineering Society
Meeting, My 1970, Los
Angeles, Ca.

228   Applied Architectural
Acoustics. Rettinger,
Michael. Chemical
Publiching, 1947, Brooklyn.

229   Architectural Acoustics:
Basic Planning Aspects.
Bolt, R. H. and Newman, R.
B. Architectural Record,
Ap 1950, Vol. CVII, P.
165-168, Je 1950, P.
166-169, S 1950, P.
148-151.

230   Architectural Acoustics.
Knudsen, V. O. Scientific
American, N 1963, P. 88.

231   Architectural Acoustics.
Knudsen, V. O. Wiley,
1932, New York.

232   Architectural Acoustics.
Engineering Record, 1900,
Vol. 41, P. 349-351,
376-379, 400-402, 426-427,
450-451, 477-478, 503-505.

233   Architectural Acoustics.
American Architect and
Building News, 1900,
P. 3-5,19-22, 35-37, 43-45,
59-61, 75-76, 83-84, Vol.
68.

234   Architecture and the
Artful Stage. Arnott,
Brian. Canadian Theatre
Review, Ap 1975, Vol. 6, P.
7.

235   Attention and the
Perception of Sound.
Broadbent. Scientific
American, Ap 1962, P. 143.

236   Audience Hears (The).
Burris-Meyer, Harold and
Cole, Edward, C.
Progressive Architecture,
O, 1947 P. 76.

237   Audio Cyclopedia.
Tremaine, Howard M. Howard
W. Sams & Co., 1969,
Indianapolis.

238   Auditorium Acoustics for
Music Performance. Johnson,
Russell. Architectural
Record , D 1960, P.
158-165, 182.

239   Auditorium Acoustics.
Shearer, Kenneth. ABTT
Newsletter, Ag 1970, P.
2-9.

240   Auditorium of a Theatre
(The). Nevill, Ralph.
Journal of the Royal
Institute of British
Architects, Ja 26, 1888
Vol. 4, P. 125-140.

241   Auditory Component
Control in the Legitimate
Theatre. Beaumont, John H.
M.F.A. Thesis, 1948, Yale
University.

242   Auditory Illusions and
Confusions. Warren.
Scientific American, D
1970, P. 30.

243   Automatic Cuing Device

for Tape Transports, (An).
Proctor, Daniel H. Theatre
Design & Technology, Wi
1979, Vol. XV, No. 4, P.
31-32.

244   Basics of Auditorium
Acoustical Design (The).
Janson, Richard W.
Lighting Dimensions, Ap
1978, Vol. 2, No. 4, P. 16.

245   Beginners' Primer of
Components. Arnett, Keith.
Theatre Craft, Mr/Ap 1980,
Vol. 14, No. 2, P. 73-79.

246   Behind the Curtains of a
Great Theater. Scientific
American, N 1924, Vol. 131,
P. 313.

247   Beyond the Dog Barks:
Thoughts on Sound Effects
Design. Harris, Gary.
Theatre Crafts O 1976.

248   Bibliography of
Acoustics of Buildings.
Watson, F. R. National
Research Council, No. 99,
Reprint and Circular
Series. see also Journal of
the American Society of
Acoustical Engineers, Jl
1931.

249   Blood on the Tracks
(With Apologies to Bob
Dylan). Harris, Gary.
Theatre Craft, My/Je 1980,
Vol. 14, No. 3, P. 79-82.

250   Building Acoustics.
Smith, T. and O'Sullivan,
P.E. Oriel Press 1971.

251   Building a Better Crash
Box. Ludwick, Michael.
Theatre Craft, Mr/Ap 1980,
Vol. 14, No. 2, P. 100.

252   Building for the
Performing Arts.
Architectural Forum, Je
1960, Vol. 112, No. 6, P.
86-103.

253   Cabinet Handbook.

Briggs, G.A. Rank
Warfedale Ltd., 1962,
Yorkshire, England.

254   Charles Bulfinch,
Architect and Citizen.
Place, Charles A. Houghton
Mifflin Co., 1925, Boston &
New York.

255   Chicago Civic Opera
Building (The). Lee, Anne.
Architectural Forum, Ap
1930, Vol. 52, P. 491-514,
599.

256   Circular 56: Copyright
for Sound Recordings.
Performing Arts Review,
1972, Vol. 3 No. 3, P. 525.

257   Codonophone (The).
Scientific American, D
1890, Vol. 63, P. 374.

258   Collected Papers on
Acoustics. Sabine, Wallace
Clement. Dover, 1964, New
York. Harvard University
Press, 1922, Cambridge.

259   Colonial Theatre and
Building (The). Blackall,
Clarence H. American
Architect, Ap 1901,
P.11-69, Vol. LXXII. Also
My Ll, 1901, P. 44; My 18,
1901, P. 51; & Je 1, 1901,
P. 67.

260   Communications System
for the Paper Mill
Playhouse. Burris-Meyer,
Harold. Theatre Arts
Monthly, Jl 1938, Vol.
XXII, No. 7, P. 536.

261   Computer-Aided Sound
Effects. Johnson, Andrew C.
and Becker, Farrel. Theatre
Crafts, Mr/Ap 1980, Vol.
14, No. 2, P. 37, 71-72.

262   Concert Shell for a
Roman Ruin. Izenour, George
C. Architectural Record, D
1970.

263   Control of Noise and

Vibration (The). Yin.
Scientific American, Ja
1969, P. 98.

264   Correction of Acoutics
of Ziegfeld Theatre.
American Architect, Ap
1930, Vol. 139, P. 41.

265   Correction of Echoes and
Reverberation in the
Auditorium. Watson, F. R.
University of Illinois,
1916, Urbana.

266   Corsican Brothers: Its
History and Technical
Problems Related to the
Production of the Play
(The). Hunter, Jack W.
Ph.D. Thesis Ohio State
Univ. 1963.

267   Creating Sound Effects.
Morgan, Howard C. Players
Magazine, My/Je 1932, Vol.
VIII, No. 5, P. 15.

268   Curing an Auditorium of
Echoes. Popular Science
Monthly; Vol. 90, F 1917,
P. 241.

269   Delicate Balance (The).
Gersh. Theatre Crafts,
Mr/Ap 1979, P.8, Vol. 13,
No. 2.

270   Design-Correlation
Towards Prefabrication of
Folk Spectacles: Scientific
Development of Sound
Reproduction Proves an
Important Influence on
Architectural Design.
Kiesler, Frederick J.
Arch. Record, Je 1937, P.
93-96.

271   Designing and
Engineering Computer
Controlled Acoustic
Flexibility for a
Multiple-Use Theater.
Izenour, George C.
Architectural Record, Mr
1974.

272   Designing Sound for

Musicals. Jacob, Abe.
Theatre Crafts, My/Je 1977,
Vol. 11, No. 3, P. 17.

273   Design of Speech
Communications Systems
(The). Beranek, Leo L.
Prod. Ind. Radio Engineers,
S 1947, Vol. 235, No. 9.

274   Destruction of Her
Majesty's Theatre. Builder,
(The), D 14, 1867, P. 903
See Also P. 945, 929.

275   Development of Speech
Acoustics Criteria : Using
an Auditorium Acoustics
Simulator. Bruce, R.D. and
Watters, B.G. Unpublished
Paper: 79th Acoustical
Society of America Meeting,
Ap 1970, Atlantic City,
N.J.

276   Development of the
Playhouse; a Survey of
Theatre Architecture from
the Renaissance to the
Present. Mullin, Donald C.
University of California
Press, 1970, Berkeley.
LOCN: Na 6821 M83 +

277   Doing It for Effect-The
Noise Gate. Lewis, Len.
ABTT (Studio Sound, My
1978).

278   Don't Walk! Wire. Dewey,
Walter S. Players, Ag/S,
1969, Vol. 44, No. 6, P.
230.

279   Double-Duty Loudspeaker.
Lighting Dimensions, Ap
1978, P.32, Vol. 2, No. 4.

280   Effect of Seating on
Theatre Acoustics. Friend,
W. K. Architecture and
Building, My, 1930, Vol.
62, P. 152.

281   Einstein on the Beach.
Simmer, Bill. Theatre
Design & Technology, Spring
1978, Vol. XIV, No. 1, P.
15.

282   Electronic Sound in the Theatre. Nemec, Boyce and Fitzberald, Richard T. and Klepper, David L. and Harris, G ary and Boutillier, Thomas and Boner, Charles R. Theatre Design and Technology, O 1970, No. 2, P. 6.

283   Electronic Systems (The). Key, Russell. Theatre Design & Technology, O 1970, No. 22, P. 27.

284   Electrons, Waves and Messages. Pierce, J.R. Hanover House, 1956, Garden City, N.Y.

285   Enquiry into the Principle Phenomenon of Sounds and Musical Strings. Young, Matthew. 1784, Dublin.

286   Enter the Sound "Designer,. Leech, Michael. Stage and Television Today (The), Je 29, 1978.

287   Equalizers-Their Uses and Abuses. Clarke, Terry. ABTT (Studio Sound, F 1978).

288   Evaluation of Acoustical Adjusting Devices Using a 1:24 Scale Model of an Auditorium. Marshall, L.G. and Watters, B.G. and Bentivegna, P.I. and johnson, F.R. and Irkegaard, R.L. Unpublished Lecture; 76th Acoustical Society of America Meeting, N 1968, Cleveland, Ohio.

289   Experimental Investigation of the Effects of Theatre Accoustics On Intelligability (An). Rabby, L.B. Ph.D. Thesis, University of Kansas, 1965.

290   Festival Hall Acoustics.

Builder, 1952, Vol. CLXXXIII, No. 5725, P. 678.

291   Finnish Theatre. Architectural Review, Ag, 1965, P. 81.

292   Folded Platform Shell for Concerts and Karuki (A). Architectural Record, N 1962, P. 157-162.

293   Folding Partition Appraised for Noise. Hardy, H. C. Architectural Record, O 1958, Vol. CXXIV, P. 220-223.

294   Further Refinements on Mic Line Tester. Corbett, Tom. Theatre Crafts, J/F 1980, Vol. 14, No. 1 P. 4.

295   Good Room Proportions Improve Acoustics. Rettinger, Michael. Progressive Architecture, Mr 1966, P. 192.

296   Guidelines for Good Sound. Wood, I.W. Architectural Record, Jl 1971, Vol. 150.

297   Handbook of Radio Production and Directing. Crews, Albert. John S. Swift & Co., Inc. 1943 Chicago.

298   Handbook of Sound Effects. Government Printing Office My 1938 Washington.

299   Hearing Matters. Harris, Bob. ABTT (Studio Sound, N, 1978).

300   Hi-Fi Loud Speakers and Enclosures. Cohen, Abraham B. Hayden Book Inc., 1956, Rochelle Park, N.J.

301   Hillingdon, Reading and Assisted Resonance. Creighton, Hugh. Tabs Sp 1978.

302   History of Theatrical
Sound Effect Devices (A).
Culver, May K. Ph.D.
Thesis, University of
Illinois, Urbana, 1979.

303   How Stage Sounds and
Storms Are Made. Popular
Mechanics, Ag 1908, Vol.
10, P. 522-523.

304   How to Build Speaker
Enclosures. Badmaieff,
Alexis and Davis, Don.
Bobbs-Merrill Co., 1973,
New York.

305   How to Create Sound
Effects for Home Recording.
Ludes, Ed and Hoffman,
Hallock B. Castle Press,
(The), 1946, Pasadena,
California.

306   How to Design an
Auditoruim Where It Is Easy
to Hear. Friend, W. K.
American Architect, S,
1930, Vol. 138, P. 50; O,
19 30, Vol. 138, P. 65.

307   Ic Op Amp Story, Part II
(The). Jung, W.G.
Broadcast Engineering, Mr
1974, Vol. 16, P. 62-66.

308   Ideal Outdoor Theatre:
Criteria and Plans for a
New Design (The). Bledsoe,
Jerry H. Ph.D. Thesis,
Purdue University, 1971.

309   II Total Teatro Di
Maurizio Sacripanti. Domus,
Ap 1966, No. 437, P. 1-11.

310   Inefficiency of Wires As
a Means of Curing Defective
Acoustics of Auditoriums
(The). Watson, F. R.
Science, New Series, Vol.
35, My 24 1912, P. 833.

311   Inexpensive Inter- Com
System. Batcheller, David
R. Players Magazine, O,
1958, Vol. 35, No. 1, P.
19.

312   Influence of Reflections
on Auditorium Acoustics.
Lochner, J. P. A. and
Burger, F. F. Journal of
Sound and Vibration, 1964,
Vol. 4, No. 1, P. 426-454.

313   Influence of Theatre
Chairs on Acoustics (The).
Gabler, W. Theatre Design
& Technology F 1970.

314   Information Sheet 2,
Recommendations and
Proposed Standards For
Sound Wiring Requirements
in a New Theatre.
Association of British
Theatre Technicians, 1979,
London.

315   Instrumentation of
Acoustic Modeling. Watters,
B.G. Journal of the
Acoustical Society of
America, F 1970, Vol. 47,
No. 2, P. 413-418.

316   Insulation, Thermal and
Acoustical: Theatre Long
Beach, California. Gibbs,
Hugh. Progressive
Architecture, Ja 1948,
P.69.

317   Integrated Circuit Tone
Control Stage (An).
Crawford, D. Audio, N
1969, Vol. 53, P. 32-34.

318   Inter-Communication
System for the Theatre.
Steward, George Erwin.
M.F.A. Thesis, Yale
University, 1960.

319   Intercommunication
System. Steward, Irwin.
Theatre Design &
Technology, O 1966, No. 6,
P. 48.

320   Introducing the
Bantam-Size Microphone.
Players Magazine, O, 1949,
Vol. 26, No. 1, P. 14.

321   Introducing the New
Metropolitan Opera House.

Seward, William.
Hifi/Stereo Review, O 1966,
P. 92-96.

322   Julliard's Movable
Ceiling. Progressive
Architecture, D 1970, P.
69.

323   Keeping "Good Buddy" Off
the Stage: the History,
Care, and Feeding of Radio
Microphones. Harris, Gary.
Theatre Crafts, Ja/f 1978,
Vol. 12, No. 1, P. 32.

324   Kennedy Opera House
Acoustics (The). Schonberg,
Harold. New York Times
(The), S 12, 1971, Col. 1,
P. 94.

325   Kicked a Building
Lately?. Huxtable, Ada
Louise. Quadrangle, 1976,
New York.

326   Lighting Can Relieve
Noise Problems. Lighting
Dimensions, N 1978, Vol. 2,
No. 9, P. 53.

327   Light and Sound for
Engineers. Stanley R.C.
Hart Publishing Co., Inc.,
1968, New York.

328   Light Weight Concert
Shells Myth or Reality.
Jaffe, C. Theatre Design &
Technology F 1966.

329   Lincoln Center for the
Performing Arts. Martin,
Ralph G. Prentice-Hall,
1971, Englewood Cliffs,
N.J.

330   Linear Systems in
Communication and Control.
Frederick, Dean K. and
Carlson, A. Bruce. Wiley,
1971, New York.

331   Little Theatre, (The).
Ingalls and Hoffman.
American Architect, D 31,
1913, Vol. 104, P. 257.

332   Louder We Can't Hear
You. Harris, Gary. Theatre
Crafts, N/D 1976, Vol. 10,
No. 6, P. 19.

333   Loudspeakers. Briggs,
G.A. Rank Warfedale Ltd,
1948, Yorkshire, England.

334   Magnetic Recordings for
Theatrical Use. Rubin, Joel
E. Educational Theatre
Journal, My, 1950, Vol. 11,
No. 2, P. 139.

335   Magnetic Recording.
Ragosine. Scientific
American, N 1969, P. 70.

336   Mechanical Noise and the
Theatre. Marshall, L.G.
Theatre Design &
Technolgoy, Fall 1979, Vol.
XV, No. 3, P. 27-31.

337   Microphones in Action.
Capel, Vivian. Fountain
Press, 1978, P. 148.

338   Modern Theater:
Architecture, Stage Design,
Lighting (The). Schubert,
Hannelore. Praeser, 1971,
New York, 222p. LOCN:
Na6821 83813

339   Movable Auditorium
Ceiling Julliard. Theatre
Design & Technology F 1970.

340   Multi-Purpose Sound
System (A). Collison,,
David. Cue Technical
Theatre Review, N/D 1979.

341   Mumbo-Jumbo on Stage
Will Be Mumbo-Jumbo in the
Auditorium Unless Theatres
Adopt Sound Techniques
Available for Half a
Century. Gibson, Ian. The
Stage and Television Today,
Ja 25, 1979.

342   Music: Heinz Hall,
Pittsburgh's Acoustical
Gem. Hughes, Alan. New York
Times (The), S 12, 1974,
Col. 6, P. 94.

343   Music, Acoustics and Architecture. Beranek, Leo L. Wiley, 1962, New York.

344   Music, Physics and Engineering. Olsen, Harry F. McGraw-Hill, 1952, New York; Also, Dover, 1967, New York.

345   Music, Sound and Sensation. Winckley. Dover, 1967, New York.

347   Music As Audio-Scenery. Galstaun, Vanick S. Players Magazine, N, 1958, Vol. 35, No. 2, P. 33.

348   Music to My Ears?. Progressive Architecture, Mr 1977.

349   New Music and Sound Effects System for Theatrical Productions (A). Dugan, D. Convention of the Audio Engineering Society, Los Angeles, Ap 1969, Reprint 652.

350   New Science of Acoustics (The). Wolf, S.K. Theatre Arts Monthly, O, 1931, Vol. XV, No. 10, P, 843.

351   New Tools for the Sound Designer. Symposium Report: the Recording Industry and the Theatre. Silbert, Irene. Theatre Crafts, S 1978, Vol. 12, No. 5, P. 101.

352   New York Building Construction. Encyclopaedia Britannica, Vol. XVI, 14th Ed. No Date.

353   Noises Off: a Handbook of Sound Effects. Napier, Frank. F. Muller, 1936, London, P. 117.

354   Noises Off-Some Sound Advice. Tabs, D 1949, Vol. 7, No. 3, P. 10.

355   Noise and Vibration Control. Beranek, Leo L. McGraw-Hill, 1971, New York.

356   Noise Control in Buildings. Architectural Record, Je 1950, P. 166-169. Also Part One: Good Hearing Conditions; S 1950, P. 148-151;.

357   Noise Control in Schools. Lane, R. N. Noise Control, Jl 1957, P. 32.

358   Noise Makers for the Futurist Concert of Noises. Sketch, Je 17, 1914, Vol. 86, P. 324.

359   Noise Makers on the Stage. Scientific American, Ja 17, 1920, Vol. 122, P. 65.

360   Noise. Baranek. Scientific American, D 1966, P. 66.

361   Notes on a Non Graphics. Eaton, Bruce. Theatre Design & Technology, Su 1978, Vol. XIV, No. 2, P. 38.

362   Notes on the Development of Architectural Acoustics, Particularly in England. Richardson, E. G. Journal of the Royal Institute of British Architects, O 1945, Vol. 52 , P. 352-354.

363   Novel Effects Used by Beerbohm Tree in His London Production of Stephen Phillips' Tragedy "Nero". Theatre Magazine, Ap 1906, Vol. 6, P. 94..

364   No Noise Is Good Noise. Sightline, ABTT Journal, Fall 1979, Vol. 13, No. 2, P. 119.

365   Oh Calcutta the Sound System Is the Thing (At). Liftin, W. Theatre Crafts N 1969.

366   On Acoustics: How to
Design an Auditorium Where
It Is Easy to Hear. Friend,
W. K. American Architect,
S 1930, Vol. 139, P. 50; O
1930, P. 65.

367   Orchestra Pits. Johnson,
Russell. Theatre Design &
Technology, Fall 1979, Vol.
XV, No. 3, P. 8-20.

368   Oxford Companion to the
Theatre (The). Hartnoll,
Phyllis (Editor). 1957
London, New York, Ontario.

369   Pandora's Box Supplies
Broadway With Stage Noise.
Mitchell, Joseph. New York
World Telegram and Sun, Ja
19, 1933,.

370   Part One - Every
Building Has Acoustical
Problems. Newman, Robert
B. Progressive
Architecture, My 1959, P.
147.

371   Perfecting Backstage
Sound. Eek, Nat. Players
Magazine, My, 1955, Vol.
31, No. 8, P. 190.

372   Performance Criteria for
Theatrical Sound Effects
Systems, Parts I & II.
Sanford, J.L. 45th
Convention of the Audio
Engineering Society, My
1973, (reprint 922), S 1973
(reprint 937).

373   Physics and the Sound of
Music. Rigden, John S.
Wiley, 1977, New York.

374   Physics of Musical
Sounds (The). Taylor.
Elsevier, 1956, New York.

375   Physics of Musical Sound
(The). Josephs, Jess J.
Van Nostrand, 1967, New
York.

376   Physics of Music (The).
Wood, Alexander. Methuen &
Co., 1962, London.

377   Physics of the Bowed
String (The). Schelleng.
Scientific American, Ja
1973, P. 87.

378   Physics of the Piano
(The). Blackham. Scientific
American, D 1965, P. 88.

379   Physics of Violins.
Hutchins. Scientific
American, N 1962, P. 78.

380   Physics of Woodwinds
(The). Benada. Scientific
American, O 1960, P. 144.

381   Pitfalls of the
General-Purpose Operational
Amplifiers As Applied Audio
Signal Processins (The).
Jung, W.G. Journal of the
Audio Engineering Society,
N 1973, Vol. 21, P.
706-714.

382   Planning for Good
Acoustics. Bagenal, Hope
and Wood, Alexander.
Methuen, 1931, London.
Dutton, 1932, New York.

383   Playback Sound System of
the Festival Theatre of
Statford, Ontario (the).
Scales, Robert. Journal of
the Audio Engineering
Society, S 1972, Vol. 20,
P. 581.

384   Play Production. Hewitt,
Barnard. J.B. Lippincott
Co., 1940, Philadelphia.

385   Practical Theatrical
Sound Console (A).
Richmond, Charles. Theatre
Design & Technology, Fall
1979, Vol. XV, No. 3, P.
21-27.

386   Practical Theatrical
Sound Console (A).
Richmond, Charles. Journal
of the Audio Engineering
Society, Ja/f 1975, Vol.
23, No. 1, P. 36.

387   Producing the Play

(Contains New Scene
Technician's Handbook).
Gassner, John and Barber,
Philip. Dryden Press, 1941,
New York. Holt, Rinehart &
Wilson, 1953, New York.
LOCN: Pn2037 G3 1953 ISBN:
0-03-005565-2

388   Production Sound
Techniques. Greenfield,
William Edward. M.F.A.
Thesis, Yale University,
1959.

389   Professional Sound
Facilities in the Theatre.
Gaiser, Gary. Theatre
Design & Technology My
1965.

390   Propagation of Sound
Across Audience Seating.
Schultz, T.J. and Watters,
B.G. Journal of the
Acoustical Society of
America, 1964, Vol. 36, P.
885.

391   Proper Record Care.
White, Melvin, R. Players
Magazine, N, 1959, Vol. 36,
No. 2, P. 33.

392   Putting Sound in Its
Place. Sightline, Sp 1979,
Vol. 13, No. 1, P. 2.

393   Radio and Television
Sound Effects. Turnbull,
Robert. Rinehart & Co.,
1951, New York.

394   Radio Sound Effects.
Creamer, Joseph and
Hoffman, William.
Ziff-Davis, 1945, New York.

395   Radio Sound Tracks: a
Reference Guide. Pitts,
Michael R. Scare Crow
Press, 1976, Metuchen, New
Jersey.

396   Rank Strand Sound. Rose,
Philip. Tabs Sp 1978.

397   Rating Scales for
Auditorium Acoustics.

Watters, B.G. and Beranek,
Leo L. and Schultz, T.J.
Unpublished Paper: 79th
Acoustical Society of
America Meeting, Ap 1970,
Atlantic City, N.J.

398   Recorded Music and Sound
Effects in Hamlet.
Scientific American, Mr
1932, Vol. 146, P. 166.

399   Recorded Music in the
Theatre. De Young, James L.
Players, Ap/My, 1968, Vol.
34, No. 4, P. 118,.

400   Remodelled Hippodrome.
Gilston, E. J. Electrical
Record, 1924, Vol. 35, P.
133-135.

401   Reproduction of Sound
(The). David. Scientific
American, Ag 1961, P 72.

402   Reverberation Time
Calculation: Time Saver
Standards. Knudsen, V. O.
and Harris, C. M.
Architectural Record, N
1948, Vol. CIV, P. 157.

403   Ripple Tank Experiments.
Rose, Keith. Architectural
Design, F 1961, P. 86-88.

404   Role of Model Testing in
the Acoustical Design of
Auditoria. Watters, B.G.
and Kirkegaard, R.L. and
Schultz, T.J. Unpublished
Paper: 74th Acoustical
Society of America Meeting,
N 1967, Miami Beach, Fla.

405   Room Acoustics
Measurements Using a
Calibrated Steady-State
Sound Source. Johnson, F.R.
and Kirkegaard, R.L. and
Watters, B.G. Unpublished
Lecture: 75th Acoustical
Society of America Meeting,
My 1968, Ottowa, Canada.

406   Safe Sound a Guide to
Electrical Safety for
Musicians. Association of

British Theatre Technicians, 1979, London.

407   Safe Sound. Signtline, Sp 1979, Vol. 13,no. 1.

408   Scenery for the Theatre. Burris-Meyer, Harold and Cole, Edward C. Little, Brown and Company 1971 Boston Toronto. LOCN: Pn2091. S8b8 1971

409   Seating and Acoustics. Friend, W. K. Architecture (New York), Jl, 1930, Vol. 62, P. 61.

410   Selecting a Compatible Sound System. Wilkins, W. Douglas. Lighting Dimensions, N 1978, Vol. 2, No. 9, P. 54.

411   Series of Experiments Investigating the Usefulness of Acoustic Absorbing Material to Modify Loudspeaker Directivity Character-istics in Theatre Sound Systems. Rand, Herb. Ph.D. Thesis, Florida State University, 1976.

412   Shakespeare's Use of Off-Stage Sounds. Shirley, Frances Ann. Universty of Nebraska Press 1963 Lincoln. LOCN: Pr3095s53

413   Shakespeare Memorial Theatre, Acoustic Diagram. Architectural Review, Je 1932, P. 226.

414   Sight Lines for the Performing Arts - an Approach Utilizing High Speed Digital Computer Technology. Frink, Peter H. M.F.A. Thesis, Yale University, 1967.

415   Simulated Sound Fields Programmed from Acoustic Model Data. Klepper, D.L. and Kirkegaard, R.L. and Terroux, Peter and Watters,

B.G. Unpublished Paper: 79th Acoustical Society of America Meeting, Ap 1970, Atlantic City, N.J.

416   Slip Disks and Backstage Sound. Yeaton, Kelly. Players Magazine, N, 1948, Vol. 25, No. 2, P. 33.

417   Some Applications of a Programmable Power Switch/Amplifier. Campbell, L.R. and Wittlinger, H.A. RCA ICAN 6048, N 1972.

418   Some Came Running. Bartram, Reg. Tabs, Fall 1977, Vol. 35, No. 3, P. 23.

419   Some Sound Advice on Stage Sound. Tabs, D 1950, Vol. 8, No. 3, P. 17.

420   Some Sound Advice. Progressive Architecture, N 1975, P. 54.

421   Sound/Being-Heard Over the Rattle of Glassware. Theatre Crafts, Mr/Ap 1976, Vol. 10, No. 2, P. 23.

422   Soundboard?. Walne, Graham. Tabs, Autumn 1976, Vol. 34, No. 3, P. 14.

423   Sounding Board for a Large Auditorium. Popular Mechanics, N 1961, Vol. 26, P. 772.

424   Sound Abosrbing Materials. Zwikker, C. and Koster, C. W. Elsevier, 1949, New York.

425   Sound Advise. Tabs, D 1938, Vol. 2, No. 3, P. 11.

426   Sound As Environment. Withey, J. A. Players Magazine, N, 1960, Vol. 37, No. 2, P. 34.

427   Sound Control for Opera. Burris-Meyer, Harold. Theatre Arts Magazine, Jl

1941, Vol. XXV, No. 7, P. 540.

428   Sound Control Techniques for the Legitimate Theatre and Opera. Burris-Meyer, Harold and Mallory, Vincent. Theatre Design & Technology, Fall 1979, Vol. XV, No. 3, P. 31-34.

429   Sound Effects: a Look into the Past. Willis, Edgar. Journal of Broadcasting, 1956/7, Vol. 1, P. 327.

430   Sound Effects. National Broadcasting Co. Mr 19 1938.

431   Sound Equipment Backstage. Yeaton, Kelly. Players Magazine, Mr 1948, Vol. 24, No. 6, P. 131.

432   Sound for the Arena. Yeaton, Kelly. Players Magazine, My, 1952, Vol. 28, No. 8, P. 179.

433   Sound Insulation and Room Acoustics. Bruel, Per Vilhelm. Chapman Hall, 1951, London.

434   Sound in the Theatre. Burris-Meyer, Harold and Mallory, Vincent. Radio Magazine, Inc., 1959, New York. LOCN: 59-13950

435   Sound in the Theatre. Wicks, K. Studio Sound, Jl 1972, Vol. 14, P. 65; and Ag 1972, Vol. 14, P. 59.

436   Sound on Stage. Nelson, Terry. Studio Sound, Ap, My, Jl, Ag 1978.

437   Sound Recording Practice. Borwick, John (Editor). Oxford University Press, 1977.

438   Sound Reproduction in the Theatre. Burris-Meyer, Harold and Mallory,

Vincent. Theatre Arts Books, 1965, New York.

439   Sound Solutions: a Portable Sound System for Outdoor Theatres. Corbett, Tom. Theatre Crafts, My 1979, Vol. 13, No. 3.

440   Sound Systems for Large Auditoriums. Beranek, Leo L. Acoustical Society of America Journal, S 1954, Vol. XXVI, P. 661-675.

441   Sound Systems. Klepper, D.L. Progressive Architecture, Ag 1961, P. 140.

442   Sound Systems. Newman, Robert B. and Cavanaugh, William J. Architectural Record, D 1961, P. 161-162.

443   Sound System Design for Legitimate Theatre (A). Stricken, Frank W. Educational Theatre Journal, O 1964, Vol. XVI, No. 3, P. 230.

444   Sound System for a Theatre. Talley, C. Horton. Players Magazine, F, 1952, Vol. 28, No.5, P. 110.

445   Sound System for the Theatre (A). Theroux, Dappy. Theatre Crafts Jl 1967.

446   Sound Technicians's Manual. Thompson, James W. M.F.A. Thesis, Yale University, 1952.

447   Sound. Watson, F. R. John Wiley, 1935, New York.

448   Speech Acoustics for the Theatre. Klepper, D.L. Theatre Design & Technology O 1973.

449   Stages of the World; a Pictorial Survey of Theatre. Theatre Arts Books, 1949, New York. LOCN: 792.084 T35 1949 4

450   Stage Effects and How to Get Them. Theatre Magazine, Jl 1924, P. 12.

451   Stage Effects. Brown, Theodore. Work, J 12, 1913, Vol. 45, P. 297.

452   Stage Management for the Amateur Theatre. Halstead, William Perdue. F.S. Crofts & Co., 1937, New York.

453   Stage Managing by Megaphone and Telephone. Popular Mechanics Vol.16 S 1911 P.412.

454   Stage Noises and Effects. Green, Michael. Herbert Jenkins, 1958, London.

455   Stage Noises. Grein, G.C. Illustrated London News, S 22, 1928, Vol. 173, P. 516.

456   Stage Sounds. Vincent, Harley. Strand Vol.28 O 1904 P.417.

457   Stage Sound Cabinet Made in Form of Trunk. Popular Mechanics Vol.24 O1915 P.508.

458   Stage Sound. Collison, David. Drama Book Specialists, 1976, New York. LOCN: Tk7881.9. C65 ISBN: 0910482659

459   State Anti-Sound Piracy Laws and a Proposed Model Statute: a Time to Consolidate the Victories Against Sound Pirates. Pesserilo, Ira M. Performing Arts Review, 1978, Vol. 8, No. 1, P. 1.

460   State Committee for Civil Construction and Architecture, Associated With Gosstre, USSR. Kremlin Palace of Congresses (The), Stroiizdatelstvo, 1966, Moscow.

461   Stevens Sound System. Theatre Arts Magazine, Jl 1932, Vol. XVI, No. 7, P. 590.

462   Story and Facts About the Krannert Center for the Performing Arts(The). University of Illinois, N.D., Urbana, Illinois. No Date.

463   Study in the Use of Sound Effects in the Elizabethan Stage (A). Brock, James W. Ph.D. Thesis, Northwestern Univ., 1950. LOCN: Diss 378 Mu 1950

464   Deleted.

465   Stuff of Radio (The). Sieveking, Lance. Cassell & Co., Ltd., 1934, London.

466   Surround Sound: Guideline for Background Entertainment and Sound Systems. Fause, Kenneth. Theatre Crafts, S 1977.

467   Sydney Opera House Affair (The). Baume, Michael. Nelson, 1967, Melbourne and London.

468   Taffy's 1978-79 Catalogue of Records and Books. Taffy's, 701 Beta Dr., Cleveland, Oh 44143.

469   Taking Pictures and Acoustics. Balbi, C. M. R. Electrical Review, (The), 1931, P 123.

470   Tale of Two Cities: Berlin's and New York's Philharmonic Halls. Architectural Forum, F 1963.

471   Talk on Opera Houses (A). Bagenal, Hope. Architectural Association Journal, Je 1956, Vol. 72, P. 16-21.

472   Technical Aspects of
Sound. Richardson, E. G.
Elsevier, 1953, Amsterdam.

473   Telephone in Theatrical
Management (The).
Scientific American
Supplement, Ag 1909, Vol.
68, P. 110.

474   Theater (The). Adler,
Dankmar. Prairie School
Review, 1965, Vol. 2, No.
2, P. 21-27.

475   Theatres; an
Architectural and Cultural
History. Tidworth, Simon.
Praeger Publishers, 1973,
New York. LOCN: Na 6821.
T48 1973

476   Theatre Acoustics: Some
Results and Warnings.
Bagenal, Hope. Royal
Institute of British
Architects, Journal, Mr 20,
1939, Third Series, Vol.
46, P. 500-504.

477   Theatre Acoustics,
Ventilating and Lighting.
Stanton, G. T.
Architectural Record, Jl
1930, Vol. 68, P. 87-96.

478   Theatre Acoustics.
Potwin, C.C. Arch. Record,
Jl 1938, P. 118.

479   Theatre and Sound.
Neilson, J.C. Builder,
(The), F 5, 1876, P. 129.

480   Theatre Arrangements.
Builder, Ag 15, 1863, Vol.
21, P. 580.

481   Theatre Chair Acoustics.
Henrikson, B.W. Theatre
Design and Technology, My
1967, P. 24.

482   Theatre Comes of
Architectural Age; New
Developments in Visual and
Aural Control Impress
Functionalism on Design
(The). Arch. Record, N
1940, P. 114-118.

483   Theatre Design. Izenour,
George C. McGraw-Hill Book
Company 1977 New York.
LOCN: Na6821 I94 Folio
ISBN: 0070320861

484   Theatre Discovers the
Tape Recorder. Wilson, John
S. Theatre Arts Magazine, F
1961, Vol. XLV, No. 2, P.
18.

485   Theatre Notes. General
Radio Experimenter (The),
1933, Vol. 8, P. 7.

486   Theatre Sound and
Communication Systems.
Klepper, D.L. Theatre
Design & Technology F 1972.

487   Theatre Sound Systems.
Culver, Max. Players,
Je/Jl, 1969, Vol. 44, No.
5, P. 195.

488   Theatre Student: Sound
and Music for the Theatre
(The). Waaser, Carol M. R.
Rosen Press, 1976, New
York.

489   Theory of Sound (The).
Rayleigh, J.W.S. Macmillan
& Co., 1894, London; Also,
Dover, 1945, New York, 2
Vols.

490   Three-Dimensional Sound
for the Legitimate Stage.
Ranger, Richard H. Theatre
Arts Magazine, N 1959, Vol.
XLIII, No. 11, P. 77.

491   Timing of "Noises-Off".
Beddow, S. Drama, O, 1937,
Vol. 16, P. 11.

492   Toward an Alternative
Theatre Technology.
Wickinson, Darryl and
Mckenzie, Ian. Theatre
Australia, Ag 1976, Vol.1,
No.1, P.49.

493   To See and Hear the
Play. Motherwell, Hiram.
Stage, O 1939, P. 27.

494   To See or to Hear;
Orientation of Outdoor
Theatres. Quinby, G.
Theatre Design & Technology
My 1966.

495   Trick Ventriloquism.
Merton, H.R. Technical
World Vol.19 Ap 1913 P.226.

496   Trinity South Repertory
File. Harvard Theatre
Collection. No Date.

497   Tubes Versus Transistors
- Is There an Audible
Difference?. Hamm, R.O.
Journal of the Audio
Engineering Society, My
1973, Vol. 21, P. 267.

498   Tuning the Hall for
Theatre. Dewey, Walter S.
Players, Ap/My, 1968, Vol.
43, No. 4, P. 102.

499   Tuning the Legitimate
Theatre. Fitzgerald, T.R.
Theatre Crafts My 1969.

500   Twin Theatres in Sweden.
Martin Tyr. Tabs, D 1970,
P.131-137.

501   Two Audio Cable Testers.
Corbett, Tom. Theatre
Crafts, S 1979, Vol. 13,
No. 4, P. 130.

502   Tyrone Guthrie Theatre
(The). Progressive
Architecture, D 1963, V ol.
XLIV, No. 12, P. 98-105.

503   University of Michigan
Repertory (The). Roche, K.
Architectural Record, My
1968, P.156-157.

504   Variable Acoustics.
Berry, Geoffrey. Tabs,
Summer, 1978, Vol. 36, No.
2, P. 9.

505   Wagner's German National
Theatre at Bayreuth.
Builder, Je 15, 1872, Vol.
30, P. 466.

506   Welsh National Theatre
Planned at Cardiff; Moving
Ceiling Controls Opera and
Drama Acoustics. Surveyor,
Ag 3, 1963, P. 963-964.

507   Whether the Theatre Is
Empty or Full, the
Acoustics Should Be the
Same. Friend, W. K.
American Architect, F,
1932, Vol. 141, P. 34.

508   Who Builds Theatres and
Why?. Reiss, A. Drama
Review (The), S 1968,
P.75-92.

509   Wonder of Our Stage
(The). Waddington, M. and
Barnett, M. Theatre Design
& Technology, Spring, 1979,
Vol. XV, No. 1, P. 8.

510   Work of the Sound
Engineers. Popular
Mechanics, My, 1937, Vol.
67, P. 702.

511   Young Vic: Theatre on a
Budget (The). Howell, Bill.
Riba Journal, Jy 1971,
London, P.287-289.

III
Lighting

512   Abc of the Electric
Light. Builder, (The), My
20, 1882, P. 603.

513   About Arcs. Tabs, S
1948, Vol. 6, No. 2, P. 11.

514   About Gas. Appleton's
Journal VII F 1872.

515   About Shop Orders.
Watson, Lee. Lighting
Dimensions D 1977.

516   Acting Area Flood and
Stage Lighting. Tabs, S
1951, Vol. 9, No. 2, P. 20.

517   Actor and Audience: a
Study of Experimental
Theatre in the United
States. Hudson, Lynton.
George Harras and Co.,
1951, London.

518   Adieu to Snuffing
Candles. Melling, John
Kennedy and Nolloth, Ann
Gloria. Tabs, D, 1957, Vol.
15, No. 3, P. 18.

519   Administrative Intern
Programs in Professional
Resident Theatres. Hardy,
Michael C. Theatre News,
S,o 1978, P.17-20, Vol. XI
No.1.

520   Adolphe Appia, Prophet
of the Modern Theatre: a
Profile. Volbach, Walther
R. Wesleyan University
Press, 1968, Middletown,
Ct.

521   Adolph Appia: the
Rebirth of Dramatic Art.
Mercier, Jean. Theatre Arts
Monthly, Ag, 1932, Vol.
XVI, No. 8, P. 61 5.

522   Aesthetics for the
Designer. Bellman, Willard
F. Educational Theatre
Journal, 1953, Vol. 5, P.
117-124.

523   Agents for Lighting
Designers. Watson, Lee.

Lighting Dimensions, N
1978, Vol. 2, No. 9, P. 16.

524   A Halleluja Hollywood.
Dwight, Michael. Tabs Sum
1975.

525   Air Fare: Inflatable
Structures. Progressive
Architecture, Ag 1972, P.
76.

526   Alexander's Brainchild.
Loney, Glenn. Theatre
Crafts, N/D 1968, P. 29-41.

527   Alhambra Theatre,
Leicester Square. Builder,
(The), D 10, 1881, P. 739.

528   All About House Wiring.
Mix, Floyd and Pritchard,
E.C. Goodheart-Wilcox Co.,
1954, Chicago.

529   All the Lighting of the
House Is Done by
Electricity. Zekiel, M.E.
Theatre Design & Technology
D 1971.

530   Alternating Current
Electricity. Timbie, W. H.
and Higbie H.H. Chapman &
Hall 1914.

531   Alternating Current
Work. Maycock, William
Perren. Pitman, 1932, New
York.

532   Alupalast: Portable
Light Metal Theatre As
Erected at Hanover.
Architect & Building News,
Ja 9, 1948, P.34-35.

533   Amateur Lighting.
Meisel, Burton E. Players
Magazine, N, 1957, Vol. 34,
No. 2, P. 33.

534   American Dramatist
(The). Montrose, J. Moses.
Little, Brown, 1925,
Boston.

535   American Electricians
Handbook. Croft, Terrell.

McGraw-Hill, 1942, New York
& London. Reprinted in
1952.

536   American Practice of Gas
Piping and Gas Lighting.
Gerhard, William P. McGraw
Pub., 1908., New York.

537   American Theater--VIII:
Theater Lighting (The).
Blackall, Clarence H.
Brickbuilder, Jl 1908, Vol.
17, P. 133.

538   American View of the
West End (An). Firmin,
Charles H. Tabs Sum 1975.

539   America Saw Us. Bundy,
William. Tabs, D, 1958,
Vol. 16, No. 3, P. 11.

540   Am I Lit Here?. Reid,
Francis. Tabs Mr 1973.

541   Analytical and
Descriptive Study of Louis
Hartman's Contribution to
Modern Theatre Lighting
(An). Lynch, Edmund. Ph.D.
Thesis, University of
Denver, 1963.

542   Analytic Survey and an
Electric Synthesis of
Current Practices in Arena
Theatre (An). Rudenshield,
Harry. M.A. Thesis,
University of Nebraska,
1961.

543   and the Lord Said.
Edwards, H. Tabs, D 1946,
Vol. 4, No. 2, P. 8.

544   and the Winner Is.
Lighting Dimensions, N
1979, P. 23-34.

545   Angles for Thrusts.
Reid, Francis. Tabs,
Summer, 1975.

546   Annie. Rasmuson, Judy.
Lighting Dimensions, Jl/Ag
1977, P. 19.

547   Another Voice-Another

Room. Ocean, Richard.
Lighting Dimensions, S
1978, Vol. 2, No. 7, P. 82.

548   ANTA Repertory Theater
Opens Temporary Quarters.
Progressive Architecture,
Mr 1965, P. 68.

549   Appia's Contribution to
the Modern Stage. Simonson,
Lee. Theatre Arts Monthly
XVI, Ag 1932, P. 631.

550   Appia Fifty Years Later
II. Albright, H.D.
Quarterly Journal of
Speech, O 1949, P.295-98,
Vol. XXXV.

551   Appia Fifty Years Later
I. Albright, H.D.
Quarterly Journal of
Speech, Ap 1949, Vol. XXXV,
P. 182-85.

552   Appia. Leeper, Janet.
Architectural Review, F
1968, Vol. 143, P. 113-118.

553   Applications of Digital
Computing Machinery to
Theatre Arts Education.
Hovar, Linn. Ph.D. Thesis,
University of Kansas, 1973.

554   Applications of Laserium
Technique to Performance
Lighting. Alvis, Arthur.
Ph.D. Thesis, Columbia
University, 1980.

555   Applications of Lasers
and Holography in Theatre
Motion Pictures. Outwater,
Chris. Theatre Design and
Technology, Fall 1978, Vol.
XIV, No. 3, P. 8-10.

556   Application and an
Evaluation of Par-38 and
R-40 Lamps and Accessories
in Low Budget
Non-Professional Theatrical
Production (The). Weiss,
David W. M.A. Thesis,
University of Wisconsin,
1951.

557   Application Data for Proper Dimming of Cold Cathode Fluorescent Tubing. Carpenter, William. Illuminating Engineering, Je 1951, Vol. XLVI, P. 306.

558   Application of the Electric Light in Theatres. Scientific American Supplement XVI, 1883, No. 10.

559   Approaches and Methods of Lighting for the Commericial Theatre. Sargent, Peter E. M.F.A. Thesis, 1963, Yale University.

560   Approaching a Tv News Setting. Hoffman, Paul S. Theatre Crafts, N/D 1979, Vol. 13, No. 6, P. 26-29.

561   Approaching Performing Arts Training: a Focused Training Program at North Carolina School of the Arts. MacKay, Patricia. Theatre Crafts, O 1978, Vol. 12, No. 6, P. 37.

562   Aquatic Circus (An). Engineer, Mr 1886, Vol. 61.

563   Architectural Approach in the Lighting of Severance Hall (The). Stedman, C.W. Transactions of the Illuminating Engineering Society, Ap 1931, Vol. XXVI, No. 4, P. 351-59.

564   Architectural Lighting Graphics. Flynn, John Edward. Reinhold Publishers, 1962, New York. LOCN: Tk4188.F56

565   Architectural Lighting. Aldrich, Walter, N. M.F.A. Thesis, 1937, Yale University.

566   Architectural Physics; Lighting. Hopkinson, R. H.M. Stationery Office, 1963, London.

567   Architect and the Emperor of Assyria: a Scenograph of Light (The). Arnott, Brian. Drama Review, Je 1973, Vol. 17, P. 73.

568   Arc Images. Jackson, J.C. Lighting Dimensions, Ap 1978, Vol. 2, No. 4, P. 18.

569   Arc Lamp and Color Screens for Stage Illumination. American Electrician, XII, S 1901, P. 463.

570   Arena for a Resident Company. Progressive Architecture, F 1962, P. 124.

571   Arena Lighting: an Analysis of Four Methods. Abbott, Stanley. Theatre Annual, 1965-1966, P. 76-87.

572   Arena Lighting, a Survey. Griffiths, Bruce. M.F.A. Thesis, Yale University, 1951.

573   Arena Staging. Skinner, Ted. Dramatics, N and D, 1953, P. 24.

574   Are Your Mirror Spots Efficient. Tabs, D 1960, Vol. 18, No. 3, P. 28.

575   Artificial Light; Its Influence Upon Civilization. Luckiesh, Matthew. Century Books of Useful Science 1920.

576   Artificial Lighting for Out-of-Dorrs. Bragdon, Claude. Theatre Arts, Ag, 1917, Vol. I, No. 4, P. 190.

577   Artificial Light and Its Application to Photography. Baxter, S.S. Recreative Science, III, 1862.

578   Artificial Light and Its Application. Westinghouse Electric and Manufacturing Company, 1940.

579   Artificial Sky Method of Stage Lighting (The). Illuminating Engineer, 1920, Vol. 13, P. 233.

581   Arts of Stage Lighting (The). Fagan, J.B. Illuminating Engineer (The) May, 1919, P. 119.

582   Art and Language of Stage Lighting (The). Rosenthal, Jean. Theatre Arts, Ag 1961, Vol. XLV, No. 8, P. 17.

583   Art and Science of Stage Lighting. Sellman, H.D. Players Magazine, N 1925, Vol. 2, No. 1, P. 4. Vol. 2 is misprinted as 5 on cover.

584   Art Conjured Out of Space and Time. Frankenstein, Alfred. San Francisco Chronicle, N 9, 1938.

585   Art in the Theatre: the Question of Reform. Telbin, William. Magazine of Art, 1894, Vol. 17, P. 44-48.

586   Art Nouveau and Art Deco Lighting. Duncan, Alastair. Simon & Schuster, 1978, New York.

587   Art of Color and Design (The). Graves, Maitland. McGraw-Hill Book Co., Inc., 1941, New York.

588   Art of Colour. Jacobs, Michel. Doubleday, Doran & Co., 1931, Garden City, New York.

589   Art of Illumination (The). Bell, Louis. McGraw, 1902, New York.

590   Art of Light (The).

Glassgold, C. Adolph. Arts, F 1929, XV, P. 133-134.

591   Art of Light (The). Kahmann, G.A. News and Views, My 1939.

592   Art of Light and Color (The). Jones, Tom Douglas. Van Nostrand Reinhold, 1972, New York.

594   Art of Stage Lighting (The). Bentham, Frederick. Taplinger Publishing Company, 1968, New York. LOCN: Pn2091 E4 B398 1970

595   Art Theatre (The). Cheney, Sheldon. Alfred Knopf, 1925, New York.

596   Assembly Hall Lighting. Progressive Architecture, Ap 1964, P. 176.

597   Astonishing New Theory of Color (An). Bello, Francis. Fortune, My 1959, P. 144.

598   As Near As Your Mail Box. Bean, Louis Burke. Dramatics, Ja 1952, Vol. 23, P. 6, 35.

599   Attachment for Arc Lamps. Electrical World, Vol. IV, O 1884.

600   Attention All Students. Watson, Lee. Lighting Dimensions, Jl/Ag 1977, P. 10.

601   At the Court of King Cotton. Williams, Michael. Tabs, Sp 1977.

602   Audience Reactions to Certain Primary Colors of Light on Actor's Faces in Dramatic Scenes. Pierce, James Franklin. M.A. Thesis, State University of Iowa, 1942.

603   Audience Sees (The) Part I, II. Burris-Meyer, Harold

and cole, Wendell.
Progressive Architecture,
Ap 1948, P. 75, Progressive
Architecture, My 1948, P.
88.

604   Audio Cyclopedia.
Tremaine, Howard M. Sams &
Co., 1969, Indianapolis.

605   Auditorium and
Stagelight Control in
Schools. Wells, L.J.
Journal of Electricity,
1926, Vol. 57, P. 61.

606   Auto-Transformer Dimmers
for Stage Lighting in
Intimate Amateur Theatres.
Hardman, Stuart Floyd. M.A.
Thesis, University of
Washington, 1949.

607   Automated Lighting
Systems at Nippon Hoso
Kyokai, Part II. Glickman,
Richard. Lighting
Dimensions, Je 1979, Vol.
3, No. 6, P. 10.

608   Automated Lighting
Systems at Nippon Hoso
Kyokai, Part I. Glickman,
Richard. Lighting
Dimensions, Ap 1979, Vol.
3, No. 4, P. 26.

609   Automatic Plotting and
Recording of Lighting
Changes. Tabs, S 1959, Vol.
17, No. 2, P. 22.

610   Automation or
Mechanization. Howard,
George T. Educational
Theatre Journal, O 1958,
Vol. X, No. 3, P. 250.

611   Automobile Theatre (An).
Theatre Magazine (The), My
1911, Vol. XIII, No. 123,
P. 168.

612   A Non-Union Response: an
Open Letter. Theatre Craft,
My/Je 1980, Vol. 14, No. 3,
P. 94.

613   B. Iden Payne Theatre:

Univ. of Texas at Austin.
Rothgeb, John R. Theatre
Design & Technology Wi
1976.

614   Baby Mirror Spotlights
Developments. Tabs, Ap
1955, Vol. 13, No. 1, P.
18.

615   Baby Spot (The).
Electrician, 1921, Vol. 87,
P. 471.

616   Ballroom: Tharon Musser
Lights the Ballroom Floor.
MacKay, Patricia. Theatre
Crafts, Mr/ap 1979, vol.
13, No. 2, P. 15.

617   Bara & Barrels. Tabs, Ap
1953, Vol. 11, No. 1, P.
16.

618   Bard Goes Abroad (The).
Tabs, Ap 1954, Vol. 12, No.
1, P. 15.

619   Basic Color. Jacobson,
Egbert. Paul Theobald,
1948, Chicago.

620   Basic Electricity.
Turner, Rufus P. Holt,
Rinehart and Winston, 1961,
New York.

621   Basic Electronics.
Volkenburgh, Van. John F.
Rider Publishing, Inc.,
1955, Vol. 1, New York.

622   Basic Home Wiring
Illustrated. Sunset Books.
Lane Publishing, Co., 1977,
Menlo Park, California.

623   Basic Stage Lighting and
Equipment. Faraday, E. E.
Furse, 1953, Nottingham.

624   Beatlemania. Andrews,
Richard. Cue Technical
Theatre Review, Ja/F 1980,
P. 18-20.

625   Before and Behind the
Curtain. Northall, William
K. Burgess, 1851, New York.

626   Beginner's Guide to
Lantern Design: I.
Anderson, Bob. Sightline,
ABTT Journal, Sp 1980, Vol.
14, No. 1, P. 41-47.

627   Beginner's Guide to
Laser Lighting (a). Lodge,
Frank. Lighting Dimensions,
F 1978, Vol. 2, No. 2, P.
38.

629   Beginning of the
Incandescent Lamp and
Lighting System (The).
Edison, Thomas Alva. Edison
Institute (The), 1976,
Dearborn, Michigan.

630   Behind the Footlights.
Coryell, John Russel.
Harper's Weekly, Je 1889.

631   Behind the Scenes at Ben
Hur. Ellsworth, William W.
Critic, Mr 1900, Vol. 36,
P. 245-49.

632   Behind the Scenes at
Drury Lane; How the Scenery
of the Pantomime Is
Illuminated. Graphic, Ja
1910, Vol. 81, P. 13.

633   Behind the Scenes at Her
Majesty's Theatre.
Electrician, Ag 21, 1885,
Vol. 15.

634   Behind the Scenes During
a Play. Fyles, Franklin.
The Ladies' Home Journal,
XVII, Ap 1890.

635   Behind the Scenes of an
Opera House. Kobbe, Gustav.
Scribners Magazine, O 1888,
Vol. 4 P. 435.

636   Behind the Scenes.
Belgravis, 1861, Vol. XLIV.

637   Belasco: Stage Realist.
Moses, Montrose J.
Independent, My 29, 1916,
P. 334.

638   Bespoke Lighting from
the Standing Rig. Walne,

Graham. Cue Technical
Theatre Review, My/Ju 1980,
P. 16.

639   Between Windward and
Lee. Fitkin, Norman. Tabs
Fall 1975.

640   Bibliographic History of
Electricity and Magnetism,
Chronologically Arranged.
Mottelay, Paul F. London,
1922.

641   Bibliography of Books
Related to Stage Lighting
(A). Harris, Judy. M.F.A.
Thesis, Carnegie-Melon
University, 1961.

642   Big Pond: a Comedy by
George Middleton (The).
Middleton, George. 1928
Prompt Book at New York
Public Library Theatre
Collection.

643   Bijou Theatre Opening.
Boston Daily Advertiser, D
12, 1882, P. 2.

644   Bill Mcmanus, Lighting
Designer. Lighting
Dimensions, Ja 1978, Vol.
2, No. 1, P. 28.

645   Birmingham Repertory
Theatre (The). Work, N,
1922, Vol. 40, P. 427.

646   Bits and Pieces.
Manning, Ferd. Lighting
Dimensions, F 1979, Vol. 3,
No. 2, P. 51.

647   Black Light. Tabs, O
1938, Vol. 2, No. 2, P. 18.

648   Black Theatre: a
Resource Directory. Primus,
Mark (Ed). Black Theatre
Alliance, 1546 Broadway,
Ny, N.Y. 10036. No Date.

649   Blessed Plot (This).
Reid, Francis. Tabs Je
1972.

650   Blinded by Science.

Schwiller, John. Tabs, Summer 1978, Vol. 36, No. 2, P. 18.

651   Blue Bird, The. Hadley, Grace T. Popular Electricity, Ja 1913, Vol. 5, P. 946-947.

652   Boise's Gastation, Houston's Ritz. Marks, Jill. Lighting Dimensions, Jl 1979, P. 26.

653   Book of the Play: Studies and Illustrations of Histrionic Story, Life, and Character (A). Cook, D. Sampson, Low, Marston, Searle & Rivington, 1876.

654   Book Reviews & a Reply. Watson, Lee. Lighting Dimensions, O 1978, Vol. 2, No. 10, P. 14.

655   Boots With Strawberry Jam at the Nottingham Playhouse. Bear, B. E. Tabs, Je 1968, Vol. 26, No.2 , P. 15.

656   Borders Are a Bore. Tabs, S 1950, Vol. 8, No. 2, P. 4.

657   Boston Opera House (The). Electrical World, LV, My 12, 1910, P. 1191.

658   Boxed to Take Away. Woodham, Peter. Tabs, D 1970, P. 138.

659   Box Truss Theory Debunked (The). Callahan, Michael. Lighting Dimensions, Ap 1979, Vol. 3, No. 4, P. 50.

660   Bricks Mortar and the Performing Arts; Report. Martin, Mayer. Twentieth Century Fund, 1970, New York.

661   Bridges and Slots. Carr, Martin. Tabs, D 1965, Vol. 23, No. 4, P. 35.

662   Brighter Stage Lighting. Legge, Brian. Tabs S 1971.

663   Bright Caravan of Light. Tabs, Autumn 1976, Vol. 34, No. 3, P. 12.

664   British Engraving of Gas Fixtures Dates from 1820-1830. Division of Prints and Photographs. Library of Congress, Lot 2728, Washington, D. C. No Date.

665   Broadcasting in America: a Survey of Television and Radio. Head, Sydney W. Houghton, Mifflin Company, 1956, Boston.

666   Bronze Lighting Fixtures; a Collection of Lamp Standards, Tripods, Lanterns, Wall Fixtures, Chandeliers, Etc. Catalogue L. Gorham Company, New York, 1916. Located at Avery Columbia University.

667   Building for the Performing Arts. Architectural Forum, Je 1960, Vol. 112, No. 6, P. 86-103.

668   Building Illumination; the Effect of New Lighting Levels. National Research Council, Building Research Institute Washington, National Academy of Sciences, 1959.

669   Build Your Own Direct Beam. Conway, John A. Players Magazine, Ja 1953.

670   Build Your Own 60 Amp, Single Phase, 3-Wire, 120/}40 Vac Power Distribution System. Wenger, David L. Lighting Dimensions, O 1978, Vol. 2, No. 10, P. 57.

671   Bursary Awards for Technicians. ABTT News, D/Ja 1980, P. 20.

672   Buxton Opera House.
Tabs, S 1938, Vol. 2, No.
1, P. 10.

673   C.I.E. Tabs Sum 1975.

674   Calculations of
Candle-Power and Color
Temperature of Tungsten
Lamps. Sant, A. and Leta,
J. Journal of the Society
of Motion Picture and
Television Engineers, D
1956, Vol. XLV, No. 12.

675   Caligari's Cabinet and
Other Grand Illusions: a
History of Film Design.
Barsacq, Leon. New American
Library, 1970, New York.

676   Canada Council and the
Performing Arts. Coffin,
Ann M. Theatre Design &
Technology, O 1966, No. 6,
P. 8.

677   Candlelight. Craig,
Edward Gordon. In: Books
and Theatres, 1925, London,
P.139-144.

678   deleted.

679   Caravaggio in College:
Jo Mielziner Creates a
Projection Spectacular.
Loney, Glenn. Theatre
Design & Technology, F
1973, No. 32, P. 25.

680   Carbon Arc and Follow
Spotting (The). Price,
Michael P. Players, N,
1962, Vol. XXXIX, No. 2, P.
42.

681   Carbon Arc As a
Theatrical Light Source
(The). Skirpan, Stephen J.
M.F.A. Thesis, Yale
University, 1956.

682   Careers and
Opportunities in the
Theatre. Darymple, Jean.
E.P. Dutton & Co., 1969,
New York.

683   Careers. Theatre Crafts,
N/d 1978, Vol. 12, No. 7,
P 86-91.

684   Carolina Playmakers'
Touring Equipment. Davis,
Harry. Theatre Arts Monthly
Jl, 1937, Vol. XXI, No. 7,
P. 581.

685   Carpentry and
Candlelight in the Theatre.
Mayor, A. Metropolitan
Museum Bulletin, F 1943,
No. 1, P. 198-203.

686   Carter on the Arts.
American Council for the
Arts, Sum-Fall 1978.

687   Cashing in on Coherent
Light. Marks, Jill.
Lighting Dimensions, S,
1979, P.7.

688   Cassandra Henning:
Developing an Indoor
Spectacular For Coca-Cola.
Lighting Dimensions, Je
1980, P. 18.

689   Catalogue of an
Important Collection of
Antique Historical Lamps
Candlesticks, Lanterns,
Relics, Etc. Norton,
C.A.Q. Parsons, 1914, New
York.

690   Catalogue of Books and
Papers Relating to
Electricity, Magnetism, the
Electric Telegraph, Etc.,
Including the Ronalds
Library. Ronalds, Francis.
London, 1880.

691   Catalog. Kliegle Bros,
1922, New York; Capitol
Stage Lighting, 1928, 1939,
New York; Century 1931,
1932; Kliegle Borther,.
located at the Harvard
Theatre Collection.

692   Catfish and Lighting
System Design. Jerit, Ron.
Lighting Dimensions, Ag
1979, P. 20.

693   Cavalcade of Stage Lighting (A). Applegate, L.G. Illuminating Engineer (The), Mr 1935.

694   CBS-knxt Computer Control System for Program Switching. Ettlinger, Adrian B. Journal of the Society of Motion Picture and Television Engineers, S 1961, Vol. 70, P. 691-695.

695   CBS Television Staging and Lighting Practices. O'brien, Richard S. Cbs-Tv General Engineering Department Publications, 1950.

696   Central Staging. Taylor, James Cleveland. Dramatics, F, 1950, Vol. 21,p. 5.

697   Central Staging. Jennings, Blandford. Bulletin of the National Association of Secondary School Principals, (The) D 1949, Vol. 33, P. 145-148.

698   Century of Signal Glass Developments (A). Killigrew, D.L. Railway Signaling and Communications, My 1949.

699   Century Theatre (The). Tabs, S 1954, Vol. 12, No. 2, P. 10.

700   Century Theatre Lighting Catalog. Century Theatre, 1957, Clifton, N.J.

701   Chamber Drama. Guthrie, John. Pear Tree Press, 1930, Flansham, Sussex, England.

702   Chapter from the Book on Architecture. Serlio, Sebastian. Mask (The), Mr, 1908, Vol. 1, No. 1, P. 14.

703   Characteristics of Down-Stage Lighting. McCandless, Stanley. Architectural Record, F 1951, Vol. 109, P. 142-145.

704   Characteristics of Incandescent Lamps for Theatre Stages, Television and Film Studios. Clark C.N. Illuminating Engineering, Jy 1966, Vol. LXI, No. 7.

705   Characteristics of Theatrical Lighting Equipment Using Tungsten Halogen Lamps. Lemons, T.M. and Levine, R.E. Theatre Design & Technology My 1968.

706   Characteristics of Tungsten Filaments As Function of Temperature(The). Jones, H. and Langmuir, L. General Electric Review, 1927, Vol. XXX.

707   Characteristic Equasions of Vacuum and Gas-filled Tungsten Filament Lamps. Barbrow and Meyer. Bureau of Standards Journal of Research, 1932.

708   Cheap and Easy Dimming. Myrick, George. Theatre Crafts, Ja/F 1979, P. 74, Vol. 13, No. 1.

709   Chelsea Theatre Centre (The). Napoleon, Davi. Theatre Crafts O 1977.

710   Chicago USA Lighting Exam. Watson, Lee. Lighting Dimensions, Jl 1979, P. 19.

711   Choosing a Spotlight. Erhardt, Louis. Theatre Design & Technology, Spring 1978, P. 11, Vol. XIV, No. 1.

712   Chormatics. Field, George. David Bogue, 1845, London.

713   Chorus Line, Computorized Lighting Control Comes to Broadway (A). Theatre Crafts, N 1975.

714   Christmas Tale, or Harlequin Scene Painter, (A). Allen, Ralph G. Tennessee Studies in Literature, 1974, Vol. 19, P. 194-161.

715   Chronological History of Electrical Development F rom 600 B. C. National Electrical Manufacturere Assn., 1946, New York.

716   Chronological History of Electricity (A). National Electrical Manufacturers Association. No Date.

717   Cid: the Latest Compact Source Arc Lamp for Film and Television. Glickman, Richard. Lighting Dimensions, My 1980, P. 10.

718   Cinema Technique in Lighting Places: Its Value on the Stage. New York Herald Tribune, Ja 24, 1937, P.20.

719   Cinemoid Colour Medium. Tabs, S 1946, Vol. 4, No. 1, P. 21.

720   Circuit Diagram Found. Lighting Dimensions, Ag 1979, P. 9.

721   Circus. Winckler, Carlton. Lighting Diemensions, S 1977, P. 20.

722   Civil Defence. Tabs, Ap 1961, Vol. 19, No. 1, P. 19.

723   Clavilux Recital Given by Wilfred. New York Times, N 2, 1940.

724   Clavilux. Runes, Dagobert D. and Harry G. Schrickel. Encyclopedia of the Arts, New York: Philosophical Library, 19 64, P. 230, 231.

725   Clavilux. Encyclopedia Britannica, 14th Ed., V, 1929, P. 784.

726   Collection of Heating and Lighting Utensils in the United States National Museum. United States National Museum, 1928, Washington.

727   Collective Barganing, Theatre With a Union Label. Eustis, Morton. Theatre Arts Magazine, N 1933, Vol. XVII, No. 11, P. 859.

728   Colonial and Early American Lighting. Hayward, Arthur H. Dover New York 1927 & 1962. ISBN: 486-20975-X

729   Colored Glass. Shreiner, E.E. McCoy & Stilwell, 1919, New York.

730   Colorimetry. Judd, Deane B. U.S. Government Printing Office, Mr 1950, Washington, D.C.

731   Coloring and Frosting Incandescent Lamps. Scientific American Supplement, My 1912, Vol. 73, P. 295.

732   Coloring Electric Light Globes. Popular Mechanics Xxi Ap 1914 P. 613.

733   Colorist. Hatt, Joseph Arthur Henry. Van Nostrand, 1913, New York.

734   Color -- a Survey in Words and Pictures. Birren, Faber. University Books, 1963, New Hyde Park, New York.

735   Color and Colors. Luckiesh, Matthew. D. Van Nostrand Co, Inc., 1938, New York.

736   Color and Design in the Decorative Arts. Burris-Meyer, Elizabeth. Prentice-Hall, Inc., 1935, Englewood Cliffs, N.J.

737   Color and Its
Applications. Luckiesh,
Matthew. Van Norstrand,
1921, New York.

738   Color and Light.
Armfield, Maxwell. Theatre
Arts Magazine III Ap 1919
P. 127.

739   Color and Light.
Snegoff, Mark. M.A. Thesis,
University of California,
Los Angeles, 1951.

740   Color As Light.
International Printing Ink
Corp., 1935, New York.

741   Color Changes in Early
Stage Lighting. Popular
Electricity III My 1910 P.
32.

742   Color Changing Ceiling
for an Office Building
Lobby. Williams, Rollo G.
Illuminating Engineer, My
1952, P.47, Vol. 5.

743   Color Characteristics of
Human Complexions, Data
Applicable To Lighting,
Television, Etc. Buck,
G.B. and froelich, H.C.
Illumination Engineering,
Ja 1948, Vol. 43, P. 27.

744   Color Comparison Chart.
Lighting Dimensions, Ap
1980.

745   Color Concepts in
Lighting Design. Watson,
Lee. Educational Theatre
Journal, O 1958, Vol. X,
No. 3, P. 254.

746   Color Control in the
Acting Area. Smith, Warren
S. Playshop (The), Ag
1951, P.12, Vol. 4.

747   Color Design in
Photography. Mante, Harold.
Van Nostrand Reinhold Co.,
1972, New York.

748   Color Effects for
Advertising and the Stage.
Luckiesh, Matthew.
Electrecal World Lxii Ap 4
1914 P. 759.

749   Color for the Stage.
Corson, Richard. Players
Magazine, O 1944, Vol. 21,
No. 1, P. 7.

750   Color Harmony and
Pigments. Hiler, Hilaire.
Favor, Fuhl, 1942, Chicago,
New York.

751   Color in Industry,
Science, and Business.
Judd, Deane B. John Wiley
& Sons, 1952, New York.

752   Color in Lighting.
Illuminating Engineering
Practice 1917 New York
P.267.

753   Color in Stage Lighting.
Arnovici, C. Theatre and
School O 1932, P. 13.

754   Color in Theatre and
Television Lighting.
Williams, Rollo G.
Illuminating Engineering,
My 1966, Vol. LXI, No. 5.

755   Color Is How You Light
It. Murphy, Winonah.
Sylvania Electric Products,
Inc., Commercial
Engineering Dept., 500
Fifth Ave, New York. No
Date.

756   Color It Color. Birren,
Faber. Progressive
Architecture, S, 1967.

757   Color Lighting in
Theatres. Transactions of
the Illuminating
Engineering Society, XVII,
F 1922, P. 68.

758   Color Metric Study of
Stage Lighting. Batcheller,
David R. Theatre Design &
Technology O 1972.

759   Color Mixture in Stage

Lighting. Mabie, E.C.
Quarterly Journal of Spech
Education (The), F 1925,
Vol. 11, P. 1-8.

760   Color Music: Scriabin's
Attempt to Compose a
Rainbow Symphony. Current
Oponion, My 1915, Vol. 58,
P. 332.

761   Color Music Introduced
at New York Concert.
Popular Mechanics, Je 1915,
Vol. 23, P. 836.

763   Color Music. Plummer,
Harry Chapin. Scientific
American, Vol. 11, Ap 10,
1915, P. 343. '

765   Color Music. Karwoski,
Theodore F. and sodbert,
Henry. Psychological
Monographs, University of
North Carolina, No. 2,
1938.

766   Color Notation (A).
Munsell, A.H. Munsell
Color Co., Inc., 1946,
Baltimore.

767   Color Organ (The).
Young, Stark. Theatre Arts
Magazine, VI, Ja 1922, P.
20.

768   Color Organ and the
Theatre (The). Young,
Stark. New Republic (The),
XXIX, Ja 18, 1922, P. 225.

769   Color Organ Exhibition.
New York Times, Ja 12,
1922.

770   Color Organ. Li, W.
Colliers Encyclopedia,
1961, Vol. 5, P. 343.

771   Color Psychology and
Color Therapy. Birren,
Faber. University Books,
1961, New Hyde Park, New
York.

772   Color Science. Wyszecki,
Gunter and Stiles, W.S.

John Wiley & Sons, Inc.,
1967, New York.

773   Color Standards and
Color Nomenclature.
Ridgway, Robert. Robert
Ridgway, 1912, Washington,
D.C.

774   Colour; a Manual of Its
Theory and Practice.
Carpenter, Henry Barrett.
Batsford, 1933, London.

775   Colour-Music. Klein,
Adrian Bernard.
Encyclopedia Britannica,
14th Ed., 1929, Vol. I, P.
168.

776   Coloured Light, an Art
Medium. Klein, Adrian
Bernard. Technical Press
Ltd. (The), 1937, London.

777   Coloured Lights for a
Small Stage. Lockett, A.
Work Vol. 50 Ja 1 1916 P.
225.

778   Deleted.

779   Coloured Light in the
Theatre. Bentham,
Frederick. Tabs, D 1960,
Vol. 18, No. 3, P. 13.

780   Coloured Light. Klein,
Adrian Bernard. C.
Lockwood, 1926, London.

781   Colours and How We See
Them. Hartridge, H. G.
Bell & Sons, Ltd., 1949,
London.

782   Colour Album. Ostwald,
Wilhelm. Winsor, 1931, New
York.

783   Colour and Light at
Work. Wilson, Robert F.
Seven Oaks Press, 1953,
London.

784   Colour Harmony, Its
Theory and Practice. Allen,
Arthur Bruce. Warne, 1937,
London, New York.

785   Colour in Theatre : No.
6. Tabs, S 1948, Vol. 6,
No. 2, P. 8.

786   Colour in Theatre - No.
2. Tabs, D 1946, Vol. 4,
No. 2, P. 11.

787   Colour in Theatre - No.
3. Tabs, S 1947, Vol. 5,
No. 2, P. 10.

788   Colour in Theatre - No.
4. Tabs, D 1947, Vol. 5,
No. 3, P. 11.

789   Colour in Theatre - No.
5. Tabs, Ap 1948, Vol. 6,
No. 1, P. 14.

790   Colour in Theatre - No.
7. Tabs, D 1948, Vol. 6,
No. 3, P. 8.

791   Colour in Theatre. Tabs,
S 1946, Vol. 4, No. 1, P.
2.

792   Colour in the Theatre,
No. 8. Tabs, Ap 1949, Vol.
7, No. 1, P. 16.

793   Colour Medium (The).
Green, F. J. Tabs, S 1949,
Vol. 7, No. 2, P. 18.

794   Colour Medium Range.
Tabs, Ap 1953, Vol. 11, No.
1, P. 21.

795   Colour Muse. Tabs, D
1972, Vol. 30, No. 4, P.
146.

796   Colour Music: the Art of
Mobile Colour. Rimington,
A. Wallace. F.A. Stokes
Co., 1911, New York.

797   Colour Music and the Art
of Lumia. Steadman, Phil.
Image, 1964, P. 17-22.

798   Colour Science. Ostwald,
Wilhelm. Windsor, 1933,
London, New York.

799   Committee for Studio
Lighting Hardware

Standardization. Lighting
Dimensions, Ap 1979, Vol.
3, No. 4, P. 32.

800   Committee Report on
Lighting for Proscenium
Type Stages. Illuminating
Engineering, Je 1968, Vol.
63, No. 6, P. 336.

801   Community Theatre:
Equipping the Stage (The).
Ramey, Howard Louis. M.F.A.
Thesis, Yale University,
1950.

802   Community Theatres:
Stage Lighting Provisions.
Burris-Meyer, Harold and
cole, Edward C.
Architectural Record, O
1930, Vol. 86.

803   Comparative
Spectrophotometric Analysis
of Representative Plastic
Color Media Used in Stage
Lighting. Houchen, Russell
Eugene. M.A. Thesis, 1976,
University of Oregon.

804   Comparative Study of the
Contributions of Steel
MacKaye and David Belasco
to the American Theatre
(A). Batcheller, Joseph
Donald. M.A. Thesis,
University of Minnesota,
1938.

805   Competing With a Legend.
Don, Robin. Cue Technical
Theatre Review, Ja/F 1980,
P. 4-5.

806   Complete Book of Garden
and Outdoor Lighting (The).
Gladstone, Bernard.
Hearthside Press, 1956 New
York.

807   Complete New Glossary of
Technical Theatrical Terms.
The Strand Electric
Company, 1947, London.

808   Composing in the Art of
Lumia. Journal of
Aesthetics, VII, D 1948, P.
79-93.

809   Composition in Light
Aesthetic and Functional
Considerations. Unruh, D.
Theatre Design & Technology
D 1974.

810   Computerized Memory
Controls for Lighting
Panecea or Toy?. Wells,
Terry. Theatre Crafts, Ja
1975.

811   Computer Aided
Theatrical Production.
Land, R.I. Theatre Design
& Technology O 1969.

812   Computorized Lighting
Control. Rubin, Joel E.
Theatre Crafts My 1975.

813   Concepts in Lighting.
Hart, Donna. Lighting
Dimensions, Ap 1978, P.54,
Vol. 2, No. 4.

814   Conceptual Approach to
Stage Lighting Design: Four
Plays in Repertory (A).
Mincher, John. Ph.D.
Thesis, Southern Illinois
University, 1973.

815   Concerning Projected
Scenery. Rubin, Joel E. and
Watson, Lee. World Theatre
(International Theatre
Institute), Autumn, 1954,
Vol. 3, No. 4.

816   Concert Lighting: How
Some of the Designers
Perceive Their Business and
Art. Moody, James L.
Theatre Crafts, Mr/ap
1979, Vol. 13, No. 2, P.
80.

817   Confessions of a Blind
Designer. Salzer, Beeb.
Theatre Design &
Technology, D 1974, No. 39,
P. 9.

818   Confidential Theatre.
Brown, Gilmor. National
Theatre Conference
Bulletin, Ag 1945, Vol. 7.

819   Conrad Hall
Cinematographer. Lighting
Dimensions, Jl/Ag 1977, P.
30.

820   Constitution and By-Laws
of the American Society of
Scenic Painters. American
Society of Scenic Painters.
American Society of Scenic
Painters, 1892, New York.

821   Constructing a Portable,
Low-Cost Manual Dissolve
System. Fishburn, Geoffrey.
Theatre Crafts, S 1978,
Vol. 12, No. 5, P. 50.

822   Constructing a Variable
Effects Projector. Stave,
H. Theatre Crafts My 1974.

823   Construction and
Installation of Stage
Lighting Equipment. Reeves,
H.H. General Electric
Review, XVII, Ap 1914, P.
412.

824   Continental Stagecraft.
Macgowan, Kenneth and
Jones, Robert Edmond.
Harcourt, Brace, & Co.,
1922, New York. LOCN:
Pn2570. M3 1964

825   Contrast: USA 829
Entrance Exams. Thomas,
Christopher A. Lighting
Dimensions, D 1978, Vol. 2,
No. 10, P. 44.

826   Controlboard and Dimmer.
Sellman, H.D. Theatre Arts
Monthly, Ju 1935, Vol. XIX,
No. 7, P. 548-49.

827   Controlled Color
Lighting. Stedman, C.W.
Architectural Forum, O
1931, Vol. LV, P. 493-98.

828   Controlling the Palace.
Lighting Dimensions, Jl
1979, P. 44.

829   Control and Application
of 5 Kw Arc Lamps.
Brauding, H.A.

Illuminating Engineering,
Je 1963, Vol. LVIII, No. 6.

830   Control Boards and
Dimmers. Theatre Arts, Je
1935, Vol. XIX.

831   Control of Lighting in
Theatres. Frank Adam
Electric Co., 1928, St.
Louis. located at the
Harvard Theatre Collection.

832   Control of Stage
Lighting (The). Overman,
Michael. Natya, Autumn
1960, Vol. 4, No. 3, P. 37.

833   Conversation With
Cassandra Henning and
Coca-Cola USA (A). Lighting
Dimensions, Je 1980, P. 16.

834   Convolux, Opus 129
Presented March 3, 1941 for
the First Time. New York
Times, Mr 8, 1941.

835   Corporate Theatre.
Moody, James L. Lighting
Dimensions, N 1978, Vol. 2,
No. 9, P. 31.

836   Correspondance (A).
Journal of Aesthetics, VII,
Mr 1948, P. 265-276.

837   Correspondence: Visible
Music. Lasker, Bruce. The
Nation, Cxv, Ag 16, 1922,
P. 168.

838   Costume and Scene
Changed by Coloured Light:
Stage Magic. Illustrated
London News, 1921, Vol.
159, P. 403.

839   Cost of Electricity.
Scientific American, XIV, O
1858.

840   Course in the
Fundamentals of Electricity
(A). Mott-Smith, Morton.
Westinghouse Electric and
Manufacturing Co., &
Science Service, 1942.

841   Covent Garden Opera
House. About the House, My
1963, Vol. 1.

842   Creating Light
Sculpture: Lasers in Three
Dimensions. Sandhaus, Dick.
Lighting Dimensions, S,
1979, P. 21.

843   Creative Artist in the
Theatre (The). Corathiel,
Elisabethe H. C. Theatre
World, N 1949, P. 61, D
1965, Vol. 45.

844   Creative Light. Kalff,
Louis Christian. Van
Nostrand Reinhold 1971, New
York. LOCN: Th7900 K34 1971
B

845   Creative Television
Lighting. Studdiford, James
Ellis. Thesis, University
of North Carolina, 1959.

846   Criterion Theatre (The).
Builder (The), Ap 1884,
Vol. XLVI, P. 558.

847   Critical Survey of
Outdoor Lighting (A).
Price, Michael P. B.A.
Thesis, University of
Minnesota. No Date. LOCN:
Mnu-M 67-82

848   Critical Survey of the
Stage Lighting Equipment in
the High Schools of
Minnesota (A). Davis, Jed
H. M.A. Thesis, University
of Minnesota, 1949.

849   Crosspatch or Inflexible
Flexibility in Lighting.
Bentham, Frederick. Theatre
Design and Technology, D
1966, No. 7.

850   Crowd That Wasn't There
and Other Secrets from
Rocky (The). Lighting
Dimensions Je 1977.

851   Cueing the Music. Moody,
James L. Theatre Crafts,
N/D 1979, Vol. 13, No. 6,
P. 90-92.

852   Curiosities of the American Stage. Hutton, Lawrence. Harper, 1891, New York.

853   Curious Use of Colored Lights. Popular Mechanics, Ap 1914, Vol. 21, P. 551.

854   Current Lighting Practice for Television Production. Illiminating Engineering, S 1951, Vol. 46, P. 9.

855   Current Trends in European Stage Design. Cole, Wendell. Educational Theatre Journal 5, 1953, P.27-32.

856   Curse of Efficiency. Tabs, S 1948, Vol. 6, No. 2, P. 17.

857   Cutting Lighting Without Losing Concept. Musser, Tharon. Theatre Crafts N 1969.

858   Cyclorama (The). Tabs, Ap 1952, Vol. 10, No. 1, P. 19.

859   Cyclorama Color Filters. Tabs, S 1955, Vol. 13, No. 2, P. 13.

860   D'Oily Carte Then and Now. Riley, Peter. Tabs, Fall 1975.

861   Damn New York Designers!. Salzer, Beeb. Lighting Dimensions, My 1980, P. 44.

862   Dance in America (The). Terry, Walter. Harper and Brothers, 1956, New York.

863   Dance Tour Lighting for Small Companies. Clark, Peggy. Theatre Design & Technology, Vol. XV, No. 2, Sum 1979, P. 17.

864   David Belasco: an Evaluation of the Man and His Contributions To American Theatre History. Forde, Gladys I. Ph.D. Thesis, Western Reserve, 1955.

865   David Belasco and the Psychology of the Switchboard. Moses, Montrose J. In the American Dramatist, 1917, Boston, P. 111.

866   David Belasco. Batcheller, Joseph Donald. Ph.D Thesis, University of Minnesota, 1942.

867   Day of the Sunspot (The). Longthorne, Robert. Tabs, S 1973, Vol. 31, No. 3, P. 97.

868   DDM - a Revolution in Lighting Control. Baker, David. Tabs D 1971.

869   Decorative and Theatrical Lighting. Bragdon, Claude. Iluminating Engineering Society Transactions, 1924, Vol. 19, P. 888.

870   Decorative Flood Lighting of Formal Landscape. Marston, Glenn. Lighting Journal, O 1916, Vol. 4, or Architect and Engineer, D 1916, Vol. 47, P. 111.

871   Demand-Controlled Lighting. Lighting Dimensions O 1977.

872   Demonstration Panel for Lighting Classes. Landry, Paul and Bowman, Ned. Players Magazine, F, 1961, Vol. 37, No. 5, P. 104.

873   Demonstration Theatre With a Difference. Tabs, D 1949, Vol. 7, No. 3, P. 23.

874   Denver's New Performing Arts Center. Chamberlain, Kathy. Lighting Dimensions, Mr 1980, P. 26-29.

875   Description of Modern
Wiring Installation in New
Theater. Electrical Review,
LXXIV, Mr 8, 1919, P. 371.

877   Designer-Director
Relationship: Form and
Process (The). Benedetti,
Robert. Theatre Crafts,
Ja/F 1979, P.36, Vol. 13,
No. 1.

878   Designer/Director
Relationship: the
Integration of Action and
Environment. Benedetti,
Robert. Theatre Crafts, O,
1979, Vol. 13, No. 5, P.
31.

879   Designers's Utopia?.
Progressive Architecture,
Jl 1971, P. 84.

880   Designers Must Design.
Tabs, S 1949, Vol. 7, No.
2, P. 8.

881   Designer Enters the Ring
(The). Wilfred, Thomas.
Players, N 1953, Vol. 30,
P. 28-29.

882   Designer Sets the Stage:
Jo Mielziner (The).
Houghton, Norris. Theatre
Arts Monthly, Ja 1937, Vol.
XXI, P. 29-31.

883   Designer Sets the Stage:
Norman Bel Geddes (The).
Houghton, Norris. Theatre
Arts Monthly, O 1936, Vol.
XX, P. 776-83.

884   Designer Talks: Richard
Pilbrow in Interview With
Robert Waterhouse (The).
Plays and Players, O 1970,
Vol. 18, P. 22.

885   Designing a Disco
Control System. Gaudio,
John. Lighting Dimensions,
Jl 1979, P. 39.

886   Designing a Mobile
Theatre. Armstrong, W.S.
Theatre Crafts S 1967.

887   Designing a Practical
Lighting Control Board.
Hamilton, John L. Players
Magazine, Mr/Ap 1939, Vol.
15, No. 4, P. 9.

888   Designing for Films.
Carrick, Edward. Studio
Publications, 1949, London.

889   Designing for TV: the
Arts and Crafts in
Television Production.
Wade, Robert J. Pellegrini
& Cudahy, 1952, New York.

890   Designing Lights for the
Mccarter Theatre. Blakeley,
C. Theatre Crafts S 1967.

891   Designing Scenery and
Lighting for the American
Place Theatre. Lundell,
Kert. Theatre Crafts Mr
1967.

892   Designing With Light.
Gillette, J. Michael.
Mayfield, 1978, Palo Alto,
Ca. LOCN: 78-51945 ISBN:
0-87484-420-7

893   Design and Construction
of an Analogue Punch Card
Theatre Lighting Control
System. Carnine, Dennis and
Kaufman, Roger. M.F.A.
Thesis, 1965, Yale
University.

894   Design and Construction
of Theatres. Morin, Roi L.
American Architect, 1922,
Vol. 121, P. 395-402,
443-450, 453-456, 493-496,
507-510, 537-542; 1923,
Vol. 122, P. 57-58, 6.

895   Design by Svoboda.
Bentham, Frederick. Tabs S
1967.

896   Design Criteria for
Lighting Interior Living
Spaces. I.E.S., 1980, New
York.

897   Design Forum. ABTT News,
Ap 1980, P. 2.

898   Design for a Cheap
Homemade Spot. Cosgrove,
Walton S. New Theatre
League, 1940, New York.

899   Design for Ballet.
Clarke, Mary and Crisp,
Clement. Hawthorn Books,
Inc. 1978, New York. ISBN:
0-8015-2020-7

900   Design for Keeping
Scenic Standards High.
Eisenberg, Lawrence.
Theatre Arts, S 1954, Vol.
XXXVIII, No. 9, P. 78.

901   Design for Portable
Low-Budget Arena Lighting
for the Educational
Theatre. Rothgeb, John R.
M.A. Thesis, University of
Michigan, 1954.

902   Design Improvements in
High Wattage Tungsten
Filament Lamps For Motion
Picture and Television
Studios. Leighton, L.G. and
Makulec, A. Journal of the
Society of Motion Picture
and Television Engineers,
Ag 1958, Vol. LXVII, No. 8.

903   Design Jobs in Public
Television. Hoffman, Paul
S. Theatre Crafts, S 1979,
Vol. 13, No. 4, P. 126.

904   Design of Control Boards
and Selection of Lighting
Equipment for High School
Stages (The). Pedrey,
Charles Paul. M.A. Thesis,
State University of Iowa,
1934.

905   Design of Electrical
Lighting and Control
Systems in the United
States (The). Burch, Roger
B. Ph.D. Thesis,
University of Illinois at
Urbana, 1972. LOCN: 792.025
B89d

906   Design of Lighting
Control Consoles With
Particular Reference to the

Techniques Used in
Television Studios in
Britain. Bentham,
Frederick. Jour. SMPTE, O
1961, Vol. 70, P.814-821.

907   Design of Theatre
'Downlights' (The). Kirk,
Edward B. Transactions of
the Illuminating
Engineering Society, Mr
1933, Vol. XXVIII, P.
280-83.

908   Design Parameters for
Use of Quartz-Iodine Lamps.
Levin, R.E. and Westlund,
A.E. Journal of the
Society of Motion Picture
and Television Engineers,
Je 1966, Vol. LXXV, No. 6.

909   Detachable Color Globes
a New Feature Embodied in
Stage Lighting Equipment.
Architecture and Building,
1924, Vol. 56, P. 79.

910   Details of an Old Gas
Batten. Tabs, S 1955, Vol.
13, No. 2, P. 17.

911   Details of Electrical
Installation in New
Pantages Theater.
Electrical Review, LXXIV,
Ja 4, 1919, P. 37.

912   Developing the Lighting
Course; a One Semester
Undergraduate Course.
Palestrant, Stephen. MFA
Thesis, 1960, Yale
University.

913   Developments in
Lighting; Technician's
Workshop. Speer, Richard
D. Theatre Arts Monthly,
Jl 1935, Vol. XIX, No. 7,
P. 550.

914   Development and Design
of Lighting Control Systems
in Am erican Theatre (The).
Markley, David J. M.A.
Thesis, Pennsylvania State
University, 1972. LOCN: 080
PO

915   and Techniques of the
American
Theatre-In-The-Round (The).
Taylor, James Cleveland.
M.A. Thesis, University of
Utah, 1958.

916   Development of
Arena-Policies and Methods
and Modifications Of Stage
Productions in the United
States Since 1925.
Freedman, Ann C. M.A.
Thesis, University of
Pittsburgh, 1951.

917   Development of Belasco's
Stage Lighting Technique
(The). Beagle, T.A. M.A.
Thesis, San Jose State,
1972. LOCN: Pn 1972 B43

918   Development of
Electrical Technology in
the 19th Century (The).
King, W. James. Bulletin
228, 1961 - 1962, Papers 28
- 30, U.S.N.M.S.

919   Development of Intensity
and Intensity Control in
Stage Lighting(The).
Roylance, Aaron Alma.
M.F.A. Thesis, University
of Utah, 1947.

920   Development of Stage
Lighting Equipment
1920-1930 (The). Holloway,
C.L. M.F.A. Thesis,
University of Texas,
Austin, 1967. LOCN: T 1967
H728

921   Development of Stage
Lighting Principles. Davis,
Jerry Leon. Ph.D. Thesis,
University of Kansas, 1968.

922   Development of Stage
Lighting Theories and
Practices in America from
the Beginnings to 1850
(The). Cordray, Laurie Ann
Stepanian. Ph.D. Thesis,
University of Missouri
(Columbia), 1973.

923   Development of Three

Color Illumination.
Electrical World, Lxv, F
1915, P. 398.

924   Dichroic Filters and the
Quartz Light. Loundsbury,
Warren C. Educational
Theatre Journal, Mr 1966,
P.73-74.

925   Die-Castings and
Pressings in the Theatre.
Tabs, D 1959, Vol. 17, No.
3, P. 15.

926   Digest and Appraisal of
Research in Stage Lighting.
Watson, Lee. M.F.A. Thesis,
Yale University, 1951.

927   Digital Computers for
Television Automatic
Switching Control.
Ettlinger, Adrian B. Jour.
SMPTE, Mr 1961, P.154-9,
Vol. 70.

928   Dillon's; Making the
Disco Beat Better. Edwards,
Brian. Lighting Dimensions,
F 1979, Vol. 3, No. 2, P.
28.

929   Dimmers for Realistic
Stage Effects. Electrical
World, LVII, Je 22, 1915,
P. 1626.

930   Dimmers for Theatrical
Lighting Control. Skirpan,
Stephen J. Skirpan
Lighting Co., 1931, Long
Island City, New York.

931   Dimmers for the
Destitute. Tabs, S 1954,
Vol. 12, No. 2, P. 17.

932   Dimmers for Tungsten
Lamps. Waller, Alfred E.
American Institute of
Electrical Engineers
Proceedings, F 18, 1915,
Vol. 34, P. 221.

933   Dimmer Differences.
Tabs, D 1955, Vol. 13, No.
3, P. 5.

934   Dimmer Memory and the Lighting Designer. Reid, Francis. Sightline, Sp 1979, Vol. 13, No. 1, P. 42.

935   Dimmer Systems for Theatrical Lighting Control. Skirpan, Stephen J. Theatre Design & Technology, Je 1961.

936   Dimmer With Colored Plates. Electrical World Lix Je 1 1912 P.1223.

937   Dinner Party (The). Kader, Don. Lighting Dimensions, N 1979, P. 37-38.

938   Directions in Kinetic Sculpture. Selz, Peter and George Rickey. Berkeley: the University Art Museum, 1966.

939   Directory of American College Theatre (1976). White, Allen S. American Theatre Association Publication, 1976.

940   Directory of Canadian Theatre Schools (A). Rubin, Don and Cranmer-Bying, Alison. Canadian Theatre Review Publications (Ontario) 1979. ISBN: 0-920644-71-6

941   Directory of Design and Technical Theatre Graduate Programs. Ray, Melanie. Theatre Crafts, F 1978, Vol. 12, No. 2, P. 37.

942   Directory of Graduate Programs in Theatre Design and Technology. Smith, R.L. USITT Education Commission, 1978.

943   Directory of Summer Theatre Design, Technical and Administrative Jobs. Ray, Melanie. Theatre Crafts, F 1978, Vol. 12, No. 2, P. 73.

944   Disappearing Footlights for School or Church. Popular Mechanics, XXVII, Mr 1917, P. 438.

945   Discharge Lamps for Photography and Projection. Bourne, H.E. Chapman and Hall Ltd., 1948, London.

946   Disco: Orchestration of Light. Lobi, Robert. Lighting Dimensions, N 1978, Vol. 2, No. 9, P. 51.

947   Disco '77. Lighting Dimensions, Mr 1978, Vol. 2, No. 3, P. 33.

948   Disco Lighting Design; More Is More. Nadon, John. Theatre Crafts, Ja/f 1980, Vol. 14, No. 1, P. 31-33, 74.

949   Disco Lighting. Lighting Dimensions, O 1977, P. 34.

950   Disco Lighting. Lighting Dimensions N 1977.

951   Disco Resources. Theatre Crafts, Ja/F 1980, Vol. 14, No. 1, P. 74.

952   Discussions. Levy, M.J. Illuminating Engineering Society Transactions, XVIII, My 1923, P. 432.

953   Discussion of Louis Hartmann's Effects on the Stage. Hall, William. Illuminating Engineering Society Transactions, XVIII, 1923, P. 427.

954   Discussion on Colored Lighting by M. Luckiesh and A.H. Taylor. Powell, A.N. Transactions Of the Illuminating Engineering Society, XIX, F 1924, P. 135.

955   Display Window Lighting and the City Beautiful. Godinez, Francisco Laurent. Comstock Co., 1914, New York.

956   Distribution and Form of Light in Space (The). Klopat, Henry Adams. M.F.A. Thesis, Yale University, 1941.

957   Dome for a Little Theatre (A). Theatre Arts Magazine, Ja 1922, Vol. VI, No. 1, P. 84.

958   Down Lighting. McCandless, Stanley. Illuminating Engineering, Ja 1951, Vol. 46, P. 46-51.

959   Down to the Cellar. Simonson, Lee. Theatre Arts Magazine, Ap 1922, Vol. VI, No. 2, P. 119.

960   Dramatic Imagination (The). Jones, Robert Edmond. Duell, Sloan & Pearce, 1941, New York.

961   Dramatic Production in the Private Secondary Schools of Connecticut. Smith, Harvey K. M.F.A. Thesis, 1948, Yale University.

962   Dramatic Value of Colour (The). Goffin, Peter. Tabs, Ap 1952, Vol.10, No. 1, P. 16.

963   Dramatizing Electricity. Fox, Edward Lyell. Greenbook Album, Je 1912, Vol. 7, P. 1120.

964   Drama in Europe in Theory and Practice (The). Jourdain, Eleanor Francis. Methuen and Company, Ltd., 1924, New York.

965   Drawing Distortion. Conway, John A. Players Magazine, O 1953.

966   Dual Role for the Safety Curtain. Tabs D 1970.

967   Duet. Rose, Philip. Tabs, Summer 1978, Vol. 36, No. 2, P. 14.

968   Eagles Part I. Johnson, Jim. Lighting Dimensions, N 1977, Vol. I, No. 5, P. 22.

969   Eagles Part 2. Gates, John C. Lighting Dimensions, N 1977, Vol. 1, No. 5, P. 24.

970   Early Australiana from Our Collection. Elizabethan Trust News, S 1975, No. 16, P. 18.

971   Early English Stage and Theatre Lighting. Lawrence, William John. In The Stage Yearbook, 1927, London.

972   Early Lighting: a Pictoral Guide. Rush Light Club. Rushlight Club, 1972, Boston. LOCN: Nk6196.R87

973   Early Lighting in New England 1620-1861. Hebard, Helen Brigham. C.E. Tuttle Company Rutland, Vermont, 1964.

974   Early Public Theatres in France (The). Wiley, W.L. Harvard University Press, 1960, Cambridge.

975   Early Uses of Electricity for the Theatre 1880-1900. Waters, Walter Kenneth, Jr. M.A. Thesis Stanford University 1951.

976   Earthing. Tabs, D 1950, Vol. 8, No. 3, P. 11.

977   Easements of Light; Modern Methods of Computing Compensation. Swarbrick, John. B.T. Batsford, London 1931.

978   Economy in Stage Lamps. Electrical Engineer, Ag 20, 1909, Vol. 44, P. 221.

979   Edmund Unique Lighting Handbook. Edmund Scientific Company, 1969, Barrington, New Jersey.

980   Education Television
Studio Requirements.
Berkeley, P.R. Tabs, Mr
1967, Vol. 25, No. 1, P.
24.

981   Edward F. Kook: Link
Between the Theatre Artist
and Technician. Olsen,
Ronald Charles. Ph.D.
Thesis, New York
University, 1978.

982   Edward F. Kook. Theatre
Arts, S, 1953, Vol. XXXVII,
No. 9, P. 64.

983   Effects for Effect.
Tabs, D 1950, Vol. 8, No.
3, P. 21.

984   Effects of Colored
Lights Shown at Yale
University. Transactions of
the Illuminating
Engineering Society, Jy
1927, Vol. XX, P. 599-601.

985   Effects of Color on the
Human Organism (The).
Birren, Faber. American
Journal of Occupational
Therapy, My-Je, 1959.

986   Effects of the Elctric
Light on the Air in
Theatres As Compared With
Gas. Scientific American,
Ag 1883, Vol. 49, P. 99.

987   Effects of Wavelengths
of Light on Physiological
Functions of Plants and
Animals. Ott, John N.
Illuminating Engineering,
Ap, 1965, Vol. 60.

988   Effect of Light and
Surroundings on Color. Cox,
Richard S. Textile World
Record, D 9, 1916, Vol. 52,
No. 2,, P. 29.

989   Deleted.

990   Einstein on the Beach.
Simmer, Bill. Theatre
Design & Technology, Spring
1978, Vol. XIV, No. 1, P.
15.

991   Electrically Controlled
Variable Color Optical
Filters. Lighting
Dimensions N 1977.

992   Electrically Operated
Stage (An). Scientific
American, LXXX, F 11, 1899.

993   Electrical Aids to the
Drama. Scientific American
D 22 1888.

994   Electrical and
Illuminating Equipment of
the Eastman theatre and
School of Music (The).
Mott, Frederick and Jones,
L. A. American Institute
of Electrical Engineers,
Journal, 1923, Vol. 42, P.
569.

995   Electrical Control for
Varying Lighting
Intensities. McCandless,
Stanley and wolf, Fred M.
Transactions of the
Illuminating Engineering
Society, Ja 1936, Vol.
XXXI, No. 7, P. 41-59.

996   Electrical Devices As
Applied to Special Effects.
Gow, John and george,
Frank. British
Cinematographer, S 1950,
Vol. 17, P. 84.

997   Electrical Diadem of the
New Ballet 'la Farandole'
(The). Scientific American,
Mr 1884, Vol. 50, P. 163.

998   Electrical Drafting.
Vangieson, D. Walter.
McGraw-Hill, 1945, New
York.

999   Electrical Entertainer's
Program (The). Curtis,
Thomas Stanley. World's
Advance, Je 1915, Vol. 30,
P. 829; Jl 1915, Vol. 31,
P. 109.

1000   Electrical Equipment and
Illumination of the Most
Artistic Theatre in

America. Schoonmaker, N.M.
Electrical World, Ja 6,
1910.

1001   Electrical Equipment of
a Buffalo Theatre.
Electrical World and
Engineer, XLVI, 1905, No.
4, P. 778.

1002   Electrical Equipment of
a Modern English Theatre.
Seager, J.A. Electrical
World, My 4, 1911, Vol. 57,
P. 1114.

1003   Electrical Equipment of
the Most Modern Theatre.
Electrical World, Ja 6,
1910, Vol. LV, P. 1.

1004   Electrical Equipment of
the Palladium. Electrician
Vol.66 Ja 20,1911 P.574.

1005   Electrical Equipment of
the Stuyvesant Theatre, New
York City. Electrical
World, D 21, 1907, P. 1219.

1006   Electrical Factor in
Gran Opera Productions
(The). Rosenfeld, Maurice.
Popular Electricity, Mr
1912, Vol. 4, P. 977.

1007   Electrical Features of
Portland Rose Festival.
Weber, F.D. Journal of
Electricity, Power and Gas,
Jl 8, 1916, Vol. 37, P. 25.

1008   Electrical Fundamentals.
TM 11-661 (Direct Current).
U.S. Army & Air Force.
Superintendent of
Documents, 1951,
Washington, D.C.

1009   Electrical Fundamentals.
TM 11-681 (Alternating
Current). U.S. Army & Air
Force. Superintendent of
Documents, 1951,
Washington, D.C.

1010   Electrical Installations
at the Kensington Theatre.
Electrician (The), XLII, D
30, 1898.

1011   Electrical Installation
in Roxy's New Theatre
(The). Electrasist, Ap
1927, Vol. 26, No. 6, P.
25-29.

1012   Electrical Layout of the
Yale Theatre. McCandless,
Stanley. American
Architect, Mr 1927, Vol.
131, P. 365.

1013   Electrical Lighting of
Drury Lane Theatre
Royal(The). Electrician
(The), S 18, 1908, Vol.
LXI, P. 865.

1014   Electrical Light Wires
in Theatres. Electrical
World, Iv, O 1884.

1015   Electrical
Manufacturers, 1875:1900.
Passer, Harold. Harvard
University Press, 1953,
Cambridge, Massachusetts.

1016   Electrical Means of
Varying the Intensity of an
Incandescent Lamp. Wolff,
Fred M. M.F.A. Thesis,
Yale University, 1935.

1017   Electrical Safety for
the Industry: Motion
Picture, Television and
Theatre. Kalbfeld, Jack W.
Lighting Dimensions, Ja
1980, P. 20-22.

1018   Electrical Safety in the
Entertainment Industry.
Davidson, Randall. Theatre
Crafts N 1977.

1019   Electrical Safety.
Dahlquist, Ron. Lighting
Dimensions, O 1979, Vol. 3,
No. 10, P. 36-37.

1020   Electrical Side of the
Theatre (The). Grau,
Robert. Electrical World Lx
Je 27 1912 P. 215.

1021   Electrical Stage
Appliances at Drury Lane
Theatre. Electrician (The),
XLII, D 30, 1898.

1022   Electrical Stage Effects. Waters, Theodore. Electric Power IX My 1896.

1023   Electrical Wiring, Fittings, Switches and Lamps. Maycock, William Perren. Pitman, 1928, London.

1024   Electrical Wiring. U.S. Department of the Army, Technical Manual Number tm5--760, 1957.

1025   Electricity--The Modern Stage Artist. Hadley, Grace T. Theatre Magazine, Ap 1919, Vol. 29, P. 212.

1026   Electricity, Magnetism and Electricity Supply. Builder (The), 1890, Vol. LVIII.

1027   Electricity and Stage Pictures. Electrical Review, Je 26, 1909, Vol. 54, P. 1171.

1028   Electricity Applied to Stage Lighting. Kliegl, John H. Electrical Review, LI, N 16, 1907, P. 801.

1029   Electricity As Appplied to Special Effects. Gow, John and George, Frank. Cine Technicial, N,d, 1950, Vol. 16, P. 188.

1030   Electricity at the New York Hippodrome. Electrical World Vol. 47 My 5 1906 P. 911.

1031   Electricity at the Savoy. Fletcher, Edward Garland. Thesis, University of Texas, Austin, 1941.

1032   Electricity at the Theatres. Electrical Engineer, F 24, 1893, Vol. 11.

1033   Electricity for the Theatre Technician. Hood, John. M.F.A. Thesis, Yale University, 1961.

1034   Electricity in Stage-Craft: Experiments With the Low Voltage Transformer. World's Advance, Ap 1915, Vol. 30, P. 547.

1035   Electricity in Stageland. Electrician, XLII, D 30, 1898.

1036   Electricity in the Modern Building. American Architecture, J 5, 1926, Vol. CXXIX, P. 150.

1037   Electricity in the Production of Joan of Arc. Electrical World, Je 24, 1909, P. 1573.

1038   Electricity in the Theatre. Guy, George. Chautauquan (The), XXVI, 1897, P. 287.

1039   Electricity Made Simple. Jacobowitz, Henry. Made Simple Books, Inc., 1959, New York.

1040   Electricity on the Stage. Wilstach, Clayton. Godey's, N 1896, Vol. 113, P. 183.

1041   Electricity on the Stage. Bissing, H. Electrical World Xxx Jl 3 1897 P. 3.

1043   Electric Arc (The). Somerville, Jack M. Methur Ltd., 1959, London.

1044   Electric Arc Lighting. Houston, Edwin James. Electrical World, 1962, New York.

1045   Electric Cables. Main, Francis Walter. Sir Isaac Pitman & Sons, 1949, London.

1046   Electric Candle (The). Niaudet, Alfred. Popular Science Monthly (The), XI, Ag 1877.

1047   Electric Fix-It Book.
Popular Mechanics Magazine
(Editors). Popular
Mechanics Press, 1953.

1048   Electric Illumination.
Krachenbuchl, John Otto.
Wiley & Sons, 1936, New
York.

1049   Electric Jewelry.
Scientific American, F
1884, Vol. 50, P. 71.

1050   Electric Lamp Industry
(The). Bright, Arthur A.
Jr. Macmillan Co. (The),
1949, New York.

1052   Electric Lighting at
Drury Lane Theatre Royal.
Electrician, F 12, 1904,
Vol. 52.

1053   Electric Lighting at the
Alhambra Theatre. Western
Electrician, Ag 20, 1904,
Vol. XXXV, P. 129.

1054   Electric Lighting at the
Brunn Theatre. Engineering,
Ap 13, 1883, Vol. 35.

1055   Electric Lighting at the
Covent Garden Theater.
Scientific American, S
1899, Vol. 81, P. 211.

1056   Electric Lighting at the
New Theatre London
Electrician, M4.
Electrician, Mr 13, 1903,
Vol. 550, P. 856.

1057   Electric Lighting at the
World in Boston. Electrical
World, My 18, 1911, Vol.
57, P. 1207.

1058   Electric Lighting in New
York. Wheeler, Schuyler S.
Harper's Weekly, Jl 27,
1889.

1059   Electric Lighting in the
New Iroquois Theatre.
Western Electrician, D 12,
1903, Vol. XXXIII, P. 437.

1060   Electric Lighting of the
Brunn Theatre (The).
Electrician, Jl 28, 1893,
Vol. 31.

1061   Electric Lighting of the
Illinois Theatre. Western
Electrician, D 15, 1900,
Vol. XXVII, P. 5377.

1062   Electric Lighting of the
Scala Theater at Milan.
Scientific American
Supplement, My 1884, Vol.
17, P. 7008, 7009.

1063   Electric Lighting of the
Theatre at Earl's Court
Exhibition (The). Engineer,
N 6, 1896, Vol. 82.

1064   Electric Lighting on the
Urania Theatre Stage.
Electrical Engineer (The),
XIII, Mr 9, 1892.

1065   Electric Lighting.
Gimson, Charles. Ulmer-Hume
Press, 1951, London.

1066   Electric Lighting.
Ferguson, Olin J. New
York: McGraw-Hill Book Co.,
1920.

1067   Electric Light (The).
Alglave, E. M. D.
Appleton, 1884, New York.

1068   Electric Light at the
Adelphi (The). Scientific
American Supplement, Mr
1889, Vol. 29, P. 11021,
11022.

1069   Electric Light at the
Criterion Theatre.
Electrician, O 11, 1884,
Vol. 13.

1070   Electric Light at the
Eden Theatre (The).
Electrical Review, II, Mr
22, 1883.

1071   Electric Light at the
Eden Theatre (The).
Engineering, Je 22, 1883,
Vol. 35.

1072   Electric Light at the
Savoy Theatre. Nature,
XXVII, Mr 1883.

1073   Electric Light at the
Theatre (The). Builder, Ja
1882, P. 10.

1074   Electric Light for a
Theatre. Scientific
American Supplement, XXI, F
6, 1886.

1075   Electric Light in a
Theatrical Performance
(The). Electrical World
(The), XVI, O 4 1890.

1076   Electric Light in
Old-Time. Popular
Electricity, O 1911, Vol.
4, P. 527.

1077   Electric Light in
Theaters. Scientific
American Supplement, D
1884, Vol. 18, P. 7452.

1078   Electric Light in
Theatres (Series).
Electrical World S 15,
1883/Ap 26, 1884/Je 4,
1884/O 18,1884.

1079   Electric Light in
Theatres (The). Scientific
American, XLIX, D 1, 1883.

1080   Electric Light in
Theatres. Electrician,
(The), XIII, S 6, 1884.

1081   Electric Light in the
British Museum (The).
Builder, (The), O 25, 1879,
P. 1184.

1082   Electric Light in the
Theatre. Robbins, Alfred
F. Notes and Queries, O 5,
1901, Vol. VIII, P. 294.

1083   Electric Power in
Theatre. Electrical Review,
My 1910, Vol. 56, P.
1026-1027.

1084   Electric Stage Lighting
Apparatus. Popular

Mechanics, Ag 1908, Vol.
10, P. 563.

1085   Electric Stage Lights.
Scientific American
Supplement, Jl 1911, Vol.
72, P. 53.

1086   Electric Theatre
Installations. Burns, S.
Electrician, Mr 7, 1913,
Vol. 70, P. 1002.

1087   Electric Torch at the
Paris Opera House.
Scientific American
Supplement, Ag 2, 1890,
Vol. 30, P. 12162.

1088   Electric Wiring ,
Fittings, Switches and
Lamps. Maycock, William
Perren. Ph.D. Thesis,
University of Minnesota,
1959.

1089   Electric Wiring of
Buildings. Raphael, F.C.
Pitman 1930.

1090   Electrifying Lighting at
the Lane. Bentham,
Frederick. Tabs Sp 1977.

1091   Electro-Calcium Lighting
Apparatus (The). Electrical
World, XVII, Ap 4, 1891, P.
262.

1092   Electromania. Williams,
W. Mattieu. Popular Science
Monthly, XXI, S 1882.

1093   Electronics Lights the
Stage. Popular Science, ag
1947, Vol. CLI, No. 2, P.
106-7.

1095   Electronic Control for
Stage Lighting. Izenour,
George C. Theatre Catalog,
Yale University, 1947-1948.
Also: U.S. Patent
2,463,463.

1096   Electronic Drama. Loney,
Glenn. Theatre Arts
Magazine, Jl 1963, Vol.
XLVII, No. 7, P. 27.

1097   Electronic Fire and Gas
Light Effect. Ney, Harold.
American Cinematographer, O
1947, Vol. 28,p. 356-357.

1098   Electronic Tube Control
for Theater Lighting.
Manheimer, J.R. and Joseph,
T.H. Journal of the
Society of Motion Picture
Engineers, Mr 1935, Vol.
XXIV, P. 221-32.

1099   Elementary Electricity.
Sick, Edgar P. McGraw-Hill
Book Co., Inc., 1931, New
York.

1100   Elements of a Work of
Living Art (The). Appia,
Adolphe. Theatre Arts
Monthly, Ag, 1932, Vol.
XVI, No. 8, P. 667.

1101   Elements of Electric
Lighting (The). Atkinson,
Philip. D. Van Nostrand
Co., 1893.

1102   Elements of Optics.
Valasek, Joseph.
McGraw-Hill, 1932, New
York.

1103   Elements of Stagecraft.
Baker, James W. Alfred
Publishing Co., 1978,
Sherman Oaks, Ca. LOCN:
Pn2086.B3 ISBN:
0-88284-053-3

1104   Elements of Stage
Design. Amberg, George.
Interiors, F 1948, Vol.
107, P. 86-89; Ap 1948, P.
105-112; Je 1948, P.
109-115.

1105   Elephant Man, Anatomy of
a Design (The). MacKay,
Patricia. Theatre Crafts,
Ja/F 1980, Vol. 14, No. 1,
P. 24-25, 80-81.

1106   Elvetham Mysteries.
Laws, James. Cue Technical
Theatre Review, N/d 1979.

1107   Emerald City: Elegance

in Fantasy. Lobi, Robert.
Lighting Dimensions, Jl
1979, P. 30.

1108   Emergency Lighting in
Theatres and Other
Buildings. Mackenzie, John
D. Electrician, Ag 16,
1912, Vol. 69, P. 781.

1109   Emotional Significance
of Color Preference (The).
Birren, Faber. American
Journal of Occupational
Therapy, Mr-Ap, 1952.

1110   Encyclopedia of American
Scenographers: 1900-1960
(An). Hippely, E.C. Ph.D.
Thesis, University of
Denver, 1966.

1111   English Stage Lighting
1575-1642. Graves, Robert.
Ph.D. Thesis, Northwestern
University, 1976. LOCN:
Diss 378 Nu 1976 G

1112   ENG and EFP Lighting
Techniques. Tucker, Clark.
Lighting Dimensions, Ap
1979, P.20, Vol. 3, No. 4.

1113   Entente Cordiale
D'eclairage. Leblanc,
Georges. Tabs, D 1956, Vol.
14, No. 3, P. 5.

1114   Episode With Gas (An).
Applebee, L.G. Tabs, Ap,
1957. Vol. 15, No. 1, P.
31.

1115   Equestrian. Illustrated
London News, O 28, 1871,
Vol. 59, P. 407.

1116   Equipment Design for the
American College and
University Theatre. Rubin,
Joel E. Interscenia, Acta
Scaenographicia
Internationalia, sp 1967,
Vol. 2, P. 16-18.

1117   Equipment for Lighting
Control. Voss, Lawrence.
Players Magazine, O 1951,
Vol. 28, P. 10-12.

1118   Equipment Leasing or
Buying. Lighting
Dimensions, O 1977, P. 54.

1119   Equipment of the School
Theatre. Smith, Milton
Myers. Ph.D. Thesis,
Columbia University, 1930.

1120   Equipping the D. E.
(Dramatic Education) Room.
Tabs Mr 1966.

1121   Ernest Klausz. Klausz,
Ernest. World Theatre,
Fall, 1954, Vol. III, No.
4, P. 57.

1122   Essentials of Stage
Lighting. Sellman, H.D.
Appleton-Century-Crofts,
1972, New York. LOCN:
Pn2091.E4 S4 ISBN:
0390795534

1123   Etched Method. Spika,
Paul J. Theatre Crafts, S
1978, Vol. 12, No. 5, P.
47.

1124   Eton College: New Hall.
Reid, Francis. Tabs Mr
1969.

1125   European Practice in the
Electric Equipment of
Theatres. Koester, Frank.
Electrical Review, Je 27,
1908, Vol. 52, P. 1023.

1126   Evaluation of the
Characteristic Curves of
Dimmers For Incandescent
Lighting Control (An).
Engle, Claude R.
Illuminating Engineer, Ap
1966, Vol. LXI, P. 320-23.

1127   Every Good Building
Needs a Foundation. Reiss,
A. Theatre Design &
Technology, O 1966, No. 6,
P. 23.

1128   Evolution of a Play.
Theatre Magazine(The), ,
1902, Vol. II, No. 21, p.
14.

1129   Evolution of Lighting
(The). Shipp, H. English
Review, XXXXIII, 1921, P.
395.

1130   Evolution of Stage
Lighting (The). Applebee,
L.A. Journal of the Royal
Society of the Arts, Ag 2,
1946, P.550-63,.

1131   Evolution of Stage
Lighting in America Since
1850 (The). Mellinger,
Maxon. M.A. Thesis,
University of Southern
California, 1930.

1132   Evolution of the Lamp
(The). Scott, Roscoe.
Illuminating Engineering
Society Transactions, IX,
1914, P. 138.

1133   Excellence in Action.
Marks, Jill. Lighting
Dimensions, O 1979, Vol. 3,
No. 10, P. 7.

1134   Excited Gasses.
Progressive Architecture, D
1968, P. 107.

1135   Exhibition of Students'
Projects for a Mobile
Theatre at the I.U.A.
Congress, London 1961.
Matthew, Robert. Architect
and Building News, Ag 30,
1961, P. 305-314.

1136   Experience of Kinesis.
Kirby, Michael. Art News,
66, F 1968, Pp. 45-47,
52-53, 71.

1137   Experimental Design of a
Stage Lighting System Using
Low Voltage Sealed Beam
Lamps. Murray, Donald
Louis. M.A. Thesis,
Michigan State University,
1956.

1138   Experimental Study of
the Effeciencies and
Adaptability of Fresnel
Lenses (An). Hearn G.
Edward. M.A. Thesis, State
University of Iowa, 1940.

1139   Experimental Study of
        the Effect of Light
        Intensity on Audience
        Perception of Character
        Dominance (An). Goltry,
        Thomas Scott. Ph.D. Thesis,
        1969, University of
        Wisconsin, Madison.

1140   Experimental Study of
        the Use of Visual Aids in
        Teaching of Stage Lighting
        (An). Dewey, Walter S.
        Ph.D. Thesis, University of
        Iowa, 1952.

1141   Experiments in Color
        Vision. Band, Edwin H.
        Scientific American, My
        1959, Vol. CC, No. 5, P.
        84.

1142   Experiment to Determine
        the Influence of Colored
        Light on Audience Reaction
        to Scenes from Plays (An).
        Kuney, Clark G. Jr. M.A.
        Thesis, State University of
        Iowa, 1940.

1143   Experiment With Lights
        for Atmosphere (An).
        Shoemaker, Elsie. Drama
        (The), D, 1929, Vol. 20, P.
        83.

1144   Experiment With
        Projected Scenery (An).
        Seigfred, Earl C. Players
        Magazine, N/D 1935, Vol.
        12, No. 2, P. 10.

1145   Experts in the
        Spotlights. Talese, Gay.
        New York Times, Mr 30,
        1958, P.1, Sec. 2.

1146   Exploring Eye (The).
        Architectural Review, Mr
        1965, Vol. 137, P. 201.

1147   Federal Theatre, 1935-39
        (The). Matthews, Jane
        Dehart. Princeton
        University Press, 1967,
        Princeton, N.J.

1148   Federal Theatre Project
        Bluprints. Federal Theatre

Project-Research Centre at
George Mason University.

1149   Federal Theatre Project
        Plates on Scenic
        Construction, Painting.
        Federal Theatre
        Project-Research Centre at
        George Mason University.

1150   Federal Theatre Project
        Script Collection (By
        Title). Federal Theatre
        Project-Research Centre at
        George Mason University.

1151   Federal Theatre Project
        Technical Purchases Card
        File. Federal Theatre
        Project-Research Centre at
        George Mason University.

1152   Fifty Years in Stage
        Lighting: a History of
        Strand Electric. Tabs Mr
        1964.

1153   Film Course Manual (A).
        Sweeting, Charles H.
        Mcgutchan Publishing
        Corporation, 1970,
        California. ISBN:
        0-8211-1821-8

1154   Final Report: a Survey
        of the Status of Theatre in
        United States High Schools.
        Peluso, Joseph L. United
        States Department of Health
        Education and Welfare,
        1970, Washington, D. C.

1155   Finances of the
        Performing Arts (The),
        Volume 1. Ford Foundation
        (The). Ford Foundation
        (The), 1974, New York.

1156   Fiorentino's Lighting
        for Industrial Shows.
        Theatre Crafts, O 1973,
        P.13-15.

1157   Fiorentino Adds New
        Light to a Sparkling
        Diamond. Kalikow, Rosemary.
        Lighting Dimensions Je
        1977.

1158   Firelight That's Real. Foster, Frederick. American Cinematographer, Mr, 1949, Vol. 30, P. 84, P. 106.

1159   Fire at the Theatre: Theatre Conflagrations in the United States from 1798 to 1950. Willis, Richard A. Ph.D. Thesis, Northwestern University, 1967. LOCN: Th9445 T3 W5 1976

1160   Fire for Hippolytos (A). Burch, Roger B. Theatre Design & Technology Sum 1978 Vol. XIV 2.

1161   Fire Risks from Electric Lighting. Nature, Ja 1882, P. 223, Vol. XXV.

1162   First Principles of Television. Dinsdale, Alfred. London, 1932. LOCN: 76-161141 ISBN: 0-405-03562-4

1163   First Theatre in London to Adopt Electrical Power (The). Building News, S 1898, Vol. 75, P. 483.

1164   First Use of Gas in Public Lighting. Leisure Hour Xxviii Mr 1879 P. 190.

1165   First Use of Limelight on the Stage. Lawrence, William John. Notes and Queries Series 7 Vol. 8 1889 P. 225.

1166   First 10 Spots (The). Reid, Francis. Tabs Ap 1974.

1167   Flexibility and Preset Control Boards. Thayer, David. Educational Theatre Journal, Mr 1961, Vol. XIII, No. 1.

1168   Flexibility in Lighting Control. Rhodes, Raymond H. Players Magazine, N 1940 , Vol. 17, No. 2, P. 9.

1169   Flexible Lighting for a Small Stage. Electricla West, Mr 1948, Vol. 100.

1170   Flickering Flames; a History of Domestic Lighting through the Ages. Thwing, Leroy Livingstone. C.E. Tuttle Company, Rutland, Vermont, 1958.

1171   Floating Theater. Progressive Architecture, Ag 1970, P. 69.

1172   Floating Theatres of the Mississippi. New York Dramatic Mirror, Ja 27, 1915, Vol. 73, P. 7.

1173   Floating Theatre (A). McClure, W. Frank. Scientific American, Ja 1904, Vol. 90, P. 24.

1174   Fluorescent and Black Light. Tabs, D 1952, Vol. 10, No. 3, P. 23.

1175   Fluorescent and Black Light. Tabs, Ap 1950, Vol. 8, No. 1, P. 22.

1176   Fluorescent and the Future. Tabs, S 1949, Vol. 7, No. 2, P. 11.

1177   Fluorescent Border Lights. Voss, Lawrence. Players Magazine, My 1956, Vol. 32, No. 8, P. 188.

1178   Fluorescent Dimming Device. Theatre World, My, 1949, Vol. 45, P. 38.

1179   Fluorescent Lighting Manual. Amick, Charles L. McGraw Hill, New York 1941.

1180   Focus: the Editor Speaks. Sokoloff, Pete. Lighting Dimensions, Ap 1978, P. 6, Vol. 2, No. 4.

1181   Focusing. Reid, Francis. Tabs S 1971.

1182   Focus on Light, New

Jersey State Museum. New York Times, My 28, 1967.

1183   Focus on Light. Bellamy, Richard. Exhibition at New Jersey State Museum Cultural Center, Trenton 1967.

1184   Foorlight Flashes. Davidge, William. American News Co. (The) 1866.

1185   Footlights--Covent Garden Theatre. Builder (The), S 5, 1857, Vol. XV, P. 516.

1186   Footlights and Spotlights. Skinner, Otis. Blue Ribbon Books 1924 New York.

1187   Footlights for Small Theatres. Motion Picture News Vol. 16 Jl 1917 P. 703.

1188   Footlights. Tabs, S 1946, Vol. 4, No. 1, P. 6.

1189   Foot Candles in Lighting Design. Tugman, J.L. Progressive Architecture, O 1957, P.129.

1190   Ford, Rockefeller and Theatre. Schechner, Richard. Tulane Drama Review, Fall 1965, Vol. 10, No. 1, P. 23.

1191   Form and Idea in Modern Theatre. Gassner, John. New York: Dryden Press, 1956.

1192   For Our Students a Memory Board Is a Panacea but Not the Answer. Clark, Peggy. Lighting Dimensions, S 1977, P. 54.

1193   For the First Time on Any Stage. Rose, Philip. Tabs Sp 1977.

1194   Fraimalite. Loundsbury, Warren C. Players Magazine, D, 1959, Vol. 36, No. 3, P. 62.

1195   French Scene (The). Leblanc, Georges. International Lighting Review, 1976, P.97, V.27,n.4.

1196   From Lighting Designer to Producer. Fisher, Jules. Theatre Crafts N 1971.

1197   From the Balcony Rail. Salzer, Beeb. Lighting Dimensions, N 1979, P. 41-42.

1198   Front Projection Process Photography With Scotchlite. Meyer, Herbert. Motion Picture Research Council Report No. 171, Hollywood, 1951.

1199   Front Screen Projection - Good News. Lefteris, George. Lighting Dimensions, O 1978, P.48-54, Vol. 2, No.10.

1200   Fuel Gas. Jenkins, C. Francis. Scientific American, S 9, 1899, Vol. LXXXI, P. 104.

1201   Functions of Stage Lighting in the Changing Concepts of the Stage (The). Walker, John A. Ph.D. Thesis, Cornell, 1952.

1202   Fundamentals and Lighting. Sturrock, Walter and Staley, K.A. General Electric Company G.E. Bulletin Ld2 Nela Park Cleveland Ohio 1956.

1203   Fundamentals of Electricity. McDougal, Wynne Luther. American Technical Society, 1954, Chicago.

1204   Fundamentals of Light and Lighting. Sturrock, Walter and Staley, K.A. Engineering Division, Lamp Department, General Electric, 1948, Cleveland.

1205   Fundamentals of Optical Engineering. Jacobs, Donald H. McGraw-Hill Book Co., Inc., 1943, New York.

1206   Fundamentals of Optics. Jenkins, Francis A. and White, Harvey E. McGraw-Hill Book Co., 1957, New York.

1207   Fundamentals of Play Production. Schonberger, Emanuel D. Northwestern Press, 1949, Minneapolis. LOCN: Pn3155. S4

1208   Furniture and Lights at Carnegie Tech. Weninger, Lloyd. Theatre Arts Magazine, Jl 1936, Vol. XX, No.7, P. 551.

1209   Furtenbach Ulm Theatre. Nagler, A.M. Theatre Annual, 1953, P.45-70, Vol. IX.

1210   Further Study of Visual Perception (A). Vernon, M. D. Cambridge University Press, 1954, Cambridge, England.

1211   Future Looks Bright for Lasers (The). Wolff, John. The Stage and Television Today, F 15, 1979.

1212   Garrick. Barton, Margaret. Faber, 1948, London.

1213   Gas-Lighting and Gas-Fitting. Gerhard, William P. Van Nostrand Co., 1913, New York.

1214   Gaslighting in America: a Guide for Historic Preservation. Myers, Denys Peter. Heritage Conservation and Recreation Service, 1978, Washington, D.C.

1215   Gas and Gas Fittings. Builder, (The), 1901, Vol. LXXXI, P.

15,35,60,82,113,139,159, 174,.

1216   Gas As a Source of Light, Heat and Power. Humphreys, C. J. Russell. A.M. Callender and Co., 1886, New York.

1217   Gas Lighting on the English and American Stages During The Nineteenth Century. Weese, Stanley. M.A.Thesis, University of Illinois, 1950.

1218   Gas Versus Electricity. Preece, W.H. Nature Xix Ja 1879 P. 261.

1219   Gel Choice Made Easy. Powell, Christopher. Tabs Sp 1976.

1220   Gem of a Job. Irving, Denis. Tabs, Autumn 1977, P.9, Vol. 35, No. 3.

1221   General Electric Lamps. Weitz, C.E. General Electric Co. Bulletin Ld-1, 1956, Cleveland, Oh.

1222   General Lighting Design. General Electric, 1964, Cleveland, Ohio.

1223   General Technical Requirements for Summer Stock Operation. Rosenthal, Jean. Blueprint for Summer Theatre - 1951 Supplement, John-Richard Press, 1951, New York.

1224   Genesis of a Ballet-Part II (The). Watson, Lee and Bookman, Kirk. Lighting Dimensions, Jy/Ag 1978, P.40, Vol. 2, No. 6.

1225   Genesis of Gas Lights (The). Wolcott, John R. Theatre Research, 1972, Vol. XII, No. 1, P. 74.

1226   Genisis of a Ballet. Watson, Lee and Bookman, Kirk. Lighting Dimensions My 1978.

1227   Geothe's Color Theory.
Van Nostrand Reinhold Co.,
1971, New York.

1228   German Projector for
Stage Effects. Popular
Electricity , S 1913, Vol.
6, P. 468-469.

1229   Getting Audited! Show
and Tell With I.R.S.
Hanlon, R. Brendan. Theatre
Crafts, O 1978, Vol. 12,
No. 6, P. 90.

1230   Getting a Design Job in
New York. Theatre Crafts,
Ja/F 1979, P.79, Vol. 13,
No. 1.

1231   Getting a Job in New
York: Part II. Clark,
Peggy. Theatre Crafts, Vol.
13, No. 3, My 1979, P. 79.

1232   Getting Jobs in
Administration. Theatre
Crafts, O 1978, P.76-78,
Vol. 12, No.6.

1233   Getting Your Foot in the
Door. Vornberger, Cal.
Theatre Craft, Mr/Ap 1980,
Vol. 14, No. 2, P. 90-91.

1234   Giant Rear Projection
Screens: Big Screens for
Small Bucks. Huggins,
Richard. Lighting
Dimensions, Ap 1978, P.36,
Vol. 2, No. 4.

1235   Give Me a Grandmaster
and Battens Any Day. Gould,
Mervyn. Tabs, Autumn 1977,
P.22, Vol. 35, No. 3.

1236   Give to Forms and Images
a Breath. Dightam, Adrian.
Cue Technical Theatre
Review, S/O 1979, P. 20-23.

1237   Glare As an Aid to Stage
Illusions. Electrical World
Lvii Ja 19 1911 P. 182.

1238   Glass Properties
Important to Stage and
Studio Lighting. Hoxie,

John. Theatre Design &
Technology D 1969.

1239   Gloria in Transit: Tent
Theatre. Progressive
Architecture, N 1975, P.
48.

1240   Glossary of Stage
Lighting. McCandless,
Stanley. Theatre Arts
Monthly, 1926, P.627-642,
Vol. 10.

1241   Going the Limit:
Realistic Repertory
Lighting for Limited
Facilities. Goldin, Toni.
Theatre Crafts, O 1978,
P.25, 58, 62, 64, Vol. 12 ,
No.6.

1242   Gordon Craig and Hubert
Von Herkomer. Craig, Edward
Gordon. Theatre Research,
1969, P.7-16, Vol. X, No.1.

1243   Gould, Mervyn. Gould,
Mervyn. Tabs Sum 1975.

1244   Graham Dances Opera at
National. Martin, John. New
York Times (The), My 15,
1945, P.23.

1245   Grand the Wonderful the
Amazing and Ever Glorious E
lectric Circus Light (The).
Theatre Crafts S 1972.

1246   Grants for the Arts.
White, Virginia. Plenum
Publishing Corporation,
1979, New York.

1247   Graphic Survey of Stage
Lighting (A). Allison,
William H. M.F.A. Thesis,
Yale University, 1952.

1248   Grauman's Metropolitan
Theatre. Tenney, George C.
Journal of Electricity,
1923, Vol. 50, P. 131.

1249   Green Limelight. Haddon,
Archibald P. Living Age,
1923, Vol. 318, P. 520.

1250   Guides to Stage Lighting Control System for High Schools, Colleges, and Television Studios. Thompson, Richard. Illuminating Engineering, Je 1966, Vol. 61, No. 6, P. 409-414.

1251   Guide to Corporate Giving in the Arts (A). Wagner, Susan E. (Editor). American Council for the Arts, 1972, N.Y.C. ISBN: 0-915400-12-X

1252   Handbook of Colorimetry. Hardy, Arthur C. Technology Press (The), 1936, Cambridge, Mass.

1253   Handbook of Dance Stagecraft. Skelton, Tom. Dance Magazine, O 1955, P.31, Mr 1957, Vol. 29.

1254   Handbook of Stage Lighting Graphics. Warfel, William B. Drama Book Specialists, 1973, New York. LOCN: Pn2091.E4 W3 ISBN: 0910482470

1255   Handcock, Fred Jason. Callahan, Michael. Lighting Dimensions N 1977, Vol. 1, No. 5, P. 27.

1256   Hanging Lanterns. Tabs, Ap 1959, Vol. 17, No. 1, P. 23.

1257   Happening. in Unlimited Total Space (A). Bogart, Jeffrey. Christian Science Monitor, Ja 20, 1969.

1258   Have a Coke and a Light. Manning, Ferd. Lighting Dimensions, Ag 1979, P. 35.

1259   Hearing the Light. Tabs, Autumn 1976, P. 2, Vol. 34, No. 3.

1260   Henry Irving's Artistic Use of Stage Lighting. Hughes, Alan. Theatre Notebook, 1979, Vol. XXXIII, No. 3, P. 100-109.

1261   Here's How: a Guide to Economy in Stagecraft. Hake, Herbert V. Row, Peterson & Co., 1942, New York. LOCN: Pn2091. S8 H25

1262   Heritage of Light, Lamps and Lighting in the Early Canadian Home (A). Russell, Loris S. University of Toronto Press, 1968, Toronto.

1263   Herkomer: Forerunner of Gordon Craig. Hewitt, Barnard. Players, My 1942, P.6, 23-24, Vol. 18.

1264   High-Brightness Xenon Compact Arc Lamps. Anderson, William T. Jr. Journal of the Society of Motion Picture and Television Engineers, S 1954, Vol. LXIII, No. 9.

1265   High-Pressure Mercury Vapour Discharge (The). Elenbaas, W. North Holland Publishing Co., 1951, Amsterdam.

1266   Highways and Sports Halls. Hunter, Moira. Sightline, ABTT Journal, Sp 1980, Vol. 14, No. 1, P. 10-15.

1267   High Brightness Xenon Lamps With Liquid-Cooled Electrodes-- Using Standard Lamp Manufacturing Techniques. Thouret, Wolfgang E. Illuminating Engineering Vol.Lx No.5 My 1965.

1268   High Intensity Xenon Lamps. Kearney, J.P. and. Rainone, N.J. Theatre Design & Technology O 1970 & My 1970.

1269   High Speed Projection System (A). Silverstein, F. Theatre Design & Technology F 1969.

1270   Historical Sketch of the

Origin, Progress, and Present State Of Gas-Lighting (An). Matthews, William. 1927, London.

1271   History of Colored Light on the Stage. Wolf, Craig. M.A. Thesis, U.C.L.A., 1967. LOCN: Ld 791.8 T3a939

1272   History of Electric Lighting. Schroeder, Henry. Smithsonian Institute (The), 1923, Washington, D.C.

1273   History of Illumination Up to the Discovery of the Incandescent Mantle. Bohm, C. Richard. Illuminating Engineer, I, 1908, P. 106.

1274   History of Lighting. Illuminating Engineering Society. Illuminating Engineering Society. No Date.

1275   History of Stage and Theatre Lighting (The). Boston Edison Co. Edison Electric Illuminating Co., 1929, Boston. LOCN: Pn2091. E4b69

1276   History of Stage Lighting (A). Rose, Forrest Hobart. M.A. Thesis, Ohio Wesleyan University, 1929.

1277   History of Stage Lighting (The). Kliegl Bros. Kliegl, 1956, Long Island City, New York.

1278   History of Stage Lighting (The). Kliegl, Herbert A. Theater Arts Books, 1947, New York.

1279   History of Stage Lighting (The). Illuminating Engineering, Ja 1956.

1280   History of Stage Lighting in America, 1879-1917 (A). Hemsley,

Gilbert V. Jr. M.F.A. Thesis, 1960, Yale University.

1281   History of Stage Lighting in the United States in the Nineteenth Century (A). Held, McDonald Watkins. Ph.D. Thesis, Northwestern University, 1955.

1282   History of Stage Lighting to 1880 (A). Dolch, Catherine. M.A. Thesis, University of Michigan, 1929.

1283   History of the Illumination of the Stage from the Beginning of The Drama to 1890 (The). Wilhelm, Dan L. M.A. Thesis, Northwestern University, 1928.

1284   History of the Incandescent Lamp. Howell, John W. and Schroeder, Henry. Magua Co. (The), 1927, Schenectady, New York.

1285   History of the United Scenic Artists Union. Habecker, Thomas James. Ph.D. Thesis, University of Illinois (Urbana), 1974.

1286   HMI: a New Name in Lights. Glickman, Richard. Lighting Dimensions Je 1977.

1287   HMI Lamps, History, Problems & Future. Lighting Dimensions, Je 1977, P. 8.

1288   HMI Update; Part II. Glickman, Richard. Lighting Dimensions, F 1979, Vol. 3, No. 2, P. 24.

1289   HMI Update. Glickman, Richard. Lighting Dimensions, Ja 1979, Vol. 3, No. 1, P. 28.

1290   Hobson's Choice.

Tarrant, Arthur. Cue Technical Theatre Review, Ja/F 1980, P. 26.

1291   Hollis Street Theatre, Boston. Theatre Scrapbook Collection, My 1, 1888, Boston Atheneaum.

1292   Holographic Process (The). Lighting Dimensions, F 1978, Vol. 2, No. 2, P. 51.

1293   Holography: Something New in Image-Making. Gatts, Strawberry. Lighting Dimensions, F 1978, Vol. 2, No. 2, P. 49.

1294   Holography: State of the Art. Lucier, Mary. Theatre Crafts S 1977.

1295   Holophane Floodlights for College/Pro Basketball. Lighting Dimensions, My 1980, P. 41.

1296   Homemade Lighting Apparatus for the Amateur Stage. Wilson, R.A. H.F.W. Deane & George Allen & Unwin Ltd., 1930, London.

1297   Home Built Lighting Equipment for the Small Stage. Fuchs, Theodore. Samuel French, 1939, New York.

1298   Home Electrical Repairs. Morgan, Alfred P. Crown Publishers, 1950, New York, 210 P.

1299   Hong Kong Arts Centre. Outhwaite, Michael. Tabs Sp 1978.

1300   House Lighting-The Poor Relation. Dewey, Walter S. Players, F/M, 1970, Vol. 45, No. 3, P. 96.

1301   How's Your Light Bridge I and II. Dewey, Walter S. Players, F/Mr and Ap/My, 1972, Vol. 47, No. 3 and 4 , p. 98 and 156.

1302   How Daylight and Moonlight Are Imitated. Gradenwitz, Alfred. Popular Electricity, Ja 1910, Vol. 2, P. 555-556.

1303   How Far That Little Canole. Dix, Cliff. Tabs, Je 1973, Vol. 31, No. 2, P. 60.

1304   How Relevant Are the Unions? Do They Hurt More Than Help?. Carson, Howard. Theatre Crafts, N/d 1978, Vol. 12, No. 7, P. 82.

1305   How Theatre Happens. Archer, Stephen. Macmillan 1978 N.Y. ISBN: 0-02-303830-6

1306   How the Arts Learned to Start Worrying and Love Big Business. ABTT News, D/Ja 1980, P. 12-13.

1307   How the New Lighting Control for the Royal Opera Was Designed. Bentham, Frederick. Tabs, S 1964.

1308   How to Condense and Project Light With Lenses. Edmund Scientific Co, 1955, New Jersey.

1309   How to Decorate and Light Your Home. Commery, E. Coward Mccann, 1955, New York.

1310   How to Make a Simple Stage, and the Scenery for It, With Diagrams. Fay, William George. French, 1931, London and New York.

1311   How to Read Schematic Diagrams. Mark, David. John F. Rider Pub. Inc., 1957, New York.

1312   How We're Failing Our Students. Goldman, Stephen. Lighting Dimensions, Je 1977, P. 46.

1313   Human Engineering Guide

to Equipment Design. U.S. Department of Defense, Joint Service Steering Committee. McGraw-Hill, 1963, New York.

1314   Hungarian Rhapsody. Fitzwater, Peter. Tabs Mr 1973.

1315   Hung Roofs. Severun, Fred N. and Corbelletti, Raniero. Progressive Architecture, Mr 1956, P. 99.

1316   Ice Show Lighting. Linder, D.S. Theatre Crafts N 1970.

1317   Ideals and Realism in Lighting Control. Bentham, Frederick. Tabs Mr 1966.

1318   Ideal Theatre Switchboard. Tabs, S 1948, Vol. 6, No. 2, P. 23.

1319   IES Lighting Handbook. Illuminating Engineering Society, 1959, New York.

1320   Illuminating Engineering Practice. Luckiesh, Matthew. McGraw, 1917, New York.

1321   Illuminating Engineering Society Lighting Handbook. Illuminating Engineering Society. Illuminating Engineering Society, 1962, New York.

1322   Illumination: the Technique of Light. Cricks, Robert. Focal Press, 1951, New York.

1323   Illumination and Architecture. Furber, William Copeland. Transactions, N 1910, Vol. 5, P. 822.

1324   Illumination and the Drama. Pollock, Arthur. Drama (The), F 1914, Vol. IV, P. 93.

1325   Illumination by the Electric Light. Scientfic American Supplement, II, S 6, 1876, P. 599.

1326   Illumination in Motion Picture Production. Linderman, R. G. and Handley, C. W. and Rodgers, A. Journal of the Society of Motion Picture Engineers, Je 1943.

1327   Illumination of Theatres. Signer, A. Journal of Royal Institute of Great Britain, II, 1831, P. 45.

1328   Illumination of Theatres. Leavy, M.J. Architecture and Building, Ja, 1918, Vol. 50, P. 3.

1329   Illumination of the Panama Pacific International Exposition. Ryan, W.D'a. Proceedings, Je 1917, Vol. 36, P. 415.

1330   deleted.

1331   Images, Images Images, the Book of Programmed Multi-Image Production. Eastman Kodak Co., 1980.

1332   Images in Light for the Living Theatre. Kook, Edward F. 1963, Copyright by Author. LOCN: Pn2091 S8 K66

1333   Images of Light in the Theatre: a History of Scenic Projection. Feher, E. Theatre Crafts, S 1970.

1334   Image Bender for Projections (An). Antos, Joseph. Theatre Design & Technology, O 1968.

1335   Image Senders. Fripo. Theatre Crafts, Ja 1970.

1336   Imitation Light. Sherman, Otto David. Lighting Dimensions, S 1978, Vol. 2, No. 7, P. 29.

1337   Impossible in Stage
Lighting Is Achieved (The).
Wallace, John J.
Scientific American, S
1925, Vol. CXXXIII, P. 154.

1338   Improved Designs for
Stage Lighting Equipment.
Brown, W.C. and Falge,
F.M. Transactions of the
Illuminating Engineering
Society, D 1927, Vol. XXII,
No. 10, P. 1144-57.

1339   Improved Lighting for
Expanded Sesame Street.
Riesengerber, G. Theatre
Crafts O 1971.

1340   Improved Mode for
Distributing or Directing
Day-Light. Arrowsmith,
John. London Journal of
Arts and Sciences, 1825,
Vol. 9, No. 54, P. 337.

1341   Improved Theatre Dimmer
(The). Electrical World,
XXXIX, F 22, 1902, P. 354.

1342   Improvements Claimed for
the Theater Spotlight.
Electrical Review, 1920,
Vol. 77, P. 399.

1343   Improvements in and
Related to Apparatus for
the Production of Color
Music. Hector, Alexander
Burnett. Patents Dept.
Australia, Victoria - A.J.
Mulet, 1912.

1344   Improvements in Stage
Lighting Control. Journal
of the American Institute
of Electrical Engineers, N
1924, Vol. 19, No. 9, P.
834-835.

1345   Improving Performance of
Lamp Dimmers. Kaddenhagen,
G.A. Theatre Design &
Technology O 1972.

1346   Incandescent Electric
Lights. Du Moncel, Compte
and Preese, Henry. Van
Nostrand, 1882, New York.

1347   Incandescent Lamps Used
for Pageant Lighting.
Popular Mechanics, XXVII,
Ja 1917, P. 79.

1348   Incandescent Lighting.
Lecey, Stanley I. Pitman
and Sons, 1922, London.

1349   Increasing Use of
Dimmers Particularly
Adapted for Use in
Theatres, Halls and
Churches. Electrical
Review, Mr 18, 1911, Vol.
58, P. 550.

1350   Incredible Slidemakers
(The). Theatre Crafts, O,
1979, Vol. 13, No. 5, P.
41.

1351   Index of Patents
Concerning Theatre
Illusions and Appliances.
Alexander, R.E. Thesis
U.C.L.A. 1964. LOCN: Ld
791.8 T3a377

1352   Indirect Lighting.
Fuchs, Theodore. Tabs, 1963
P.39, Vol. XXI, No.3.

1353   Indirect Lighting.
Fuchs, Theodore. Tabs,
1963, Vol. XXI, No. 3, P.
39.

1354   Indoor and Outdoor
Stage-Lighting Outfit (An).
Electrical Review and
Western Electrician Lxix O
14 1916 P. 678.

1355   Indoor Sporting Events
for Television. Manning,
Ferd. Lighting Dimensions,
Ap 1979, Vol. 3, No. 4, P.
41.

1356   Industrial Electricity
and Wiring. Moyer, Jas.A.
and Wostreh, John F.
McGraw-Hill Book Co, Inc.,
1943, New York.

1357   Industrial Theatre-It
Ain't Shakespeare but It
Pays The Bills. Lighting
Dimensions, Je 1980, P. 34.

1358   Industry Organizations.
    Watson, Lee. Lighting
    Dimensions, O 1977, P. 15.

1359   Industry Speaks Out On:
    Innovations of the 70's.
    Theatre Crafts, Ja/f 1980,
    Vol. 14, No. 1, P. 20.

1360   Inexpensive Homebuilt
    Lighting Equipment for The
    Low Budget Theatre. Lutton,
    Richard B. M.A. Thesis,
    State University of Iowa,
    1950.

1361   Inexpensive Multiscene
    Preset System. Orro, F.B.
    and Cyrus, E.A. Theatre
    Crafts, My 1974.

1362   Inflatables for
    Environments. Smith, C.
    Ray. Theatre Crafts My
    1976.

1363   Inflated Roof Tops-
    Boston Tent Theatre.
    Progressive Architecture, O
    1959, P. 83.

1364   Influences of Artificial
    Illumination Upon the
    Theatre. Mahovlick, Frank.
    M.A. Thesis, University of
    Southern California, 1951.

1365   Influence of Light in
    Drama, Greek Period to the
    Present. Comerford, Sister
    M. Abrosine. M.A. Thesis,
    Catholic University, 1952.

1366   Influence of the
    Aesthetics of Adolphe Appia
    on the Theory and Practice
    of Stage Lighting in the
    Contemporary American
    Theatre (The).
    Vandervennet, Mary
    Elizabeth. M.A. Thesis,
    Catholic University of
    America, 1964.

1367   Inspired by the
    Clavilux. Ashbrook, Carolyn
    S. Design, Xxxxi, S 1939,
    P.18-20.

1368   Installation of Flaming
    Arc Lamps in a Theatre.
    electrical Review and
    Western Electrician, LVII,
    S 3, 1910, P. 488.

1369   Instant Colour. Wolfe,
    Michael and Schwiller,
    John. Tabs, Sp 1977.

1370   Instant Interiors after
    Instant Food. Progressive
    Architecture, Je 1967, P.
    176.

1371   Instant Lighting. Flymm,
    Patricia. Theatre Crafts Mr
    1969.

1372   Instant Light for the
    Drama Room. Walker, Donald.
    Tabs Sp 1976.

1373   Instruction Sheets for
    the General Shop
    Electricity. Lewis, Melvin
    S. and Dillon, John H.
    McGraw-Hill, 1932, New
    York.

1374   Ins and the Outs of a
    Labor Union (The). Maronek,
    James. Theatre Crafts, O,
    1979, Vol. 13, No. 5, P.6.

1375   Interaction of Color.
    Albers, Josef. Yale
    University Press, 1971, New
    Haven.

1376   Interior Lighting for
    Environmental Designers.
    Nuckolls, James L.
    Wiley-Inter Science, 1967,
    New York. ISBN: Tk4175.N82

1377   Interior Lighting. De
    Boer, J.B. and Fischer, D.
    Scholium International,
    1978, Flushing, New York.

1378   International: Mobile
    Theatres. Goss, Anthony.
    Interbuild, Ag 1961, P.
    16-17.

1379   International Centennial
    of Light. Lighting
    Dimensions, N 1978, P.22,
    Vol. 2, No.9.

1380   International Music Hall, Radio City. Transactions of the Illuminating Engineering Society, F 1933, P.112-113, Vol. XXVIII, No.2.

1381   Introducing Our North Countries Repertory. Tabs, S 1955, Vol. 13, No. 2, P. 8.

1382   Introduction: Kinetic Art (An). Image (England), 1964, P.23-27.

1383   Introduction to Color (An). Evans, Ralph M. John Wiley & Sons, Inc., 1948, New York.

1384   Introduction to Stage Lighting. Educational Drama Association Pamphlet, No. 2. No Date.

1385   Inventory of Gas Lighting Equipment in the Theatre Royal, Hull 1877. Brokaw, J.W. Theatre Survey, My 1974.

1386   Inverse Square Law (The). Strange, Eric. Sightline, ABTT Journal, Sp 1980, Vol. 14, No. 1, P. 15-20.

1387   Investigation into the Techniques and Problems Associated With 35 Millimeter Projections As Scenic Elements in the Design Of Shakespeare's Much Ado About Nothing. Williams, Rodger. University Microfilm Order Number M-5012 Xi//04. No Date.

1388   Investigation of Current Trends in Light Projection (An). Kremptz, R.E. M.A. Thesis, San Jose State, 1967. LOCN: Pn 1967 K7

1389   In an English Country Garden. Reid, Francis. Tabs, D 1970.

1390   In Lighting Design: What Makes a Winner?. Lighting Dimensions, N 1979.

1391   In the Eye of the Beholder. Bryan, Robert. Tabs, Sp 1975.

1392   Iodine Incandescent Lamps-- Principles. Van Tijen, J.W. Technical Review, My 1966, Vol. LXI, No. 5.

1393   Iodine Incandescent Lamp With Virtually 100% Lumen Maintenance (An). Zubler, E.G. and Mosby, F.A. Illuminating Engineering, D 1959, Vol. LIV, No. 12.

1394   Ipswitch Theatre Book (An). Rosenfeld, Sybil. Theatre Notebook, Su 1959, Vol. XIII, No. 4, P. 129.

1395   Iron and Brass Implements of the English and American Home. Lindsay, J.S. The Medici Society, 1937, Boston.

1396   Irving and Stage Lighting. Stoker, Bram. Nineteenth Century and After, My 1911, Vol. 69, P. 903.

1397   Jack and Jill Went Down the Strand to Patch and Plug a Socket. Reid, Francis. Tabs, S 1973, Vol. 31, No. 3, P. 130.

1398   John Denver: Concert in the Round. Moody, James L. Lighting Dimensions, Ja 1979, Vol. 3, No. 1, P. 36.

1399   John Gleason-Lighting Designer: Practitioner and Professor. Lighting Dimensions, Mr 1979, Vol. 3, No. 3, P. 36.

1400   Joining the Union. United Scenic Artists of America (Local 829). Theatre Crafts, My/Je 1978, P. 70.

1401   Joining United Scenic
Artists Local 829: Follow
Up. Webb, Elmon. Theatre
Crafts, S 1978, Vol. 12,
No. 5, P. 9-12.

1402   Jones, Robert Edmond.
Current Biographies, 1947,
P.276-77.

1403   Josef Svoboda: Theatre
Artist in the Age of
Science. Burian, Jarka M.
Educational Theatre
Journal, My 1970, Vol.
XX11, No. 2, P. 123.

1404   Joseph Svoboda and His
Czech Scenographic Millieu.
Heymann, Henry. Theatre
Design & Technology F 1970.

1405   Joseph Svoboda Portfolio
(A). Svoboda, Josef.
Theatre Design & Technology
D 1966.

1406   Joys of Gas Lighting
(The). Willis, Richard A.
Theatre Design & Technology
My 1969.

1407   Jo Mielziner Approaches
Fifty Years in the Theatre.
Theatre Crafts My 1970.

1408   Jo Mielziner. Isaacs,
Hermine Rich. World
Theatre, 1951, Vol. II, No.
2, P. 41.

1409   Jules Fisher
(Interview). Lighting
Dimensions, Mr 1978, Vol.
2, No. 3, P. 23.

1410   Karl Lautenschlaeger:
Reformer of Stage Scenery.
Schoene, Guenter. In:
Innovations in Stage and
Theatre Design; Papers of
the Sixth Congress,
International Federation
for Theatre.

1411   Keep It Dark. Woulf, S.
Tabs, Ap 1953, Vol. 11, No.
1, P. 20.

1412   Kinetics?. Bentham,
Frederick. Tabs D 1970.

1413   Kinetic Art. London
Magazine, Iv, Ag 1964, P.
37-45.

1414   Kinetic Art. Gadney,
Reg. Granta, N 30, 1963,
Vol. LXIII, P. 24-26.

1415   Kinetic Electric
Environment (The).
Progressive Architecture, O
1968, P. 198.

1416   Kings Island Dark Ride.
Theatre Crafts, S 1977,
Vol. 11, No. 4, P. 45.

1417   Kiss. Paine, Zoe.
Lighting Dimensions, Ja
1979, Vol. 3, No. 1, P. 24.

1418   Kit for Establishing
Lighting Positions (A).
Woodman, Katherine Bowers.
M.F.A. Thesis, Yale
University, 1960.

1419   Kleig-Light Kliegl. New
Yorker, Jl 13, 1957, Vol.
33, P. 20.

1420   Kliegl
Theatrical-Decorative-Spect
Lighting Catalog 40. Kliegl
Brothers, 1936, New York.

1421   Laboratory Method
Applied to Stage Lighting
(A). Bullock, Robert.
M.F.A. Thesis, Yale
University, 1948.

1422   Lamentations!. Manning,
Ferd. Lighting Dimensions,
N 1978, Vol. 2, No. 9, P.
27.

1423   Lamp-Lighter (The).
Sheringham, G. English
Review, 1923, Vol. 36, P.
146.

1424   Deleted.

1425   Lamps and Maintenance.
Tabs, Ap 1953, Vol. 11, No.
1, P. 15.

1426   Lamps and Other Lighting Devices. Pyne Press. Pyne Press (The), 1972, Princeton.

1427   Lamps for a Brighter America. Keating, Paul W. McGraw-Hill, 1954, New York.

1428   Lamps for Garrick's Footlights. Mullin, Donald C. Theatre Notebook, 1972, Vol. XXVI, No. 3, P. 92.

1429   Lamps for Projection. Westinghouse Electric Co., Bloomfield, N.J. No Date.

1430   Lamp and Lighting Book (The). Newman, Thelma R. and Newman, Jay H. and Newman, Lee S. Crown, 1976, New York. LOCN: 75-43564 ISBN: 0-517-51863-5

1431   Lamp Bulletin, Ld-1. Weitz, C.E. General Electric Co., Lamp Division, 1950, Cleveland, Ohio.

1432   Lamp Data Files. Kliegl Bros. Kliegl Bros., 1929, Long Island City, NY.

1433   Lantern for Spot and Colored Lights. Popular Mechanics, N 1914, Vol. 22, P. 790.

1434   ·Large Theater-Dimmer Installation in Oakland's New Municipal Auditorium. Electrical Review and Western Electrician, Jl 1, 1916, Vol. 69, P. 40.

1435   Laserium. Lighting Dimensions, F 1978, Vol. 2, No. 2, P. 36.

1436   Lasers and Holography. Kock, Winston E. Anchor Books, Doubleday & Co., Inc., 1969, Garden City, NY.

1437   Laser and Holographic Companies. Lighting Dimensions, F 1978, P.52, Vol. 2, No. 2.

1438   Laser Graphics. Morris, Jennifer. Lighting Dimensions, O 1979, Vol. 3, No. 10, P. 24-26.

1439   Laser Process May Help Keep Color Film Fadeproof. Lighting Dimensions, Ja/ag 1978, Vol. 2, No. 6, P. 13.

1440   Laser Produces Color Images from Digital Data. Lighting Dimensions, F 1978, Vol. 2, No. 2, P. 40.

1441   Laser Projections for Performance Lighting: Three Approaches. Alvis, Arthur. Theatre Crafts, N/d 1978, Vol. 12, No. 7, P. 45.

1442   Laser Regulations: This Time It's for Real. Sandhaus, Dick. Lighting Dimensions, Mr 1978, Vol. 2, No. 3, P. 21.

1443   Laser Safety in Entertainment. Rogers, Bruce and Levenberg, Gary. Lighting Dimensions, F 1978, Vol. 2, No. 2, P. 33.

1444   Laser Theatre Technology. O'Brien, Dr. Brian B. Lighting Dimensions, My 1980, P. 28.

1445   Laser. Sapan, Jason. Lighting Dimensions, F 1978, Vol. 2, No. 2, P. 23.

1446   Las Vegas Spectacular. Theatre Crafts Mr 1976.

1447   Latest in Portables - Shakespeare. Progressive Architecture, S 1964, P. 93.

1448   Laws of Contrast to Colour (The). Chevreul, Michel Eugene. Roetledge and Sons. No Date.

1449   La Rouldtte: a Mobile Theatre for the Young. Tabs, D 1967, Vol. 25, No. 4, P. L2.

1450   La Rouldtte: a Moble Theatre for the Young. Tabs, S 1956, Vol. 14, No. 2, P. 6.

1451   League of Professional Theatre Training (The). Watson, Lee. Lighting Dimensions, Ju 1980 P. 12.

1452   Lee Ragonese on Saloon Lighting. Moody, James L. Lighting Dimensions, D 1979, P. 26-33.

1453   Lee Simonson: Obituary. Thornton, Frank J. Theatre Design & Technology, F 1967, No. 8, P. 35.

1454   Legit or Concert Lighting?. Hausman, Lee. Lighting Dimensions, Ja/ag 1978, Vol. 2, No. 6, P. 54.

1455   Lenses and Reflectors for Railroad Service. Beuford, Frank. General Electric Review, F 1927, Vol. XXXX.

1456   Letter of Thomas Wilfred to J. Handel Evans. Leonardo, Vol. 3, 1970, P. 467.

1457   Letter to the Editor. Dean, Basil. Tabs, 1963, Vol. XXI, No. 1, P. 4.

1458   Let Newton Be! and All Was Light. Corbett, Tony. Tabs, Autumn 1976, Vol. 34, No. 3, P. 7.

1459   Let There Be Footlight. Corry, Percy. Tabs, Ap 1939, Vol. 3, No. 1, P. 9.

1460   Let There Be Light. Theatre Design & Technology My 1971.

1461   Let There Be Light. Ivan, Rosalind. Theatre Magazine, F 1925, Vol. 41, P. 20, 50.

1462   Let There Be Light. Oenslager, Donald. Theatre Arts, S 1947, Vol. XXVI, P. 46-52. Also USITT Publication.

1463   Let There Be Light. Matz, Mary Jane. Opera News, Ap 3, 1971, Vol. 35, Np. 8-11.

1464   Let There Be Neon. Stern, Rudi. Abrams, 1979.

1465   Life of David Belasco (The). Winter, William. Jefferson Winter, 1925, New York, 2 Vols.

1466   Life of David Belasco. Winter, William. Moffat Yard & Co., 1918, New York.

1467   Light-Link Lighting Control System, (The). Cox, Charles H. III. Theatre Design & Technology, Wi 1979, Vol. XV, No. 4, P. 16-20.

1468   Light-Play. Brodsky, Nina. Studio, F 1939, Vol. 117, P. 68-69.

1469   Light, Color and Environment. Birren, Faber. Van Nostrand Reinhold Co., 1969, New York.

1470   Light, Colour and Vision. Legrand, Yves. John Wiley & Sons, Inc., 1957, New York.

1471   Light, Motion Space. Walker Art Center, Minneapolis. Exhibition Milwaukee Art Center 1967.

1472   Lightboard. Pilbrow, Richard. Tabs, Fall 1975.

1473   Lighter Side of Laser (The). Horn, Richard. New York Times Magazine (The), S 30, 1979, Part 2, P. 96.

1474   Lighting/Glitter and Glamorize. Theatre Crafts, Mr/Ap 1976, Vol. 10, No. 2, P. 14.

1475   Lighting/More Than a Paper Moon. Theatre Crafts, S 1975, Vol. 9, No. 4, P. 26.

1476   Lighting, Awareness & Discipline. Feder, Abe H. Lighting Dimensions, Ap 1978, Vol. 2, No. 4, P. 38.

1477   Lighting, Stage: History. Byrne, Muriel St. Clare. Oxford Companion to the Theatre, Oxford University Press, 1967.

1478   Lighting at the R.K.O. Roxy. Transactions of the Illuminating Engineering Society, S 1933, Vol. 28, No. 7, P. 665-666.

1479   Lighting and Brightness for Selling. Welch, Kenneth C. Illuminating Engineering, My 1946, Vol. XLI, No. 5, P. 386.

1480   Lighting and Control Equipment for Legitimate Theatre. Electrical Record Vol. 28 1920 P. 108.

1481   Lighting and Control Equipment for the Theatre: Where Are The Standards?. Pincu, Thomas L. Theatre Crafts, Ja/f 1978, Vol. 12, No. 1, P. 73.

1482   Lighting and Its Design. Larson, Leslie. Whitney Library of Design, 1964, New York. LOCN: Th7703.L3

1483   Lighting and Lamp Design. Cox, Warren E. Crown, 1952, New York.

1484   Lighting and Speech. Casson, J. Tabs, S 1952, Vol. 10, No. 2, P. 13.

1485   Lighting an Opera. Bristow, Charles. Opera, Ap 1963, Vol. 14, P. 220.

1486   Lighting Archive at Pennsylvania State University (The). Tabs Sp 1976.

1487   Lighting Art; Its Practice and Possibilities. Luckiesh, Matthew. McGraw-Hill, 1917, New York.

1488   Lighting Artists Must Light. Tabs, D 1947, Vol. 5, No. 3, P. 4.

1490   Lighting As an Art. Nightingale, F.B. Knight Publishing Co., 1962, Sky Forest, California.

1491   Lighting As Part of the Course in Play Production. McCandless, Stanley. Players Magazine, Mr/Ap 1932, Vol VIII, No. 4.

1492   Lighting at the Aldwych. Wickham, John. Tabs, Ap 1961, Vol. 19, No. 1, P. 8.

1493   Lighting at the Juilliard School. Feinburg, Andrew. Lighting Dimensions, Ap 1980, P. 18-20.

1494   Lighting at Yale and Lighting at Talladega. Theatre Arts Monthly, Jl, 1940, Vol. XXIV, No. 7, P. 533.

1495   Lighting a Pageant. Wetherby, Esther. Drama, N 1930, Vol. 21, P. 23.

1496   Lighting a Play. Greppin, Ernest. School Arts Magazine, 1924, Vol. 23, P. 548.

1497   Lighting a Show With John Murray Anderson. Gressler, Thomas H. Players, O/N 1975, Vol. 51, P. 28.

1498   Lighting a Theatre in
Wilkinsburg Pa. Stehley,
J. C. Lighting Journal, Ag
1913, Vol. 1, P. 199.

1499   Lighting Book (The); a
Manual for the Layman
Setting Forth the Practical
and Esthetic Sides of Good
Lighting for the Home.
Godinez, Francisco Laurent.
Mcbride, Nast and Company,
New York, 1913.

1500   Lighting Book (The).
Stair, J.L. Curtis
Lighting, Inc., 1930,
Chicago.

1501   Lighting by Linnebach.
Tabs, S 1965, Vol. 23, No.
3, P. 14.

1502   Lighting by Logic.
Anderson, Bob. Tabs Mr
1973.

1503   Lighting by the Book.
Reid, Francis. Cue
Technical Theatre Review,
S/O 1979, P. 10-11.

1504   Lighting Circuits and
Switches. Croft, Terrell.
McGraw-Hill, 1923, New
York.

1505   Lighting Control and
Concepts of Theatre
Activity. Barlow, Anthony
D. Educational Theatre
Journal, My 1973, Vol. 25,
No. 2, P. 135.

1506   Lighting Control and
Intelligent Machines.
Colvin, R.H. and malkin.
Theatre Crafts, O 1975.

1507   Lighting Control and Its
Operator (The). Bentham,
Frederick. Tabs, D, 1958,
Vol. 16, No. 3, P. 28.

1508   Lighting Control
Equipment of Theatre and
Television. Skirpan,
Stephen J. Metropolitan
Lighting, Inc., 1958, Long
Island City, N.Y.

1509   Lighting Control for Tv
Studios. Tabs, D 1955, Vol.
13, No. 3, P. 18.

1510   Lighting Control III.
Tabs, Ap, 1957, Vol. 15,
No. 1, P. 20.

1511   Lighting Control in
Germany. Fritz, Heinz J.
Tabs, Fall 1978, Vol. 36,
No. 3, P. 16-18.

1512   Lighting Control Is
Something Wrong With
Simplicity. Ashby, C.
Theatre Crafts O 1972.

1513   Lighting Control Systems
for Television. Thompson.
Broadcast Journal, Mr 1970.

1514   Lighting Control
Systems. Kliegl Bros.
Kliegl Bros., 1961, Catalog
S-65, New York.

1515   Lighting Control System
Warranty (The). Benson,
Robert. Theatre Crafts, O
1977, Vol. II, No. 5, P. 9.

1516   Lighting Control VI.
Bentham, Frederick. Tabs,
Ap, 1958, Vol. 16, No. 1 P.
6.

1517   Lighting Control V.
Bentham, Frederick. Tabs,
D, 1957, Vol. 15, No. 3, P.
22.

1518   Lighting Control 1.
Tabs, Ap 1956, Vol. 14, No.
1, P.13.

1519   Lighting Control 2.
Tabs, D 1956, Vol. 14, No.
3, P. 10.

1520   Lighting Designer in the
Theatre (The). Pilbrow,
Richard. Tabs, S 1963, Vol.
21, No. 2, P. 12.

1521   Lighting Designs of Jean
Rosenthal (The). Sesak,
Mary Margaret. Ph.D.
Thesis, Ohio State
University, 1976.

1522   Lighting Design for
Television. Watts, John
Ransford. Thesis, Yale
University, 1953.

1523   Lighting Design in
Buildings. Boud, John.
Peter Pergrinus, 1973,
Stevenage.

1524   Lighting Design in
Germany. Tabs, Autumn 1977,
Vol. 35, No. 3, P. 7.

1525   Lighting Design Comes of
Age. Rubin, Joel E. and
Watson, Leland H. Players
Magazine, Ap, 1955, Vol.
31, No. 7, P. 164.

1526   Lighting Design. Moon,
Parry Hiram. Addison-Wesley
Press, 1948, Cambridge,
Ma.

1527   Lighting Director With
Ringling Brothers, Barnum
and Bailey Circus. Powers,
Erick. Lighting Dimensions
S 1977.

1528   Lighting Effects for War
Training. Tabs, S 1946,
Vol. 4, No. 1, P. 7.

1529   Lighting Effects on the
Stage. Hartmann, Louis
(Hartman). Transactions of
the Illuminating
Engineering Society, XVII,
My 1923, P. 419.

1531   Lighting Equipment for
the Educational Theatre.
Minter, Gordon. Players,
Magazine, J/F 1946, Vol.
22, No. 3, P. 8.

1532   Lighting Equipment for
X-Hall Theatre, University
of Texas. McCormic, Ralph.
M.A. Thesis, Stanford
University, 1949.

1533   Lighting Fittings
Performance and Design.
Bean, Arthur Robert.
Pergamon Press, 1968, New
York. LOCN: Th 7960. B4
1968

1534   Lighting Fixtures and
Lighting Effects. Luckiesh,
Matthew. McGraw-Hill, 1925,
New York.

1535   Lighting Fixtures for
the Home, the Church and
Public Buildings.
Pettingell- Andrews Co.
1910, Boston.

1536   Lighting for Amateur
Productions. Hobbs, Mabel
F. Playground, 1925, Vol.
18, P. 604-606.

1537   Lighting for Armchair
Theatre. Campbell, Gavin.
Tabs, 10 1963, Vol. 21, No.
1, P. 16.

1538   Lighting for Color and
Form: Principles, Equipment
and Applications. Williams,
Rollo G. Sir Isaac Pitman
& Sons 1954 London.

1539   Lighting for Color Tv.
Winkler, E.C. Theatre
Design & Technology O 1970.

1540   Lighting for Colour
Television. Ackerman, K.R.
Lighting Research &
Technology, 1969, Vol. 1,
No. 3, P.123-131.

1541   Lighting for E N G
(Electronic News
Gathering). Tello, Steve.
Lighting Dimensions, Jl/Ag
1977, P. 48.

1542   Lighting for
Entertainment 1961. Strand
Electric. Strand Electric &
Engineering Co., Ltd.
(The), 1961, London.

1543   Lighting for Isolation
on the Thrust Stage.
Williams, Charles. Theatre
Design & Technology F 1969.

1544   Lighting for
Non-Professional Stage
Production. Powell, Alvin
A. and Rodger, A. Krieger
Pub., 1931, New York. LOCN:
Pn 2091 E4p6 (Mwep)

1545   Lighting for Open Stage
Realism. Kurtz, K. N.
Theatre Crafts N 1973.

1546   Lighting for Opera and
Ballet in Repertory.
Sondheimer, Hans. Theatre
Crafts, Ja/F 1973, P.13-19.

1547   Lighting for Repertory
at the Vivian Beaumont.
Gleason, John. Theatre
Crafts N 1968.

1548   Lighting for the Arena
Stage. Averyt, William
Bennet. M.F.A. Thesis,
University of Texas, 1967.

1549   Lighting for the Arena
Stage. Garness, Jon
Michael. M.F.A. Thesis,
1964, Yale University.

1550   Lighting for the Arena
Theatre. Rubin, Joel E. In
Blueprint for Summer
Theatre, John Rochard
Press, 1954, New York.

1551   Lighting for the
Audience. McCandless,
Stanley. Illuminating
Engineering, Ag 1951, Vol.
8, P. 46.

1552   Lighting for the
Audience. McCandless,
Stanley. Theatre Arts, F,
1954, Vol. XXXVIII, No. 2,
P. 76.

1553   Lighting for the Modern
Stage: a Handbook for
Architects, Engineers, and
Drama Directors. Davis
(Ariel) Mfg. Co., 1959,
Salt Lake City.

1555   Lighting for the Stage.
Rosenthal, Jean. Opera
News, Ap 13, 1968, P.8-11.

1556   Lighting for the Stage.
Landry, Paul. Players, N,
1961, Vol. XXXVIII, No. 2,
P. 54.

1557   Lighting for the
Theatre. Rosenthal, Jean.
Music America, F 15, 1954,
Vol. LXXIV, P. 13, 223.

1558   Lighting from Concealed
Sources. Stair, J.L. and
and the Engineering
Department. National X-Ray
Reflector Co. 1919.

1559   Lighting Gas by
Electricity. Scientific
American Supplement, II, Jl
15, 1876, P. 456. Second
Source Says 1896.

1560   Lighting Handbook, 4th
Edition. GTE Sylvania Inc.,
1972, Danvers, MA.

1561   Lighting Handbook.
Westinghouse Electric and
Manufacturing Co.
Westinghouse Electric &
Manufacturing Co., 1943,
Bloomfield, Ny.

1562   Lighting in America:
from Colonial Rushlights to
Victorian Chandelier s.
Cooke, Lawrence. Main
Street/   Universe Books,
1976, New York. LOCN:
Nk6196. L53

1563   Lighting in
Architectural Design.
Phillips, Derek.
McGraw-Hill, 1964, New
York.

1564   Lighting in
Architecture. Kohler, Dr.
Walter. Reinhold, 1959, New
York.

1565   Lighting in Awkward
Areas. Tabs, S 1952, Vol.
10, No. 2, P. 22.

1566   Lighting in Early
Playhouses. Brown, Frank
Chouteau. Theatre Magazine,
Jl 1918, Vol. 28, P. 36.

1567   Lighting in Industry.
British Electrical
Development Association.
1953, London. Located at
the Boston Public Library.

1568   Lighting in Minature.
Segrin, R. Theatre Design
& Technology, F 1969.

1569   Lighting in New York.
Musser, Tharon. Class
Paper, Yale University
Drama Library, 1950.

1570   Lighting in the Radio
City Theatres. McCandless,
Stanley. Transactions of
the Illuminating
Engineering Society, S
1933, Vol. XXVIII, No. 9,
P. 665-83.

1571   Lighting in the Rock'n
Roll Business. Kerr, David.
Cue Technical Theatre
Review, S/O 1979, P. 14-15.

1572   Lighting in the Theatre.
Bergman, Gosta M. Almovist
& Wiksell Intn'l., 1977,
Stockholm, Sweden; Rowman &
Littlefield, 1977, Totwa,
N.J. LOCN: Pn 2091 E4 B45
1977

1574   Lighting Is Important.
Williams, E. Tabs, S 1947,
Vol. 5, No. 2, P. 10.

1575   Lighting Layout for High
School Auditoriums and
Stages: Basic Standards and
Minimum Specifications (A).
Kleiner, Anne May. M.F.A.
Thesis, Yale University,
1942.

1576   Lighting Marlene
Dietrich. Davis, Joe. Tabs
Sum 1976.

1577   Lighting Modern Dance.
Emmons, Beverly. Theatre
Design & Technology O 1970.

1578   Lighting of Buildings
(The). Hopkinson, Ralph
Galbraith. Praeger, 1969,
New York. LOCN: Th 7703 H65
1969 B

1579   Lighting of Buildings
(The). H.M. Stationery
Office, London 1944.

1580   Lighting of Museums
(The). Grossi, Olindo.
Pencil Points Xix, S 1938,
P. 569.

1581   Lighting of Open-Air
Performances (The). Bonnat,
Yves. World Theatre, Su,
1960, Vol. IX, No.2, P.
149.

1582   Lighting of Severance
Hall: the New Home of the
Cleveland Symphony
Orchestra. Holden, Dean H.
Transactions of the
Illuminating Engineering
Society, Ap 1931, Vol.
XXVI, No. 4, P. 331-50.

1583   Lighting of Theatres:
the Paris Opera House
(The). Builder (The), Ag,
3, 1861, P. 521.

1584   Deleted.

1585   Lighting of Theatres
(The). Builder, D 13, 1862,
Vol. 20, P. 888.

1586   Lighting of Theatres
(The). Builder, (The), Ap
2, 1881, P. 422.

1587   Lighting of Theatres and
Auditoriums. Powell, A.L.
Edison Lamp Works 1923.

1588   Lighting of the Savoy
Theatre (The). Engineering,
Mr 3, 1882, Vol. 33, P.
204.

1589   Lighting of the Savoy
Theatre (The). Tabs, S
1962, Vol. 20, N. 2, P. 29.

1590   Lighting of the Stage of
the Berlin Grand Opera
House. Grimshaw, Robert.
Illuminating Engineer, O
1911, Vol. 6, P. 432.

1591   Lighting on a Small
Budget. Weiss, David W.
Players Magazine, D, 1952,
Vol. 29, No. 3, P. 64.

1592   Lighting Peter Pan.
Moody, James L. Theatre
Design& & Technology F
1972.

1593   Lighting Plan for the
Auditorium of St. Mary's
College, Oanier, Kansas
(Xavier Auditorium).
Papousek, Mary Lou. M.A.
Thesis, Stanford
University, 1948.

1594   Lighting Plot for
Irving's 'Merchant of
Venice'. Educational
Theatre Journal, 1972, Vol.
24, P. 265.

1595   Lighting Plot. Tabs, Ap
1962, Vol. 20, No. 1, P.
18.

1596   Lighting Problem (The).
Mortensen, A.L. Players
Magazine, My 1950, Vol. 26,
P. 126-28.

1597   Lighting Problem Again
(The). Mortensen, A.L.
Players Magazine, Mr, 1950,
Vol. 26, No. 6, P. 126.

1598   Lighting Problem Solved
(A). Maurer, John. Players
Magazine, My/Je 1926, Vol.
11, No. 4, P. 5.

1599   Lighting Projection
Screen Surroundings.
Cravath, J.R. Illuminating
Engineering, Jl 1951, Vol.
46, P. 361.

1600   Lighting Rehearsals.
Tabs, D 1951, Vol. 9, No.
3, P. 25.

1601   Lighting Requirements of
a New Professional Color
Film for Motion Pictures.
Blount, Richard.
Illuminating Engineering,
Ag 1951.

1602   Lighting Stage History.
Bryne, M. St. Clare. In the
Oxford Companion to the
Theatre by Phyllis Hartnoll

(Ed) Oxford University
Press.

1603   Lighting Street and
Stage. Craig, Edward
Gordon. London Mercury, My
1936, Vol. XXXVI, P. 30-6.

1604   Lighting Techniques in
Strange Companions. Marks,
Jill. Lighting Dimensions O
1979, Vol. 3, No. 10, P.
28-34.

1605   Lighting Theories of
Jules Fisher. Fisher,
Jules. Theatre Crafts N
1971.

1606   Lighting the Amateur
Production. Stratton,
Clarence. Theatre Magazine,
Je 1920, Vol. XXXI, P. 539,
557.

1607   Lighting the Amateur
Stage. Nelms, Henning.
Theatre Arts, Inc., 1931,
New York.

1608   Lighting the Amateur
Stage. Nelms, Henning. W.
Heffer and Sons, Ltd.,
1930, New York.

1609   Lighting the Amateur
Stage. Say, Maurice George.
Albyn Press, 1949,
Edinbourgh.

1610   Lighting the Arena
Stage. Mullin, Donald C.
Tabs Je 1965.

1611   Lighting the Big Top.
Fox, C. P. Lighting
Dimensions, S 1977, P. 25.

1612   Lighting the Center
Stage. Loundsbury, Warren
C. Players Magazine, F,
1955, Vol. 31, No. 5, P.
114.

1613   Lighting the Dance.
Rosenthal, Jean. New York
Times, Jy 21, 1963, Sec.
10, P. 6.

1614   Lighting the Dorothy
Hamill Special. Klages,
William. Lighting
Dimensions, D 1977, P. 27.

1615   Lighting the Flying
Dutchman. Bristow, Charles.
Tabs, Ap1959, Vol. 17, No.
1, P. 12.

1616   Lighting the Hardware
Way. Bentham, Frederick.
Tabs Je 1969.

1617   Lighting the Industrial
Show: Tricks of the Trade.
Hagan, John. Lighting
Dimensions, Je 1980, P. 25.

1619   Lighting the Legitimate
Theatre. McCandless,
Stanley. Architectural
Forum (The), S 1932, Vol.
LVII, P. 279-86.

1620   Lighting the Modern
Play. Hadley, Grace T.
Theatre Magazine Vol.Xxx Jl
1919 P.36.

1621   Lighting the Modern
Stage. Davis, Ariel R.
Ariel Davis Manufacturing
Co., 1958, Salt Lake City.

1622   Lighting the New York
World's Fair. Engelken,
Richard C. Electrical
Engineering, My 1940.

1624   Lighting the Open Stage.
Tabs, D 1954, Vol. 12, No.
3, P. 16.

1625   Lighting the Pageant of
Lexington. Porter, L.C.
Electrical World, Jl 24,
1915, Vol. LXVI, P. 209.

1626   Lighting the Play.
Feder, Abe H. In:
Producing the Play
(Gassner, John, Editor),
Dryden, 1958, New York.

1627   Lighting the School
Auditorium and Stage.
McCandless, Stanley. School
Executive, Je 1946.

1628   Lighting the School
Auditorium and Stage.
Allen, C.J. Illuminating
Engineering, Mr 1951, Vol.
46, P. 131.

1629   Lighting the School
Auditorium and Stage.
Allen, C.J. Progressive
Architecture, Ag 1951, P.
89.

1630   Lighting the School
Stage. Watson, Lee.
Nation's Schools, D 1949,
Vol. 44, P. 6.

1631   Lighting the Stage: Art
and Practice. Bellman,
Willard F. Chandler Pub.
Co., 1967, 1974, New York.
LOCN: Pn2091.E4b39 1974
ISBN: 0-8102-0040-6

1632   Lighting the Stage by
Tallow Candle, Oil and Gas.
Baugh, Christopher. Tabs
Sum 1976.

1633   Lighting the Stage for
Amateur Dramatics. Stanton,
Walter H. Players
Magazine, Ja 1952, Vol. 28,
P. 95.

1634   Lighting the Stage
Setting. Springer, Angus.
Players Magazine, Ap 1945,
Vol. 21, No. 7, P. 7.

1635   Lighting the Stage
Without a Proscenium.
Molette, Carlton. Players
Magazine, O/n 1968, Vol.
44, No. 1, P. 26.

1636   Lighting the Stage With
Homemade Equipment. Knapp,
Jack Stuart. Walter Baker
Co., 1933, Boston. LOCN: Tk
4399.T6k6 (Mwep)

1637   Lighting the Stage.
Builder, Je 28, 1851, Vol.
9.

1638   Lighting the Stage.
Builder (The), My 4, 1872,
XXX, P. 342.

1639   Lighting the Stage.
Burris-Meyer, Harold.
Theatre Arts Monthly, Jy
1932, Vol. XVI, P. 573-80.

1640   Lighting the Stage.
Corry, Percy. Pitman
Publishing Corp., 1954, New
York.

1641   Lighting the Stage.
Watson, Lee. Church
Property Administration,
Mr/d 1950, Vols. 2-6, P.
14.

1642   Lighting the Unknown
Soldier and His Wife.
Fisher, Jules. Theatre
Crafts, N/D 1967, P.9-12.

1643   Lighting the World's
Largest Theater. Electrical
World, 1920, Vol. 76, P.
777.

1644   Lighting through the
Years: the Light in the
Darkness. Poese, Bill.
Wallace-Homestead Book
Company, 1976, Des Moines,
Iowa. LOCN: 75-36635 ISBN:
0-87069-137-6

1645   Lighting Translucent
Backgrounds. Garmes, Lee.
American Cinematographer,
N, 1949, Vol. 30, P. 398.

1646   Lighting Up the Ghost at
the Royal Polytechnic.
Illustrated London News, Ja
16, 1875, Vol. 66, P. 54.

1647   Lighting Without Tears.
Rose, Philip. Dancing
Times, Ja 1954, P.223.

1648   Lighting With Military
Precision. Rich, Peter G.
Tabs, Summer 1978, Vol. 36,
No. 2, P. 16.

1649   Lighting Your Home: a
Practical Guide. Gilliatt,
Mary and Baker, Douglas.
Pantheon Books, 1979, New
York.

1650   deleted.

1651   deleted.

1652   Lighting. Pichel,
Irving. Theatre Arts, Ja
1928, Vol. IX, P. 24.

1653   Lighting. Pichel,
Irving. Theatre Arts
Monthly, S 1925, Vol. IX,
P. 614-24.

1654   Lighting. Theatre
Crafts, Mr/Ap 1973,
P.25-27, My 1971, P.17-2 2.

1655   Lighting. Theatre
Crafts, S 1973, P.12-13.

1656   Lighting. Phillips,
Derek. Macdonald, 1970,
London. LOCN: Th7703.P52

1657   Lighting. Prichard,
David Christopher. American
Elsevier, 1969, New York.
LOCN: Th7703.P69

1658   Lights, Camera, Music.
Manning, Ferd. Lighting
Dimensions, Ja 1979, Vol.
3, No. 1, P. 49.

1659   Lights in Theatres.
Builder, O 27, 1866, Vol.
24, P. 800.

1660   Lights in the Dark.
Kaufman, W. Tabs, D 1952,
Vol. 10, No. 3, P. 12.

1661   Light and Air; a Text
Book for Architects and
Surveyors. Fletcher,
Banister. 1886, London.

1662   Light and Color in
Advertising and
Merchandising. Luckiesh,
Matthew. Van Nostrand Co.,
1923, New York. LOCN:
Hf5839.L8

1663   Light and Color in
Relation to Stage Effects.
Scientific American, Je 21,
1924, Vol. 88. Second
Source Lists Je 21, 1925,
P. 23.

1664   Light and Colour Theories and Their Relation to Light and colour Standardization. Lovibond, Joseph Williams. Spon, 1915, London.

1665   Light and Illumination. Steinmitz, P. Scientific American Mr 25& Ap 1 1916.

1666   Light and Life of Electric Filament Lamps. Tabs, Ap 1948, Vol. 6, No. 1, P. 19.

1667   Light and Lighting. Bentham, Frederick. Tabs Mr 1969.

1668   Light and Music Drama: the Aesthetic Basis and Technical Practice Of Stage Lighting at the Bayreuth Festspielhaus. Lucas, John Robert. M.F.A. Thesis, Yale University, 1964.

1669   Light and Shade and Their Applications. Luckiesh, Matthew. Van Nostrand, 1916, New York.

1670   Light and Shade. Sellman, H.D. Drama Vol.18 Ja 1928.

1671   Light and Shadow. Jones, Robert Edmond. Theatre Arts Magazine, F 1941, Vol. XXV, No. 2, P. 120.

1672   Light and Shadow. Craig, Edward Gordon. Mask (The), Ja, 1929, Vol. 15, No. 1, P. 19.

1673   Light and the Artist. Journal of Aesthetics, VII Je 1947, P. 247-251.

1674   Light and Work. Luckiesh, Matthew. Van Nostrand Co., 1924, New York.

1675   Light Art. Piene, N.R. Art in America, 55, My 1967, P. 24-47.

1676   Light As an Architectural Material. Feder, Abe H. Progressive Architecture, S 1958, Vol. XLIX, P. 124-31.

1677   Light As an Element of Design in the Evolution of Stage Setting in the Late 19th Century. Osgood, Chester W. M.A. Thesis, State University of Iowa, 1931.

1678   Light As a Scene Painter. Literary Digest, Je 1924, Vol. 81.

1679   Light Biggest Aid to Stage Wizards. Murray, Fred S. New York Times Part 2 My 16, 1915.

1680   Light Facts About Light Bulbs. Large Lamp Department General Electric Company Nela Park Cleveland, Ohio Ap 1966.

1681   Light Furnishes Ballroom Decoration. Scientific American, Vol. 142, No. 6, Je 1930, P. 464-465.

1682   Light in Art. Hess, Thomas B. and Ashbery, John. Colier Books/ Art News Series, 1969, New York; Also Macmillan, New York (Paperback).

1683   Light in Holland (The). Bailey, Anthony. Knopf, 1970, New York.

1684   Light in the Theatre. Rosse, Herman. Chapter One, D 1957, Vol. 4, P. 1.

1685   Light in Visual Communication. Ackerman, K.R. International Lighting Review, 1976, Vol. 27, No. 4, P. 86-89.

1686   Light Language (A). Progressive Architecture, F 1977, P. 64.

1687   Light Motives.
Progressive Architecture,
Ap 1979, P. 92.

1688   Light on the Matter.
Read, John B. Dance and
Dancers, F 1971, Vol. 22,
P. 17-21.

1689   Light Paint (A).
Waterhouse, Robert. Plays
and Players, O 1971, Vol.
19, P. 24-25.

1690   Light Plays. Kraft,
Irma. New York Herald
Tribune, Ag,11,1929.

1691   Light Plot for the Glass
Menagerie Produced on Penn
State's Center Stage
Theatre. Yeaton, Kelly.
Players Magazine, My 1950,
Vol. 26, P. 180-2.

1692   Light Shade and Balance.
Devine, G. Tabs, Ap 1953,
Vol. 11, No. 1, P. 6.

1693   Light Sources of the
Past and Present. Sturrock,
Walter and Staley, K.A.
General Electric Company
Lamp Divisions, Nela Park,
Cleveland, Ohio, 1952.

1694   Light Tree Solutions.
Bailey, Allan. Theatre
Crafts, O, 1979, Vol. 13,
No. 5, P. 71.

1695   Light Waves and Their
Uses. Michelson, A. A.
University of Chicago
Press, 1903.

1696   Light Without Light:
Phosphorescent Stage
Effects. Sketch, 1923, Vol.
121, P. 323.

1697   Light. Morris, Richard.
Bobbs-Merril Company, 1979,
New York. LOCN: Qc 358.5 M
67 ISBN: 0-672-52557-7

1698   Lime-Light (The).
Baxter, S.S. Recreative
Science, II, 1861.

1699   Lime-Light (The).
Hardwich, T. Frederick.
Scientific American
Supplement, XI, 1881.

1700   Lime Light (The).
Chamber's (Edinburgh)
Journal Xxxvii 1862.

1701   Lime Light Without
Oxygen. Scientific American
Supplement, III, 1877.

1702   Lime Light. New York
Herald Series, Ap 1, 1845,
Ap 3, 1845, Ap 2, 1845, Ap
7, 1845.

1703   Lincon Conspiracy
Lighting. Maehl, Ross.
Lighting Dimensions, Je
1977, P. 12.

1704   Line Forms to the Right
(The). Thibeau, J.
Lighting Dimensions, N
1978, Vol. 2, No. 9, P. 70.

1705   Line Material Industries
- Outdoor Lighting Design
Manual. McGraw-Edison
Company, Milwaukee, 1962.

1706   Linnebach Projections.
Voss, Lawrence. Players
Magazine, My 1956, Vol. 32,
No. 8, P. 188.

1707   List of Works in the New
York Public Library
Relating to Illumination.
Bulletin of the New York
Public Library, D 1908,
Vol. 12, P. 686.

1708   List of Works on
Electricity in the New York
Public Library. Bulletin of
the New York Public
Library, N 1901-Ja 1903,
Vol. 6-7.

1709   Livingston Platt's
Lighting Experiments at the
Toy and Castle Square
Theatres. New York Dramatic
Mirror, My 28, 1913.

1710   Living Art or Still

Life?. Appia, Adolphe.
Theatre Annual (The), Vol.
1943, P. 38-46.

1711   Living Pictures.
Electrical World, Ja 1895,
Vol. 25, P. 45.

1712   Lobby of Light.
Architectural Forum, Ja
1952.

1713   Loie Fuller, the Fairy
of Light. De Morinni,
Clare. Chronicles of
American Dance, Henry Holt,
1948, New York.

1714   Loie Fuller, the Great
White Lilly, a Study of the
Contributions Of Loie
Fuller to the Development
of Stage Lighting.
Holloway, Elizabeth Rhodes.
M.F.A. Thesis, 1966, Yale
University.

1715   Loie Fuller. Kermode,
Frank. Theatre Arts, S
1962, Vol. XXVI, P. 6-21.

1716   London Coliseum, The.
Electrician, Ja 27, 1905,
Vol. 54, P. 575-580.

1717   London in the Eighteenth
Century. Besant, Sir
Walter. Black, 1902,
London.

1718   London Opera Centre.
Walne, Graham. Tabs, Autumn
1977, Vol. 35, No. 3, P.
14.

1719   Long-Forgotten Magic
Lantern, from the
Old-Fashioned Slide
Projector, (The).
Interiors, D 1948, Vol.
108, P. 84-95.

1720   Long Range 1000 Watt
Spot Light. Tabs, D 1954,
Vol. 12, No. 3, P. 19.

1721   Louis Hartman:
Electrician, Inventor and
Stage Lighting Designer.

Weidner, R.W. Thesis, Penn
State University, 1973.
LOCN: 080 Po1973m

1722   Low-Cost Rear Projection
Screens: a Technical
Production Case-Book in
Developing Three Surfaces
on Visqueen. Janesick,
Gerald. Theatre Crafts,
Mr/ap 1978, Vol. 12, No.
3, P. 30.

1723   Lumia: the Eighth Fine
Art. Westchester County
Fair, Wi 1932, P. 10-13.

1724   Lumia: Visions in Form,
Color and Motion. Bogart,
Jeffrey. Kansas City Star,
Je 30, 1968.

1725   Luminal Music. Time, Ap
28, 1967, P. 78.

1726   Luminescence As a Means
of Scenic Expression.
Jaroslakrska, Jaroslav.
Interscena, Acta
Scaenogrphica
Internationalia, Su 1967,
Vol. 3, P. 31-34.

1727   Luminography, the New
Academy, and Chauvinism.
Salzer, Beeb. Lighting
Dimensions, F 1978, Vol. 2,
No. 2, P. 70.

1728   Luminous Ceilings for
United Nations Auditoriums.
Electrical World, O 26,
1946, Vol. CXXVI, P. 60-61.

1729   Luminous Surfaces for
Architectural Lighting.
Lyon, John A. Reprinted
from Transactions of the
Illuminating Engineering
Society, Jl 1937, Vol.
XXXII, No. 7, P. 723-733.

1730   Luminous Tube Lighting.
Miller, Henry A. Chemical
Publishing Co., 1946,
Brooklyn, New York.

1731   Deleted.

1732   Lux Et Veritas. Manning, Ferd. Lighting Dimensions, D 1978, P.18, Vol. 12, No. 10.

1733   Madame Ristori on Stage Science. Saturday Review (The), Je 9, 1888, LXV, P. 693.

1734   Made to Dwell in a Dungeon Cell. Bentham, Frederick. Tabs, Ap 1960, Vol. 18, No. 1, P. 19.

1735   Maerz and Paul Dictionary of Color. McGraw-Hill, New York. No Date.

1736   Magic: Stage Illusions and Scientific Diversions, Including Trick Photography. Hopkins, Albert A. Munn and Co., 1901, New York.

1737   Deleted.

1738   Magic is in the Lighting Praque's Black Light Theatre Floats Props in Space. Theatre Crafts Ja 1972.

1739   Magic Lanterns. Rosse, Herman. Chapter One, Ap/My 1960, Vol. 7, P. 1.

1740   Magic Lantern Is Coming to London. Stage, S 15, 1960, London.

1741   Magic Lantern. Deshong, Andrew. Yale Theatre, Fall 1970, P.38-50.

1742   Magic of Light (The). Rosenthal, Jean and Wertenbaker, Lael T. Little, Brown, 1972, Boston. LOCN: Pn2091.E4 R68 ISBN: 0316931209

1743   Magic of Light (The). Kernodle, George R. Theatre Arts, N 1942, Vol. XXVI, P. 717-22.

1745   Magnetic Amplifiers: Theory and Application. Platt, Sidney. Prentice-Hall, 1958, Englewood, New Jersey.

1746   Major Renovation: Dade County Auditorium- Miami, Florida (A). Mix, Richard I. Lighting Dimensions, Ap 1978, Vol. 2, No. 4, P. 27.

1747   Maker of Moons (A). Parker, Grosvenor A. Theatre Magazine, S 1913, Vol. XVII, P. XII.

1748   Make Your Own Electrical Repairs. Morgan, Alfred P. Fawcett Publications, 1956, Greenwich, CT.

1749   Making of the Electrical Age: from The Telegraph to Automation. Sharlin, Harold. Abelard-Shuman, 1963, New York.

1750   Making Originals for Photographic Slides. Conway, John A. Players Magazine, My 1953.

1751   Making Reflections Work. Aronstein, M. Theatre Crafts My 1969.

1752   Making the Theatre Go Round. Egolf, Clem. Blueprint for Summer Theatre, 1951, Supplement.

1753   Making Varicolored Flash Papers for Stage Effects. Popular Mechanics, 1922, Vol. 38, P. 803.

1754   Making Your Own Gobos by Photofabrication. Pollock, S.P. Theatre Crafts S 1976.

1755   Malillumination: a New Dimension in Lighting. Ott, John N. Lighting Dimensions, N 1978, Vol. 2, No. 9, P. 41.

1756   Mammoth Stage Lighting

Control for Roxy Theatre.
Electrical World, F 5,
1927, Vol. LXXXIX, P. 297.

1757   Manager's Point of View
(The). Townsend, Percy.
Theatre (The), I, Ap 5,
1886.

1758   Manual Dissolve Unit:
Further Suggestions.
Howard, John T. Jr.
Theatre Crafts, Ja/f 1979,
Vol. 13, No. 1, P. 4.

1759   Manual of Lighting Data;
an Activity of the
Committee on Lighting
Service of the Illuminating
Engineering Society To Help
Lighting Service
Departments. Illuminating
Engineering Society.
Committee on Lighting
Service, 1929, New York.

1760   Manufacturer Profiles,
Part I. Lighting
Dimensions, Je 1979, Vol.
3, No. 6, P. 18.

1761   Manufacturing of Glass
for Illuminating Purposes
(Review Of). Bostock, E.H.
Illuminating Engineer, N
1911, Vol. VI, No. 9, P.
495.

1762   Man Behind the Gun
(The). Maxwell, Perriton.
Theatre Magazine (The), S
1916, Vol. XXIV, No. 187,
P. 132.

1763   Marquee Flasher for
Sweet Charity. Shook, R.
Theatre Design & Technology
D 1973.

1764   Marvels of Modern
Mechanics. Wilkins, Harold
T. London, 1926.

1765   Mass Producing Mirror
Spots. Tabs, S 1955, Vol.
13, No. 2, P. 10.

1766   Mathematical and
Physical Bases for

Incandescent Lamp
Exponents. Vanhorn, D.
Illuminating Engineering,
Ap 1965, Vol. LX, No. 4.

1767   Mathematics for
Electricians. Kuehn, Martin
H. McGraw-Hill, 1949, New
York.

1768   Maude Adams Invents
Stage Lighting Device. New
York Times, O 15, 1931,
P.23.

1769   Max and Mabel. Theatre
Crafts N 1974.

1770   Max Reinhardt and the
U.S.A. Pinthus, Kurt.
Theatre Research, 1963,
Vol. V, No. 3, P. 151-65.

1771   Measurement of Color
(The). Wright, William D.
Hilger and Watts, Ltd.,
1964, London.

1772   Measurement of Visual
Acuity in Lighting the
Actor's Face. Draegert,
Gayland L. M.A. Thesis,
State University of Iowa,
1937.

1773   Measurement Standards
for Theatre, Tv and Film
Lighting. Neenan, Charles.
Theatre Design & Technology
O 1966.

1774   Medium-Priced
Solid-State Control System
(A). Bentham, Frederick.
Theatre Design &
Technology, O 1966, No. 6,
P. 44.

1775   Meet Jean Rosenthal.
Goodman, Saul. Dance
Magazine, F 1962, P.19-23.

1776   Membrane Structures for
Living and Learning to Be
Pioneered on Three
Campuses. Efl College
Newsletter, S 1970, P.2-7.

1777   Memoirs of Thomas

Drummond. McLennan, John F.
Edmonston & Douglas, 1867,
Edinburgh.

1778   Memorabilia. Bentham,
Frederick. Tabs, Fall 1978,
Vol. 36, No. 3, P. 7-12.

1779   Memorial to the
Legislature of the State of
New York for the
Investigation of the
Conditions Surrounding Gas
and Electrical Lighting in
the City of New York.
Merchants Association of
New York, 1905, New York.

1780   Memorial Tribute to Jean
Rosenthal. Houseman, John.
United States Institute for
Theatre Technology
Newsletter, My/j3 1969,
Vol. VIII, P. 4-5.

1781   Memoria 80: Meditation
Upon. Bentham, Frederick.
Sightline, ABTT Journal, Sp
1980, Vol. 14, No. 1, P.
34-40.

1782   Memory Assisted
Controlled Lighting
Designed for the Operator.
Gilchrist, D. and Zeller,
F. Riddle, L. Theatre
Crafts My 1976.

1783   Memory Assisted Lighting
Control Systems. Tawic,
M.N. and Cramer, M.
Theatre Crafts N 1974.

1784   Memory Explosion (The).
Anderson, Bob. Sightline
(ABTT Journal), Autumn
1978, Vol. 12, No. 2, P.
99.

1785   Memory Explosion II
(The). Anderson, Bob.
Sightline, Sp 1979, Vol.
13, No. 1, P. 36.

1786   Memory Lighting Control
for Rada. Reid, Francis.
Tabs Sum 1976.

1787   Memory Revolution (The).
Tabs Ap 1974.

1788   Merging the Disciplines.
Progressive Architecture, S
1973.

1789   Mescal and Mechanisms of
Hallucinations. Kluver,
Heinrich. University of
Chicago Press, 1966.

1790   Method for Analuyzing
Promp Book Notations for
Evidences of Gas Lighting
Practices (A). Bagman, P.
Jerald. OSU Theatre
Collection Bulletin, 1961,
Vol. 8, P. 34.

1791   Method of Lighting the
Stage (A). McCandless,
Stanley. Theatre Arts
Books, 1932, 1939, 1947,
1958, New York. LOCN:
Pn2091. E4 M3 1958

1792   Midwestern Discos.
Watson, Lee. Lighting
Dimensions, Ap 1979, Vol.
3, No. 4, P. 17.

1793   Mielziner. Genauer,
Emily. Theatre Arts, S
1951, Vol. XXXV, P. 34-37,
86-87.

1794   Million Dollar Musicals.
MacKay, Patricia. Theatre
Crafts, My/Je 1978, Vol.
12, No. 4, P. 13.

1795   Miniature Switchboard
Will Light Small Stage.
Architectural Record, Ja
1956, Vol. 119, P. 206.

1796   Minimum Equipment Needed
for the All-Purpose High
School Stage (The).
Heckert, Floyd H. M.F.A.
Thesis, Ohio University,
1952.

1797   Minimum Standards for
the Accredatation of
Theatre Degree Programs in
Colleges and Universities.
Theatre News (The), Mr
1978.

1798   Mini Spots and the

Theatre. Tabs, D 1967, Vol. L25, No. 4, P. 15.

1799   Miracle in the Evening. Bel Geddes, Norman. Doubleday and Company, 1960, Garden City.

1800   Mirrors, Prisms, and Lenses. Southall, James P. Macmillan, 1933, New York.

1801   Mixed Red, White Light Makes All Other Colors. Toth, R.C. Illuminating Engineering, Ja 1958, Vol. 53, Supp 18a.

1802   MMS for Glyndebourne. Reid, Francis. Tabs Sp 1977.

1803   Mobile Color and Stage Lighting. Jones, Bassett. Electrical World, Jl 31, 1915, Vol. LXVI, P. 245/ Ag 7, 1915, P. 294/ Ag 14 1915, P. 346/ Ag 21, 1915 P. 407/.

1804   Mobile Painting - Art's Newest Expression. Seidenberg, Roderick. International Studio, Mr 1922, LXXV, P. 84-86.

1805   Mobile Stage for Summer Touring. Kelly, Timothy L. Theatre Crafts, My/Je 1978, Vol. 12, No. 4, P. 36.

1806   Mobile Theatre for Hair (In Holland). Johns, Eric. Stage (The), S 23, 1970, P. 16-17.

1807   Models for Money: Obtaining Government and Foundation Grants and Assistance. Urgo, Louis A. Suffolk University Management Education Center. No Date.

1808   Model Stage Lighting Equipment. Tabs, Ap 1949, Vol. 7, No. 1, P. 14.

1809   Model Stage Lighting.

Tabs, S 1938, Vol. 2, No. 1.

1810   Model Theatre for Lighting Study (A). Welt, Jahrg. Halbjalr Ap 2 1910.

1811   Modern Cinemas. Architectural Press, (The), 1936.

1812   Modern Developments of Stage Lighting. Groom, H.R. Lester. Electricity, 1925, Vol. 39, P. 145-147, 160-161, 187-188.

1813   Modern Dilemma in Art: the Reflections of a Color-Music Painter(The). Belmont, I.J. Harbinger House, 1944, Chapter 21, New York.

1814   Modern Illumination: Theory and Practice. Hurstmann, Henry Charles and Tousley, Victor H. F.J. Drake & Co., 1912, Chicago.

1815   Modern Lamps in Old Instruments. Volkman, Rudy. Theatre Craft, Mr/Ap 1980, Vol. 14, No. 2, P. 98.

1816   Modern Lenses and Their Uses. Dawes, J.A. Photo-Era N 1918.

1817   Modern Lighting Equipment and Visual Accompaniment in Light. Encyclopedia Britannica, 14th Ed., Xxi, 1929, P. 289-291.

1818   Modern Lighting Technique. Hewitt, Harry. Edward Arnold & Co., 1952, London.

1819   Modern Lighting With Control Lenses. Logan, H.L. Transactions of the I.E.S., D 1930, Vol. XV, P. 10.

1820   Modern Methods of Using

Gas. Builder (The) S 7, 1907, Vol. XCIII.

1821   Modern Stage Effects. Davids, Edith. Munsey, Jl 1901, Vol. XXV, P. 524-532.

1822   Modern Stage Illumination. Scientific American Supplement, Ap 1910, Vol. 69, P. 244, 245.

1823   Modern Stage Lighting: the Blackburn-Starling System. Electricity, 1923, Vol. 37, P. 139.

1824   Modern Stage Lighting in England. Applebee, L.G. Oxford Companion to the Theatre (The), Phyllis Hartnoll, Editor, 1967, Third Edition, P.571.

1825   Modern Stage Lighting. Turner, W. J. London Mercury, 1922, Vol. 7, P. 649.

1826   Modern Stage Lighting. Era, F 8, 1913, Vol. 76, P. 19.

1827   Modern Stage Lighting. Electrical Review, 1923, Vol. 92, P. 406, 447.

1828   Deleted.

1829   Modern Switchboards. Herrick, Albert B. Cutter Electrical Mfg. Co., 1898, Philadelphia.

1830   Modern Theater: Architecture, Stage Design, Lighting (The). Schubert, Hannelore. Praeser, 1971, New York, 222p. LOCN: Na6821 83813

1831   Modern Theatres. Pichel, Irving. Harcourt, Brace & Co., 1925, New York. Edition on Building a Theatre, 1920. LOCN: 792 P583m

1832   Modern Theatre

Installation in New York City (A). Smith, Irving B. Electrical World and Engineer, Mr 14, 1903, Vol. XLI, P. 4, 55.

1833   Modern Theatre Lighting. Bowman, Wayne. Harper & Bros., 1957, New York. LOCN: 57-10574

1834   Modern Theatre Practice. Heffner, Hubert C. and selden, Samuel and sellman, Hunton D. and walkup, Fairfax P. Prentice-Hall, 1973, Englewood Cliffs, N.J. LOCN: 72-89404 ISBN: 0-13-598805-5

1835   Modification of Spectrum of Tungsten Filament Quartz-Iodine Lamps Due to Iodine Vapor. Studer, F. and Van Beers, R. Journal of the Optical Society of America, Jl 1964, Vol. LIV, No. 6.

1836   Modular Scenic System (The): a Designer/Director Manual. Kramer, William W. Hampshire Theatre, Hampshire College, Amherst, Ma. No Date.

1837   Money Business: Grants & Awards for Creative Artists. Artists Foundation, Inc. (The), 1978, 100 Boylston St., Boston, 02116. ISBN: 0161-5866

1838   Monster Motor Truck to Carry Scenery. Popular Mechanics, Ja 1912, Vol. 17, P. 22-23.

1839   Mood Master of Light. Schiller, Ronald. Coronet, O 1951, Vol. XXX, P. 98-101.

1840   More About Optical Effects. Tabs, S 1951, Vol. 9, No. 2, P. 18.

1841   More About the U.S.A.
829 Lighting Design Exam.
Brand, Robert. Lighting
Dimensions, D 1977.

1842   More Light on the Lime
Light. Goodman, L.P.
Theatre Survey, N 1969.

1843   Mormon Tabernacle (The).
Olsen, Ronald Charles.
Tabs, Mr 1973.

1844   Motion Picture
Operation, Stage Electrics
and Illusions. Horstmann,
Henry Charles. F.J. Drake &
Co., 1914, Chicago. LOCN:
Pn 1994.H7

1845   Movable Theatres. Goss,
Anthony. Architects'
Journal, Jl 5, 1961, P.
10-11.

1846   Movement and Light in
Today's Art. Popper, Frank.
The Unesco Courier, S 1963,
P. 13-23.

1847   Moving Pictures from a
Linnebach. Stell, W.
Joseph. Theatre Crafts Ja
1969.

1848   Moving Scenic
Projection. Conway, John
A. Players Magazine, Ja
1954.

1849   Multi-Image As a
Lighting Tool. Fowler,
Lowell. Lighting
Dimensions, Mr 1980, P.
30-37.

1850   Programming: Hardware
and Software. Lucier, Mary.
Theatre Crafts, O 1979,
Vol. 13, No. 5, P. 40.

1851   Multi-Lantern Complexity
- Why? (A). Pilbrow,
Richard. Tabs, S 1967.

1852   Multi-Media Projected
Scenery at NYC Opera 3
Productions by Frank
Grisara. Guttman, Gilda.

Ph.D. Thesis, New York
University, 1980.

1853   Multi-Projector
Complexity (A). Tabs, Je
1973, Vol. 31, No. 2, P.
57.

1854   Multi-Q. Tabs Sp 1977.

1855   Multiplex and Projected
Holograms. Howell, Robert.
Theatre Design and
Technology, Fall, 1978,
Vol. XIV, No. 3, P. 11-12.

1856   Munsell Book of Color.
Munsell Color Co., 1929,
London.

1857   Museum Devoted Only to
Holography (A). Lighting
Dimensions, F 1978, P.6,
Vol. 2, No. 2.

1858   Musical Comedy Design.
Bay, Howard. Michigan State
University Press, 1961.

1859   Music & the Art of the
Theatre. Appia, Adolphe.
Hewitt, University of Miami
Press, 1963; Books of the
Theatre, No. 3. ISBN:
0-87024-018-8

1860   Music and Scene by Appia
in Translation. Moore,
Ulric. Ph.D. Thesis,
Cornell University, 1929.
LOCN: Pn 1624 1929 M821

1861   Music Hall (The). Reid,
Francis. Cue Technical
Theatre Review, My/Ju 1980.

1862   Music in Colors.
Electrical Experimenter, My
1915, Vol. 3, P. 1.

1863   Music on the Band Rail
First. Gould, Mervyn. Tabs,
Summer 1978, P. 7, Vol. 36,
No. 2.

1864   Name in Lights: J.
Rosenthal. Violett, Ellen.
Theatre Arts, D 1950, Vol.
34, P. 24-27.

1865   Nananne Porcher. Watson, Lee. Lighting Dimensions, Ap 1980, P. 34-36.

1866   National Arts Centre Ottawa. Bentham, Frederick. Tabs, Mr 1970, Vol. 28, No. 1, P. 16.

1867   National Directory for the Performing Arts/ Educational. Handel, Beatrice (Editor). John Wiley & Sons, 1978, New York. LOCN: Pn 1s77 N3rff 1978 ISBN: 0-471-03304-9

1868   National Directory for the Performing Arts and Civic Centers. Handel, Beatrice (Editor). John Wiley & Sons, 1978, New York. LOCN: Pn 2289 N38 1978 Ref ISBN: 0-471-03303-0

1869   National Electric Code (The). Theatre Design & Technology, O 1970.

1870   National Electric Code Handbook. Abbott, Arthur L. McGraw Hill, 1952, New York.

1871   National Physical Fitness Divison, Department of National Health and Welfare, Simplified Stage Lighting. Minister of National Health and Welfare, Canada. No Date.

1872   National Theatre, Budapest. Szucs, K. International Lighting Review, Vol. 70, No. 4, P. 130. No Date.

1873   Natural Lighting for Television. Trussell, Hal. Lighting Dimensions, Ap 1980.

1874   Nature of Light and Color in Air (The). Minart, Marcel G. Dover Press, 1954, New York.

1875   Naval Electrical Manual. H.M. Stationery Office 1928.

1876   NBC Presents Twlicms (The World's Largest Indoor Country Music Show). Manning, Ferd. Lighting Dimensions, Jy/ag 1978, Vol. 2, No. 6, P. 16.

1877   Needed: a New Approach to Teaching Lighting. Sassone, Rich. Lighting Dimensions, N 1978, Vol. 2, No. 9, P. 44.

1878   Nefertiti. MacKay, Patricia. Tabs N 1977.

1879   Nefrtiti. MacKay, Patricia. Theatre Crafts, N/D 1977, Vol. 11, No. 6, P. 17.

1880   Neil Diamond. Fiorentino, Imero. Lighting Dimensions, Je 1977, P. 20.

1881   Nevada Showbiz. Watson, Lee. Lighting Dimensions, Mr 1979, Vol. 3, No. 3, P. 24.

1882   Newest Art(The). Peters, Rollo. Theatre Arts Magazine, 1918, Vol. II, No. 3, P. 119, 127.

1883   Newest Thing in Lighting Controls (The). Salzer, Beeb. Lighting Dimensions, D 1977.

1884   News and Editorial, Stanley R. McCandless. Rubin, Joel E. Theatre Design and Technology, D 1967, No. 11, P. 3.

1885   New Alhambra Theatre (The). Builder, (The), N 10, 1883, P. 636.

1886   New Art of Light (The). Craig, Edward Gordon. Arts and Decoration, N 1921, Vol. XVI, P. 52.

1887   New at the Albery
Theatre. Tabs, Autumn 1977,
Vol. 35, No. 3, P. 5.

1888   New Baby Mirror Spot.
Tabs, Ap 1953, Vol. 11, No.
1, P. 9.

1889   New Ballet of Electra at
Her Majesty's Theatre
(The). Illustrated London
News, My 5, 1849, Vol. 14,
P. 293.

1890   New Control-Board;
Remodeling of an Old Board
after a Fire. Davis, Harry.
Carolina Playbook, D 1940,
P. 172-176.

1891   New Designs Demonstrate
the Versatility of Xenon
High-Pressure Lamps.
Thouret, Wolfgang E. and
Strauss, Herbert S.
Illuminating Engineering,
Mr 1962, Vol. LVIII, No. 3.

1892   New Design Problem:
Multi-Media Effects (The).
Weiss, David W. Players,
Ag/s 1970, Vol. 45, P.
264-67.

1893   New Developments.
Lighting Dimensions, O
1979, Vol. 3, No. 10.

1894   New Dimmer for Theatre
Work (A). Electrician, N
11, 1904, Vol. 54, P. 131.

1895   New Disappearing
Footlight Furnished in
Complete Finished Sections
(A). Electrical Review and
Western Electrician, N 11,
1916, Vol. 69, P. 86;
Electrical World, N 11,
1916,.

1896   New Disco Light
Controller (A). Lighting
Dimensions, S 1978, Vol. 2,
No. 7, P. 55.

1897   New Electrical
Apparatus. Scientific
American Supplement, Jl
1896, Vol. 42, P. 17107.

1898   New Electrical Energy
Saving Light Bulbs.
Lighting Dimensions, O
1977, P. 44.

1899   New from Rank Strand.
Rose, Philip. Tabs, Fall
1978, Vol. 36, No. 3, P.
12-15.

1900   New Hunter Theatres.
Simonson, Lee. Theatre
Arts, Mr 1940, Vol. XXIV,
No. 3, P. 215-216.

1901   New Idea for Theatre
Stage Illumination.
Fitzkee, D. Architect and
Engineer, S, 1931, Vol.
106, P. 118.

1902   New King of Painting
Uses Light As Medium. New
York Times, D 8, 1931.

1903   New Klieglight (The).
Kliegl, Herbert A. Journal
of Motion Picture
Engineers, D 1934, Vol.
XXIII, P. 359-62.

1904   New Lamps for Old in the
Theatres. Shipp, H.
English Review (The),n
1921, P.395-398.

1905   New Lanterns. Tabs, Ap
1963, Vol. 21, No. 1, P. 5.

1906   New Lighting at the Met.
Transactions of the
Illuminating Engineering
Society, F 1935, Vol. 30,
No. 2, P. 212-221.

1907   New Lighting at the
Roxy. Transactions of the
Illuminating Engineering
Society Jl 1927, Vol. 22,
No. 7, P. 456.

1908   New Light for the
Theatre. Bailey, Ralph
Sargent. Theatre Magazine,
Jy 1930, P.23-24.

1909   New Light on Old Lamps.
Freeman, Larry. Century
House, 1968, New York.

1910   New Light Sources and
Associated Optical Systems
for Theatre and Television.
Lemons, T.M. and Levin,
R.E. Illuminating
Engineering, N 1965, Vol.
LX, No. 11.

1911   New Methods and
Materials in Stage Design.
Yves-Bonnat. World Theatre,
Sp, 1963, Vol. XII, No. 1,
P. 5.

1912   New Method of Stage
Lighting(A). Scientific
American Vol. XCIV My
19,1906 P.414.

1913   New Method of Stage
Lighting (A). Feeney,
Joseph M. Lighting Journal
O 1915.

1914   New Mode of Lighting
Theatres. Scientific
American, Ag 1861, Vol. 5,
P. 101.

1915   New Par and R-Type Lamps
Using Compact Quartz-Iodine
Sources. Beesley, E.M. and
Stone, M.L. Illuminating
Engineering, F 1966, Vol.
LXI, No. 2.

1916   New SCR Dimmer Speeds
Light-Control Progress.
Langer, Robert A.
Electrical Construction and
Maintainance, F 1959, Vol.
58, P. 70-72.

1917   New Stagecraft:
Developmets in Scenery and
Lighting on the New York
Stage Between 1900 and 1915
(The). Arnold, Richard.
Ph.D. Thesis, Northwestern
University, 1962.

1918   New Stage Mechanics
Exibited in London. Musical
Courier, Ap 29, 1914, Vol.
68, P. 5.

1919   New Strand P. R. Control
System. Tabs, S 1955, Vol.
13, No. 2, P. 5.

1920   New System of Lighting
Control. Players Magazine,
Ja/F 1930, Vol. VI, No. 2,
P. 5.

1921   New System of Lighting
Theatres in Paris. American
Gas Light Journal, Ja 1,
1863, Vol. 4, P. 197.

1922   New Technology in
Lighting Control Equipment.
Levy, Walter A. Journal of
the Society of Motion
Picture and Television
Engineers, Vol. 69,
P.253-8. No Date.

1923   New Theatres for Old.
Gorelik, Mordecai. Samuel
French, 1955, New York.

1924   New Theatres in Paris
(The). Builder (The), O 25,
1862, Vol. XX, P. 761, See
Also P. 777.

1925   New Theatre on Wheels
(A). Scheff, Aimee. Theatre
Arts, F, 1953, Vol. XXXVII,
No. 2, P. 86.

1926   New Types of Theatre
Dimmers. Electrical World,
S 23, 1899, Vol. 34, P.
465.

1927   New Type of Footlight
(A). Fuchs, Theodore. Drama
(The), O 1925, Vol. XVI, P.
23ff.

1928   New U.S.A. 829 - League
Pact. Theatre Crafts, Ja/f
1979, Vol. 13, No. 1, P. 8.

1929   New Uses for Reflector
Lamps. Kimberly, George B.
Theatre Arts Magazine, Jl
1944, Vol. XXVIII, No. 7,
P. 430.

1930   New Use for Cinemoid
(A). Hudson, E. O. Tabs, S
1955, Vol. 13, No. 2, P.
12.

1931   New Ways of Servicing
Buildings. De Mare, Eric

Samuel. The Architectural
Press, 1954.

1932   New Way of Lighting
Stages (A). Scientific
American, Ap 1910, Vol.
102, P. 342.

1933   New Way of Outlining
Theater Scenery (A).
Scientific American, Ja
1877, Vol. 36 P. 4.

1934   New York's Roseland
Ballroom. Lighting
Dimensions, F 1980, P.
18-24.

1935   New York Theatre Fires.
New York Herald, Ja 10,
1896, P. 7, Mr 28, 1889, P.
12, O 23, 1888, P. 3.

1936   Night Skies. Tabs, D
1952, Vol. 10, No. 3, P. 9.

1937   Nikolais Dance Theatre's
Uses of Light (The).
Nickolich, Barbara E.
Drama Review, Je 1973, Vol.
17, P. 80-91.

1938   Non-Flying Dutchman (A).
Corry, Percy. Tabs S 1972.

1939   Non-Lighting for the
Theatre. Theatre Crafts S
1971.

1940   Non Technical Guide to
Hollography (A). Cocetti,
R.A. Tech Paper,
University of Montana,
1963.

1942   Norman Bel Geddes.
Bliven, Bruce. Theatre
Arts, Jl 1919, Vol. III,
No. 3, P. 179.

1943   Norman Bel Geddes:
Designer, Director, Stage
Architect. Weller, Betty
H. Ph.D. Thesis,
University of Iowa, 1959.

1944   Norman Bel Geddes, Man
of Ideas. Works, Bernhard
R. Ph.D. Thesis,

University of Wisconsin,
1960.

1945   Norman Bel Geddes and
the Art of Modern Theatre
Lighting. Bogusch, George.
Educational Theatre
Journal, D 1972, Vol. 24,
No. 4, P. 415.

1946   Norman Bel Geddes
Artistic Lighting Designer.
Mecham, E. J. M. F. A.
Thesis, University of
Texas, Austin, 1966.

1947   Northern Lights.
Roberts, Peter. Plays and
Players, Ja, 1961, P. 6.

1948   Notes & Queries 2.
Scientific American, N
1877, Vol. 37, P. 315.

1949   Notes & Queries 3.
Scientific American, My
1877, Vol. 36, P. 283.

1950   Notes & Queries 38.
Scientific American, Mr
1877, Vol. 36, P. 139.

1951   Notes & Queries 323.
Scientific American, S
1876, Vol. 35 P. 171.

1952   Notes and Queries   83.
Scientific American, Ap
1875, Vol. 32, P. 251.

1953   Notes and Queries.
Scientific American, Ap
1875, Vol. 32, P. 251.

1954   Notes on Lighting Design
for the Elizabethan Stage.
Thayer, David. Educational
Theatre Journal, 1959, Vol.
11, P. 222-28.

1955   Notes on Network Tv
Lighting Practice. Thayer,
David. Educational Theatre
Journal, O 1957, Vol. 9,
P.223-230.

1956   Notes on the Application
of the Silicon Controlled
Rectifier. General Electric

Company. General Electric
Company, D 1958, Auburn,
New York.

1957   Notes. Electrician (The)
Xii S 6 1884 P. 381.

1958   Not So Good Old Days
(The). Tabs, Ap 1950, Vol.
8, No. 1, P. 25.

1959   Novel Gas Apparatus at
the Paris Grand Opera.
Scientific American, Je
1875, Vol. 32, P. 388.

1960   Novel Mobile Stage (A).
Pitkin, W. Theatre Crafts
Mr 1968.

1961   Now Is the Time for All
Good Men. Gould, Mervyn.
Cue Technical Theatre
Review, S/O 1979, P. 29.

1962   No Longer a Sci-Fi
Dream: Make Way for
Technological Revolution!.
ABTT News, S 1979, P. 15.

1963   No Volts: No Amps No
Watts. Tabs, S 1953, Vol.
11, No. 2, P. 20.

1964   Numbers Game (The).
Bentham, Frederick. Tabs,
Autumn 1976, Vol. 34, No.
3, P. 19.

1965   Obscure Pioneer of the
Newest Art in the Theatre.
Current Opinion, Ag 1916,
P. 101-102.

1966   Observations on an
Improved Oxyhydrogen Lime
Light As Adapted by the
Universal Lime Light
Company Limited. Renton, A.
H. Henery Hansard, 1859,
London.

1967   Observations on Scenic
Projection in Northern
Europe and in the U.S.A.
Bellman, Willard F.
Theatre Design &
Technology, D 1969.

1968   Occupational Safety and
Health Effects Associated
With Reduced Levels of
Illumination (The). U.S.
Dept. of H.E.W., 1975,
Cincinnati. LOCN:
Th7700.022

1969   Off Broadway Television.
Manning, Ferd. Lighting
Dimensions, Jl 1979, P. 61.

1970   Of Music and Painting.
New York Times, Ja 5, 1941.

1971   OISTT Reports on Theatre
Training. Theatre Design &
Technology, Fall 1976.

1972   Old Instruments, New
Images. Rynkiewicz, Robert.
Theatre Crafts, N/D 1979,
Vol. 13, No. 6, P. 89.

1973   Old Lamps of Central
Europe and Other Lighting
Devices. Benesch, Ladislav
Von. C.E. Tuttle Co., 1963,
Rutland,vt., for Rushlight
Club. LOCN: Nk8360,b45

1974   Old Vic (The). Tabs, D
1950, Vol. 8, No. 3, P. 22.

1975   One-Eyed Theatre?. Tabs,
S 1951, Vol. 9, No. 2, P.
5.

1976   Only Preset Controls
Will Do. Tabs Mr 1971.

1977   On Bellman's
Scenography. Arnold,
Richard. Lighting
Dimensions, Ag 1979, P. 50.

1978   On Development of a
Lighting Score. Kliegl,
Herbert A. Impulse, 1952,
P. 13.

1979   On October's Electrical
Safety. Gill, George.
Lighting Dimensions, Ja
1980, P.34.

1980   On Stage Color. Withey,
J. A. Players Magazine,
My, 1959, Vol. 35, No. 8,
P. 177.

1981   On the Illumination of
Lighthouses. Drummond,
Lieut. Thomas.
Philosophical Transactions
of the Royal Society of
London, 1830.

1982   Opening Light in Sydney.
Ornbo, Robert. Tabs Ap
1974.

1983   Open Faced Instruments:
New Possibilities in
Theatre. Moody, James L.
Theatre Design & Technology
F 1971.

1984   Open Stage and the
Modern Theatre in Research
and Practice (The).
Southern, Richard. Faber
and Faber, 1953, London.

1985   Opportunities for the
Artistic Use of Light to
Convey a Play's Images.
Mostepanenko, E.I. ABTT
News, N 1978, P. 4.

1986   Opryland. Lighting
Dimensions, O 1977, P. 28.

1987   Optical Control of
Light; a Brief Survey of
the Physical Properties of
Light and Optical Means of
Controling Its
Distribution. Hughes,
Marjorie A. M.F.A. Thesis,
Yale University, 1935.

1988   Optical Design of
Reflectors (The). Elmer,
William B. Elmer, 1974, 2
Chestnut St., Andover, M.A.
01810. LOCN: Th 7970 R4 E37
1974

1989   Optical Illusions and
Lights at Barnum's (The).
Scientific American
Supplement, Ap 1890, Vol.
29, P. 11938.

1990   Optical Projection.
Gage, S.R. and Gage, H.P.
Comstock Publishing Co.,
1914, Ithaca, N. Y.

1991   Optical Properties of
Ellipsoidal Reflectors
(The). Holeman, John M.
General Electric Review,
1923-26. Reprinted by
USITT.

1992   Optics for the Theatre
Technician. Price, Michael
P. M.F.A. Thesis, 1963,
Yale University.

1993   Optics. Journal of
Science, 1827, VI.

1994   Optics. Sears, Francis
W. Addison-Wesley
Press,inc 1938, Cambridge,
Mass.

1995   Optics. Newton, Sir
Isaac. Dover, 1952, New
York. Also Published by
Mgraw Hill, 1931, New York.

1996   Optimum Level of
Illumination for Maximum
Visual Efficiency in the
Theatre. Felton, John G.
Jr. M.A. Thesis, State
University of Iowa, 1938.

1997   Organo Ad Libitum: or
Prometheus Not Yet Unbound.
Bentham, Frederick. Tabs,
Autumn 1977, Vol. 35, No.
3, P. 19.

1998   Organ of Color(The).
Literary Digest, F 4, 1922,
Vol. LXXII, P. 26.

1999   Origins and Development
of Kenetic Art. Popper,
Frank. Graphic Society,
1969, New York.

2000   Our Theatre Today.
Bricker, Herschel (Editor).
French, 1936, New York.

2001   Outline of an Elementary
Course in Stage Lighting
(An). Part I. Currie, Dean
N. M.A. Thesis, Carnegie
Institute of Technology,
1931.

2002   Overhead Projectors.

Lighting Dimensions, O 1978, Vol. 2, No. 10, P. 58.

2003   Oxford Companion to the Theatre (The). Hartnoll, Phyllis (Editor). Oxford Press, 1957, London.

2004   Oxyhydrogen Light (The). Scientific American Supplement I 1876.

2005   Painting Scenery With Electric Lights. Literary Digest, D 10, 1921, Vol. 71, P. 23.

2006   Painting the Stage With Light. Benke, M. Design, D 1952, Vol. 54, P. 66.

2007   Painting With Light. Alton, John. Macmillan Co., 1949, New York.

2008   Deleted.

2009   Panel: National Electric Code. Theatre Design and Technology, O 1970, P.29-33.

2010   Panic Circuits Lighting for Safety. Safford, David. Theatre Design & Technology, F 1969.

2011   Pani of Candle Street. Tabs Fall 1975.

2012   Papers Presented at the Eighth Ann Arbor Conference: the Theatre. University of Michigan College of Architecture and Design, 1950, Ann Arbor, Michigan.

2013   Paris Theatre Des Varietes. Leblanc, Georges. Tabs Sum 1976.

2014   Parthenon: an Essay on the Mode by Which Light Was Introduced Into Greek and Roman Theatres (The). Fergusson, James. J. Murray, 1883, London. ISBN: Na260. F35

2015   Parts of a Survey of the Lighting Design Industry. Lighting Dimesions, N 1979.

2016   Passing of Stage Scenery(The). Literary Digest, (The), O 14, 1922, Vol. LXXV, P. 36.

2017   Patented Lighting. Rushlight Club (The), 1979, Boston.

2018   Pattern 23w, a New Use. Tabs, Ap, 1958, Vol. 16, No. 1, P. 27.

2019   Paulie Jenkins: Lighting Director for the Los Angeles Actors' Theatre. Lighting Dimensions, Ap 1978, Vol. 2, No. 4, P. 24.

2020   Pennsylvania State University Theatre Lighting Archives. Tabs, O 1975.

2021   Penthouse Production in High School. Hughes, Glenn. Quarterly Journal of Speech, D 1949, Vol. 35, P. 456-463.

2022   Performing Arts and Entertainment Related Occupations. G.P.O. 029-001-02100-3. No Date.

2023   Period Lighting Fixtures. Gould, George G. and Gould, Mrs. Florence Pearl, Holden. Dodd, 1928, New York.

2024   Period Lighting. Wells, Stanley. Pelham, 1975, London. LOCN: Th7703.W44

2025   Peter Cheeseman Talks Around Lighting. Tabs, D 1972, Vol. 30, No. 4, P. 148.

2026   Peter Harris-Tm. Anderson, Bob. Tabs Ap 1974.

2027   Pete Edwards. Lighting Dimensions D 1977.

2028   Particular Movable
Theatre, (A). Architects
Journal (The), Ag 1961,
Vol. 134, P. 299.

2029   Art of Scenic Design and
Staging for Children's
Theatre. Davis, Jed H.
Ph.D. Thesis, University of
Minnesota, 1958.

2030   Phaedra and the Lion.
Hewes, Henry. Saturday
Review, Je 5, 1954, Vol.
37, P. 25-26.

2031   Photographic Techniques
for Creating Projected
Effects. Lessley, Merrill.
Lighting Dimensions, O
1978, Vol. 2, No. 10, P.
26-44.

2032   Photographic
Transparencies As a Means
of Teaching Stage Lighting.
Utterback, James. Ph.D.
Thesis, Southern Illinois
University, 1976.

2033   Picture Booth Control.
Voss, Lawrence. Players
Magazine, Ap 1954, Vol. 30,
No. 7, P. 163.

2034   Pierre Patte: Late 18th
Century Lighting Innovator.
Theatre Crafts, S 1969, P.
28.

2035   Pinball: Making the
Lighting Sparkle for Dr.
Pepper. Winston, William.
Lighting Dimensions, Ja
1978, Vol. 2, No. 1, P. 25.

2036   Planning and Equipping
the Educational Theatre.
Gillette, A.S. National
Thespian Society, 1945,
Cincinnati, Ohio.

2037   Planning for Lighting
Control Systems. Thayer,
David. Theatre Design &
Technology My 1965.

2038   Planning Lighting on a
Model. Stanbury, R. Tabs,
S 1952, Vol. 10, No. 1, P.
5.

2039   Planning of the "Oliver"
National Tour. Albery, Ian
B. Tabs Mr 1966.

2040   Planning the Small
Stage. Corry, Percy. Tabs,
D 1953, Vol. 11, No. 3,.

2041   Plan and Working
Drawings for a Multiple-Use
Stage Setting Suitable for
a Touring Theatre. Pannett,
Murrell. M.A. Thesis,
University of Washington,
1948.

2042   Plan for Replugging (A).
Eggleston, W. Theatre
Crafts Jl 1967.

2043   Plastics Research and
Technology at the National
Bureau Of Standards. Kline,
Gordon M. United States
Government Printing Office,
Je 1950, Washington, D. C.
National Bureau of
Standards Circular 494.

2044   Player King and the
Theatre at Drottingholm
(The). Ewer, Monica.
Theatre Arts Magazine, Mr
1931, Vol. XV, No. 3, P.
228.

2045   Playing With Light.
Theatre Arts Magazine, Ag
1917, Vol. 1 No. 4 P. 195.

2046   Please, Darling, Bring
Three to Seven. Sargeant,
Winthrop. New Yorker, F 4,
1956, Vol. 31, P. 33-59.

2047   Plea for Simplicity (A).
Kenny, Sean. World Theatre,
1963, Vol. 12, P. 45-48.

2048   Plotting for a Pageant.
Tabs, S 1949, Vol. 7, No.
2, P. 15.

2049   Plug Analyzer (A).
Corbett, Tom. Theatre
Crafts, Mr/Ap 1977, Vol.
II, No. 2, P. 70.

2050   Polarized Lights.
Sporre, Dennis J. Theatre
Crafts O 1969.

2051   Polyethylene: a Superb
Non Conductor of Electrical
Current. Lighting
Dimensions, O 1977, P. 18.

2052   Polyethylene Turns on
the Wire and Cable
Business. Lighting
Dimensions O 1977.

2053   Pool of Light:
Suggestions for Lighting
Central Staging (A).
Yeaton, Kelly. Players
Magazine, Ap, 1949, Vol.
25, No. 7, P. 152.

2054   Portable Dimmer Board
(A). Risser, Arthur C.
Players, O, 1962, Vol.
XXXIX, No. 1, P. 24.

2055   Portable Dimmer Cases
Used by Traveling Shows.
Electrical Review, 1921,
Vol. 78, P. 195.

2056   Portable Proscenium.
Pearson, Talbot. Theatre
Arts, Jl 1942, Vol. XXVI,
No. 7, P. 474.

2057   Portable Stage-Lighting
Control. Lewis, Richard B.
and Herndon, Leroy T.
Players Magazine, Jl/Ag
1939, Vol. 15, No. 6, P.
20.

2058   Portable Stage Lighting
Control. Lewis, Richard B.
and Herndon, Leroy T.
General Radio Experimenter,
Jy 1938, Vol. 2, P. 13.

2059   Portable Stage Light
Simulator (The). Proctor,
Daniel H. M.F.A. Thesis,
1970, Yale University.

2060   Portable Switchboard.
Wilson, Asher. Players
Magazine, N 1953, Vol. 30,
No. 2, P. 45.

2061   Porto Theatre.
Oenslager, Donald and Kook,
Edward F. Theatre Crafts
My 1969.

2062   Porto Theatre. Kook,
Edward F. and Oenslager,
Donald. USITT Publication.
No Date.

2063   Possibilities in Gas
Lighting. Scientific
American Supplement, 1879,
VII.

2064   Possibilities of Stage
Lighting Together With an
Account of Several Recent
Publications (The). Jones,
Bassett. Transactions of
the Illuminating
Engineering Society, Jl 20,
1916, Vol. XI, No. 5, P.
547.

2065   Postwar Developments in
Stage Lighting. Smedberg,
George. Educational Theatre
Journal, O 1953, Vol. 5,
No. 3, P. 253.

2066   Post Modern Words or Is
Ther Art after Death?.
Salzer, Beeb. Lighting
Dimensions, Je 1980, P. 43.

2067   Potpourri. Watson, Lee.
Lighting Dimensions, Ag
1979, P. 15.

2068   Powerful Light Produced
With Nitrogen Lamp. Popular
Mechanics Vol. 24 N 1915 P.
646.

2069   Practical Application of
the Laser to Performance
Lighting (The). Alvis,
Arthur and Hansen, Richard.
Lighting Dimensions, F
1978, P.28, Vol. 2, No. 2.

2070   Practical Dreams: the
Theatre of Robert Edmond
Jones. Pendleton, Ralph.
Wesleyan University Press,
1958, Middletown,
Connecticut.

2071   Practical Electrical Wiring. Richter, Herbert P. McGraw-Hill, 1952, New York.

2072   Practical Electricity and House Wiring. Richter, Herbert P. Frederick J. Drake & Co., 1952, Chicago.

2073   Practical Stage Lighting. Bogar, Emmet W. R. Rosen Press, 1971, New York. LOCN: Pn2091.E4 857 ISBN: 0823902242

2074   Practical Treatise on the Manufacture and Distribution of Coal Gas. Richards, William. Spon, 1877, New York.

2075   Pre-Set, Proportional Dimming Portable Switchboard. Voss, Lawrence. Players Magazine, O 1951, Vol. XXVIII, P. 10.

2076   Prefocus Lampholders. Tabs, S 1950, Vol. 8, No. 2, P. 10.

2077   Preparing the Professional Designer. Elder, E. Theatre Crafts My 1969.

2078   Press the Button-See the Show. Jungmann, A. M. Popular Science Monthly, Ja 1919, Vol. 94, P. 43.

2079   Price of Economy (The). Whitehouse, A.K. Tabs Sp 1978.

2080   Primary Colors the Watt Wasters. Tabs, D 1954, Vol. 12, No. 3, P. 22.

2081   Primer of Lamps and Lighting. Allphin, Willard. Addison-Wesley, 1973, Reading, Ma. ISBN: Th7703. A43 1973

2082   Principles of Color Technology. Billmeyer, Fred W. Jr. and Saltzman, Max. Wiley, 1966, New York.

2083   Principles of Harmony and Contrast of Colours and Their Application to the Arts (The). Chevreul, Michel Eugene. G. Bell and Sons, London, England. No Date.

2084   Principles of Natural Lighting. Lynes, J. Elsevier Publishing Company, New York 1968.

2085   Principles of Optics (The). Hardy, Arthur C. and Perrin, Fred H. McGraw Hill, 1932, New York.

2086   Principles of Physics, III, Optics. Sears, Francis W. Addison-Wesley Press, 1948, Cambridge, Ma.

2087   Private Foundations & Business Corporations Active in Arts/ Humanities/Education (2 Vols.). Millsaps, Daniel. Washington International Arts Letter, 1974, Washington. ISBN: 0-912072-05-9

2088   Problems of the Stage Designer. Whistler, Rex. In: Footnotes to the Theatre, (R.D. Charques, Ed.), Peter Davies, 1938, London, P.117-32.

2089   Problems of Touring Opera (The). Aston, Tom A. Theatre Crafts, Mr/Ap 1969, Vol. 3, No. 2, P. 15-17.

2090   Problem of the Switchboard (The). McCandless, Stanley and wolf, Fred M. Players Magazine, J/F, 1947, Vol. 23, No. 3, P. 55.

2091   Process of Play Production (The). Crofton, Allen and Royer, Jessica. Crofts, 1928, New York.

2092   Producing America's Outdoor Dramas. Selden,

Samuel. Univ. of North Carolina, 1954, Chapel Hill.

2093   Producing the Play (Contains New Scene Technician's Handbook). Gassner, John and Barber, Philip. Dryden Press, 1941, New York. Holt, Rinehart & Wilson, 1953, New York. LOCN: Pn2037 G3 1953 ISBN: 0-03-005565-2

2094   Production and Stage Management at the Blackfriars Theatre. Isaacs, Jacob. Oxford University Press, 1933, London.

2095   Production and Utilization of Light(The). Drysdale, C.V. Illuminating Engineer, (The), 1908, Vol. I, P. 196, 295.

2096   Production of Late American Drama (The). Leverton, Garrett H. Teachers College, Bureau of Publications, 1936.

2097   Product Listings, Part II. Lighting Dimensions, Je 1979, Vol. 3, No. 6, P. 25.

2098   Product News. Cue Technical Theatre Review, Mr/Ap 1980, P. 23-27.

2099   Professor Pepper's Phantasmagoria. Tabs S 1971.

2100   Profile of a Pioneer. Corry, Percy. Tabs, D, 1957, Vol. 15, No. 3, P. 7.

2101   Progress in Stage Lighting. Electrician, 1921, Vol. 87, P. 299.

2102   Progress in 1961--Our Expanding Universe. Illuminating Engineering, Ja 1962, Vol. LVII, No. 1.

2103   Projected Images. Deubel. Theatre Crafts Ja 1970.

2104   Projected Opera Settings. Planer, Paul. Opera News, F 15, 1954, Vol. 18, P. 4-5.

2105   Projected Scenery: Its Design, Preparation, and Technique. Payne, Robert B. M.A. Thesis, San Jose College, 1958.

2106   Projected Scenery-Pro & Con. Arnovici, C. Theatre and School, O 1933, Vol. 12, P. 20.

2107   Projected Scenery-Static and Dynamic - Its Uses and Limitations. Moore, P. L. M.A. Thesis, Syracuse University, 1952.

2108   Projected Scenery, a Technical Manual. Wilfred, Thomas. Drama Book Shop, 1965, New York. LOCN: Pn 2091 S8 W54

2109   Projected Scenery at the Questors. Anderson, Bob. Tabs S 1970.

2110   Projected Scenery for the School Stage. Santos, Louisa. Baker's Plays, 1949, Boston.

2111   Projected Scenery Using a Large Plastic, Fresnel Lens. Klappert, Walter R. and Domser, Ira. Theatre Crafts, S 1978, Vol. 12, No. 5, P. 52-53.

2112   Projected Scenery. Butler, D.E. M.A. Thesis, University of Washington, 1955.

2114   Projected Scenery. Unruh, Walter. World Theatre (International Theatre Institute), Spring, 1953, Vol. 2, No. 4.

2115   Projected Scenery.
Conway, John A. Players
Magazine, Mr, 1952, Vol.
28, No. 6, P. 129.

2116   Projected Scenery. Tabs,
Ap 1939, Vol. 3, No. 1, P.
8.

2117   Projected Scenery.
Minter, Gordon. Players,
Magazine, Jl/Ag 1946, Vol.
22, No. 6, P. 8.

2118   Projected Scenery.
Brown, Ralph. Theatre Arts
Monthly, Jl, 1945, Vol.
XXIX, No. 7, P. 4 18.

2119   Projected Scenery.
Friedrich, W. F. Players
Magazine, N, 1952, Vol. 29,
No. 2, P. 42.

2120   Projected Scenic
Backgrounds Used at the
Catholic University
Theatre. Brown, Ralph.
Catholic University,
December, 1944, Washi
ngton, D.C.

2121   Projected Setting: a
Symposium (The). Rubin,
Joel E. and Kook, E. F.
and Wilfred, Thomas and
Planer, Paul and Clark,
Peggy and McCandless,
Stanley and Conway, John
A. and Educational
Theatre Journal, O, 1954,
Vol. 6 P. 260.

2122   Projected Setting (The).
Wilfred, Thomas.
Educational Theatre
Journal, My 1954, Vol. VI,
No. 2, P. 136.

2123   Projected Window
Patterns. Yeaton, Kelly.
Players Magazine, My 1956,
Vol 32 No 8, P. 188.

2124   Projecting Backgrounds.
Gross, Mark. Theatre Craft,
My/Je 1980, Vol. 14, No. 3,
P. 41.

2125   Projecting Strindberg.
McKinney, George W.
Players Magazine, N 1957,
Vol. 34, No. 2, P. 33.

2126   Projections: Towards a
Theatre of Light. Feher,
E. E. Feher 250 Davenport
Rd. Toronto. No Date.

2127   Projection - the New
Popularity. Tawil, Andrea.
Lighting Dimensions, O
1978, Vol. 2, No. 10, P.
24-25.

2128   Projection Developments.
Tabs Ap 1974.

2129   Projection. ABTT News,
Ja 1980,.

2130   Project for a Theatrical
Presentation of the Divine
Comedy Of Dante Alighieri.
Bel Geddes, Norman. Theatre
Arts, Inc., 1924, New York.

2131   Project in Functional
Staging and Lighting (A).
Kenna, James Gratton. M.A.
Thesis, University of
Denver, 1948.

2132   Project Seagull
Chichester. Bear, B. E.
Tabs, S 1973, Vol. 31, No.
3, P. 115.

2133   Project Sphinx.
Chamberlain, Kathy.
Lighting Dimensions, D
1979, P. 34-39.

2134   Prometheus and
Melpomene. Wilfred, Thomas.
Theatre Arts Magazine, S
1928, Vol. XII, P. 639.

2135   Prometheus Unbound.
Ostoja-Kotkowski, J.S.
Tabs, Fall 1978, Vol. 36,
No. 3, P. 3-6.

2136   Prompt on Cueing (A).
Tabs, D 1948, Vol. 6, No.
3, P. 14.

2137   Proper Grounding.

Fackert, Jim. Lighting Dimensions, Jl 1979, P. 8.

2138   Proposed Guide for Teaching Stage Lighting in the High School Dramatic Arts Program. Elmor, John L. M.A. Thesis, University of Southern California, 1955.

2139   Proposed National Lighting Training Symposium. Watson, Lee. Theatre Design & Technology, Su 1980, Vol. XVI, No. 2, P. 4.

2140   Proscenium and Sight-Lines. Southern, Richard. Theatre Arts, 1964, New York & Faber and Faber, 1964, London. LOCN: Pn 2091 S8 S63 1964

2141   Protective Alliance of Scene Painters. New York Dramatic Mirror, N 14, 1896, P. 12.

2142   Protest at Arts Grant to Region. Morris, Michael. The Guardian, Mr 15, 1979.

2143   Psychedelic Experience (The). Leary, Timothy and Metzner, Ralph and Alpert, Richard. University Books, 1964, New Hyde Park, New York.

2144   Psychedelic Lighting Manual, the. Lightwork Company, New York. Lightwork Company, 1968, New York.

2145   Psychological Aspects of Color and Illumination. Evans, Ralph M. Illuminating Engineering Vol.46 Ap 1951 P.176.

2146   Psychological Implications of Color and Illumination. Birren, Faber. Illuminating Engineering, My 1969, P.397-402.

2148   Psychology of Lighting and Color As It Pertains to Stage Lighting Wih Emphasis on the Director's Viewpoint (The). Scanga, Richard V. M.A. Thesis, Carnegie Institute of Technology, 1952.

2149   Psychology of Perception (The). Vernon, M. D. Penguin Books, 1966, Harmondsworth, Middlesex, England.

2150   Psychology of the Switchboard(The). Moses, Montrose J. Theatre Magazine, Ag 1909, Vol. 10, P. 64.

2151   Public Lighting by Gas and Electricity. Dibdin, William Joseph. The Sanitary Publishing Company, Limited, 1902.

2152   Purchasing Guide for Ellipsoidal Reflector Spotlights. Benson, Robert. Theatre Crafts, S 1978, Vol. 12, No. 5, P. 13-16.

2153   Quartz-Iodine Infrared Heat Lamp (The). Heinlein, L.T. and Stephens, W.R. Illuminating Engineering, Ja 1966, Vol. LXI, No.1.

2154   Quartz-Iodine Lamps: Limitations Lead to New Designs. Lemons, T.M. Illuminating Engineering, S 1964, Vol. LIX, No. 9.

2155   Quartz-Iodine Lamps and Reflectors for Set Lighting. Peek, S.C. Journal of the Society of Motion Picture and Television Engineers, S 1962, Vol. LXXI, No. 9.

2156   Quartz-Iodine Lamp Limitations Lead to New Designs. Lemons, T.M. and Meyer, E.R. Illuminating Engineering, N 1964, Vol. LIX, No. 11.

2157   Quartz-Iodine Tungsten
Lamp: Mechanism, Design and
Performance. Moore, J.A.
and Jolly, C.M. Journal of
Science and Technology, F
1962, Vol. XXIX, No. 2.

2158   Quartzcolor Ianiro. Tabs
Sp 1977.

2159   Quartz Lighting Lamp
Applications. Paugh, R.L.
and Allen, C.J.
Illuminating Engineering, D
1959, Vol. LIV, No. 12.

2160   Questions and Answers on
Light Sources. Ies Light
Sources Committee.
Illuminating Engineering,
Mr 1967, Vol. LXII, No. 3.

2161   R.A.'s Ideas of Scenery
(A). Desprez, Frank. Era, O
15, 1913, Vol. 77, P. 21.

2162   R.K.O. Roxy Theatre,
Radio City. Transactions of
the Illuminating
Engineering Society, Mr
1933, Vol. XXVIII, No. 3,
P. 213-15.

2163   Rainbow Shines, (The).
Dexter, Paul. Lighting
Dimensions, Ag 1979, P. 16.

2164   Ralph Holmes: Lighting
and Art Director for Dance
in America. MacKay,
Patricia. Theatre Crafts, O
1979, Vol. 13, No. 5, P.
25.

2165   Ranked High in the
Lighting Business. ABTT
News, F 1980, P. 11.

2166   Realism on the Stage.
Westminster Review, 1891,
CXXV.

2167   Realistic Sky for the
Stage. Popular Mechanics,
1922, Vol. 38, P. 821.

2168   Reccommendation for
Permanent Lighting
Installation & Wiring For

Existing Broadway Theatres.
American National Theatre
Academy, 1950, New York.

2169   Recent Advances in
Lighting. Luckiesh,
Matthew. Scientific
American, Ja 1922, CXXVI,
P. 27.

2170   Recent Applications of
Color in Lighting. Curtis,
Augustus D. and Stair,
J.L. Transactions of the
Illuminating Engineering
Society, D 30, 1920, Vol.
XV, P. 678.

2171   Recent Developments in
Electric Incandescent Lamps
in Relation to Illuminating
Engineering. Morris, J.T.
Illuminating Engineer, Ja
1916, Vol. 9, P. 6.

2172   Recent Developments in
Light "Music". Riddle,
Laura. The World Observer,
Ja 1938, P. 1-3, Offprint.

2173   Recent Developments in
Stage Lighting Control.
Sellman, H.D. Theatre
Arts, Jy 1941, Vol. XXV,
No. 7, P. 543.

2174   Recent Developments in
Stage Lighting Control.
Sellman, H.D. Quarterly
Journal of Speech, D 1950,
Vol. 36, P. 530-533.

2175   Recent Developments in
the U.S. Office of
Education. Grove, Richard.
Theatre Design &
Technology, O 1966, No. 6,
P. 7.

2176   Recollections and
Reflections. Dean, Basil.
Tabs, D 1962, Vol. 20, No.
3, P. 5.

2177   Records of the New York
Stage from 1750 to 1860.
Ireland, Joseph N. T.H.
Morrell, 1867, New York.

2178   Records of the Office of the Chief of Engineers, Fortification File, 1776-1920. National Archives, Record Group 77, Washington, D. C. No Date.

2179   Record Keeping for the Performing Arts Taxpayer. Hanlon, R. Brendan. Theatre Crafts, N/D 1978, P. 80.

2180   Redgrave Patch Panel. Laws, James. Tabs Sp 1976.

2181   Redgrave Patch Panel. Counsell, John. Tabs Sp 1976.

2182   Reflections: the Roxy Theatre. Transactions of the Illuminating Engineering Society, Jy 1925, Vol. XXII, No. 6, P. 652-654.

2183   Regulations and Rules for Electrical Installations in Places of Public Entertainment. London County Council. No Date.

2184   Rehearsal of a Play (The). Fyles, Franklin. Ladies' Home Journal (The), Ja 1900, XVII.

2185   Rehearsal Work Light. Howard, John T. Jr. Theatre Crafts, O, 1979, Vol. 13, No. 5, P. 93.

2186   Relationship of Stage Lighting Sources and Methods to Acting Style in Theatres, 1850 to 1915 (The). Barsness, Lawrence. M.A. Thesis, University of Oregon, 1950.

2187   Relative Lantern Performances. Tabs, S 1953, Vol. 11, No. 2, P. 30.

2188   Remodelled Hippodrome. Gilston, E. J. Electrical Record, 1924, Vol. 35, P. 133-135.

2189   Remote Control Circuits and Theatre Circuits. Croft, Terrell. Lighting Circuits and Switches, 1923, P. 270, New York.

2190   Remote Control for Theater Lighting. Electrical World, 1919, Vol. 74, P. 747.

2191   Renaissance Stage: Documents of Serlio, Furttenbach. Serlio, Sebastian. University of Miami Press 1958.

2192   Repertory Theatre: the Problem of a Complete Concept in Lighting and Sound. Hemsley, Gilbert V. Jr. Theatre Crafts, My/Je 1967, P.16-21.

2193   Replacing the Arc Lamp in Stage Lighting by 1000-Watt Nitrogen Lamp Equipment. Electrical Review Vol.Lxxi Jl 14,1917 P.77.

2194   Report from the 15th Photokina. Glickman, Richard. Lighting Dimensions, D 1978, Vol. 12, No. 10, P. 22.

2195   Requirements of Theatre Lighting (The). Rose, S.L.E. and Mahan, H.E. General Electric Review, O 1913, Vol. XVI, P. 745.

2196   Research in Theatre Architecture and Design. Educational Theatre Journal, Je 1967, Vol. XIX, No. 2a, P. 255.

2197   Residential Lighting. Fahsbonder, Myrtle. D. Van Nostrand Company, 1947, New York.

2198   Retrospect, I. Watson, Lee. Lighting Dimensions, F 1978, Vol. 2, No. 2, P. 16.

2199   Retrospect - II. Watson,

Lee. Lighting Dimensions, Mr 1978, Vol. 2, No. 3, P. 14.

2200   Revolution in Light. Izenour, George C. Theatre Arts, O 1947, Vol. XXXI, No. 10, P. 72-75.

2201   Revolution in Stage Lighting. Living Age, 1921, Vol. 310, P. 495.

2202   Revolution in Stage Scenery(A). Kitchen, Karl B. Theatre Magazine Vol.13 Ap 1911, P.113.

2203   Rewiring Commercial 35mm Slide Projectors for Theatre Use. Mardon, David and Wade, Sharon. Theatre Design & Technology, Fall 1979, Vol. XV, No. 3, P. 35.

2204   Rheostats for Stage Lighting. Loebreke, E. Institution of Civil Engineers Proceedings, 1890, Vol. 101, P. 396.

2205   Richard Pilbrow. Corathiel, Elisabethe H. C. Theatre World, N 1963, Vol. 59, P. 28.

2206   Right Light (The). Wechsborg, Joseph. New Yorker, O 22, 1960, P.49-84.

2207   Rise of Spectacle in America, The. Lawrence, William John. Theatre Magazine, the Ja 1917, Vol. XXV, P. 44.

2208   Rise of the American Professional Lighting Designer to 1960. Murray, Donald Louis. Ph.D. Thesis, University of Michigan, 1970. LOCN: Pn2091 E4m8 1976

2209   Riviera Theatre, Broadway and 97th Street, New York. Versteeg, Robert.

Architecture and Building, Ap 1914, Vol. 46, P. 168-169.

2210   Robertson's Phantasmagoria in Madrid, 1821. Varey, J. Theatre Notebook, 1954, Vol. 9, P. 84.

2211   Robert Edmond Jones: Poetic Artist of the New Stagecraft. Black, Eugene. Ph.D. Thesis, University of Wisconsin at Madison, 1955.

2212   Rocky Lighting. Schellerup, Glenn. Lighting Dimensions, Je 1977, P. 12.

2213   Rock & Roll Tour Lighting: What You Need to Know before You Begin to Design. Moody, James L. Theatre Crafts, Mr/ap 1978, Vol. 12, No. 3, P. 78.

2214   Rock Show Tour Lighting: Personnel and Unions. Moody, James L. and Hausman, Lee. Theatre Crafts, S 1977, Vol. 11, No. 4, P. 104.

2215   Rock Tour Lighting: the Contract and Technical Riders. Moody, James L. Theatre Crafts, N/d 1978, Vol. 12, No. 7, P. 69.

2216   Role of Contemporary Scene Building Houses for Broadway Theatre(The). Collom, Jeffrey Robert. Ph.D. Thesis, Michigan State University, 1975. LOCN: Pn 2091 S8c6 1979

2217   Role of the Light (The). Whithey, J.A. Players Magazine, Ja, 1958, Vol. 34, No. 4, P. 80.

2218   Romantic Realism and the Cosmic. Loney, Glenn. Theatre Crafts, O 1978, Vol. 12, No. 6, P. 29-33, 40-46.

2219   Romeo and Juliet at East
        15. Haley, Geoffrey. Tabs
        Je 1971.

2220   Roxy As Host to the New
        York Section, I.E.S.
        Transactions of the
        Illuminating Engineering
        Society, Mr 1927, Vol.
        XXII, P. 231-32.

2221   Roxy Theatre, New York
        City (The). Journal of the
        Theatre Historical Society
        (The), 1979, Vol. II, No.
        1.

2222   Roxy Theatre (The).
        Transactions of the
        Illuminating Engineering
        Society, Jy 1927, Vol.
        XXII, P. 652-53.

2223   Royal Festival Hall: the
        Arena Stage. Tabs, D 1951,
        Vol. 9, No. 3, P. 18.

2224   Royal Opera House,
        Covent Garden. Tabs, D
        1965, Vol. 22, No. 4, P.
        L4.

2225   Ruined Lady Asks Revenge
        (A). Aston, Frank. New York
        World Telegram and Sun, My
        6, 1958, P.26.

2226   Sadler' S Wells at the
        London Coliseum. Bentham,
        Frederick. Tabs, D 1968,
        Vol. 26, No. 4, P. 10.

2227   Salute to Hans (A).
        Watson, Lee. Lighting
        Dimensions, D 1978, Vol. 2,
        No. 10, P. 12.

2228   Samuel Pepys and the
        World He Lived in.
        Wheatley, Henry Benjamin.
        Bickers & Son, 1895,
        London.

2229   Sante Fe Opera's
        Apprentice Technician
        Training Program (The).
        Ohl, Theodore G. Lighting
        Dimensions, Jy/ag 1978,
        Vol. 2, No. 6, P. 33.

2230   Sante Fe Opera
        (Background). Wanek,
        Catherine. Lighting
        Dimensions, Ja 1978, Vol.
        2, No. 1, P. 30.

2231   Sante Fe Opera (Stephen
        Ross). Lighting Dimensions,
        Ja 1978, Vol. 2, No. 1, P.
        35.

2232   San Diego Shakespeare
        Festival Rises from the
        Ashes. Earle, Vicki.
        Theatre Design &
        Technology, Winter 1978,
        Vol. XIV, No. 4, 4p. 16.

2233   Saturday Night and
        Sunday Morning at the
        London Palladium. Bentham,
        Frederick. Tabs D 1966.

2234   Saturday Night Fever.
        Nadon, John. Lighting
        Dimensions, F 1979, Vol. 3,
        No. 2, P. 32.

2235   Savoy Theatre (The).
        Building News, S 23, 1881,
        Vol. 41, P. 389.

2236   Savoy Theatre (The).
        Builder, (The), S 24, 1881,
        P. 402.

2237   Scenery: a Manual of
        Scene Design. Helvenston,
        Harold Finley. Stanford
        University Press, 1931.

2238   Scenery and Panoramic
        Views. Builder (The), Ap
        13, 1850, Vol. VIII, No.
        375.

2239   Scenery by Projection:
        Boris Aronson's Ideas for
        Simplified Stage Settings.
        Newsweek, J. 7, 1947, Vol.
        30, P. 82.

2240   Scenery for Projection.
        Brodsky, Nina. Studio, F,
        1939, Vol. 117, P. 68.

2241   Scenery Projected in
        Space. Lyon, J.D. Theatre
        Design & Technology O 1971.

2242   Scenes in the Theatre.
Bentham, Frederick. Tabs S
1971.

2243   Scene Changing by Light
Applied to Shakespeare:
M.Pitoeff's Remarkable
Single Setting for Macbeth
at Geneva. Illustrated
London News, 1921, Vol.
159, P. 718.

2244   Scene Designing As a
Business. Eustis, Morton.
Theatre Arts Monthly, Jl,
1934, Vol. VIII, No. 7, P.
499.

2245   Scene Design and Stage
Lighting. Parker, W. Oren
and Smith, Harvey K. Holt,
Rinehart & Winston, 1963,
1968, 1974, New York, 597
P. LOCN: Pn2091.S8p3 1974
ISBN: 0-03-089446-8

2246   Scene. Craig, Edward
Gordon. H. Milford, 1923,
London.

2247   Scenic-Art. Herkomer,
Hubert Von. Magazine of
Art, 1892, Vol. 15, P.
259-64.

2248   Scenic Artist News.
United Scenic Artists,
1931, Vol. 1-28.

2249   Scenic Artist. United
Scenic Artists of America
(Local 829). M.L.A. Oxford
Univ. Press, 1940, London.

2250   Scenic Art in Mr.
Irving's Faust. Weers,
Lyman H. Dramatic Year:
1887-1888, Ticknor and Co.,
1889.

2251   Scenic Design and
Lighting. Eckart, Jean and
Eckart, William. Theatre
Arts Magazine, Jl 1960,
Vol. XLIV, No. 7, P. 55.

2252   Scenic Projection:
Current Equipment and
Practice in the U.S.

2252 (cont.) Senie, Curtis Jay. M.F.A.
Thesis, 1966, Yale
University.

2253   Scenic Projection on a
Budget Do It Yourself
Scenes and Machines.
Segrin, R. Theatre Crafts
My 1976.

2254   Scenic Wonders of the
Theater. Popular Mechanics,
1926, Vol. 45, P. 67-71.

2255   Scenic World (The).
Cornhill Magazine, LII,
1886.

2256   Scenographer's Work:
Josef Svoboda's Designs,
1971-1975. Burian, Jarka
M. Theatre Design &
Technology Sum 1976.

2257   Scheme for Arena Theatre
Lighting Grid Design in
Terms of Grid Spacing,
Walkway Space, and Masking
by Louvres. Bock, Fred
Clinton. Ph.D. Thesis,
1966, Ohio State
University.

2258   Schwabe Hasart System of
Stage Lighting at St.
Martin's Theatre, London.
Spectator, Mr 17, 1923,
Vol. 130, P. 446.

2259   Science and Art of
"Light" Painting for the
Stage: a Study of What
Color Does to Color (The).
Bauer, Mary V. M.A.
Thesis, Northwestern
University, 1928.

2260   Science in the Theater.
Scientific American
Supplement, Mr 1902, Vol.
53, P. 21924, 21925.

2261   Science in the Theatre.
Scientific American, LVI,
Je 18, 1891.

2262   Science of Color (The).
Jacobson, Egbert. American
Photo-Engravers
Association, 1937, Chicago.

2263   Science of Color (The).
Committee on Colormetry.
Thomas Y. Crowell Co.,
1953, New York.

2264   Science of Seeing (The).
Luckiesh, Matthew and Moss,
Frank K. D. Van Nostrand
1948 New York.

2265   Scientific Basis of
Illuminating Engineering
(The). Moon, P.
McGraw-Hill Book Co., Inc.,
1936, New York.

2266   Scientific Lantern
(The). Hopkins, George.
Scientific American
Supplement, Ag 19, 1905,
Vol. 1546, P. 24768.

2267   Scottish Opera' Fidelio.
Bristow, Charles. Tabs D
1970.

2268   Scottish Opera at the
Theatre Royal Glasgow.
Sugden, Derek. Tabs Sum
1976.

2269   Script to Stage; Case
History of a Set. Loucheim,
Aline. New York Times
Magazine, D 9, 1951, P. 24.

2270   Sculpture and Light:
Toronto and Montreal. Arts
Canada, 25, D 1968, P. 43.

2271   Season in Federal
Street: J.B. Williamson and
the Boston Theatre,
1796-1797 (A). Alden, John.
Proceedings of the American
Antiquarian Society, 1955,
Vol. 65, P. 9-74.

2272   Secret Regions of the
Stage (The). Logan, Olive.
Harper's New Monthly
Magazine, Ap 1874, No. 287,
P. 628.

2273   Secret Spring (The).
Bragdon, Claude. Andrew
Dakers, Ltd., 1938, London.

2274   Seeing Music in Color.

Person, Charles W.
Illustrated World, S 1915,
Vol. 24, P. 44.

2275   Seeing Things--In the
Round. Brown, John Mason.
Saturday Review of
Literature, Ap 3, 1948,
Vol. 31, P. 24.

2276   Selected 'Still'
Projection Apparatus for
Scenic and Effects
Projection. Lipschutz,
Mark. U.S.I.T.T., Room
1408, 1501 Broadway, Ny,
N.Y. No Date.

2277   Selecting a Lighting
Control System. Benson,
Robert. Theatre Crafts N
1977.

2278   Self Instruction for
Students in Gas Supply.
Mentor. Ernest Bond Ltd.,
1926, London,.

2279   Sensory Deprivation.
Leiderman, Herbert and
mendelson, Jack H. and
wexler, Donald and
solomon, Phillip. Archives
of Internal Medicine, F,
1958.

2280   Series Stage Arc Lamp.
Electrical Review Vol.67 Jl
15,1910 P.89.

2281   Setting Sail for Yet
Another Part of the Forest.
Don, Robin. Cue Technical
Theatre Review, My/Ju 1980,
P. 7.

2282   Severance Hall,
Cleveland. Better Theatres,
S 26, 1931, P. 19.

2283   Severance Hall,
Cleveland. Architectural
Forum, O 1931, P. 493.

2284   Shadows in the Light.
Fisher, Jules. Theatre
Crafts Ja 1974.

2285   Shakespeare's

Blackfriars Playhouse: Its History and Design. Smith, Irwin. New York University Press 1964.

2286   Shakespeare from Betterton to Irving. Odell, G.C.D. Scribner, 1920, New York, 2 Vols.

2287   Shakespeare Memorial Theatre. Smith, P. P. Tabs, D 1951, Vol. 9, No. 3, P. 5.

2288   Shakespeare Returns to Australia. Tabs, S 1953, Vol. 11, No. 2,.

2289   Sharks. Cooper, Gary. Theatre Craft, My/Je 1980, Vol. 14, No. 3, P. 40.

2290   Sharper Projected Images in T.V. Hoffman, Paul S. Lighting Dimensions, O 1978, Vol. 2, No. 10, P. 19-21.

2291   Shedding Some Light on Religion. Moody, James L. Lighting Dimensions, Ja 1978, Vol. 2, No. 1, P. 39.

2292   Shooting a Low Budget Film. Landau, David. Lighting Dimensions, S 1978, Vol. 2, No. 7, P. 47.

2293   Shop-Built Manually Controlled Light Chaser. Gillette, J. Michael. Theatre Crafts, Ja/F 1980, Vol. 14, No. 1, P. 106.

2294   Shops and Stores. Ketchum, Morris Jr. Reinhold, 1948, New York.

2295   Shop Experiments With Miniature Lighting Devices and Fabric Lamination. Corey, Irene. Theatre Crafts, My/Je 1977, Vol. 11, No. 3, P. 13.

2296   Shorewood High School Auditorium (The). Fuchs, Theodore. Northwestern University Press, 1949.

2297   Short Story of Holography-The Vision of Tomorrow (A). Sapan, Edith. Lighting Dimensions, F 1978, P.42, Vol. 2, No.2.

2298   Show Boats: the History of an American Institution. Graham, Philip. University of Texas Press, 1951, Austin.

2299   Sic-Act Drama Sells Westinghouse Lighting. Industrial Marketing, Ja 1949, Vol. 34, P. 74.

2300   Side Lighting. Tabs, D 1950, Vol. 8, No. 3, P. 26.

2301   Siemans Stage Lighting Control With Magnetic Amplifiers. Kolbe, Alfred. Siemans Review, Je 1959, Vol. XXVI, No. 4, P. 105-114.

2302   Significant Developments in Tv Studio Lighting Layouts. Williams, Rollo G. Journal of the Society of Motion Picture and Television Engineers, Ag 1959, Vol. 68, P.545-7.

2303   Signs of the Times. Electrical World, My 25, 1895, XXV, P. 605.

2304   Silencer Box for Kodak Carousels. Mardon, David and Mckay, Art. Theatre Design & Technology, Fall 1979, Vol. XV, No. 3, P. 35-36.

2305   Silicon Controlled Rectifier (The). Lee, B.H. M.A. Thesis, Indiana University, 1963. LOCN: Pn4000 L477

2306   Silicon Controlled Rectifer Dimmers and Iodine Lamps Demonstrated. Tabs, D 1961, Vol. 19, No. 3, P. 8.

2307   Silicon Controlled Rectifier Dimmer (The).

More, Herbert R. and Malang, Albert W. Journal of the Society of Motion Picture and Television Engineers, O 1959.

2308   Silicon Controlled Rectifier Manual. General Electric Company. General Electric Company, 1961, Auburn, New York.

2309   Simone Forti's Holographic Angel. Minarik, Fran. Theatre Design & Technology, Fall 1978, Vol. XIV, No. 3, P. 17-18.

2310   Simonson, Lee. Current Biographies, 1948, P.574-575.

2311   Simple Dimmer (A). Hake, Herbert V. Players Magazine, Jl/Ag 1937, Vol. 13, No. 6, P. 16.

2312   Simple Home Built Lighting Equipment for the Low Budget Theatre. Lutton, Richard B. M.A. Thesis, University of Iowa, 1950.

2313   Simplified Light Control System. Voss, Lawrence. Players Magazine, O, 1955, Vol. 32, No. 1, P. 19.

2314   Single Source Arena Light. Yeaton, Kelly. Players Magazine, D, 1951, Vol. 28, No. 3, P. 74.

2315   Single Source Lighting. Morgan, R. Theatre Crafts Mr 1970, P. 12.

2316   Six-Act Drama Sells Westinghouse Lighting. Industrial Marketing, Ja 1949, Vol. 34, P. 74.

2317   Six Discos Reviewed. Watson, Lee. Lighting Dimensions, F 1979, Vol. 3, No. 2, P. 16.

2318   Slight on Stage Lighting. Tabs D 1971.

2319   Smithsonian's New Tent Theatre. Theatre Design and Technology, O 1969, No. 18, P. 15.

2320   Smoke Clouds. Voss, Lawrence. Players Magazine, F, 1952, Vol. 28, No. 5, P. 110.

2321   Social History of Lighting (The). O'dea, William T. Macmillan, 1958, New York. Routledge, 1958, London.

2322   Sodium Iodide Lighting Equipment. Benson, Robert. Theatre Design & Technology, O 1966, No. 6, P. 46.

2323   Solid-State Packaged Dimmer. Becker, E. K. Theatre Design & Technology, O 1966, No. 6, P. 47.

2324   Solving Stage Lighting Problems. Lawrence, William John. New York Dramatic Mirror (The), Mr 3, 1917, P.5.

2325   Solving the Cinematographer's Problems With Light Control Media. Holmes, David. American Cinematographer, S 1974, P.1082.

2327   Something New in Dimmers. Skirpan, Stephen J. Official Bulletin, IATSE, Wi 1961-62, Sp 1962.

2328   Some Advise on Stage Lighting. Bear, B. E. Tabs, S 1966, Vol. 24, No. 3, P. 27.

2329   Some Emotional Reactions of a Theatre Audience With Regard to Colored Light. Huntley, Stirling Louis. Ph.D. Thesis, Stanford University, 1956.

2330   Some Needed Equipment

for the High School Stage.
Leeper, H.T. High School
Thespian, Ja/f 1937, Vol.
3, P. 8.

2331   Some Observations on
Manually Operated Stage
Switchboards in the
Professional Theatre. Tabs,
S 1953, Vol. 11, No. 2, P.
23.

2332   Some of the Industrial
Uses of Calcium Compounds.
Bolas, Thomas. Scientific
American Supplement, XII,
1882.

2333   Some Possibilities of
Stage Lighting. Jones,
Bassett. Illuminating
Engineering Society
Transactions, 1916, Vol.
XI, P. 647.

2334   Some Problems of "Arena"
Presentation. Mitchley, J.
Tabs, D 1954, Vol. 12, No.
3, P. 7.

2335   Some Properties of SCR
Dimmers in the Field.
Cramer, M. Theatre Design
& Technology, O 1966.

2336   Some Recent Staging by
C. Raymond Jonson. Drama
(The), My/je 1923, Vol.
XIII, P. 302.

2337   Some Secrets of
Electrical Stagecraft.
Popular Electricity, 1912,
Vol. 4, P. 982, 1094; 1912,
Vol. 5, P. 13, 221, 422,
548.

2338   Some Secrets of
Starwars. Lighting
Dimensions, O 1977, P. 24.

2339   Some Stage-Trades.
Chamber's (Edinburgh)
Journal, 1888, Vol. LXV.

2340   Some Views of Lighting
for Theatre and Television
in Europe. Rose, Philip.
Illuminating Engineering, F
1966, Vol. LXI, No. 2.

2341   Source Book in
Theatrical History (A).
Nagler, A.M. Dover
Publications, Inc. 1952 New
York.

2342   Southern Cross. Irving,
Denis. Tabs, D 1972, Vol.
30, No. 4, P. 137.

2343   Special Effects in
Disco. Nadon, John.
Lighting Dimensions, Jl
1979, P. 32.

2344   Special Lighting Effects
on the Late Nineteenth
Century Stage. Held,
McDonald Watkins. Furman
Studies, XXXIII, Sp 1950,
P. 61.

2345   Special Stage Lighting
and Flood Lighting of a
Great Outdoor Pageant.
Electrical Review and
Western Electrician, S 9,
1916, Vol. 69, P. 483.

2346   Specifications for Stage
Lighting Equipment for a
University Theatre. Brink,
C.L. M.A. Thesis, State
University of Iowa, 1932.

2347   Spectacular Stage
Lighting at the Circus
Schumann, Berlin.
Electrical World, F 10,
1910, Vol. 55, P. 361.

2348   Spectral Emissivity of
Tungsten. Larrabee, R.
Journal of the Optical
Society of America, Je
1959, Vol. XLIX, No. 6.

2349   Spectrophotometric
Comparisons of the Effects
of Stage Lighting On New
Developed Expendable Color
Media. Courtade, T.
Theatre Design & Technology
My 1973.

2350   Spectrophotometric
Comparison of Effects of
Light on Expendable Color
Media. Gaiser, Gary and

Rootes, Minor. Theatre
Design & Technology My
1967.

2351   Spectrophotometry (200
to 1000 Millimicrons).
Gibson, Kasson S. U.S.
Government Printing Office,
S 1949, Washington D.C.

2352   Spectro Photometric
Analysis of the Yale Color
Master System. Butler, Paul
Lindsay. M.F.A. Thesis,
1971, Yale University.

2353   Speech Communication and
Theater Arts: a Classified
Bibliography of Theses and
Dissertations 1973-1978.
Merenda, Merilyn D. and
Polichak, James. Plenum
Publishing Corporation,
1979, New York.

2354   Splash, Sensitivity, or
Structure-Styles of
Lighting Design. Watson,
Lee. Lighting Dimensions,
Ja 1978, Vol. 2, No. 1, P.
17.

2355   Spot-Light Dimmer.
Electrical World, Jl 22,
1911, Vol. 58, P. 235.

2356   Spotlight Efficiency.
Sellman, H.D. Theatre
Arts, Jl 1936, Vol. 20.

2357   Spotlight on Lake
Placid. McKenna, Steve.
Lighting Dimensions, My
1980, P. 22.

2358   Spotlight Stories. Kook,
Edward F. Saturday Review,
N 5, 1960, P. 49.

2359   Spots - Cheaper by the
Dozen. Matthews, Arthur C.
Playbill, The, 1950, P. 6.

2360   Spot Dimmers. Ackler,
Bryan H. Theatre Crafts,
Mr/ap 1979, Vol. 13, No.
2, P. 89.

2361   Spot Lamp Dimmer.

Electrical World Vol. 67 Je
24, 1916 P. 1488 Electrical
Review and Western
Electrician Vol. 69 Je 22
1916 P.

2362   Square One. Reid,
Francis. Tabs Je 1971.

2363   Stability of Lighting
Towers. Corbett, Tom.
Lighting Dimensions, D
1979, P. 40-45.

2364   Stagecraft from the
Director's Point of View.
Stewart, Hal D. Pitman,
1949, London.

2365   Stagecraft. Pausback,
Nicholas J. Pausback
Scenery Co., 1928, Chicago.

2366   Stages and Scenery.
Pilbrow, Richard. Twentieth
Century, 1961, Vol. 169, P.
118-28.

2367   Stage and Its Equipment.
Wilson, R.A.
Small-Harcourt, 1932, New
York.

2368   Stage and Players.
Hutton, Lawrence. Hurd and
Houghton, 1875, New York.

2369   Stage Director Looks
Back (A). Tabs, S 1953,
Vol. 11, No. 2, P. 10.

2370   Stage Effects Produced
by Electricity. Electrical
World (The), Ap 30, 1892,
XIX, P. 301.

2371   Stage Equipment and
Lighting. Berry, R. D.
Architectural Forum, Ap,
1930, Vol. 52, P. 605.

2372   Stage in the Twentieth
Century (The). Broadway
Publishers, 1912, New York.

2373   Stage Lighting:
Principles and Practice.
Ridge, C. Harold and
Alfred, F.S. Sir Isaac

Pitman & Sons, Ltd., 1935, London.

2374   Stage Lighting: Survey Since 1906. McCandless, Stanley. Illuminating Engineering, Ja 1956, Vol. LI, No. 1, P. 113-22. ISBN: 0-87024-018-8

2375   Stage Lighting; Principles and Practice. Alfred, Frederick Samuel. Pitman, 1935, London & New York.

2376   Stage Lighting--Illumination, Design and Environment. Commons, Milton D. M.A. Thesis, University of Kansas, 1950.

2377   Stage Lighting-A Survey from 1906. Illuminating Engineering Society Journal, Ja, 1966, Vol. LI, P. 115.

2378   Stage Lighting-Summary of Essential Equipments And Layouts. Falge, Francis and Weitz, C. D. General Electric Co. Lamp Division, Nela Park, Cleveland, Ohio. No Date.

2379   Stage Lighting, Its Illuminative Power in the Theatre. Jones, Robert Edmond. New York Times, N 21, 1914, P.12.

2380   Stage Lighting, Nineteenth Century American. Weese, Stanley. M.A. Thesis, University of Illinois, 1950.

2381   Stage Lighting - Its History, Mechanics, Art. Hall, Elmer E. Emerson Quarterly, My 1926, Vol. 6, P. 15-16; S.A. N 1926, Vol. 7, P. 5-8; S.A. Ja 1927, P. 17-18.

2382   Stage Lighting - the Oxford Companion to the Theatre. Hartnoll, Phyllis (Editor). London: Oxford University Press, 1962, 2nd Edition.

2383   Stage Lighting Apparatus in England and America During the Nineteenth Century. Walker, John A. M.A. Thesis, University of North Carolina, 1939.

2384   Stage Lighting Apparatus. Electrical World, My 7, 1898, Vol. 31, P. 566.

2385   Stage Lighting by Electricity. Scott, Graham. Electrical Engineer, Mr 9, 1892, Vol. 13, P. 259.

2386   Stage Lighting by Zones. Rae, F.B. Illustrated World, Ag 1917, Vol. 27, P. 875.

2387   Stage Lighting Control Board for Allegheny College. Hulburt, John W. Alleghney College Department of Dramatic Art. No Date.

2388   Stage Lighting Control Incorporating a Procedural Guide for Operating the Electronic Onsole. Lindauer, Frederic A. M.F.A. Thesis, 1966, Yale University.

2389   Stage Lighting Demonstrated. Tabs, Ap 1954, Vol. 12, No. 1, P. 23.

2390   Stage Lighting Design. Howard, John. Los Angeles State College Department of Speech and Drama, 1963, Los Angeles. No Date.

2391   Stage Lighting Equipment. Springer, Angus. Player's Magazine, My 1945, Vol. 21, P. 8.

2392   Stage Lighting for

"Little" Theatres. Ridge, C. Harold. W. Heffer & Sons, Ltd., 1925, Cambridge, England.

2393   Stage Lighting for Amateurs: With an Appendix on Drama in Education. Goffin, Peter. J. Garnet Miller, 1955, London.

2394   Stage Lighting for High School Theatres. Rubin, Joel E. National Thespian Society, College Hill Station, 1951, Cincinnati, Ohio.

2395   Stage Lighting for Little Theatres. Ridge, C. Harold. Houghton, 1929, New York.

2396   Stage Lighting for Theatre in the Round. Tabs S 1964.

2397   Stage Lighting for the Amateur Producer. Wilson, Angus. Pitman, 1960, London.

2398   Stage Lighting Handbook (The). Reid, Francis. Theatre Arts Books, 1976, New York. LOCN: Pn2091.E4 R4 ISBN: 0878301569

2399   Stage Lighting Handbook. Howard, John. Dept. of Speech & Drama, Los Angeles State Col., 1962, Los Angeles.

2400   Stage Lighting in American Theatres Between 1800 and 1850. Hamilton, John L. M.A. Thesis, University of Minnosota, 1941.

2402   Stage Lighting in the Baden State Theatre, Karlsruhe. Niethammer, H.E.W. International Lighting Review, 1976, Vol. 27, No. 4, P. 103-105.

2403   Stage Lighting in the

Opera House. Dace, Wallace. M.F.A. Thesis, Yale University, 1948.

2404   Stage Lighting in the United States. McCandless, Stanley. Oxford Companion to the Theatre (The), Phyllis Hartnoll, Ed., 1967, Third Edition.

2405   Stage Lighting in the 19th Century. Legge, Brian. Tabs, S 1968, Vol. 26, No. 3, P. 12.

2406   Stage Lighting Methods: Eighteenth Century American Theatre. Peterson, Rita. M.A. Thesis, University of Wisconsin, 1950.

2407   Stage Lighting Principles and Practice. Ridge, C. Harold and Alfred, F.S. Sir Isaac Pitman & Sons, 1940, London.

2408   Stage Lighting Projector Lamp. Tabs, Ap 1953, Vol. 11, No. 1, P. 14.

2409   Stage Lighting Remote Control System of C 1895. Howard, T. E. Tabs, D, 1973, Vol. 31, No. 4, P. 188.

2410   Stage Lighting Theory , Equipment, and Practice in The United States from 1900 to 1935. Scales, Robert. Ph.D. Thesis, University of Minnesota, 1969. LOCN: Pn2091 E4 S28

2411   Stage Lighting the Broadway Practice. Holm, Klaus. Theatre Design & Technology D 1976.

2412   Stage Lighting Up To, and Including the Introduction of Electricity. Gray, Arthur Coe. Thesis, Cornell, University, 1931.

2413   Stage Lighting With
Home-Made Equipment.
Hoerner, George R.
Visitext, 1950, Ithaca, New
York.

2414   Stage Lighting. Sellman,
H.D. Extension Division
Bulletin of the University
of Arizona, Mr 1928, Vol.
V, P. 5-8.

2415   Stage Lighting. Ridge,
C. Harold. W. Heffer &
Sons, 1928, Cambridge.

2416   Stage Lighting. Powell,
A.L. and Fuchs, Theodore.
General Electric Co.,
Harrison, N.J., Bulletin
Ld146a. No Date.

2418   Stage Lighting. Jones,
Robert Edmond. New York
Times, N 21, 1914.

2419   Stage Lighting. Fuchs,
Theodore. B. Blom, 1963,
New York. Little, Brown &
Co., 1929, New York. LOCN:
Tk4399

2420   Stage Lighting.
Cutler-Hammer Mfg., 1911,
Milwaukee.

2421   Stage Lighting.
Illuminating Engineering,
Ja 1956, Vol. LI, P.
113-22.

2422   Stage Lighting. Ost,
Geofry. Herbert Jennings
1957 London.

2424   Stage Lighting. Pilbrow,
Richard. D. Van Nostrand
Co., 1971, New York. LOCN:
Pn2091. E4 P5 1970 ISBN:
0-442-26556-5

2425   Stage Lighting. National
Recreation Association. No
Date.

2426   Stage Lighting. Powell,
A.L. and Fuchs, Theodore.
Edison Lamp Works, 1923.

2427   Stage Lighting.
Stainton, Walter H.
Players Magazine, F, 1953,
Vol. 29, No. 5, P. 102.

2428   Stage Lights and Other
Effects. Corbould, William.
Work Vol. 6 1893 P. 245.

2429   Stage Lights of
Theatres. Builder, (The), F
7, 1863, P. 105.

2430   Stage Machinery and
Lighting Equipment for
Small Theatres and
Community Buildings.
Pichel, Irving. Theatre
Arts Magazine, Ap 1920,
Vol. IV, P. 137-52.

2431   Stage on Wheels (A).
Scientific American, O
1937, Vol. 157, P. 221.

2432   Stage Science. Saturday
Review (The), LXIV, O 29,
1887, P. 588.

2433   Stage Skies. Jewett,
William A. M.F.A. Thesis,
Yale University, 1948.

2434   Stage Switchboard Design
II. Tabs, Ap 1949, Vol. 7,
No. 1, P. 19.

2435   Stage Switchboard Survey
(A). Tabs, D 1955, Vol. 13,
No. 3, P. 10.

2436   Staging a Spectacular
Revue. Short, Hassard.
Theatre Magazine, XL, F
1924, P. 22.

2437   Staging Miniature Fires
for Amateur Defense Films.
Fulton, John P. American
Cinematographer, D, 1942,
Vol. 23, P. 521.

2438   Staging the Dance.
Melcer, Fannie Helen. W.C.
Brown, 1955, Dubuque, Iowa.

2439   Standardization of Color
Media, Photographic and
Processing F Filters,

Polyester Camera and Color Printing Filters. Holmes, David. Lighting Dimensions, Ap 1978, Vol. 2, No. 4, P. 33.

2440   Standards for Designer's Portfolios. Graham, Lawrence L. Theatre Design & Technology, Winter 1975, No. 43, P. 23. USITT Publication.

2441   Stand By. and Hit It. Brown, Steve. Lighting Dimensions N 1977.

2442   Stanley R. McCandless. Rubin, Joel E. Theatre Design & Technology, D 1967, No. 11, P. 3.

2443   Star Lighting. Edison Monthly (The), IX, Mr 1917, P. 389.

2444   Star Wars Craze That Swept the Nation (The). Rogers, Bruce. Lighting Dimensions, S 1978, Vol. 2, No. 7, P. 26.

2445   Steele MacKaye's Ideas and Theories As Incorporated in The Lyceum Theatre. Vorenberg, William. A.M. Thesis, Stanford University, 1949.

2446   Storage Batteries on the Stage. Bissing, H. Electrical World, XXX, O 30, 1897.

2447   Storing Gelatines. Voss, Lawrence. Players Magazine, D 1953, Vol. 30, No. 3, P. 68.

2448   Story of Color (The). Birren, Faber. Crimson Press (The), 1941, Westport, Ma.

2449   Story of the Lamp (And the Candle) (The). Robins, Frederick William. Oxford University Press, 1939, New York, London.

2450   Story of the Meininger (The). Grube, Max. University of Miami Press, 1963, Coral Gables, Fla.

2451   Strands of Incandescent Carbon. Legge, Brian. Tabs, Fall 1978, Vol. 36, No. 3, P. 22-23.

2452   Stratford-On-Avon in London. Tabs, D 1960, Vol. 18, No. 3, P. 6.

2453   Stratford at Twenty Five. Loney, Glenn. Theatre Crafts My 1978.

2454   Stratford Ontario Festival Theatre New Lighting Installation. Buck, Bruce. Tabs Mr 1972.

2455   Stratford Revisted. Bentham, Frederick. Tabs, Mr 1972.

2456   Striking Use of Electric Lights on the Stage (A). Electrical World, Mr 12, 1892, Vol. 19, P. 182.

2457   Studies in Elizabethan Theatre. Prouty, Charles. Shoestring Press, 1961, New York.

2458   Studies in the Projection of Light/ Optical Properties of Ellipsoidal Reflectors (The). Benford, Frank and Holeman, John M. USITT Publication (General Electric Review, 1923-1926).

2459   Study of Colour, With Lessons and Exercises. Doubleday, 1927, Garden City, N.Y., 219 P., 2 Vols.

2460   Study of Nineteenth Century Gas Lighting Methods As Evidenced in Some Existing Prompt Scripts (A). Bangham, P. Jerald. M.A. Thesis, Ohio State University, 1959.

2461   Study of Problems
Involved in Lighting the
Negro Actor on the Stage
(A) M.A. Thesis, Tennessee
Agricultural & Industrial
College, 195 1. Cox,
William D. M.A. Thesis,
Tennessee Agricultural &
Industrial College, 1951.

2462   Study of Projected
Scenery- History ,
Technology, Design.
Litwack, Sydney Zanville.
M.A. Thesis, North Carolina
University, 1954.

2463   Study of the History and
Methods of Production for
Theatre-In-The-Round (A).
Hutchinson, William C.
M.A. Thesis, West Texas
State College, 1958.

2464   A Study of the
International Alliance of
Theatrical Stage Employes
and Moving Picture Machine
Operators of the United
States and Canada. Cauble,
J.R. M.A. Thesis,
U.C.L.A., 1964. LOCN: Ld
791.8 T3031

2465   Study of the Influence
of Conventional Film
Lighting on Audience
Response. Thayer, David.
Ph.D. Thesis, State
University of Iowa 1960.

2466   Study of the Lighting
Equipment, Facilities, and
Practices In Ten Mid-West
Television Stations (A).
Davis, John Aaron, Jr.
Thesis, State University of
Iowa, 1954.

2467   Study of the Physical
Principles and Mechanical
Equipment Employed in
Present-Day Theatrical
Lighting (A). Strawcutter,
Clair. M.A. Thesis,
University of Washington,
1951.

2468   Study of the

Requirements for Stage
Lighting (A). Marks,
Kilborn. M.A. Thesis,
Michigan State, 1956.

2469   Style in Lighting
Design. Palmer, Richard H.
Educational Theatre
Journal, My 1967, Vol. XIX,
No. 2, P. 142.

2470   Stylizing Slide Images
Photography through
Patterned Glass to Modify
Source Material. Dehm, G.
Theatre Design & Technology
Sum 1975.

2471   Subsidized Theatre of
West Germany (The).
Sievers, W. David.
Educational Theatre
Journal, Mr 1960, Vol. XII,
No. 1, P. 1.

2472   Subsidy-A Stimulus or
Soporific. Tabs, D 1955,
Vol. 13, No. 3, P. 25.

2473   Subsidy and the
Performing Arts. Mayleas,
Ruth. Theatre Design &
Technology, O 1966, No. 6,
P. 4.

2474   Suggested Layouts of
Stage Lighting Equipment
for the School and College
Auditorium. Fuchs,
Theodore. Pub. by Author,
Northwestern University,
1950, Evanston, Illinois.

2475   Summer Theatre Directory
(1979). Hoggard, Kevin
(Editor). American Theatre
Association, Publications
1979.

2476   Sunburner (The). Tabs, D
1956, Vol. 14, No. 3, P.
23.

2477   Sun System, a Workable
Gel Filing System (The).
Soare, Thomas F. Lighting
Dimensions, O 1977, P. 20.

2478   Super Projection in the

Garden at the Garden. Tabs Mr 1971.

2479   Supplement to Selected 'still' Projection Apparatus For Scenic and Effects Projection. Lipschutz, Mark. U.S.I.T.T. Publisher. No Date.

2480   Supply, Demand and the Performing Arts.A Critical Look at The Business of Supplying Show Business. Thompson, Richard and Jones, Ted and Tawil, Joseph and Davis, James. Theatre Design & Technology, Winter 1975, No. 43, P. 27.

2481   Support for the Arts. Levene, Victoria. Performing Arts Review, Vol. 6, No. 3, P. 393. No Date.

2482   Survey of the Use of Projected Scenery in the Theatre (A). Lacy, Robin. A Yale Class Paper in the Drama Department Library, 1948.

2483   Swan Lake. Scientific American, Mr 1883, Vol. 48, P. 134.

2484   Swiss Spectacular. De Jonge, Alex. Tabs Sp 1978.

2485   Switchboard of Stage Lighting (The). Bissing, H. Electrical World, XXXI, F 19, 1898.

2486   Switchboard Survey. Tabs, D 1951, Vol. 9, No. 3, P. 23.

2487   Sydney Opera House. Drijver, F. and Waldram, J.M. International Lighting Review, Vol. 73, No. 4, P. 113. No Date.

2488   Syllabus of Stage Lighting (A). McCandless, Stanley. Whitlock's

Bookstore, 1927, New Haven, Conn.

2489   Symphonies in Color: Silent Music. Etude, Xxxx, Je 1922, Pp. 379-380.

2490   Symphony in Red. Baldwin, Chris. Cue Technical Theatre Review, S/O 1979, P. 18-19.

2491   System of Portable Stage Settings and Lighting (A). Peet, Telfair B. Alabama Polytechnic Institute, 1950, Auburn, Alabama.

2493   Tables of Spectral Lines. Zardel, A. Pergamon Ltd., 1961, London.

2494   Tabs and the Times before. Bentham, Frederick. Sightline, ABTT Journal, Fall 1979, Vol. 13, No. 2, P. 114.

2495   Tag Technical Library and Information Sheets. Tag Foundation, Ltd., (Technical Assistance Group), 463 West St., Ny,ny 10014. No Date.

2496   Take a Good Look at Lighting. Stainton, Walter H. Players Magazine, Ja, 1952, Vol. 28, No. 4, P. 95.

2497   Tale of a Switchboard and the Key to St. Peters. Tabs S 1970.

2498   Tale of Three Switchboards (A). Bentham, Frederick. Tabs Mr 1972.

2499   Talking to Followspots. Heath, Rosemary F. Lighting Dimensions, F 1980, P. 26-28.

2500   TCS Survey 1979. Theatre Communications Group, Inc. Theatre Communication Group Inc., 1980,new York.

2501   Teatro Alla Scala. Tabs Sum 1976.

2502   Tea or Coffee?. Tabs, 1952, Vol 10, No. 2, P. 25.

2503   Technical Advancements for the American Theatre. Weaver, Clark. Players Magazine, Mr 1959, Vol. 35, No. 5, P. 134.

2504   Technical Advancements in American Theatre. Weaver, Clark. Players Magazine, My, 1959, Vol. 35, No. 6, P. 134.

2505   Technical Development of Stage Lighting Apparatus in the United States, 1900-1950 (The). Rubin, Joel E. Ph.D. Thesis, Stanford University, 1960. LOCN: Pn2091 E4 R79 1976

2506   Technical Development of Television. Shiers, George (Introduction). Arno Press, 1977, New York. LOCN: 75-23902 ISBN: 0-405-07761-0

2507   Technical Method of Removing Distortion from Lens Projections (A). Lown, Charles. M.A. Thesis, State University of Iowa, 1945.

2508   Technical News Article. Lonberg-Holm, K. Architectural Record, Jl 1930, P. 94.

2509   Technical Possibilities (The). Flanagan, Arena Hallie. Federal One, D 1977, Vol. 2,no. 3, Published Occasionally by the Research Center for the Federal Theatre Project,.

2510   Technical Theatre Takes to the Streets. Theatre Crafts Mr 1972.

2511   Techniques of Stage Lighting. Tabs Je 1970.

2512   Technique for the Elimination of Distortion from Projected Images In Stage Lighting. Kyvig, Edward. M.A. Thesis, State University of Iowa, 1937.

2513   Technique of Lighting for Television and Motion Pictures (The). Millerson, Gerald. Hastings House, 1972, New York. LOCN: Tr 899. M48

2514   Technique of Special Effects Cinematography (The). Fielding, Raymond E. Hastings House, 1965, New York. ISBN: 8038-7031-0

2515   Technique of Stage Lighting (The). Williams, Rollo G. Sir Isaac Pitman & Sons, 1952, London. First Published 1947.

2516   Technology As Art: the American Contemporaty Theatre. Kirby, E. T. Theatre Design & Technology, Sum 1978, Vol. XIV.

2517   Deleted.

2518   Technology Update: Holography. Goldberg, Larry. Lighting Dimensions, F 1978, Vol. 2, No. 2, P. 46.

2519   Ted Fuchs. Watson, Lee. Lighting Dimensions, Mr 1980, P. 19-24.

2520   Televising the Large Arena Theatrical Event. Klages, William. Lighting Dimensions, S 1977, P. 32.

2521   Television and the Art of "No". Manning, Ferd. Lighting Dimensions, S 1978, Vol. 2, No. 7, P. 23.

2522   Television Design. Greenough, Richard. Tabs, D 1965, Vol. 23, No. 4, P. 28.

2523   Television En Brochette.
Manning, Ferd. Lighting
Dimensions, Mr 1979, Vol.
3, No. 3, P. 51.

2524   Television Lighting.
Kliegl Bros. Kliegl Bros.,
Catalog TV-6, 1960, New
York.

2525   Television Lighting 2000
or Even 1984. Ackerman,
K.R. Tabs Je 1971.

2526   Textbook of Illuminating
Engineering. Walsh, J.W.T.
Sir Isaac Pitman & Sons,
Ltd., 1947, London.

2527   Textbook of Illumination
(A). Kunerth, William. J.
Wiley & Sons, 1936, New
York.

2528   Thanks for the Memory.
Rose, Philip. Theatre
Crafts O 1974.

2529   Tharon Musser Interview.
Lighting Dimensions, Je
1977, P. 16.

2530   Theater Without
Footlights (A). Scientific
American, S 1917, Vol. 117,
P. 201.

2531   Theatre: Camelot Partly
Enchanted. Taubman, Howard.
New York Times, D 5, 1960,
P.42.

2532   Theatre: Tragic Journey.
New York Times, N 9, 1956,
P.37.

2533   Theatre--An
Unforgettable Visit (The).
New York Times, My 6, 1958,
P.34.

2534   Theatre-In-The-Round.
Architectural Forum, S
1950, Vol. 93, P. 130-133.

2535   Theatres on Ocean
Liners. Theatre Arts
Monthly, Mr 1930, Vol. 14.

2536   Theatres. Shaw, Eyre M.
Practical Magazine, 1873,
Vol. 2, P. 84.

2537   Theatres. Building News,
O 26, 1894, Vol. 67, P.
566-69.

2538   Theatres. Transactions
of the Illuminating
Engineering Society, S
1922, Vol. XVII, P. 392.

2539   Theatre Among the
Fiords. Reid, Francis.
Tabs, Autumn 1976, Vol. 34,
No. 3, P. 16.

2540   Theatre and Its People
(The). Fyles, Franklin.
Ladies Home Journal, Ap
1900, XVII.

2541   Theatre and Seats.
Design, Ap 1969, P. 67.

2542   Theatre and Stage, Vols,
I & II. Downs, Harold
(Editor). Greenwood Press,
Inc., Westport, Ct., 1978.
LOCN: Pn2035.D6 1978 ISBN:
0-313-20222-2

2543   Theatre Archaeology: the
Projected Picture Trust.
ABTT News, F 1980 P. 19.

2544   Theatre Arrangements.
Builder, Ag 15, 1863, Vol.
21, P. 580.

2545   Theatre Art. D'Amico,
Victor Edmond. Manual Arts
Press, 1931, Peoria, Il.

2546   Theatre Between Covers
(The). Bailey, Ralph
Sargent. Theatre Magazine,
My 1930, Vol. LI, P. 8.

2547   Theatre Construction and
Maintenance. Buckle, James
G. The Stage" Office,
1888.

2548   Theatre Designed by
Fuller and Sadao,
Inc.,/Geometric, Inc. (A).
Fuller, Buckminster and

Sadao, Shoji. Drama Review, Sp 1968, Vol. 12, P. 117-120.

2549   Theatre Designed With Light Meters. Architectural Record, N 1948, Vol. 104, P. 121-144.

2550   Theatre Design in Britain. Bentham, Frederick. Tabs, Je 1966.

2551   Theatre Dimmers. Wirt, Charles. Electrical World, Mr 9, 1901, Vol. 37, P. 411.

2552   Theatre Dimmers. Electrical World, My 14, 1904, Vol. 43, P. 928.

2553   Theatre Dimmers. Rollins, D.M. Society of Motion Picture Engineers Journal, Je 1948, Vol. 50, P. 607-612.

2554   Theatre Dimmer. Electrical World, Mr 7, 1896, Vol. 27, P. 264.

2555   Theatre Dimmer. Electrical World, Je 1909, Vol. 54, P. 696.

2556   Theatre Dimmer. Electrical World, Ja 14, 1905, Vol. 45, P. 118.

2557   Theatre Fittings; Improved Safety Footlights. Builder (The), O 18, 1862, XX, P. 745.

2558   Theatre Form through Light. Feder, Abe H. American Institute of Architects' Journal, O 1960, Vol. XXXIV, P. 81-83.

2559   Theatre Goes North (The). Wiik, Karl Eilert. Tabs, S 1959, Vol. 17, No. 2, P. 24; D 1959, Vol. 17, No. 3, P. 23.

2560   Theatre Illumination Battens and Stage Arc

Lamps. Electrical Review, O 19, 1906, Vol. 59, P. 626.

2561   Theatre Illumination. Harris, H.C. Electrical Review, Ap 19, 1913, Vol. 62, P. 805.

2562   Theatre Illumination. Levy, M.J. Architecture and Building Vol. 50 No. 1 Ja 1918.

2563   Theatre Illumination. Vaughn, F.A. and Cook, G.H. Transactions of the Illuminating Society D 1911.

2564   Theatre in Canada (The). Hendry, Tom. World Theatre, Vol. XVI, 1967, No. 5/, P. 423-426.

2565   Theatre in Hungary (A). Wooderson, Michael. Tabs, Ap 1961, Vol. 19, No. 1, P. 19.

2566   Theatre Lighting: an Illustrated Glossary. Wehlburg, Albert F. C. Drama Book Specialists, 1975, New York. LOCN: Pn2091.E4 W4 ISBN: 0910482691

2567   Theatre Lighting: a New Era of Technological Development. Rubin, Joel E. Journal of the American Institute of Architects, Ag 1961, Vol. 36, P. 78-81.

2568   Theatre Lighting; a Manual of the Stage Switchboard. Hartmann, Louis (Hartman). Drama Book Specialists, 1970, New York. LOCN: Pn2091.E4 H3 1970

2569   Theatre Lighting , the Savoy Theatre. Times (The), O 3, 1881, P. 7; O 6, 1881, P. 9; O 10, 1881, P. 8.

2570   Theatre Lighting Control Today. Hamilton, John L.

Players Magazine, Ja 1941,
Vol. 17, No. 4, P. 13.

2571   Theatre Lighting
Control. Burke, B.S. and
Rollins, D.M. Electrical
Journal, N 1935, Vol.
XXXII, P. 477-481.

2572   Theatre Lighting
Instruments: Determining
Your Needs And Evaluating
Units. Benson, Robert.
Theatre Crafts, Mr/Ap 1978
P.13, Vol. 12, No. 3.

2573   Theatre Lighting in the
Age of Gas. Rees, Terence.
Society for Theatre
Research (The), 1978,
London.

2574   Theatre Lighting Past
and Present. Ward Leonard
Company Bulletin 75 Ja
1928.

2575   Theatre Lighting.
Applebee, L.G. Notes and
Queries, N, 1945, P. 217.

2576   Theatre Lighting.
Wilkinson, Henry. Journal
of the Royal Society of
Arts, Ap 6, 1928, LXXVI, P.
533.

2577   Theatre Lighting. Era,
Ap 19, 1913, Vol. 76, P.
11.

2578   Theatre Lighting. Flage,
Francis M. and Weitz, C.E.
General Electric Co., 1938,
Cleveland.

2579   Theatre Lighting.
Hartmann, Louis (Hartman).
D. Appleton & Co., 1930,
New York.

2580   Theatre Lighting 2000: a
Darkling View. Bentham,
Frederick. Tabs Je 1971.

2581   Theatre Lights of the
Past. Edison Monthly (The),
F 1917, Vol. IX, P. 338.

2582   Theatre Lit by Gas.
Austin, Roland. Notes and
Queries, Jl 5, 1913, Vol.
VII.

2583   Theatre Mutochrome
(The). Smith, C.F. Optical
Convention, 1926,
Proceedings, London, Part
1, P.215-224.

2584   Theatre of George Jean
Nathan (The). Goldberg,
Isaac. Simon & Schuster,
1926.

2585   Theatre of Performing
Lights (The). Brill, Louis
M. Lighting Dimensions, S,
1979, P. 16.

2586   Theatre of the Universe.
Dines, Richard. Tabs Fall
1974.

2587   Theatre of Tomorrow.
Macgowan, Kenneth.
Liverright, 1921. Harcourt,
Brace & Co., 1922, New
York.

2588   Theatre People: Tharon
Musser. Widem, Allen M.
Hartford Times, Jy 18,
1965, P.21.

2589   Theatre Plans in
Harsdoerffer's Frauenzimmer
- Gespraechspiel. Jordan,
Gilbert J. Journal of
English and Germanic
Philology, 1943, Vol. 42,
P. 475.

2590   Theatre Royal Back
Drawing Room. Legge, Brian.
Tabs Je 1970.

2591   Theatre Royal Drury
Lane. Tabs, D 1954, Vol.
12, No. 3, P. 11.

2592   Theatre Technician Faces
Life (The). Klain, James.
Theatre Design and
Technology, O, 1972, Vol.
30, P. 31.

2593   Theatre through Its

Stage Door (The). Belasco, David. Harper & Brothers, 1919, New York. Benjamin Bloom Reprint 254pp.

2594   Theatre Union: a History (The). Winsten, Lynne Robin. Ph.D. Thesis, University of California, Los Angeles, 1978.

2595   Theatre Union: a History 1933-1937 (The). Weisstuch, Mark. Ph.D. Thesis, C.U.N.Y., 1978.

2596   Theatrical Deserts (The). Theatre Quarterly, O, 1973, Vol. III, No. 12,p. 18.

2597   Theatrical Electrical Plant (A). Electrical World, Mr 7, 1896, Vol. 27, P. 250.

2598   Theatrical Lighting; Specification Plan. Architecture and Building, 1926, Vol. 58, P. 51-53.

2599   Theatrical Lighting Box. Work Vol.46 O 25 1913 P.79.

2600   Theatrical Lighting Graphics Package (A). Gemsath, W. and Seawright, J. and Ghent, E. and Garrard, M. Byte Vol.3 No. 6 Je1978 P. 153.

2601   Theatrical Lighting in a Church. Bagwell, Richard. Players, My, 1963, Vol. XXXIX, No. 8, P. 245.

2602   Theatrical Lighting Practice. Rubin, Joel E. and Watson, Leland H. Theatre Arts Books, 1954, New York. LOCN: Pn2091.E4 R8

2603   Theatrical Lighting. Kliegl Bros. Kliegl Bros., 1957, Catalog T-61, New York.

2604   Theatrical Mechanism.

Scientific American Supplement Xxi My 22 1886 P. 8648.

2605   Theory and Design of Illuminating Engineering Equipment (The). Kliegl, Herbert A. Chapman & Hall, Ltd., 1930, London.

2606   Theory and Practice of Alternating Currents (The). Dover, A.T. Pitman 1929.

2607   Theory of Colors. Geoth, Johann Wolfgang Von. John Murray, 1840, London.

2608   Theory of the Lighting Controlboard Applied. Hamilton, John L. Players Magazine, F 1941, Vol. 17, No. 5, P. 9.

2609   This Month's Products. Progressive Architecture, 1948, Continuing Feature.

2610   Thomas Drummond. O'Brien, R. Barry. Kegan Paul Trench and Co., 1889, London.

2611   Thomas Drummond. Westminster Review Cxxxii 1889.

2612   Thomas Wilfred, Lumia: a Retrospective Exhibition: the Corcoran Gallery of Art, Washington D.C., April 16-May 30, 1971. Stein, Donna M. Corcoran Gallery of Art 1971 Washington. LOCN: N8219 L5s7x

2613   Thomas Wilfred in Lumia Recital. Jewell, Edward Alden. New York Times, Ja 10, 1942.

2614   Thomas Wilfred 1889-1968. Stein, Donna M. The Museum of Modern Art Members Newsletter, D 1968.

2615   Three A's of Store Lighting; Attraction Appraisal, Atmosphere.

Ketch, James M. Cleveland Electric, 1946.

2616   Three Ways to Program Variable Lighting. Polizzano, P. and Williams, Rollo G. Control Engineering, Jl 1961, Vol. 8, No. 7, P. 123-127.

2617   Throwing a New Light on the Drama. Ford, Hugh. Sunday Magazine New York Tribune D 28 1913.

2618   Thyratron Reactors. General Electric Review, D 1931, Vol. 34, No. 12, P. 716.

2619   Thyratron Reactor Lighting Control. Schneider, E. D. Electrical Engineering, Je 1938.

2620   Thyratron Reactor Theater Lighting Control. Manheimer, J.R. Journal of the Society of Motion Picture Engineers, Jy 1936, P.107-12, Vol. XXVII.

2621   Tom Skelton's Lighting Is a Primer for Teaching and Practice. Skelton, Tom. Theatre Crafts, My/Je 1973, P.16-23.

2622   Tony for Jennifer Tipton, (A). Lighting Dimensions, Jl/Ag 1977, P. 14.

2623   Tools of Lighting Design: Color. Skelton, Tom. Dance Magazine, Ja 1956, P.60-64.

2624   Tools of Lighting Design: Introduction. Skelton, Tom. Dance Magazine, N 1956, P160-63.

2625   Tools of Lighting Design: Lighting a Modern Dance. Skelton, Tom. Dance Magazine, Mr 1956, P.54-58.

2626   Torch of Civilization. Luckiesh, Matthew. G.P. Putnam's Sons, 1940, New York.

2627   Tourable Neon. Bottari, Michael and Case, Ronald. Theatre Craft, My/Je 1980, Vol. 14, No. 3, P 41.

2628   Touring Equipment. Bock, Frank. Players Magazine, F 1957, Vol 33 N0 5, P. 104.

2629   Touring Scenery. Payne, Darwin Reid. Players Magazine, N, 1959, Vol. 36, No. 2, P. 31.

2630   Touring the Educational Theatre. Billings, Alan G. Educational Theatre Journal, O 1964, Vol. XVI, No. 3, P. 242.

2631   Towards an Ideal Lighting Control. Bentham, Frederick. Tabs, D 1965, Vol. 23, No. 4, P. 16.

2632   Toward an Alternative Theatre Technology. Wickinson, Darryl and Mckenzie, Ian. Theatre Australia, Ag 1976, Vol.1, No.1, P.49.

2633   Training of Lighting Designers, Part II. Gleason, John. Theatre Crafts, O 1977, Vol. 11, No. 5, P. 71.

2634   Deleted.

2635   Training Technicians Theatre Engineers and Scenographers (On). Mielziner, Jo. Theatre Design & Technology, S 1976.

2636   Training the Lighting Designer. Clark, Peggy and Gleason, John. Theatre Crafts, N 1976.

2637   Transistor Manual. General Electric Company.

General Electric Company, 1960, New York.

2638   Trend of Modern Lighting (A). Davis, Jed H. Tabs, S 1949, Vol. 7, No. 2, P. 5.

2639   Trials of School Lighting Design. Whitehouse, A.K. Tabs, Fall 1975.

2640   Trial Stage for Lighting Investigation (A). Winds, Adolf. Buhne Und Welt, Ap 1910.

2641   Tribute to John Watson (A). Watson, Lee. Lighting Dimensions, Ja 1980, P. 16-19.

2642   Tungsten Halogen or Quartz Iodine. Tabs, Mr 1969.

2643   Tungsten Iodine Lamps and Their Application. Strange, J.W. and Stewart, J. Transactions of the Illuminating Engineering Society, Ja 1963, Vol. XXVIII, No. 1, London.

2644   Turned on Lights. Nuckolls, James L. Theatre Crafts My 1968.

2645   Turning a Manuscript into a Play. Theatre Magazine, S 1918, Vol. XXVIII, P. 153.

2646   Tv Lighting Then & Now. Gaitti, Carl. Lighting Dimensions, S 1977, P. 17.

2647   Twelve Pound Switchboard (A). Vincent A. Drama, Ap, 1939, Vol. 17, P. 111.

2648   Twentieth-Century Innovations in Stage Design, Stage Machinery, and Theatre Architecture in Austria. Dietrich, Margret. In: Innovations in Stage & Theatre Design (Papers of the 6th Congress,

Internat'l. Federation for Theatre, 1969, New York).

2649   Twenty-Five Years of Stage Lighting. Bentham, Frederick. Transactions of the Illuminating Engineering Society, 1961, London, P 79.

2650   Twenty Years of Starlighting. Marcus, Keva. International Photographer, D 1947.

2651   Two Hundred Candles Simulated for the Drottningholm. Theatre Design & Technology D 1966.

2652   Two Solutions from the Vassar Shop. Ackler, Bryan H. Theatre Crafts, My/Je 1976, Vol. 10, No. 3, P. 56.

2653   Typical Lighting Problems. Corry, Percy. Tabs, Ap 1955, Vol. 13, No. 1, P. 7.

2654   Typical School Stage. Tabs, S 1953, Vol. 11, No. 2, P. 15.

2655   Tyrone Guthrie on Lighting. Guthrie, Tyrone. Tabs, Ap 1961, Vol. 19, No. 1, P. 14.

2656   Tyrone Guthrie Theatre (The). Progressive Architecture, D 1963, Vol. XLIV, No. 12, P. 98-105.

2657   Tyrone Guthrie Theatre Minneapolis. Corry, Percy. Tabs, D 1963, Vol. 21, No. 3, P. 32.

2658   Tyrone Guthrie. Tabs, Ap 1952, Vol. 10, No. 1, P. 10.

2659   Ultraviolet Luminescent Effects and Their Uses. Strobl, Alexander and Zahour, Robert L. Transactions of the

Illuminating Engineering Society, Jy 1933, Vol. XXVIII, P. 612-618.

2660   Understanding Lights/sound and Power. Wilkens, W. Douglas and Wenger, Dave L. Lighting Dimensions, S 1978, Vol. 2, No. 7, P. 62.

2661   Under a Bunch Light. Goodman, Minnie Buchanan. Harper's Weekly, Ap 5, 1890, XXXIV, P. 269.

2662   Unearned Income: Fund Raising. Culman, Peter. Theatre Craft, Mr/Ap 1980, Vol. 14, No. 2, P. 84-86.

2663   Uniform Numerical Color Media Coding System (A). Little, W.D. Theatre Design & Technology O 1972.

2664   Unintentional Lighting. Dewey, Walter S. Players, D/J, 1969, Vol. 44, No. 2, P. 42.

2665   Unionization of the Stage Designer: Male and Female. Stowell, Don. Theatre Design and Technology, O 1974.

2666   Unions: Questions and Answers. Webb, Elmon. Theatre Crafts, Vol. 13, No. 3, My 1979, P. 91.

2667   Unique Dance Given in a London Theatre. Popular Mechanics, S 1913, Vol. 20 , P. 412.

2668   Unique Lighting Effect on the Stage. National Electric Light Association Bulletin, 1920, Vol. 7, P. 811.

2669   Unique Lighting Handbook, No. 9100. Edmund Scientific Co., 1969, New Jersey.

2670   United Scenic Artists

and Associates, Local 829. Chassman, Arthur. M.F.A. Thesis, Yale University, 1955.

2671   United Scenic Artists Local 829: Questions and Answers. Webb, Elmon. Theatre Crafts, N/d 1978, Vol. 12, No. 7, P. 16.

2672   United States and British Patents for Scenic and Lighting Devices for the Theatre from 1861 to 1915. Johnson, Raoul Fenton. Ph.D Thesis, University of Illinois Urbana Champaign, 1966. LOCN: Pn 2091 S8 J6 1976

2673   United States Patents Pertaining to Theatre. Hild, Stephen Glenn. Ph.D. Thesis, Univ. of Missouri-Columbia, 1972.

2674   Unsinkable Molly at Winter Garden. Aston, Frank. New York World Telegram and Sun, N 4, 1960, P.30.

2675   U.S.A. 829 Annual Lighting Associates Entrance Examination. Watson, Lee. Lighting Dimensions, Jy/Ag 1978, P.30, Vol. 2, No. 6.

2676   Uses of Projected Scenery. Ornbo, Robert. Theatre Quarterly, Jl 1972, Vol. II, No. 7, P. 60.

2677   Use of Black Light. Magon, Jero. Players Magazine Vol.28 F 1952 P.115.

2678   Use of Camera Color Filters for Quick Changes. Life, N 12, 1951, Vol. 31, P. 119.

2679   Use of Dyed Cellulose Acetate and Methyl Methocrylate As Color Media (The). Dewey, Walter S.

M.A. Thesis, State
University of Iowa, 1947.

2680   Use of Gas in Theatres
(The). Collins, Wilkie.
Mask (The), O, 1924, Vol.
10, No. 4, P. 163.

2681   Use of Lasers in the
Damnation of Faust (The).
Helbing, Terry. Theatre
Design and Technology, Fall
1978, Vol. XIV, No. 3, P.
15-16.

2682   Use of Lime Light in the
English and American
Theatre 1825-1900(The).
Held, McDonald Watkins.
M.A. Thesis, Northwestern
University, 1937.

2683   Use of Mazda C. Lamps
for Stage Lighting (The).
Powell, A.L. and Cook,
L.W. Lighting Journal,
1916, Vol. 4, P. 3.

2684   Use of Projection in
Arena (The). Petit, Paul
B. Players Magazine, Ja,
1956, Vol. 32, No. 4, P.
89.

2685   Use of the Linnebach
Projector for Scenic
Projection (The). Renolds,
L.L. M.A. Thesis,
Stanford, 1950. LOCN: 3781
S78tr ISBN: 0-06-031560-1

2686   Use of Visual Aids in
Teaching Stage Lighting
(The). Dewey, Walter S.
Ph.D. Thesis, University of
Iowa, 1953.

2687   Using Photometric Data
Sheets. Bullock, Robert.
Theatre Design &
Technology, Spring 1979,
Vol. XV, No. 1, P. 23.

2688   Using Your Spotlight.
Erhardt, Louis. Theatre
Design & Technology, Su
1980, Vol. XVI, No. 2, P.
14-16.

2689   USITT Recommended
Symbols Standards for
Lighting Equipment. Wolff,
Fred M. Theatre Design and
Technology, D 1973.

2690   Vacuum Technique.
Dushman, S. J. Wiley &
Sons, 1949, New York.

2691   Variable-Beam Reflector
Spotlight for Quartz-Iodine
Lamps. Levin, R.E. Journal
of the Society of Motion
Picture and Television
Engineers, Mr 1964, Vol.
LXXIII, No. 3.

2692   Variacs Used As Controls
in Flexible Stage Lighting
Unit. McElroy, P.K.
General Radio Experimenter
(The), Mr 1938, Vol. 10, P.
10.

2693   Variacs Used With
Incandescent Lamps. Smiley,
Gilbert. General Radio
Experimenter (The), S 1948,
Vol. 4, P. 23.

2694   Variac Lighting Control
in the Little Theatre.
General Radio Experimenter
(The), F 1936, Vol. 10, P.
9.

2695   Variac Ratings. Smiley,
Gilbert. General Radio
Experimenter (The), O 1948,
Vol. 5, P. 23.

2696   Variety Is More Than
Spice. Dewey, Walter S.
Players, F/M, 1968, Vol.
43, No. 3, P. 82.

2697   Vaudeville Theatre
(The). Builder, Ap 23,
1870, Vol. 28, P. 319.

2698   Veni, Video, Vici -
Audio. Manning, Ferd.
Lighting Dimensions, O
1978, Vol. 2, No. 10, P.
60-62.

2699   Ventilation and Lighting
of Theatres and Hospitals

(Review of Le Theatre Et L'Architecte). Builder, Mr 16, 1861, Vol. 19, P. 172.

2700   Versatility of Application of Selsyn Equipment (The). Corby, R.A. General Electric Review, D 1930, Vol. XXX, P. 706-711.

2701   Video and Tv Reader. Lucier, Mary. Theatre Crafts, My/Je 1978, Vol. 12, No. 4, P. 72b.

2702   Viewpoint on Lighting for Dance (A). Bates, Ronald L. Lighting Dimensions, Jy/ag 1978, Vol. 2, No. 6, P. 42.

2703   Views of the Panama Pacific International Exposition, San Francisco. General Electric Company. General Electric Company, Schenectady, New York, 1915.

2704   Visible Music: the Birth of a New Art. Vail, George. Nation (The), Ag 2, 1922, Vol. CXV, P. 120.

2705   Visions in Space; Seminar on Scenic Projections. Theatre Design & Technology My 1970.

2706   Visual Adaptation and Stage Lighting. Sporre, Dennis J. Theatre Design & Technology My 1969.

2707   Vivian Beaumont Theatre and Its Stage Lighting Facilities. Feher, E. Interscaena, Sp 1968, Vol. 2, P. 40.

2708   Wagner, Appia, and the Idea of Musical Design. Kernodle, George R. Educational Theatre Journal, 1954, Vol. 6, P. 223-30.

2709   Wagner Said Let There Be

Light but Not Too Much (And). Loney, Glenn. Theatre Crafts S 1969.

2710   Wavelength Tables for Spectral Analysis. Twgum, Frank. A Hilger Ltd., 1923, London.

2711   Waves Switch Light. Nuckolls, James L. Progressive Architecture, D 1968, P. 113.

2712   West Side Story in Winter Garden. New York Times, S 27, 1957, P.14.

2713   What's New in MMS (Modular Memory System). Bertenshaw, David. Tabs, Autumn 1976, Vol. 34, No. 3, P. 10.

2714   What's New. Rose, Philip. Tabs Sp 1976.

2715   What in Me Is Dark Illumine. Ormerod, Roland. Tabs Fall 1975.

2716   What Is Good and Sufficient Lighting?. Kook, Edward F. Theatre Arts Monthly, Jy 1931, P.619-22.

2717   What the Swedish State Allows the Theatres. Topelius, G. Z. World Theatre, Sp, 1955, Vol. IV, No. 2, P. 57.

2718   When I Consider How My Light is Spent. Gould, Mervyn. Tabs, S 1971.

2719   White-Light Holographic Displays. Lighting Dimensions, F 1978, Vol. 2, No. 2, P. 44.

2720   White Is Black. Carroll, Sidney. Coronet, N 1938, Vol. 4 No. 7.

2721   White Light--What Is It?. Williams, Rollo G. Illuminating Engineering, Ag 1960, P.431-4.

2722   Whole Thing Is All With
Lights (The). Kobler, John.
New Yorker, N 15, 1947.

2723   Who Lights the Set?.
Wrench, K. G. Tabs, S
1954, Vol. 12, No. 2, P.
23.

2724   Wilfred, Thomas
(Obituary). New York Times,
Ag 16, 1968.

2725   Wilfred, Thomas.
Weinstock, Herbert.
Encyclopedia Americana, 28,
1969, P. 763.

2726   Windows in Modern
Architecture. Bake,
Geoffrey. Architectural
Book Publishing Company,
1948, New York.

2727   Wireless on Off
Switching. Nuckolls, James
L. Theatre Crafts Mr 1970.

2728   Wiring for Light and
Power. Croft, Terrell.
McGraw-Hill Book Company,
Inc., 1921, New York, Vol.
42.

2729   Wiring of a Theatre
(The). Electrical Review
and Western Electrician, O
10, 1914, Vol. 65, P. 708.

2730   Work of Living Art and
Man Is the Measure of All
Things (The). Appia,
Adolphe. University of
Miami Press, 1960, Coral
Gables, Fla.

2731   World's Largest Indoor
Stage Brings a New Method
of Light Control.
Electrasist, 1924, Vol. 23,
P. 35.

2732   World and the Theatre
(The). Theatre Arts
Monthly, Ag 1932, Vol. XVI,
P. 605-606.

2733   World of Colour (The).
Katz, David. Kegan Paul,

Tranch, Trubner and
Company, 1935, London.

2734   World of Quartz (The).
Light, Ja 1962, Vol. XXXI,
No. 1.

2735   World of Shakespeare at
the New Heritage Theatre
(The). Aveline, Joe.
Sightline, ABTT Journal,
Fall 1979, Vol. 13, No. 2,
P. 104-108.

2736   World of Tomorrow-A
Vision (The). Watson, Lee.
Lighting Dimensions, D
1979, P. 24-25.

2737   Xenon Arc Light Source
for the Theatre. Ward,
W.A. Thesis, U.C.L.A.,
1967. LOCN: Ld 791.8 T3w129

2738   Xenon Arc Projection
Lamp (The). Reese, Warren
B. Journal of the Society
of Motion Picture and
Television Engineers, Je
1958, Vol. LXVII, No. 6.

2739   Xenon Compact Arcs With
Increased Brightness
Through the Addition of
Hydrogen. Thouret, Wolfgang
E. and Strauss, Herbert S.
Illuminating Engineering,
My 1963, Vol. LIX, No. 5.

2740   Xenon Compact Arc Lamps.
Anderson, William T. Jr.
Journal of the Optical
Society of America, Je
1951, Vol Xli, No. 6.

2741   Xenon File (The).
Sandhaus, Dick. Lighting
Dimensions, F 1979, Vol. 3,
No. 2, P. 40. see also
'Xenon' in Lighting
Dimentions, N 1978, Vol. 2,
No. 9, P. 29.

2742   Xenon High-Pressure
Lamps in Motion Picture
Theatres. Ulffers, Heinz.
Journal of the Society of
Motion Picture and
Television Engineers, Je
1958, Vol. LXVII, No. 6.

2743   Xenon Projection Lamps:
        a Resume. Kloepfel, Don V.
        Journal of the Society of
        Motion Picture and
        Television Engineers, Je
        1964, Vol. LXXIII, No. 5.

2744   Xy Scanning in Laser
        Entertainment. Rogers,
        Bruce and Levenberg, Gary.
        Lighting Dimensions, Ap
        1978, Vol. 2, No. 4, P. 21.

2745   Yale Theatre Electrical
        Layout. McCandless,
        Stanley. American
        Architect, 1927, Vol. 131,
        P. 365-368.

2746   Your Career in Theater,
        Radio Television or Film
        Making. Allosso, Michael.
        Arco Publishing, 1978, New
        York. LOCN: Pn 1580 A4 1978

2747   Your Career in the
        Theatre. Savan, Bruce.
        Doubleday Co., 1961, New
        York.

2748   Your Own Turn on Thing.
        Skirpan, Stephen J.
        Theatre Crafts My 1970.

2749   You Must Have Gas. Tabs,
        D 1949, Vol. 7, No. 3, P.
        18.

2750   Zamora Trial Makes TV
        History (The). Tello,
        Steve. Lighting Dimensions,
        Mr 1978, Vol. 2, No. 3, P.
        39.

2751   1958 Achievements -
        United States Theatre
        Illuminating. Lighting
        Dimensions, N 1978, Vol. 2,
        No. 9, P. 29.

2752   2000-Watt Iodide Quartz
        Lamps. Lemons, T.M.
        Theatre Design &
        Technology, O 1966, No. 6,
        P. 49.

2753   3000 Years of Drama,
        Acting, and Stagecraft.
        Cheney, Sheldon. Longmann,
        1952, New York.

IV
Properties

2754   Advanced Woodworking and Furniture Making. Feirer, John L. Charles A. Bennett, 1963, Peoria, Illinois.

2755   Alternative Solutions. Brauner, Leon. Theatre Crafts, O 1977, Vol. 11, No. 5, P. 22.

2756   American Belt Axe 1650 to 1870 (The). Wheeler, Robert F. American Arms Collector (The), O 1957, P. 127-130.

2757   American Bulleted Cartridges. Waters, Kenneth L. Gun Digest 1968 P.265.

2758   Ancient Carpenters' Tools. Mercer, Henry C. Bucks County Historical Society, 1950.

2759   Ancient Mask Making Techniques for an Indian Ritual: the Chhau Dance of Purulia. Barua, D.S. Theatre Crafts, Mr/Ap 1979, P. 29, Vol. 13, No. 2.

2760   Armor Without Hammers. Manwaring, David. Theatre Crafts N 1977.

2761   Armourer and His Craft (The). Ffoulkes, Charles J. Benjamin Blom, 1912, New York.

2762   Arms and Armour of the Greeks. Snodgrass, A. M. Cornell University Press, 1967, Ithaca.

2763   Arms and Equipment of the Civil War. Coggins, Jack. Doubleday & Co. 1962 New York.

2764   Art of Caning a Chair (The). Esbach, Barbara B. Sampler of Early American Craft Projects, the Early American Society, 1979, Gettysburg, P. 1-3.

2765   Bankside Stage-Book. Whanslaw, H.W. W. Gardner, 1924, London.

2766   Basic Pistol Marksmanship. National Rifle Association 1959 Washington , D.C..

2767   Basic Rifle Marksmanship. National Rifle Association 1960 Washington, D.C.

2768   Basic Shotgun Instruction. National Rifle Association 1962 Washington, D.C.

2769   Beg, Borrow, Buy, or. Zimmerman, Joe. Players Magazine, Mr, 1948, Vol. 24, No. 6, P. 131.

2770   Blacksmiths' and Farriers' Tools at Shelburne Museum. Smith, H.R. Bradley. Shelburne Museum, 1966, Shelburne, Vt.

2771   Book of Pistols and Revolvers (The). Smith, W.H.B. Stackpole Co., 1962, Harrisburg, Pa.

2772   Book of Rifles (The). Smith, W.H.B. Stackpole Co., 1961, Harrisburg, Pa.

2773   Bristol Theatre Royal Inventory (A). Southern, Richard. In: Studies in English Theatre History (Society for Theatre Research, 1952, London), P.98-113.

2774   British Gun Laws Don't Stop Crime. Kleber, Louis C. Guns Ag 1966 P.28, 50.

2775   British Military Firearms. Blackmore, Howard L. Herbert Jenkins, 1961, London.

2776   Broad Swords for the Period Play. Chavez, Edmond

M. Players, O, 1961, Vol. XXXVIII, No. 1, P. 14.

2777   Buckram Masks: a How-To Casebook on Mask-Making. Holen, Rick. Theatre Crafts, Ja/F 1979, P.35, Vol. 13, No. 1.

2778   Casting Stage Statuary from Life. Baston, Paul. M.F.A. Thesis, 1977, San Diego State University.

2779   Choosing Electric Light Fitting for the Stage Setting. Tabs, S 1954, Vol. 12, No. 2, P. 5.

2780   Code of Practice for Pyrotechnics & Smoke Effects. In: Code of Practice for the Theatre Industry, London. No Date.

2781   Collection of Heating and Lighting Utensils in the United States National Museum. United States National Museum, 1928, Washington.

2782   Colonial Craftsmen and the Beginning of American Industry. Tunis, Edwin. World Publishing, 1965, Cleveland.

2783   Comparative Study - Celastic, Plastic, Rok, Papier Mache. Opsvig, Virginia. Players Magazine, My 1954, Vol. 30, No. 8, P. 187.

2784   Complete Guide to Handloading. Sharpe, Philip B. Funk and Wagnalls Co., 1953, New York.

2785   Confederate Arms. Albaugh, William A. Stackpole Co. 1960 Harrisburg.

2786   Construction Plastic-Ceramic Masks for Stage Use. Park, Ralph Kennedy. Players Magazine,

F 1957, Vol 33, No5, P. 104.

2787   Control of Firearms. Rakusan, Jerome. Guns My 1967 P.9.

2788   Crystal Coffin, the. Carrington, Hereward. Modern Mechanics, Mr 1915, Vol. 30, P. 393-394.

2789   Curtain-Maker's Handbook (The). Moreland, F. A. E.P. Dutton, 1979, New York.

2790   Detailing With Dough. Fitzpatrick, Susan. Theatre Crafts, Ja/F 1980, Vol. 14, No. 1, P. 41.

2791   Development of Machine Tools in New England. Hubbard, Guy. American Machinist, 1923 Vol.59, 1924 Vol.60, 1924 Vol.61.

2792   Documents Relating to the Office of the Revels in the Time Of Queen Elizabeth. Feuillerat, Albert (Ed). A. Uystpruyst, 1908, Louvain.

2793   Duelling Pistols. Atkinson, J.A. Gassell & Co., 1964, London.

2794   Elizabethan Scenes of Violence and the Problem of Their Staging. Mitchell, Lee. Ph.D. Thesis, Northwestern University, 1941.

2795   Engines of War. Wilkinson, Henry. Longman, Orme, Brown, Green, and Longmans, 1841, London.

2796   English and American Tool Builders. Roe, Joseph W. McGraw Hill, 1926, New York.

2797   English Master of Arms (The). Aylward, J. D. Routledge and Kegan Paul, 1956, London.

2798   European and American
Arms. Blair, Claude. London
and Crown Publishers, 1962,
New York.

2799   European Hand Firearms
of the 16th, 17th, and 18th
Centuries. Jackson, H.J.
and Whitlaw, C.E. The
Holland Press 1959 London.

2800   Experimenting With New
Materials for Masks and
Props. Skow, M. and Ackler,
B. Theatre Crafts S 1976.

2801   Fatal Firearm Accidents
in the United States.
Statistical Bulletin
Metropolitan Life Insurance
Company Vol.Xxxxvi S 1966
P.1.

2802   Federal Gun Laws. Henry
Schlesinger 1963 New York.

2803   Fine Furniture for the
Amateur Cabinetmaker.
Marlow, A. W. Bonanza
Books 1955, New York.

2804   Firearms in American
History, 1600-1800. Sawyer,
Charles W. Published by
the Author, 1910, Boston.

2805   Firearms in the Theatre.
Hinderick, Leslie. Ph.D.
Thesis, Northwestern
University, 1968. LOCN:
Diss 378 Nu 1968

2806   Firearms. Ricketts,
Howard. G.P. Putnam's Sons,
1962, New York.

2807   Firearm Accidents Costly
in Lives. Statistical
Bulletin Metropolitan Life
Insurance Company Vol.Xxxx
S 1959 P.8.

2808   Firearm Safety in the
Theatre. Archer, Stephen.
News, Secondary School
Theatre Conference, 1966,
P.5-9.

2809   Fires for Fireplaces.
Chavez, Edmond M. Players
Magazine, N 1955, Vol 32 No
2, P. 42.

2810   Flame Texturing Wood,
Follow Up. Arnett, Keith.
Theatre Crafts, Mr/Ap 1978,
Vol. 12, No. 3, P. 86.

2811   Flying Monkeys on
Wheels: Evillene's
Motorcycle Gang. Theatre
Crafts, N/D 1978, P.29,
Vol. 12, No. 7.

2812   Foldaway Furniture.
Kramer, Jack. Cornerstone
Library, 1978, New York.
ISBN: 346-12341-0

2813   For the Young Hunter.
Madson, John and Kozicky,
Edward. Olin Mathieson
Chemical Corp., 1963, East
Alton, Illinois.

2814   Furniture of the Greeks,
Etruscans, and Romans
(The). Richter, G.M.A.
Phaidon, 1967, London,.

2815   Furniture Upholstery &
Repair. Johnstone, James
E. Lane Publishing Co.,
1970, Minlo Park,
California.

2816   Gathering Old Furniture
for Stage Atmosphere. New
York Times, N 22, 1914,
Section 7, P. 7.

2817   Gelatine Moulds for
Masks. Kreier, George, Jr.
Players Magazine, D, 1949,
Vol. 26, No. 3, P. 58.

2818   German Mask Industry.
Scientific American, S
1900, Vol. 83, P. 198.

2819   Getting the Most Out of
Your 22. Mckenty, John G.
Prentice-Hall, Inc., 1967,
Englewood Cliffs, New
Jersey.

2820   Goodbye to Gunpowder.
Chidsey, Donald Barr. Crown
Publishers, 1963, New York.

2821   Guns: the Development of
Firearms, Rifles. Moore,
Warren. Grosset & Dunlap
1963 New York.

2822   Guns on the Early
Frontier. Russell, Carl P.
University of California
Press, 1957, Berkeley.

2823   Guns through the Ages.
Boothroyd, Geoffrey.
Sterling Publishing Co.,
1962, New York.

2824   Gun Collecting. Chapel,
Charles E. Coward-Mccann,
1939, New York.

2825   Gun Report Noise. Maxim,
Hiram P. U.S. Government
Printing Office, 1917,
Washington, D.C., P. 193.

2826   Gun Which Shoots Sounds
Only. Scientific American,
1919, Vol. 121, P. 192.

2827   Hammer and Tongs. Hogg,
Garry. 1964, London.

2828   Hatcher's Notebook.
Hatcher, Julien S.
Stackpole Co., 1962,
Harrisburg, Pa.

2829   History, Iconology and
Uses of Masks in the
Theatre Past and Present
With Procedures, Materials
and Techniques for Modern
day Use on the Stage (The).
Quittner, C. James. Ph.D.
Thesis, University of Utah,
1970.

2830   History of Archery
(The). Burke, Edmund.
Heinemann, 1958, London.

2831   History of Spanish
Firearms (A). Lavin, James
D. Arco Co. 1965 New York.

2832   History of the
Incandescent Lamp. Howell,
John W. and Schroeder,
Henry. Magua Co. (The),
1927, Schenectady, New
York.

2833   History of Weaponry (A).
Canby, Courtland. Hawthorne
Books 1963 New York.

2834   Home Furnishings on the
Stage. Harris, W.L. Good
Furniture, 1917, Vol. 9, P.
74-78.

2835   Hoppe's Guide to Gun
Cleaning. Frank A. Hopee,
Inc., 1967, Jenkintown, Pa.

2836   How Firearm Accidents
Occur. Statistical
Bulletin, Metropolitan Life
Insurance Company, S 1956,
P. 6-8, Vol. XXXVII.

2837   How to Build Your Own
Furniture. Decristoforo, R.
J. Harper & Row, 1965, New
York.

2838   How to Make Flexible
Model Moulds. Ferrari, E.
Modern Plastics, 1954, Vol.
31, No. 11, P. 93.

2839   How to Rent Props.
Zimmerman, Joe. Players
Magazine, My, 1948, Vol.
24, No. 8, P. 179.

2840   Imitation Arms and
Armor. Popular Mechanics
Vol. 12 D 1909.

2841   Imitation Guns Need a
Licence, Court Rules. The
Guardian, Sat. Ap 7, 1979.

2842   International Armaments.
Johnson, George B. and
Lockhoven, Hans B.
International Small Arms
Publishers, 1965, Cologne,
Germany.

2843   Introduction to Plastic
Stage Properties. Pecker,
Sumner C. M.F.A. Thesis,
1957, Yale University.

2844   Islamic Armourers and
Their Works. Mayer, L. A.
Albert Kundig, 1962,
Geneva.

2845   Lamp and Lighting Book
(The). Newman, Thelma R.
and Newman, Jay H. and
Newman, Lee S. Crown,
1976, New York. LOCN:
75-43564 ISBN:
0-517-51863-5

2846   Light, Touch, Pratical
Armor. Sargent, James M.
Players Magazine, O, 1949,
Vol. 26, No. 1, P. 9.

2847   Lighting and Lamp
Design. Cox, Warren E.
Crown, 1952, New York.

2848   Lighting Design and
Human Environment. Daggy,
E. Progressive
Architecture Pencil Points
My 1946, P. 81.

2849   Lighting Fittings
Performance and Design.
Bean, Arthur Robert.
Pergamon Press, 1968, New
York. LOCN: Th 7960. B4
1968

2850   Lighting Fixtures and
Lighting Effects. Luckiesh,
Matthew. McGraw-Hill, 1925,
New York.

2851   Lighting Fixtures for
the Home, the Church and
Public Buildings.
Pettingell- Andrews Co.
1910, Boston.

2852   Lighting through the
Years: the Light in the
Darkness. Poese, Bill.
Wallace-Homestead Book
Company, 1976, Des Moines,
Iowa. LOCN: 75-36635 ISBN:
0-87069-137-6

2853   Light Sources of the
Past and Present. Sturrock,
Walter and Staley, K.A.
General Electric Company
Lamp Division Nela Park
Cleveland, Ohio 1952.

2854   Lyman Reloading
Handbook. Lyman Gunsight,
1964, Middlefield, Ct.

2855   Machine Guns and Certain
Other Firearms. Code of
Federal Regulations, 1954,
U.S. Treasury Dept.,
Internal Revenue Service,
Title 26, Part 179.

2856   Making Masks for the
Berliner Ensemble. Fischer,
Eduard. World Theatre, Sp,
1960, Vol. X, No. 1, P. 54.

2857   Masks for the Great God
Brown. Original Masks,
1926. located at the
Harvard Theatre Collection.

2858   Mask and False Nose
Industry (The). Scientific
American Supplement, Ap
1895, Vol. 39, P. 16105,
16106.

2859   Masterpieces As Stage
Properties. The Upholsterer
Ap 15 1913 P. 81.

2860   Master Prop Builder for
Broadway and Television.
Nihda, Fred. Theatre
Crafts, My/Je 1977, Vol.
11, No. 3, P. 7.

2861   Materials and Methods of
Sculpture (The). Rich,
J.C. New York Oxford
University Press, 1947, New
York.

2862   Materials of the Scene:
an Introduction to
Technical Theatre. Wolfe,
Welby B. Harper & Row,
1977, New York. LOCN:
2085.W6 ISBN: 0-06-047184-0

2863   Mechanical Devices in
the Home. Allen, Edith.
Manual Arts Press, 1922,
Peoria, Ill.

2864   Modern Theatre Practice.
Heffner, Hubert C. and
Selden, Samuel and Sellman,
Hunton D. and   walkup, Fa
irfax P. Prentice-Hall,
1973, Englewood Cliffs,
N.J. LOCN: 72-89404 ISBN:
0-13-598805-5

2865   Modified Hand Guns for
Stage Use. Ackler, Bryan
H. Theatre Crafts J 1977.

2866   Museum of Early American
Tools (A). Sloane, Eric.
Wilffred Funk, 1964, New
York.

2867   Museum of Historical
Arms,(The) Catalogue No.
21. Owners (The), Miami
Beach, Fl. No Date.

2868   New Faces for Old Ones:
the Stage Masks of Ancient
Greece Revived by W. T.
Benda. Bird, Carol. Theatre
Magazine, F 1921, Vol.
XXXIII No. 239, P. 92.

2870   New Model Casting
Materials. Scientific
American, S 1933, Vol. 149,
P. 123.

2871   New Products and Where
to Buy. Corson, Richard.
Players Magazine, 1952,
Vol. 29, No. 2,.

2872   Notes Towards a
Reconstruction of Le
Mystere Des Actes Des
Apotres As Presented at
Bourges, 1536. Hasim,
James. Theatre
Research/Recherches
Theatrales, 1972, Vol. 12,
P. 29-73.

2873   Note on Masks (A).
Balance, John. Mask (The),
1908, Vol. 1, P. 9.

2874   NRA Home Firearm Safety.
National Rifle Association,
1962, Washington, D.C.

2875   NRA Hunter Safety
Handbook. National Rifle
Association, 1957,
Washington, D.C.

2876   Organizing the Property
Crew. Tolch, John. Players
Magazine, Mr 1961, Vol. 37,
No. 6, P. 131.

2877   Pageant of the Gun.
Peterson, Harold L.
Doubleday & Co., 1967,
Garden City, N.Y.

2878   Papier-Mache in Great
Britain and America.
Toller, Jane. C.T.
Branford, 1962, Newton, Ma.

2879   Patented Lighting.
Rushlight Club (The), 1979,
Boston.

2880   Period Lighting
Fixtures. Gould, George G.
and Gould, Mrs. Florence
Pearl, Holden. Dodd, 1928,
New York.

2881   Period Lighting. Wells,
Stanley. Pelham, 1975,
London. LOCN: Th7703.W44

2882   Peter Shaffer's Equus in
the Ring. Theatre Crafts,
J/F 1975, Vol. 9, No. 1, P.
20.

2883   Pictorial Booklet on
Early Jamestown Commodities
and Industries (A). Hudson,
J. Paul. Virginia 350th
Anniversary Celebration
Corp., 1957, Jamestown,
Va..

2884   Pierced Tin Lantern.
Daniele, Joseph. Sampler of
Early American Craft
Projects, the Early Americn
Society, 1979, Gettysburg,
P. 26-29.

2885   Pistols, Rifles, and
Machine Guns. Allen,
W.G.B. English
Universities Press, 1953,
London.

2886   Plastico Masks. Players
Magazine, D, 1951, Vol. 28,
No. 3, P. 68.

2887   Plastic People: Extras
for Milwaukee Repertory
Theatre. Baun, J.T. and
Foster, E. Theatre Crafts
N 1975.

2888   Play Production. Nelms, Henning. Barnes & Noble, Inc., 1950, New York.

2889   Play Production. Hewitt, Barnard. J.B. Lippincott Co., 1940, Philadelphia.

2890   Pneumatic Stage Furniture That Collapses to Economize Space in Transport. Scientific American, F 1917, Vol. 116, P. 205.

2891   Prehistoric Technology: an Experimental Study of the Oldest Tools and Artifacts from Traces of Manufacture and Wear. Semenov, S.A. Barnes & Noble, 1964, New York.

2892   Preparing the Stage Meal Behind the Scenes. Theatre Magazine, (The), S 1913, Vol. XVIII, No. 151, P. 96.

2893   Principles of Firearms. Balleisen, Charles E. John Wiley and Sons, 1956, New York.

2894   Production and Staging of Plays (The). Carter, C. and Bradbury, A.J. and Howard, W.R.B. Arc Books, 1953, New York.

2895   Products & Services: the Publishers Association. ABTT News, Ap 1980, P. 23.

2896   Properties & Dressing the Stage. Bruder, Karl C. Rosen Richards, 1969, New York. ISBN: 0823901505

2897   Property Man (The). Josaphare, L. Harper's Weekley, S. 14, 1912, Vol. 55, P. 14.

2898   Prop Masterpieces. Payne, Darwin Reid. Players Magazine, Ap 1954, Vol. 30, No. 7, P. 163.

2899   Questions and Answers:

Loading Blanks. Harrison, E.H. American Rifleman, N 1962, P.83 Vol.110.

2900   Ralph Lee's Festival Figures for Halloween and Other Appearances. Spector, Susan and Urkowitz, Steven. Theatre Crafts, O 1977, Vol. 11, No. 5.

2901   Realistic Deer. Jones, Kris. Theatre Crafts, Ja/F 1980, Vol. 14, No. 1, P. 40.

2902   Real Antiques As Stage Properties. Upholsterer Vol.57 F 15 1917 P.59.

2903   Remington (Catalogue). Remington Arms Company, Inc., 1966, Bridgeport, Ct.

2904   Remodelled Hippodrome. Gilston, E. J. Electrical Record, 1924, Vol. 35, P. 133-135.

2905   Renovation Concepts, Unique Product Resource: Architectural Catalogue. Renovation Concepts, P.O. Box 3720, Minneapolis, Minnesota 55403.

2906   Rethinking Equus Heads: Pop-Riveted Aluminum Heads for 10.00. Hansen, Robert C. Theatre Crafts, Vol. 13., No. 3, My 1979, P. 25.

2907   Rethinking Equus Heads. Haupt, John. Theatre Crafts, Vol. 13, No. 3, My 1979, P. 24.

2908   Rifle Book (The). O'Connor, Jack. Random House 1948 New York.

2909   Roman Soldier. Forester, Amedee. A. and C. Black, 1928, London.

2910   Royal Progress at the Barbican. Tabs, Je 1968, Vol. 26, No. 2, P. 5.

2911   Rubber Mask
Construction. Randall,
Dorothy Myrick. Players
Magazine, Ap, 1951, Vol.
27, No. 7, P. 152.

2912   Runnin' the Show; a
Practical Handbook. Whorf,
Richard B. and Wheeler,
Roger. W.H. Baker, 1930,
Boston.

2913   Safety With Firearms.
American Rifleman (The),
Reprint R13, National Rifle
Association, 1965,
Washington, D.C.

2914   Scenery and Furniture.
Brown, Frank Chouteau.
House Beautiful, N 1914, P.
180-183.

2915   Scenery and Stage
Decorations; Color - Light
- the New Art. Hewlett,
J.M. American Architect
(The), Ap 1918, Vol. 113,
Pt. 2, P. 425-430.

2916   Scenery and Stage
Decoration. Hewlett, J.M.
Brooklyn Museum Quaterly
(The), 1917, Vol. 4, P.
115-123.

2917   Scenery for the Theatre.
Burris-Meyer, Harold and
Cole, Edward C. Little,
Brown and Company 1971
Boston Toronto. LOCN:
Pn2091. S8b8 1971

2918   Scene Technician's
Handbook (The). Barber,
Philip W. Whitlock's Book
Store, 1928, New Haven,
Ct., 93 P.

2919   Secrets of the Property
Room. Mclaughlin, J.M.
Theatre Magazine Vol.41 F
1925 P.10.

2920   Sewing Machine: Its
Invention & Development
(The). Smithsonian
Institution Press, 1976,
Washington. LOCN: Tj 1507

C6 1976, Folio ISBN:
0-87474-330-3

2921   Shakespeare at the
Globe. Beckerman, Bernard.
Macmillan, 1962, New York.

2922   Shall I Try Celastic.
Prisk, Bernice. Players
Magazine, Mr, 1953, Vol.
29, No. 6, P. 129.

2923   Shooter's Bible:
Reloader's Guide.
Steindler, R.A. Follett
Publishing Co., 1968,
Chicago.

2924   Short History of Armor
and a Method of
Constructing Armor for The
Stage (A). Zirke, Larry
Edwin. M.A. Thesis,
University of Washington,
1958.

2925   Short History of Costume
Armour (A). Kelly, F. M.
and Schwabe, R. Benjamin
Blom, 1931, New York.

2926   Shrubs for 5 Dollars
Each. Shawger, David C.
Theatre Crafts, Vol. 13,
No. 3, My 1979, P. 29.

2927   Silencers. Sterett,
Larry S. Gun Digest, 1964,
18th Ed., P. 135-138.

2928   Silencers. Armsco Corp.,
1967, Seattle.

2929   Small Arms and
Ammunition in the United
States Service. Lewis,
Berkley R. Smithsonian
Institute (The), 1956,
Washington, D.C.

2930   Small Arms of the World.
Smith, W.H.B. Stackpole,
Co., 1962, Harrisburg,pa.

2931   Small Stage Properties
and Furniture. Cookson,
Mrs. Nesfield. George Allen
& Unwin Ltd., 1934, London.

2932   Deleted.

2933 Soldier's Manual (The).
Nesmith, J. H. Riling and
Lentz, 1963, Philadelphia.

2934 Something Out of
Nothing: Ideas for Making
Armor, Fur, and Glass.
Lynne, Klonda. Players
Magazine, My/Je 1936, Vol.
12, No. 5, P. 22.

2935 Some Thoughts on Props.
Tabs, S 1955, Vol. 13, No.
2, P. 24.

2936 Spear (The). Ellehauge,
Martin. Olaf Moller, 1948,
Copenhagen.

2937 Special Effects:
Photographer's Flash Gun.
Pope, Karl T. Theatre
Crafts, N/D 1978, P.92,
Vol.12, No.7.

2938 Specifications Booklet:
Lightweight, Glassless
Mirrors. Kamar Products,
Inc., 2 South Buckhout,
Irvington-On-Hudson, New
York, 10533. No Date.

2939 Speer Manual for
Reloading Ammunition.
Speer, Inc., 1964,
Lewiston, Idaho.

2940 Stagecraft and Scene
Design. Philippi, Herbert.
Houghton Mifflin Co., 1953,
Boston. LOCN: Pn2091. S8
P48

2941 Stagecraft. Bradbury,
A.H. and Howard, W.R.B.
Herbert Jenkins, 1953,
London.

2942 Stages, Scenery, and
Props. Yerian, Cameron John
and Yerian, Margaret.
Childrens Press, 1975,
Chicago. LOCN: Pn2091.S8 Y4
1975 ISBN: 0516013138

2943 Stage Armor
Construction. Prisk,
Bernice. Players Magazine,
N, 1950, Vol. 26, No. 2, P.
40.

2944 Stage Automobile
Constructed to Blow Up.
Popular Mechanics, Mr 1913,
Vol. 19, P. 462.

2945 Stage Craft for
Non-Professionals. Buerki,
F.A. University of
Wisconsin, 1945, Madison.
LOCN: Pn2091 S8 B74 1972

2946 Stage Fights. Gordon,
Gilbert. Theatre Arts
Books, 1973, New York.

2948 Stage Management for the
Amateur Theatre. Halstead,
William Perdue. F.S. Crofts
& Co., 1937, New York.

2949 Stage Properties and How
to Make Them. Kenton,
Warren. Drama Book
Specialists, 1974, New
York. LOCN: Pn2091 S8 K4
1974

2950 Stage Properties.
Conway, Heather. Barrie &
Jenkins, 1960, England.

2951 Stage Scenery: Its
Construction and Rigging.
Gillette, A.S. Harper and
Row, 1972, New York. LOCN:
Pn2091. S8 G5 1972 ISBN:
Pn2091 S8 G5

2952 Stage Scenery,
Decoration, Upholstery,
Furniture and Effects.
Lancaster, Harry. Furniture
Gazette, Ap 10, 1875, Vol.
3; F 19, 1867, Vol. 5.

2953 Stage Violence. Katz,
Albert M. Richard Rosen
Press, 1976, New York.
LOCN: Pn 2071 F5k3 ISBN:
0-8239-0336-2

2954 Stage Warfare. Cassell's
Magazine, London, 1901,
Vol. 31, P. 227-231.

2955 Staging of the
Donaueschingen Passion
Play. Modern Language
Review, 1920, Vol. 15, P.
65:76, 279-297.

2956   Staging TV Programs and Commercials: How to Plan and Execute Sets, Props and Production Facilities. Wade, Robert J. Hastings House, 1954.

2957   State Pistol Laws. Henry Schlesinger, 1962, New York.

2958   Strange Guns in Hollywood. Pollexfen, Jack. American Rifleman, N 1947, Vol. 95, P. 29-31.

2959   Suicide Specials. Webster, Donald E., Jr. Stackpole Co., 1958, Harrisburg , Pa.

2960   Sword, Lance and Bayonet. Ffoulkes, Charles J. and Hopkinson, Captain E. C. Cambridge, 1938, London.

2961   Swords and Daggers. Wilkinson, Frederick. Ward, Lock, 1967, London.

2962   Swords on Stage. Gregoric, Michael T. M.A. Thesis, University of Michigan, 1956.

2963   Techniques of the Stage Fight. Hobbs, William. Theatre Arts Books, 1967, New York.

2964   Template Spun Polystyrene Foam for Stage Furniture. Chapman, Richard H. Theatre Crafts N 1977.

2965   Ten Commandments of Safety (The). Gun Digest, 1964, P. 336.

2966   Terrible to the Eye Alone. Popular Science Monthly, Mr 1917, Vol. 90, P. 379.

2967   Theatre Lighting. Flage, Francis M. and Weitz, C.E. General Electric Co., 1938, Cleveland.

2968   Theatre Props. Motley, Pseud. Drama Book Specialists, 1975, New York. LOCN: Pn2091 S8 M73

2969   Theatre Scenecraft: for the Backstage Technician and Artist. Adix, Vern. Children's Theatre Press, 1956, Anchorage, Ky.

2970   Theatre Student: Properties and Dressing the Stage (The). Bruder, Karl C. Richards Rosen Press 1969 New York. LOCN: Pn2091.S8 B68

2971   Theatre Unbound (The). Bakshy, Alexander. Cecil Palmer, 1923, London.

2972   Theatrical Firearms. Scientific American Supplement, My 1887, Vol. 23, P. 9477.

2973   Theatrical Tricks. Walker, Gladys R. Players Magazine, Mr/Ap 1933, Vol. IX, No. 4, P. 5.

2974   This Kind of War. Fehrenback, T.R. Macmillan Co., (The), 1963, New York.

2975   To Make a Mask. McPharlin, Paul. Theatre Arts Monthly Vol.9 1925 P.593.

2976   Treasure. Hunt, Ridgely. Chicago Tribune Sunday Magazine, My 14, 1967, P.70-72.

2977   Treasury of the Gun (The). Peterson, Harold L. Golden Press, 1962, New York.

2978   Ultra-New in Stage Decoration, The. Upholsterer, The, Ap 1915, P. 71-72.

2979   Useful Gummed Paper Tape. Raines, Lester and Settles, O. B. Players

Magazine, S/O 1936, Vol.
13, No. 1, P. 18.

2980   Weapons in the Theatre.
Wise, Arthur. Barnes and
Nobel, 1968, New York.

2981   Weapons of the British
Soldier. Rogers, Col.
H.C.B. Seeley Service &
Co. 1960 London.

2982   What Stars Eat on the
Stage. Gregory, J.P.
Theatre Magazine Vol.42 Ag
1925 P. 12.

2983   Wheelwright's Shop
(The). Stuart, George.
1923, Cambridge, Reprinted
1958.

2984   Woodworking Tools at
Shelburne Museum. Wildung,
Frank H. Shelburne Museum,
1957, Shelburne, Vt., 79 P.
Also, Hobby House,
Washington, D.C.

2985   Woodworking Tools
1600-1900. Welsh, Peter C.
Contributions from the
Museum of History and
Technology, Smithsonian
Institution, 1966,
Washington, D.C.,.

2986   1967 Redbook of Used Gun
Values (The). Publisher's
Development Corp., 1967,
Skokie, Illinois.

V
Scenery

2987   A.B.T.T. Trade Show:
About Theatre and About
People. Walne, Graham. The
Stage and Television Today,
Mr 29, 1979.

2988   Abc's of Electrical
Soldering. Dezettel, Louis
M. Howard W. Sams, 1971,
Indianapolis.

2989   About Shop Orders.
Watson, Lee. Lighting
Dimensions D 1977.

2990   Abrasive Metal
Finishing, Employee Health
and Safety Practices.
G.P.O. 017-033-00122-7 45c.
No Date.

2991   ABTT 1979. Moody, James
L. Theatre Crafts, S 1979,
Vol. 13, No. 4, P. 20.

2992   Accidents Will Happen.
Bell, Archie. Theatre
Magazine, Ja 1926, P. 10.

2993   Achim Freyer: Designer
of Interpretative Imagery.
Riddell, Richard. Theatre
Crafts, O, 1979, Vol. 13,
No. 5, P. 17.

2994   Acrylics. Modern
Plastics, 1956, Vol. 33,
No. 5, P. 88.

2995   Actors Who Have Died
Upon the Stage. Bates,
William. Notes and Queries,
1873, P. 338-340, Vol. 11.

2996   Adaptable Stages and
Inflexible Minds!. Jones,
Disley. Tabs, S 1961, Vol.
19, No. 2, P. 5.

2997   Adaptation of Commercial
Scafolding to the Problem
of Stage Platforming (The).
Mckennon, H.D. M.A. Thesis
U.C.L.A. 1967. LOCN: Ld
791.8 T3m199

2998   Adaption of Modern
Painting to Stage Design.
Johansen, Waldemar.

Players, F 1943, Vol. 19,
P. 8.

2999   Addendum to "Robert
Edmond Jones and His Art: a
Bibliographic Portrait"H.
Larson, Orville K. Theatre
Design & Technology, O
1971, No. 26, P. 28.

3000   Adequacy of Colorado
High School Auditoriums,
Stages, and Stage Equipment
for the Purpose of Play
Production (The). Grout,
Homer. M.A. Thesis,
University of Denver, 1945.

3001   Adhesives and Coatings
for Dow Foam Plastics. Dow
Chemical Co. Midland: The
Dow Chemical Company, Co.,
1967.

3002   Adjustable Caster Base
(An). Wedwick, Daryl M.
Theatre Design &
Technology, Winter 1977,
Vol. XIII, No., P. 31.

3003   Adolphe Appia:
Catalogue. Stadler, Edmund.
Victoria and Albert Museum,
1970, London.

3004   Adolphe Appia's Theories
of Production. Kaucher,
Dorothy. Quarterly Journal
of Speech Education, Je
1928, P. 411-422.

3006   Adolphe Appia, Prophet
of the Modern Theatre: a
Profile. Volbach, Walther
R. Wesleyan University
Press, 1968, Middletown,
Ct.

3007   Adolphe Appia. Museum
Victoria and Albert. St.
Clements Fosh & Cross,
1970, London. LOCN: Pn 2096
A657

3008   Adolph Appia: His Life
and Work. Beck, Gordon.
Players, Ja, 1962, Vol. 38,
No. 4, P. 118.

3009   Adolph Appia: the Rebirth of Dramatic Art. Mercier, Jean. Theatre Arts Monthly, Ag, 1932, Vol. XVI, No. 8, P. 61 5.

3010   Advanced Woodworking and Furniture Making. Feirer, John L. Charles A. Bennett, 1963, Peoria, Illinois.

3011   Adventures With Plastics. Newkirk, L. V. D. C. Heath and Co., 1947, Chicago, Illinois.

3012   Aesthetics for the Designer. Bellman, Willard F. Educational Theatre Journal, 1953, Vol. 5, P. 117-124.

3013   After the Practice the Theory, Gordon Craig and Movement. Rood, Arnold. Theatre Research 1971, Vol. XI, No. 2,3, P. 81.

3014   Aider and Abettor. Johnston, Alva. New Yorker, O 23, 1948, Vol. 24, P. 37-51; O 30, 1948, P. 28-39.

3015   Ain't Misbehavin. MacKay, Patricia. Theatre Crafts, O 1978, Vol. 12, No. 6, P. 13.

3017   Air and Gas Compression. Gill. Thomas T. John Wiley and Sons, Inc., 1941, New York.

3019   Air Bearing Turntables. Seemann, Jim. Theatre Design & Technology, Fall 1978, Vol. XIV, No. 3, P. 19-20.

3020   Air Fare: Inflatable Structures. Progressive Architecture, Ag 1972, P. 76.

3021   Air of Art Is Poisoned (The). Mallary, Robert. Art News, Ag 1966, P. 36.

3022   Air Power Helps Make Good Furniture. Smallwood, J.P. Compressed Air Magazine, Ap, 1959, Vol. 62, N. 4, P.98.

3023   Air Stapler and Scenic Construction. Miller, William. Theatre Crafts, N/D 1975, Vol. 9, No. 6, P. 48.

3024   Album of Designs, An. Appia, Adolphe. Art Institute, Zurich, 1929.

3025   Alexander Johnson, Machinist. Burnim, Kalman and Highfill, Philip, Jr. Theatre Notebook, S 1969, Vol. XXIII, No. 3, P. 100.

3026   Alice Dar Sarzamina Ojoyeb: the Adventures of Andre in Wonderland. Cortesi, Leslie. Theatre Design & Technology, My 1972, No. 29, P. 19.

3027   Aline Bernstein: a History and Evaluation. Barton, Mike Alan. Ph.D. Thesis, Indiana University, 1971.

3028   Alphabet Soup. Watson, Lee. Lighting Dimensions N 1977.

3029   Altes Werkzeug. Bernt, Walter. Georg D. W. Callwey, 1939, Munich.

3030   Aluminum Apron for Oxford Playhouse. Engineering, Mr 29, 1957, Vol. CLXXXIII, P. 393-394.

3031   Aluminum Framed Scenery. Sidlauskas, Francis Walter. M.F.A. Thesis, 1948, Yale University.

3032   Amateur Acting and Play Production. Campbell, Wayne. Macmillan, 1931, New York.

3033   America's First

Revolving Stage. Cole, Wendell. Western Speech Journal, Wi 1963, Vol. 27.

3034   American Artist and the Stage (The). Cheney, Sheldon. International Studio, 1921, Vol. 74.

3035   American Collection in Prague (An). Rothgeb, John R. Theatre Design & Technology, Sp 1980, Vol. XVI, No. 1, P. 13-14.

3036   American Dramatic Theatres VII. Fox, John A. American Architect and Building News 6, S 1879, P. 74.

3037   American Note-Book Abroad (An). Macgowan, Kenneth. Theatre Arts Magazine, O 1922, Vol. VI, No. 4, P. 299.

3038   American Opera Designs. Architectural Forum (The), Ja 1942, Vol. 76 Supplements P. 14,16.

3039   American Scenography: 1716-1969. Gillette, A.S. In: American Theatre: a Sum of Its Parts (The) - Samuel French, 1971, New York, P. 180-96.

3040   American Stage Wizard, (An). Ranck, Edwin Carty. Theatre Magazine, Ag 1915, Pp. 83, 92-93.

3041.   American Theater--IX: the Stage (The). Blackall, Clarence H. Brickbuilder, Ag 1908, Vol. 17, P. 163-166; S 1908, Vol. 17, P. 185-186, 211-213.

3042   American Theatre: A Sum of Its Parts, (The). Williams, Henry B. Samuel French, 1971, New York.

3043   American Theatres. Townsend, Horace. Transactions of the Royal

Institute of British Architects, 1891-92 Vol. 8,p. 65-85.

3044   American Theatre Designers. I. Albert Johnson. Reed, Edward. Magazine of Art, My 1940, Vol. 33, P. 274-279, 314, 316-317, P. 576-580, 594-595.

3045   American Woodworking Tools. Kebabian, Paul and Witney, Dudley. New York Graphic Society, 1978, Boston. ISBN: 0-8212-0731-8

3046   Analysis and Investigation of Current German Scenic Materials. Dryden, Dan. M.A. Thesis Univ. of Wisconson 1972. LOCN: Awo D799 D365

3047   Analysis of Structural Adhesives for the Theatre (An). Buccolo, Robert Daniel. M.F.A. Thesis, Yale University, 1956.

3048   Analytical and Descriptive Study of the Contributions of Edward Gordon Craig to Modern Theatre Art (An). Miller, Charles James. Ph.D. Thesis, University of Southern California, 1957.

3049   Analytical Study of Production Facilities of Contemporary Professional American Repertory Companies (An). Whaley, Frank L. Ph.D. Thesis, Florida State University, 1970.

3050   Anatomy of an Illusion; Studies in Nineteenth-Century Scene Design. International Congress on Theatre Research. Lectures of the Fourth International Congress on Theatre Research, 1965, Amsterdam. LOCN: Pn 2091 S8 I47 1965aa

3051   Ancient Egyptian
Masonry, the Building
Craft. Clarke, Somers and
Engelbach, R. Oxford
Univeristy Press, 1930,
London.

3052   Animated Scenery.
Arnold, Richard.
Educational Theatre
Journal, O 1964, P.
249-252.

3053   Annals of Conjuring
(The). Clarke, Sidney W.
In: Magic Wand (The)-Edited
by George Johnson, Mr-N,
1924, Vol. XIII, Nos.
121-123.

3054   Annotated Bibliography
of Scene and Costume Design
in the Past Hundred Years.
Pevitts, Robert. Ph.D.
Thesis, Southern Illinois
University, 1977.

3055   Annotated Translation:
Theatrical Machinery: Stage
Scenery And Devices by
George Moynet. Paul,
Charles Robert. Ph.D.
Thesis, University of
Southern California, 1970.

3056   Anthropomorphic Scenery.
Maronek, James. Theatre
Crafts, My/Je 1967, Vol. 1,
No. 2, P. 35-39.

3057   Anything Can Be Made
from Corrugated. Lee, B.H.
Theatre Design & Technology
F 1973.

3058   An American in Paris;
Norman Bel Geddes Produces
Jean D'arc. Bogusch,
George. Theatre Design &
Technology, O 1969, No. 18,
P. 4.

3059   Aphra Draws Off a Scene.
Southern, Richard. Life and
Letters To-Day, N 1941,
Vol. 31, P. 106-114.

3060   Appia's L'oeuvre D' Art
Vivant. Bayles, E.R. M.A.

Thesis, University of
Washington, 1935.

3061   Appia. Leeper, Janet.
Architectural Review, F
1968, Vol. 143, P. 113-118.

3062   Applications of Digital
Computing Machinery to
Theatre Arts Education.
Hovar, Linn. Ph.D. Thesis,
University of Kansas, 1973.

3063   Apprentices in the Scene
Room: Toward an American
Tradition in Scene
Painting. Wolcott, John R.
Nineteenth Century Theatre
Research, 1976, Vol. 4, No.
1, P. 23.

3064   Approaching Performing
Arts Training: a Focused
Training Program at North
Carolina School of the
Arts. MacKay, Patricia.
Theatre Crafts, O 1978,
Vol. 12, No. 6, P. 37.

3065   Approach to Special
Effects for Limited
Television Production (An).
Traband, Roy Edward.
Thesis, University of
Tulsa, 1959.

3066   Aqua Scenes at Sadler's
Wells Theatre. Jackson,
Allan S. and Morrow, John
C. OSU Theatre Collection
Bulletin, 1962, Vol. 9, P.
22-47.

3067   Arbitrator of Theatre
Staff Dispute. Jongh,
Nicholas De. The Guardian,
Mr 13, 1979.

3068   Arc-Welding Manual.
General Electric Company.
Kenfield-Davis Publishing,
Co., 1928, Chicago.

3069   Architectural and
Perspective Designs.
Bibiena, Giuseppe Galli.
Dover, 1964, New York.

3070   Architectural

Considerations in the
Design Of Special Purpose
Machines. Daley, Leslie
Norbert. University of
Illinois, 1975, Urbana.
LOCN: Qa76. I4

3071   Architectural Drawing.
Field, Wooster Bard.
McGraw-Hill, 1922, New
York.

3072   Architectural Stage
(The). Cheney, Sheldon.
Theatre Arts Monthly, Jl,
1927, Vol. XI, No.7, P.
478.

3073   Architecture, Theatrale.
Publisher Unknown, Located
at Boston Public Library,
Good Illustrations. No
Date.

3074   Architecture,
Scenography, and Theatre.
Bortnovski, Paul. Romanian
Review, 1966, Vol. 20, No.
4, P. 100-104.

3075   Architecture for the
Educational Theatre.
Robinson, Horace W.
University of Oregon, 1970,
Portland, Or. LOCN: Lb
3221. R55

3076   Architecture for the New
Theatre. Harmon, Arthur
Loomis. Theatre Arts
Monthly, F 1936, Vol. XX,
No. 6, P. 145.

3077   Architecture of
"Coriolanus" at the Lyceum
Theatre. Spiers, Richard
Phene. Architectural
Review, 1901, Vol. 10, P.
3-21.

3078   Architecture on Stage
and Screen. Lanchester,
H.V. Builder (The), Ja
1946, Vol. 104, P. 31-32.

3079   Architect As Stage
Designer (The). Leacroft,
Richard. Architect and
Building News (The), Ja
1947, Vol. 189, P. 68.

3080   Are Designers
Necessary?. Marshall,
Herbert. Plays and Players,
N 1962, Vol. 10, P. 18.

3081   Are You Protected. Lago,
B.P. Theatre Design &
Technology Sp 1976.

3082   Armbruster Scenic Studio
(The). Joyce, Robert S.
OSU Theatre Collection
Bulletin, 1965, Vol. 12, P.
6-19.

3083   Armor Without Hammers.
Manwaring, David. Theatre
Crafts N 1977.

3084   Armstrong Expandofoam.
Armstrong Cork Co., 1968,
Lancaster, Penn.

3085   Army Stage Illusion.
Popular Mechanics, 1913,
Vol. 10, P. 34.

3086   Artificial Clouds in
Third Dimension. Waxman,
Harry. Cine Technician,
Jl:ag, 1946, Vol. 12, P.
86, P. 93.

3087   Artist's Aid to Broadway
(The). Parker, Robert A.
Arts and Decoration, O
1921, P.364.

3088   Artist's Approach to the
Theatre. Jones, Robert
Edmond. Theatre Arts
Monthly, S 1928, Vol. XII,
No. 9, P. 629.

3089   Artistic and
Scenographic Experiments in
the Czezechoslovak Theatre.
Trager, Josef. Interscena
Acta Scaenopgraphica
Internationalia, Sp 1967,
vol. 2, P. 36-41.

3090   Artistic Approach of
Filippo Juvarra, Late
Baroque Scene Designer
(The). West, William
Russell. Ph.D. Thesis, Ohio
State University, 1962.

3091   Artistic Approach of the Grieve Family to Selected Problems of Ninteenth-Century Scene Painting. Hamblin, Junus N. Ph.D. Thesis, Ohio State University, 1966.

3092   Artistic Partnrship, (The). New York Dramatic Mirror, Jl 1898, P. 23.

3093   Artists and Technicians File. Harvard Theatre Collection. No Date.

3094   Artist in the American Theatre: Illustrated by the Work of American Stage Craftsmen (The). Touchstone, Ap 1919, Vol. 5, P. 40-50, 77-79.

3095   Artist Life. Soria, Dorle J. High Fidelity-Musical America, N 1973, Vol. 23.

3096   Arts Management: an Annotated Bibliography. Coe, L. and Benedict, S. 1978. LOCN: Z 5956 A7 C65, Ref. Art

3097   Art & the Law, Index: Volumes I-III. Volunteer Lawyers for the Arts, 36 West 44 St., Suite 1110, Ny, N.Y. 10036. No Date.

3098   Art and Architecture on the Stage; "Harod" at Her Majesty's Theatre. Spiers, Richard Phene. Architectural Review, 1901, Vol. 9, P. 3-12.

3099   Art and the Stage in the 20th Century; Painters and Sculptors Work for the Theater. Rischbieter, Henning. New York Graphic Society, 1968, Greenwich Ct. LOCN: N 6490 R5473

3101   Art in the Theatre: Boris Aronson. Glassgold, C. Adolph. Arts, Ja 1928, Vol. 13, P. 46-47.

3102   Art in the Theatre: Spectacle. Harris, Augustus. Magazine of Art, 1889, P.109-13, Vol. 12.

3103   Art in the Theatre: the Decline of Scenic Art in America. Marston, Richard. Magazine of Art, 1894, Vol. 17, P. 163-168.

3104   Art in the Theatre: the Painting of Scenery. Telbin, William. Magazine of Art, 1889, P.195-201, Vol. 12.

3105   Art Must Work for Its Living. Mannes, Marya. Theatre Guild Magazine, O 1931, Vol. 9, P. 30-35.

3106   Art of Ballet, The. Perugini, Mark E. J.B. Lippincott Co., 1915, P. 339.

3107   Art of Escape (The). Novak, John. Canada's Micky Hades, 1979.

3108   Art of Japanese Joinery (The). Seike, Kiyosi. Weatherhill/Tankosha, 1977, New York.

3109   Art of Joseph Urban (The). Theatre Magazine (The), S 1915, Vol. XXII, No. 175, P. 124.

3110   Art of Knotting and Splicing. Day, Cyrus Lawrence. U.S. Naval Institute, 1955, Annapolis, Maryland.

3111   Art of Play Production. Dolman, John Jr. Harper & Row, 1946, New York. ISBN: 0-06-041680-7

3112   Art of Robert Edmond Jones (The). Shipp, H. English Review, 1922, Vol. 34, P. 355-357.

3113   Art of Scene Painting (The). Samuel French, 1879, New York.

3114   Art of Scenic Design; a
Pictorial Analysis of Stage
Setting and Its Relation to
Theatrical Production.
Simonson, Lee. Harper,
1950, New York, 174 P.;
Also Musson, Toronto.

3115   Art of Scenography
(The). Ricci, Corrado. Art
Bulleting, Mr 1928, P. 231.

3116   Art of Stage Decoration
1940-1955 (The).
Hillestrom, Gustaf. World
Theatre, Sp, 1955, Vol. IV,
No. 2, P. 27.

3117   Art of the Gauze (The).
Shanks, Alec. Tabs, Ap,
1957, Vol. 15, No. 1, P. 4.

3118   Art of the Minor
Theatres in 1860.
Armstrong, William A.
Theatre Notebook, 1956,
Vol. 10, P. 89.

3119   Art of the Scenic
Designs of Lee Simonson
(The). Springer, N. J.
Creative Art, My 1928, Vol.
2, P. 335.

3120   Art of the Theatre: Mr.
C. Lovat Designs for "As
You Like It.".
International Studio, Au
1919, Vol. 68, P. 63.

3121   Art of the Theatre: the
Designs of W. Bridges Adams
(The). Hoppe, E. O.
International Studio,
1919-1920, Vol. 69, P.
156-159.

3122   Art of the Theatre--Mr.
Norman Macdermott's
Settings (The). Hoppe, E.
O. International Studio,
1919-1920, Vol 69, P.
65-69.

3123   Art of the Theatre, The.
Brochner, George.
International Studio (The),
O 1919.

3124   Art of the Theatre, The.
Cheney, Sheldon. Knopf,
1925, New York.

3125   Art of Woodturning.
Klenke, William. Charles A.
Bennett, 1954 Peoria,
Illinois.

3126   Art on the Stage.
Building News, Jy 29, 1881,
P.34.

3127   Art on the Stage.
Scientific American
Supplement, 1881, Vol. XII.

3128   Art on the Stage.
New-York Daily Tribune, D
27, 1880, P.5.

3129   Art Versus Craft.
Mielziner, Jo. Theatre
Design & Technology, Sum
1976, Vol. XII, No. 2, P.
9.

3130   Ascension Images in Art
and Theatre. Larson,
Orville K. Gazette Des
Beaux Arts, O 1959, Vol. 6,
P. 161.

3131   Aspects of Staging
Adelgitha. Adelsperger,
Walter. OSU Theatre
Collection Bulletin, 1960,
P. 14.

3132   Asphaleia Theatre in
Vienna. Builder, (The), N
4, 1882, P. 587.

3133   Astra Trunk Mystery
Explained. Popular
Electricity, Vol. 29, S
1914, P. 283.

3134   At the Bottom of It
All-The Studio Floor.
Holmstock, Toni. Dance
Magazine, My 1952, P.
42-43.

3135   Audels Carpenters and
Builders Guide 2. Graham,
Frank D. and Emery, Thomas
J. Audel and Co.,
Publishers, 1939, New York.

3136   Audience Will Accept
Almost Anything Except
Boredom. Close, Robin. Tabs
Sp 1977.

3137   Audio-Visual Equipment
Directory, 1978-79 (The).
Herickes, S.H. (Editor).
1978. LOCN: Ts 2301 A7 A8
Audio-Visual

3138   Auditoria, Stages and
Ancillary Spaces, Fixtures
and Equipment. Architects'
Journal, Ag 5, 1964, Vol.
140, P. 405-412, Ag 12,
1964, P. 345-360, Ag 26
1964, P. 511-525.

3139   Augustus Welby Northmore
Pugin's Influence in the
Theatre. Marlis, Alan
Philip. Ph.D. Thesis, 1974,
City University of New
York.

3140   Automated Theatre Sound
and Light Show at Ford's
Theatre. Mintz , D.
Theatre Crafts Mr 1971.

3141   Automation or
Mechanization. Howard,
George T. Educational
Theatre Journal, O 1958,
Vol. X, P. 250.

3142   Away from Scenic
Realism. Philippi, Herbert.
Players Magazine, F 1954,
Vol. 30, No. 5, P. 105.

3143   Awful Handyman's Book.
Daniels, George. Harper &
Row, 1966, New York. Paper
Cornerstone 1969, New York.

3144   B. Iden Payne Theatre:
Univ. of Texas at Austin.
Rothgeb, John R. Theatre
Design & Technology Wi
1976.

3145   Back-Stage Toilers
(The). Tabs, Ap 1954, Vol.
12, No. 1, P. 11.

3146   Backstage at the
Metropolitan Opera House.
Sargent, W. Life, Ja 14,
1946, Vol. 20, P. 51.

3147   Backstage in the Music
Hall. Davenport, W.
Colliers D 30, 1933, Vol.
92, P. 15.

3148   Ballet Decor. Terry,
Walter. New York Herald
Tribune, O 5, 1941.

3149   Ballet Design. Smith,
Oliver. Dance News Annual,
1953, P. 92-103.

3150   Ballroom: Tharon Musser
Lights the Ballroom Floor.
MacKay, Patricia. Theatre
Crafts, Mr/ap 1979, Vol.
13, No. 2, P. 15.

3151   Band Saw and the Jig Saw
(The). Haines, Ray E. Van
Nostrand, 1953, New York.

3152   Banishing the Actor from
the Theatre. Current
Literature, Ap 1912, P.
457.

3153   Bankside Stage-Book.
Whanslaw, H.W. W. Gardner,
1924, London.

3154   Banvard's Panorama.
Scientific American, D
1848, Vol. 4, P. 100.

3155   Baroque and Romantic
Stage Design. Scholz, Janos
(Ed.). H. Bittner, 1950,
New York.

3156   Baroque Theatre (The).
Baur-Heinhold, Marharet and
Whittall, Mary Translation.
McGraw-Hill 1967 New York.

3157   Basic Course of
Practical Metalwork, (A).
Bedford, John R. John
Murry, 1960, London.

3158   Basic Sheet-Metal
Practice. Giachino, Joseph
W. Van Nostrand, 1952 New
York.

3159 Basic Sheet Metal Work. Wilkinson, H. St. Martin's Press, 1964, New York.

3160 Bats That Fly in the Night. Theatre Crafts O 1977.

3161 Bayreuth Festival: a Centenary Ring Cycle (The). Theatre Crafts, Mr/Ap 1977, Vol. II, No. 2, P. 16.

3162 Bay Area (The). MacKay, Patricia. Theatre Crafts, S 1980, Vol. 14, No. 4, P. 18.

3163 Bay Area Theatre Spaces. Loney, Glenn. Theatre Crafts, S 1980, Vol. 14, No. 4, P. 23.

3164 Behind, Above, and Below the Curtain. Graphic, Ja 1874, Vol. 9, P. 3.

3165 Behind, Below, and Above the Scenes. Bunce, Oliver Bell. Appleton's Journal, 1870, Vol. 3, P. 589-94.

3166 Behind the Curtains of a Great Theater. Scientific American, N 1924, Vol. 131, P. 313.

3167 Behind the Motion Picture Screen. Lescarboura, Augustin Celestin. Scientific American Publishing Co., 1922, New York.

3168 Behind the Scenes: the Framework. Stevenson, Florence. Opera News, F 24, 1962, Vol. 26, P. 26-29.

3169 Behind the Scenes at Ben Hur. Ellsworth, William W. Critic, Mr 1900, Vol. 36, P. 245-49.

3170 Behind the Scenes at Drury Lane; How the Scenery of the Pantomime Is Illuminated. Graphic, Ja 1910, Vol. 81, P. 13.

3171 Behind the Scenes at Her Majesty's Theatre. Electrician, Ag 21, 1885, Vol. 15.

3172 Behind the Scenes at the Opera. Sphere Vol. 36 Ja 23 1909 P. 88.

3173 Behind the Scenes of an Opera House. Kobbe, Gustav. Scribners Magazine, O 1888, Vol. 4 P. 435.

3174 Behind the Scenes of Noonameena. Elizabethan Trust News, S 1973, P. 13, No. 8.

3175 Behind the Scenes of Operatic Make Believe. Theatre Magazine, My 1922, P. 315.

3176 Behind the Scenes. Clark, Peter. Architectural Forum, S 1932, P. 266.

3177 Behind the Scenes. Theatre Notebook, Vol. 10, P. 82, Pl. 4. No Date.

3178 Behind the Soviet Scenes Lawrence and Lee Tour USSR. Loney, Glenn. Theatre Design & Technology, My 1973.

3179 Behind the Wings in the Hoftheater in Dresden. Scientific American Supplement, F 1, 1902, Vol. 53, P. 21812-15.

3180 Bel-Geddes-Master of the Scenic Art. Vernon, Grenvile. Theatre Magazine, Ap 1924, P. 20.

3181 Belasco Magic. Mcglinchee, Claire. Players, O/N, 1967, Vol. 34, No. 1, P. 12.

3182 Bel Geddes' Hamlet, a Melodramma (The). Brown, Frank Chouteau. Drama, D 1929, Vol. 20, P. 73-74.

3183   Benwell on Victorian
Scene Painting. Theatre
Notebook, O, 1946, Vol. 1,
No. 5, P. 67.

3184   Bergenz Festival (The).
Theatre Crafts, Mr/Ap 1977,
Vol. II, No. 2, P. 22.

3185   Berkeley Shakespeare
Festival. Theatre Crafts, S
1980, Vol. 14, No. 4, P.
26.

3186   Best of Families: David
Jenkins Designs
Turn-Of-The-Century New
York for the New Television
Series (The). MacKay,
Patricia. Theatre Crafts,
Ja/F 1978, Vol. 12, No. 1,
P. 11.

3187   Better Grip for
Adhesives. Chemical World,
S 17, 1955, Vol. 77, P. 61.

3188   Bibiena Family (The).
Mayor, A. H. Bittner,
1945, New York.

3189   Bibliography of
Conjuring and Similar
Deceptions. Clarke, Sidney
W. and Blind, Adolphe.
1920, London.

3190   Bibliography of Plastic
Sources (A). USITT
Publication (Seminar on
Plastic Sources, Ap 1974,
Suny, Albany).

3191   Bibliography of Theatre
& Stage Design: a Select
List of Books and Articles.
Cheshire, David F. British
Theatre Institute, (Roger
Hudson), 30 Clarevill e
St., London Sw 7 Saw
England ABTT, 1960-1970.
ISBN: 0-904512-01-0

3192   Bibliography of the Art
of Turning and Lathe and
Machine Tool History.
Abell, Sidney and Leggat,
John and Ogden, Warren G.
Jr. Society of Ornamental

Turners (The), 1956,
Isleworth, Middlesex &
South Lincoln, M.A.

3193   Bil-Jax Scaffolding
(Catalog No. 40). Bil-Jax
Inc. Bil-Jax, Inc., 1966,
Archbold, Ohio.

3194   Biographical Dictionary
of Actors, Actresses,
Musicians, Dancers,
Managers, & Other Stage
Personnel in London,
1660-1800, (A). Highfill,
Philip H. Jr. Southern
Illinois University Press,
1973-75.

3195   Birth of Blitz (The).
Kenny, Sean. Plays and
Players, My 1962, P. 9.

3196   Bishop of Broadway:
David Belasco (The).
Timberlake, Craig. Library
Publishing, 1954, New York.
LOCN: Pn 2287 B4 T5

3197   Black Art Redivivus.
Scientific American Ag
1907, Vol. 97, P. 148.

3198   Black Box: an Experiment
in Visual Theatre (The).
Epstein, John, Et Al.
Latimer Press, 1970,
London.

3199   Blaster's Handbook. Du
Pont De Nemuors & Co.,
1958, Wilmington, Delaware.

3200   Blow Me a House. Vogue,
O 15, 1969, Vol. 154, No.
7, P. 138.

3201   Boggling the Eye Or: How
to Make an Effect in Opera.
Bowers, Faubian. Opera
News, Ja 8, 1972, Vol. 36,
No. 7, P. 9.

3202   Book of Formulas,
Recipes, Methods and Secret
Processes. Popular Science
Publishing Co., 1932, New
York.

3203   Book of Play Production
(The). Smith, Milton Myers.
D. Appleton & Co., 1926,
New York.

3204   Book of Successful
Bathrooms. Schram, Joseph
F. Structures Publishing
Co., 1976, Farmington,
Michigan. LOCN: 75-31489
ISBN: 0-912336-16-1

3205   Book of the Play:
Studies and Illustrations
of Histrionic Story, Life,
and Character (A). Cook,
D. Sampson, Low, Marston,
Searle & Rivington, 1876.

3206   Booth's Theatre - Behind
the Scenes. Booth's Theatre
(Pamphlet Issued By), 1870,
New York. Henry L. Hinton,
1870, New York.

3207   Borders: Their
Origins/Their Decline.
Lawrence, William John.
Stage (The), Jl 14, 1932,
P. 9, Jl 28, 1932, P. 13.

3208   Boris Aronson Sketchbook
(A). Jenkins, Speight.
Opera News, Ja 2, 1971,
Vol. 35, P. 20-23.

3209   Boris Aronson. Hersh,
Burton. Show, F 1962, Vol.
2, P. 8.

3210   Boris Aronson. Truabe,
Shepard. Theatre Guild
Magazine, Ja 1931, Vol. 8,
P. 26-30.

3211   Box Set in Charles
Kean's Productions of
Shakespearean Tragedy.
Wilson, M. Glen. OSU
Theatre Collection
Bulletin, 1958, Vol. 5, P.
7-26.

3212   Bringing Svoboda Sets to
Life. Times, My 17, 1967,
P. 6.

3213   Bring Him Backalive!.
Dewey, Walter S. Players,

O/N, 1968, Vol. 44, No. 1,
P. 2.

3214   Bristol Hippodrome
Stage, Its Machinery and
Mechanical Equipment.
Macrae, F. G. H. Stage
Year Book, 1916, P. 37-39.

3215   Bristol Theatre Royal
Inventory (A). Southern,
Richard. In: Studies in
English Theatre History
(Society for Theatre
Research, 1952, London),
P.98-113.

3216   British Gun Laws Don't
Stop Crime. Kleber, Louis
C. Guns, Ag 1966, P. 28,
50.

3217   British Stage Designers
Bring Home the Golden
Triga. Bury, John (O.B.E.).
Cue Technical Theatre
Review, S/O 1979, P. 6-8.

3218   Broadway and Hollywood:
George Jenkins for Film and
Theatre Designs On Both
Coasts. Fielding, Eric.
Theatre Craft, Mr/Ap 1980,
Vol. 14, No. 2, P. 20,
55-59.

3219   Buckle Up: Safety in the
Parks. Davidson, Randall.
Theatre Crafts, S 1977,
Vol. 11, No. 4, P. 54.

3220   Budget Settings for Off
Off Broadway. Crane,
Cynthia. Theatre Craft,
My/Je 1980, Vol. 14, No. 3,
P. 43.

3221   Budget Technology Four
Solutions. Raddell, B. and
Lyon, N. Theatre Crafts My
1973.

3222   Builder S Hardware
Samples on File in
Washington, D.C. U.S.
Government Printing Office
Washington, D.C.. No Date.
ISBN: 051-000-00098-6

3223   Building Arches an Easy
Way. Chavez, Edmond M.
Players Magazine, F 1954,
Vol. 30, No. 5, P. 111.

3224   Building a Giant for
Jack and the Beanstalk; a
Peep Behind the Scenes at
Drury Lane. Graphic, Ja
1911, Vol. 83, P. 25.

3225   Building a Model Set.
Robinson, Marion. Players
Magazine, N, 1956, Vol. 33,
No. 2, P. 38.

3226   Building a Portable
Theatrical Stage. Corbould,
William. Work, Je 1903,
Vol. 25, P. 294-295.

3227   Building Block Theatre.
Maceachron, Grace. Theatre
Crafts, Ja/F 1968, P.
12-20.

3228   Building Codes, Building
Costs, and Building Safety.
Colean, Miles L. American
City, Ap 1946, Vol. LVI, P.
93.

3229   Building Code for
California. California
State Chamber of Commerce.
John Kitchen Printing Co.,
1939, San Francisco.

3230   Building Code of the
City of New York (The).
Publication of the
Department of Building of
the City of New York, 1901.

3231   Building for
Self-Sufficiency. Clarke,
Robin. Universe Books,
1977, New York. LOCN:
76-5093 ISBN: 0-87663-230-4

3232   Building for the
Performing Arts.
Architectural Forum, Je
1960, Vol. 112, No. 6, P.
86-103.

3233   Building Plays. Nathan,
George Jean. Bohemia N
Magazine, Ag 1909.

3234   Building Stage Platforms
With Slotted Metal Angle.
Stewart, Craig. Educational
Theatre Journal, Mr 1966,
Vol. XVIII, No. I, P. 77.

3235   Building the Illusion of
Size. Wade, Robert F.
Theatre Arts Magazine, Jl
1944, Vol. XXVIII, No. 7,
P. 428.

3236   Building Your Own Home.
Yeck, Fred. Arco Publishing
Co., 1975, New York. LOCN:
74-16918 ISBN:
0-668-03656-7

3237   Build Your Own Model
Theatre. Parker, Anthony.
S. Paul, 1959, London.
LOCN: Pn2091. M6p3

3238   Bulgarian Scenography.
Dinova-Ruseva, Bera.
Interscaena-Acta
Scaenographica, Sp 1974,
Vol. 4, P. 32-48; Fall
1974, P. 13-50; Wi 1974, P.
1-36.

3239   Bulletin Ig1:311,
Casting With Plaster and
Hydrocal Gypsum Cements.
United States Gympsum Co.,
Chicago. No Date.

3240   Busby Berkeley on a
Budget. Harvey, Peter.
Theatre Crafts, O 1969, P.
7.

3241   Business of Producing
(The). Musser, Tharon.
M.F.A. Thesis, 1949, Yale
University.

3242   Buying Consulting
Services. Benson, Robert.
Theatre Crafts, N/D 1979,
Vol. 13, No. 6, P. 86-88.

3243   C.I.E.. Tabs Sum 1975.

3244   Cabaret Du Neant (The).
Scientific American, Mr
1896, Vol. 74, P. 152.

3245   California Institute of

the Arts Ends Design and Technical Training Modular Theatre Paralized. Theatre Crafts N 1973.

3246   California Tours!. Wallach, Susan Levi. Theatre Crafts, S 1980, Vol. 14, No. 4, P. 31.

3247   Caligari's Cabinet and Other Grand Illusions: a History of Film Design. Barsacq, Leon. New American Library, 1970, New York.

3248   Calling on Craig. Marks, Claude. Theatre Arts, S 1957, Vol. 41, P. 78.

3249   Camelot. Original Rendering, 1960, New York. located at the Harvard Theatre Collection.

3250   Camera and the Scene (The). Bruguiere, Francis. Theatre Arts Monthly, 1924, Vol. 8, P. 166.

3251   Camille (Act III & IV) 1932, Devil and Daniel Webster, 1939. Jones, Robert Edmond. Original Drawing at Harvard Theatre Collection, Harvard University.

3252   Canadian Theatre Checklist (1979-80). Rubin, Don and Mekler, Mimi. Canadian Theatre Review Publications (Ontario) 1979. ISBN: 0705-5064

3253   Can We Afford to Discard Ornamental Plaster?. Progressive Architecture, Mr 1967, P. 162.

3254   Caravaggio in College: Jo Mielziner Creates a Projection Spectacular. Loney, Glenn. Theatre Design & Technology, F 1973, No. 32, P. 25.

3255   Carolina Playmakers' Touring Equipment. Davis,

Harry. Theatre Arts Monthly Jl, 1937, Vol. XXI, No. 7, P. 581.

3256   Carpentry and Building Construction. Feirer, John L. and Hutchings, Gilbert R. Chas. a Bennett Co., 1976, Peoria, Ill.. LOCN: 76-2144 ISBN: 87002-004-8

3257   Carpentry and Candlelight in the Theatre. Mayor, A. Metropolitan Museum Bulletin, F 1943, P.198-203, No. 1.

3258   Case in for Scenery. Kase, Robert. Players Magazine, My, 1950, Vol. 26, No. 8, P. 192.

3259   Case of Augusta Sohlkevs John Depol (The). Baker, Barbara. Education Theatre Journal, My 1978, P. 233.

3260   Case of Gordon Craig (The). Simonson, Lee. Theatre Guild Magazine, F 1931, Vol. 8, P. 18.

3261   Case Study of American Production: English Source and American Practice. Wolcott, John R. OSU Theatre Collection Bulletin, 1968, Vol. 15, P. 9.

3262   Castle and School Theatres in Czech Lands. Bartusek, Antonin. Interscaena, Sum 1970, Vol. 4, P. 1-23.

3263   Catalog of the Norman Gel Geddes Theatre Collection. Hunter, Frederick J. G. K. Hall, 1973, Boston. LOCN: Pn2096 G37t4 ISBN: 0-8161-0137-9

3264   Catalog of the Theatre: Scenery, Lighting, Hardward Painting. Throckmorton, Cleon. Cleon Throckmorton, 1938, New York.

3265   Caused by Black and
White; the Ghost Girls.
Sketch, F 1914, Supplement,
Vol. 85, P. 8.

3266   Cave of Phantoms (The).
Scientific American
Supplement, N 1895, Vol.
40, P. 16578.

3267   Centenary of the
Panorama (The). Southern,
H. Theatre Notebook, 1950,
Vol. 5, No. 11, P. 67.

3268   Center for Building
Technology, a Perspective.
U.S. Government Printing
Office Washington, D.C..
No Date. ISBN:
003-003-01575-0

3269   Century of
Scene-Painting. Lawrence,
William John. Gentleman'
Magazine, Mr 1888, Vol.
264, P. 282-94.

3270   Chamber Drama. Guthrie,
John. Pear Tree Press,
1930, Flansham, Sussex,
England.

3271   Changable Scenery for
Plays on the Caroline
Stage. Richards, Kenneth
R. Theatre Notebook, Ja
1968, Vol. XXIII, No. 1, P.
6.

3272   Changeable Scenery, Its
Origin and Development in
the British Theatre.
Southern, Richard. Faber &
Faber, 1952, London.

3273   Changing Concepts of
Realism in Scenery on the
New York Stage 1900-1915,
(The). Arnold, Richard.
Ph.D. Thesis, Northwestern
University, 1962.

3274   Changing Pattern of
Spectacle on the New York
Stage. Oliver, George B.
Ph.D. Thesis, Pennsylvania
State University, 1956.

3275   Chapter from the Book on
Architecture. Serlio,
Sebastian. Mask (The), Mr,
1908, Vol. 1, No. 1, P. 14.

3276   Characteristics of the
Yale Spotline Winch.
Martin, Craig T. M.F.A.
Thesis, 1971, Yale
University.

3277   Character of Australian
Technology (The). Irving,
Dennis. Theatre Australia,
S 1976, Vol.1, No.2 , P.52.

3278   Charles Ciceri and the
Background of American
Scene Design. Duerr, E.
Theatre Arts, D 1932, Vol.
16, P. 983-990.

3279   Chases Electric
Cyclorama. Scientific
American, F 1896, Vol. 74,
P. 120.

3280   Checklist of Scene
Painters Working in Great
Britain And Ireland in the
18th Century (A).
Rosenfeld, Sybil and
Croft-Murray, Edward.
Theatre Notebook, Fa 1964,
Vol. XIX, No. 1, P. 6, No.
2, P. 49, No. 3, P. 102,
Vol. XX, No. 4,.

3281   Check List of Books and
Periodicals Written
Designed and Edited by
Edward Gordon Craig.
Fletcher, Ifan Kyrle.
Theatre Notebook, 1955,
Vol. 10, P. 50.

3282   Chelsea Theatre Centre
(The). Napoleon, Davi.
Theatre Crafts O 1977.

3283   Chemical Magic. Ford,
Leonard A. Fawcett
Publications, 1959,
Greenwich, Ct.

3284   Chemistry of Powder and
Explosives (The). Davis,
Tenney L. John Wiley &
Sons, Inc. 1941 - 1943, New
York.

3285   Chicago: Tony Walton
Designs in Black Vinyl and
Neon. Dunham, Richard B.
Theatre Crafts, O 1975,
Vol. 9, No. 5, P. 6.

3286   Chicago Auditorium
(The). Adler, Dankmar.
Architectural Record.
Ap/je 1892, Vol. 1, P.
415-34.

3287   Chicago Building Code.
Atlantic, O 1950, Vol.
CLXXXVI, P. 21.

3288   Chicago Code of 1911
(The). Brundage, Edward J.
Editor. 1911, Chicago.

3289   Chicago Tackles Its
Building Code.
Architectural Record, Mr
1946, P. 66.

3290   Chichester Festival:
Programming for Profits
(The). Loney, Glenn.
Theatre Crafts, My/Je 1979,
Vol. 13, No. 3, P. 23.

3291   China: Technical. ABTT
News, Ap 1980.

3292   China at Work: An
Illustrated Record of the
Primitive Industries of
China's Masses, Whose Life
Is Toil, and Thus an
Account of Chinese
Civilization. Hommel,
Rudolf P. Day, for Bucks
County Historical Society,
1937, New York.

3293   Christian Rite and
Christian Drama in the
Middle Ages. Hardison, O.
B. Baltimore, 1965.

3294   Christmass Tale, or,
Harlequin Scene Painter,
(A). Allen, Ralph G.
Tennessee Studies in ·
Literature, 1974, Vol. 19,
P. 194-161.

3295   Church Visible (The).
Tabs Sum 1976.

3296   Cinema Workshop: Part
12, Special Effects (The).
Loring, Charles. American
Cinematographer, Je 1947,
Vol. 28, P. 208, 225.

3297   Circular 56: Copyright
for Sound Recordings.
Performing Arts Review,
1972, Vol. 3 No. 3, P. 525.

3298   Civic Theatres and the
Amateurs. Corry, Percy.
Tabs Je 1965.

3299   Clarkson Stanfield, R.A.
Scene Painter, Artist,
Gentleman and Friend.
Bogusch, George. Quarterly
Journal of Speech, O 1970,
Vol. LVI, No. 3, P. 245.

3300   Clarkson Stanfield and
the Spectacularist. Pugh,
Anthony. Cue Technical
Theatre Review, N/D 1979.

3301   Classical Antiquity: the
Theatre and the Artist.
Webster, Thomas B. L.
Apollo, Ag 1967, Vol. 86,
P. 94-101.

3302   Classics in a Chinatown
Loft: the Shade Company.
Theatre Crafts, Mr/Ap 1974,
Vol. 8, No. 2, P. 14.

3303   Claud Lovat Fraser,
1890-1921. Battersby,
Martin. Art and Artists N
1969, Vol. 4, P. 38-41.

3304   Cleveland Museum's
Theatre Models.
Architecture and Building,
Ag, 1942, P. 4.

3305   Clouds in Captivity.
Living Age, 1923, Vol. 317,
P. 180.

3306   Code of Practice for
Pyrotechnics & Smoke
Effects. Code of Practice
for the Theatre Industry,
Chapter 1 Part 5. No Date,
England.

3307   Cold Bending and
Forming. Kervick, Richard
J. and Springborn, R. K.
Society of Manufacturing
Engineers, 1966, Dearborn,
Michigan.

3308   Collaboration and
Synthesis: Gunilla
Pamstiema-Weiss Discusses
Design and Directors.
Loney, Glenn. Theatre
Crafts, N/D 1978, Vol. 12,
No. 7, P. 38.

3309   Collection in the
Huntington Library. Bliss,
Cary S. OSU Theatre
Collection Bulletin, Sp
1956, Vol. 2, No. 2, P. 4.

3310   Collection of
Eighty-Three Patents.
United States Patent
Office, 1901, Washington,
D. C.

3311   Collective Bargaining,
Theatre With a Union Label.
Eustis, Morton. Theatre
Arts Magazine, N 1933, Vol.
XVII, No. 11, P. 859.

3312   Colored Fires. Kennedy,
E.J. Scientific American
Supplement, Mr 1893, Vol.
35, P. 14359.

3313   Colored Lights for
Tableaux. Scientific
American, Ja 1886, Vol. 54,
P. 36.

3314   Colored Lights in Parlor
Theatricals. Roy, W.K.
Scientific American, Ja
1881, Vol. 44, P. 24.

3315   Color Codes for Tools
and Uses for Cardboard
Tubing. Bowman, Wayne.
Players Magazine, N, 1956,
Vol. 33, No. 2, P. 35.

3316   Color Design in
Photography. Mante, Harold.
Van Nostrand Reinhold Co.,
1972, New York.

3317   Color for the Curtain.
Architectural Forum, Ap,
1930, Vol. 52, P. 496.

3318   Color for the Stage.
Corson, Richard. Players
Magazine, O 1944, Vol. 21,
No. 1, P. 7.

3319   Columns: an Easy Way.
Chavez, Edmond M. Players,
Mr, 1963, Vol. XXXIX, No.
6, P. 174.

3320   Commedia Dell'arte; a
Study in Italian Popular
Comedy, (The). Smith,
Winifred. Columbia
University Press, 1913,
Vol. XV, P. 290.

3321   Commentary on the
'Historical Development of
the Box Set' (A). Larson,
Orville K. Theatre Annual,
1945, Vol. XII, P. 28-36.

3322   Common Hazards of the
School and College Theatre.
Smith, Harvey K.
Educational Theatre
Journal, Mr 1950, Vol. II,
No. 1, P. 32.

3323   Comparative Analysis of
Five Structural Component
Part Systems for Use in
Platform Construction on
the Stage. Adducci,
Alexander F. M.A. Thesis,
Northern Illinois
University, 1966.

3324   Comparative Study -
Celastic, Plastic, Rok,
Papier Mache. Opsvig,
Virginia. Players Magazine,
My 1954, Vol. 30, No. 8, P.
187.

3325   Competing With a Legend.
Don, Robin. Cue Technical
Theatre Review, Ja/F 1980,
P. 4-5.

3326   Complete Do-It-Yourself
Manual. Reader's Digest.
Readers Digest Assoc.,
1973, Pleasantville, New
York. LOCN: 72-87867

3327   Complete Guide to
Amateur Dramatics. Melvill,
Herald. Citadel, 1958, New
York. LOCN: Pn3151. M4 1958

3328   Complete Metalworking
Manual. Cooley, R.H. Arco
Publishing Company, 1967,
New York.

3329   Complete New Glossary of
Technical Theatrical Terms.
The Strand Electric
Company, 1947, London.

3330   Complete Woodworking.
Adams, J. and Stieri, E.
Arco, 1960, New York.

3331   Composite Tool for the
Lighting Technician.
Hanson, Thomas L. Theatre
Design & Technology My
1971.

3332   Composition and
Rendering. Bishop, Albert
Thornton. Wiley, 1933, New
York, 128 P., Also, Chapman
& Hall, London.

3333   Compressed Air and Gas
Handbook (The). Compressed
Air and Gas Institute
(The), 1961, New York.

3334   Compressed Air Practice.
Richards, Frank.
McGraw-Hill Book Company,
Incorporated, 1913, New
York.

3335   Compressed Air. Hiscox,
Gardner D. Norman W.
Henley and Company, 1901,
New York.

3336   Compressed Air.
Richards, Frank. John Wiley
and Sons, 1907, New York.

3337   Computerized Ticketing.
Theatre Crafts, S 1970,
Vol. 4, No. 4, P. 24-26,
36-38.

3338   Computer Drafting Speeds
Motel Design. Progressive
Architecture, S 1968, P.
151.

3339   Concerning Diagonal
Curtain Tracks. Byles,
R.S. Theatre Notebook,
1953-54, Vol. 8, P. 11-15.

3340   Concerning Gauzes. Tabs,
Ap 1950, Vol. 8, No. 1, P.
10.

3341   Concise Guide to
Plastics. Simonds, Herbert
R. and Church, James M.
Van Nostrand, 1963, New
York.

3342   Concise Guide to
Structural Adhesives.
Guttman, Werner H.
Reinhold Publishing Co.,
1961, New York.

3343   Conjurers of the
Sixteenth Century
Translated by J. B. Mussey.
Volkmann, Kurt. The Sphinx,
Mr 1953, Vol. LII, Pp.
30:36, 53.

3344   Constructing and
Repairing Stage Netting.
Kunz, J. Theatre Crafts S
1976.

3345   Constructing a Remote
Control Smoke Machine.
Cooper, Alec and Scales,
Robert. Theatre Crafts J
1977.

3346   Constructing Model
Buildings. Cleaver, John.
Scopas Handbook (A), 1973,
Academy Editions, London,
St. Martins Press, New
York. ISBN: 0-85670-043-7

3347   Construction
Plastic-Ceramic Masks for
Stage Use. Park, Ralph
Kennedy. Players Magazine,
F 1957, Vol 33, No5, P.
104.

3348   Constructivism in Scene
Design: an Historical and
Critical Study of The Basis
and Development of
Constructivism. Vagenas,
Peter T. Unpublished Ph.D.

Thesis, University of
Denver, 1966.

3349   Constructivism. Cheney,
Sheldon. Theatre Arts
Monthly, N, 1927, Vol. XI,
No. 11, P. 857.

3350   Consultant (The): Then
and Now. Izenour, George
C. Theater Design and
Technology, Summer 1975,
No. 41.

3351   Consulting in the
Theatre. Rosenthal, Jean.
Theatre Design &
Technology, O 1966, No. 6,
P. 38.

3352   Contemporary Polish
Stage Design. Strzelecki,
Zenobiusz. World Theatre,
Su, 1957, Vol. VI, No. 2,
P. 119.

3353   Contemporary Rigging
Systems and Their
Relationship to Theatre
Types. Reinert, Thomas
David. Ph.D. Thesis,
Bowling Green State Univ.,
1976.

3354   Contemporary Scene
Design As Seen by a Chilean
Designer. Trumper,
Bernardo. Interscaena, Fall
1970, Vol.4, No. 4, P. 1-8.

3355   Contemporary Stage and
Costume Design in Hungary.
Corvina Press, 1973,
Budapest.

3356   Contemporary Stage
Design, U.S.A.. Burdick,
Elizabeth B. and Hansen,
Peggy C. and Zanger, Brenda
(Eds). Wesleyan University
Press, 1975, Middletown,
Connecticut. LOCN: Pn 2091
S8 C62

3357   Contemporary Stage
Design in the U.S.S.R.
Korolev, Ivan. Drama, Ja
1930, Vol. 20, P. 99.

3358   Contemporary Survey of
Recent Trends and
Developments in Technical
Theatre at Representative
Colleges and Universities
(A). Gaultney, Richard.
Ph.D. Thesis, University of
Southern Illinois, 1973.

3359   Continental Method of
Scene Painting. Plounin,
V. Beaumont, 1927, London.
Reprint by Da Capo Press,
1979, New York.

3360   Continental Stagecraft.
Macgowan, Kenneth and
Jones, Robert Edmond.
Harcourt, Brace, & Co.,
1922, New York. LOCN:
Pn2570. M3 1964

3361   Contour Curtains.
Billings, Alan G. Players,
N, 1961, Vol. XXXVIII, No.
2, P. 52.

3362   Contribution of the
Robert Bergman Scenic
Studio to Contemporary
American Scene Design
(The). Coughenour, Kay L.
Ph.D. Thesis, Kent State
University, 1973.

3363   Control of Firearms.
Rakusan, Jerome. Guns, My
1967, P. 9.

3364   Conversation With
Svoboda. Casson, Sir Hugh.
Royal Institute of British
Architects Journal, My
1967, Vol. 74 P. 202-203.

3365   Cook Coro-Foam. Cook
Paint & Varnish Co., Kansas
City, Missouri. No Date.

3366   Corinth: Results of
Excavations Conducted by
the American School Of
Classical Studies at
Athens. Stillwell, R.
Theatre (The), 1952, Vol.
II.

3367   Correct Explanation of
the Ghost. Scientific

American, Ag 1863, Vol. 9,
P. 132.

3368   Correspondence About New
Theatres for Old. Gorelik,
Mordecai and Jones, Robert
Edmond. Educational Theatre
Journal, Mr 1968, Vol. XX,
P. 32.

3369   Costume and Scenery for
Amateurs; a Practical
Working Handbook. MacKay,
Constance D'arcy. Holt,
1915, 1932, New York.

3370   Counter View of Multi
Media (A). Clark, Peggy.
Theatre Crafts, O 1970.

3371   Court Theaters of
Drottningholm and
Gripsholm. Beijer, Agne.
Benjamin Blom, 1972, New
York. LOCN: Na6840.S9 B412
1972

3372   Coventry Corpus Christi
Plays. Craig, Hardin.
Oxford Press, 1957. LOCN:
Pr 111.9 E5 N087

3373   Covent Garden's New
Stage. Sphere, My 1901,
Vol. 5, P. 167.

3374   Cpr Urethane Foam:
Pour-Spray-Froth. Upjohn
Co., Cpr 38j6, Torrance,
Calif. No Date.

3375   Craftsman's Approach to
Scenery (The). Buerki,
F.A. M.S. Thesis,
University of Wisconsin,
1935. LOCN: Awm B 8619

3376   Craftsman, (The).
Bernstein, Aline. Theatre
Arts Monthly, Ap 1945, Vol.
XXIX, No. 4, P. 208.

3377   Crafts in Plastic Foam.
Barnsley, Alan.
Watson-Guptill, 1973, New
York. LOCN: Tt 297 B37 1973

3378   Craft and the Theater.
Palmstierna-Weiss, Gunilla.

Craft Horizons, My-Je 1968,
Vol. 28, P. 24-30, 68-69.

3379   Craft of Horace
Armistead (The). Kirstein,
Lincoln. Chrysalis, 1957,
Vol. 10, Nos. 1-2, P. 3-15.

3380   Craig's Greatness. Stage
and Television Today, N 9,
1967, P. 15.

3381   Craig-Shakespeare
Macbeth (The). Ross,
Douglas. Drama, D 1928,
Vol. 19, P. 69.

3382   Creating With Aluminium.
Mattson, Elmer B. Bruce,
1961, Milwaukee.

3383   Creative Artist in the
Theatre (The). Corathiel,
Elisabethe H. C. Theatre
World, N 1949, P. 61, D
1965, Vol. 45.

3384   Creative Crafts for
Everyone. Turner, G. Alan.
Viking Press, 1959, New
York.

3385   Credits. Houghton,
Norris. Theatres Arts
Magazine, N 1946, Vol. XXX,
No. 11, P. 657.

3386   Crisis at Columbia.
Grossman, Bernard A.
Theatre Design &
Technology, My 1971, No.
25, P. 25.

3387   Critical Study of Fluid
Powered Machinery in the
United States (A).
Hufstetler, Lorin. Ph.D.
Thesis, University of
Southern California, 1978.

3388   Crucifer of Blood: John
Wulp Carries on the
Painterly Tradition(The).
MacKay, Patricia. Theatre
Crafts, Ja/f 1979, Vol.
13, No. 1, P. 21.

3389   Crunch of the Curtain
(The). The Guardian, Mr 19,
1979.

3390   Crystal Coffin (The).
Carrington, Hereward.
Modern Mechanics, Mr 1915,
Vol. 30, P. 393-394.

3392   Current Information
Needs for the Performing
Arts Technician. Bowman,
Ned A. Theatre Design &
Technology, Su 1975, No.
41, P. 25.

3393   Curtain-Maker's Handbook
(The). Moreland, F. A.
E.P. Dutton, 1979, New
York.

3394   Curtains for Stage
Settings. Napier, Frank. F.
Muller, 1937, London, 146
P.; S.J.R. Saunders,
Toronto. LOCN: Pn 2091 S8
N27

3395   Curtain Down-To Begin.
Bartram, Reg. Cue Technical
Theatre Review, My/Ju 1980,
P. 19.

3396   Curtain Down on Theatre
Fires. Willis, Richard A.
Theatre Survey N 1972.

3397   Cutting the Expense of
Backdrops With Electricity.
Decker, Hermine Duthie.
Players Magazine, S/O 1932,
Vol. IX, No. 1, P. 9.

3399   Cyclorama (The). Tabs,
Ap 1952, Vol. 10, No. 1, P.
19.

3400   Cyclorama (The).
Scientific American, N
1886, Vol. 55, P. 287, 296.

3402   Czechoslovakian Stage
Design and Scenography
1914-1938: a Survey Part 1.
Burian, Jarka M. Theatre
Design & Technology, Su
1975, No. 41, P. 14.

3403   Czechoslovakian Stage
Design and Scenography
1914-1938: a Survey Part
II. Burian, Jarka M.
Theatre Design &

Technology, Fa 1975, No.
42, P. 23.

3404   Daguerre Et La Lumiere.
Tabs, D 1972, Vol. 30, No.
4, P. 156.

3405   Dance Production.
Lippincott, Gertrude Lawton
(Ed). American Association
for Health, Physical
Education, and Recreation,
1956, Washington, D. C.

3406   Dangerous Properties of
Industrial Materials. Sax,
Irving. Van Nostrand, 1975,
New York.

3407   Davenant, Father of
English Scenery. Southern,
Richard. Life & Letters
To-Day, F 1942, Vol. 32, P.
114-126.

3408   David Belasco:
Naturalism in the American
Theatre. Marker, Lise-Lone.
Princeton University Press,
1975, Princeton, New
Jersey.

3410   David Garrick, Director.
Burnim, Kalman A.
University of Pittsburgh
Press, 1961, Pittsburgh.

3411   Dawn Chiang. Theatre
Crafts, S 1980, Vol. 14,
No. 4, P. 45.

3412   Death, Destruction, and
Detroit at the Schaubuhne
Am Halleschen Ufer.
Butzmann, Volker. Theatre
Design & Technology, Su
1980, Vol. XVI, No. 2, P.
10.

3413   Death in the Pit.
Saturday Review of
Politics, Literature,
Science And Art (The), Ja
1884, Vol. LVII, P. 73-74.

3414   Death of a Painter.
Mielziner, Jo. American
Artist, N 1949, Vol. 13, P.
32-37, 61-63.

3415   Decapitation Mystery
Explained, (The). Newlin,
T. J. Popular Electricty,
Jl 1914, Vol. 29, P. 28-30.

3416   Decor for Arena Staging.
Philippi, Herbert. Players
Magazine, D, 1951, Vol. 28,
No. 3, P. 56.

3417   Decor for Dance.
Ter-Arutunian, Rouben. New
York Times, Jl 14, 1963.

3418   Decor of the New Opera,
(The). Hart, Jerome.
International Studio ,
1926, Vol. 38, P. 67-70.

3419   Degaetani, Rubin and
Swinney-Define the U.S.
Institute For Theatre
Technology. Theatre Crafts,
N/D 1967, P. 18-23.

3420   Deluge - the Show That
Electricity Made Possible
(The). Holmes, George.
Electrical Experimenter, F
1918, Vol. 5, P. 668-669.

3421   Demountable, Disposable
Module Stage Platform (A).
Parola, Gene. Theatre
Design & Technology F 1967.

3422   Deriving Precise
Measurements from Scenic
Sketches: Perspective
Rendering by Hand-Held
Calculator, Part II.
Hoffman, Paul S. Theatre
Design & Technology, Summer
1979, Vol. XV, No. 2, P. 5.

3423   Description of
Stephenson's Theatre
Machinery. Birch, J. B.
Institution of Civil
Engineers. Proceedings, Je
1841, Vol. 1, P. 153.

3424   Description of the
Festum Praesentationis
Beataem a Fourteenth
Century Prompt Book.
Mexieres, Phillippe De. A.
Kner, New Haven. No Date.

3425   Descriptive Study of
Scenic Styles in the
Productions of Successful
Serious American Drama on
the New York Stage of the
1920's. Kadlec, Anthony
Lawrence. Ph.D. Thesis,
Michigan Stage University,
1969.

3426   Design: Discipline.
Armstrong, W.S. Theatre
Crafts, Mr/Ap 1967, Vol. 1,
No. 1, P. 16-19.

3427   Designer's Delemma.
Strike, Maurice. Canadian
Theatre Review, Wi 1974,
No. 1, P. 45.

3429   Designer's Portfolio,
(A). Kerr, Mary. Canadian
Theatre Review, Sp 1974,
No. 2, P. 34-39.

3430   Designer-Director
Relationship: Form and
Process (The). Benedetti,
Robert. Theatre Crafts,
Ja/f 1979, Vol. 13, No. 1,
P. 36.

3431   Designer/Director
Relationship: the
Integration of Action and
Environment. Benedetti,
Robert. Theatre Crafts, O,
1979, Vol. 13, No. 5, P.
31.

3432   Designers Difficulties.
Lees, Alan. Theatre
Australia, D 1976, Vol. 1,
No. 5, P.50.

3433   Designers for the Dance.
Fatt, Amelia. Dance
Magazine, F 1967, Vol. 41,
P. 42-50; Ap 1967, P.
55-58.

3434   Designer (The).
Hastings, Baird. Dance
Magazine, My 1951, Vol. 25,
P. 24.

3435   Designer As Taxpayer
(The). Hanlon, R. Brendan.
Theatre Crafts, Ja/f 1978,
Vol. 12, No. 1, P. 69.

3436   Designer for Exotic Movement, (A). Williams, Peter. Dance and Dancers, Mr 1952, Vol. 3, P. 14-15.

3437   Designer in the Theatre (The). Siminson. International Exhibition of Theatre Arts, Museum of Modern Art, 1934, New York.

3438   Designer Sets the Stage; Jo Mielziner Aline Bernstein. Houghton, Norris. Theatre Arts Magazine, F 1937, Vol. XXI, No. 2, P. 115,.

3439   Designer Talks: Oliver Smith in Interview With Robert Whaterhouse, (The). Plays and Players, N 1970, Vol. 18, P. 20-21.

3440   Designer Talks: Patrick Robertson in Conversation With Michael Billington. Robertson, Patrick. Plays and Players, Ap 1970, P. 16-17.

3441   Designer Talks: Timothy O'Brienin Conversation With Michael Billington (The). O'Brien, Timothy. Plays and Players, O 1969, P. 44-45.

3442   Designing and Building a Solar House: Your Place in the Sun. Watson, Donald. Garden Way Publishing, 1977, Charlott, Vt.. LOCN: 76-53830 ISBN: 0-88266-086-1

3443   Designing and Making Stage Scenery. Warre, Michael. Studio Vista Ltd, London; Reinhold Book Corp., New York, 1968. LOCN: Pn2091. S8 W34 1966 ISBN: 289 36885 5

3444   Designing and Painting for the Theatre. Pecktal, Lynn. Holt, Rinehart and Winston, 1975, New York, 412 P.. LOCN: Pn2091.S8 P37 ISBN: 0030122767

3445   Designing and Painting Scenery for the Theatre. Melvill, Herald. Barrie & Rockliff, 1963, London.

3446   Designing at the Centre. Laufer, Murray. Canadian Theatre Review, Sum 1974, No. 3, P. 42-45.

3447   Designing a School Play. Chilver, Peter and Jones, Eric. Taplinger Publisher, 1970, New York. ISBN: 0-8008-2171-8

3448   Designing for a New Vision: Director-Designer Jean-Pierre Ponnelle's Controversial Settings. Loney, Glenn. Theatre Crafts, Mr/Ap 1978, Vol. 12, No. 3, P. 15.

3449   Designing for Ballet. Williams, Peter. Dance and Dancers, My 1950, P. 18.

3450   Designing for Films. Carrick, Edward. Studio Publications, 1949, London.

3451   Designing for Gilbert and Sullivan. Coffin, Peter. Studio Pub, 1941, New York.

3452   Designing for Moving Pictures. Carrick, Edward. Studio Publishers (The), 1941, New York.

3453   Designing for the Stage. Zinkesen Noris. Studio (The), 1945, New York. LOCN: Pn2091 S8f 382

3454   Designing for the Stage. Svoboda, Josef. Opera, Ag 1967, Vol. 18, P. 631-636.

3455   Designing for the Theatre: a Memoir and a Portfolio. Mielziner, Jo. Atheneum, 1965, New York.

3456   Designing for the Theatre: Continental Methods at the Slade

School. Laver, James.
Studio, D 1934, Vol. 108,
P. 261.

3457   Designing for Tv: the
Arts and Crafts in
Television Production.
Wade, Robert J. Pellegrini
& Cudahy, 1952, New York.

3458   Designing Hamlet With
Appia. Van Wyck, Jessica
Davis. Theatre Arts
Monthly, Ja, 1925, Vol. IX,
No. 1, P. 17.

3459   Designing of Stage
Scenery and the Present
Chaotic Condition of the
Art in America. Meyer,
Baron De. Vanity Fair, N
1916, Vol. VII, P. 69.

3460   Designing Scenery and
Lighting for the American
Place Theatre. Lundell,
Kert. Theatre Crafts Mr
1967.

3461   Designing With Levels.
Batcheller, David R.
Players, My, 1962, Vol.
XXXVIII, NO. 8, P. 248.

3462   Designs by Inigo Jones
for Masques & Plays at
Court. Jones, Inigo.
Russell & Russell, 1966,
New York.

3463   Designs for the First
Movable Scenery on the
English Public Stage,
(The). Keith, William
Grant. Burlington Magazine,
Ap 1914, Vol. 25, P. 29-33;
My 1914, P. 85-98.

3464   Design and Construction
of Theatres. Morin, Roi L.
American Architect, 1922,
P.395-402,443-450,453-456,4
93-496,507-510,537-542,533-
Vol. 122; 1923, P.57-58,6.

3465   Design and Technology of
the Federal Theatre
Project. Saltzman, Jared.
Ph.D. Thesis, New York
(School of the Arts), 1980.

3466   Design for Acting..
Russell, John A. Royal
Architectural Institute of
Canada Journal, My 1941,
Vol. 18, P P. 79-82.

3467   Design for a Living.
Hellman, Geoffrey T. New
Yorker, F 8, 1941, Vol.
16-17; F 15, 22, 1941.

3468   Design for a New Kind of
Theatre. Bel Geddes,
Norman. New York Times
Magazine, N 30, 1947, P.
24-25.

3469   Design for Ballet.
Clarke, Mary and Crisp,
Clement. Hawthorn Books,
Inc. 1978, New York. ISBN:
0-8015-2020-7

3470   Design for the Ballet.
Beaumont, Cyril William.
The Studio Publications,
1937, New York. LOCN: Gv
1787 B38

3471   Design for the Musical
Stage. Bay, Howard. Theatre
Arts, N 1945, Vol. 29, P.
650.

3472   Design for the Stage:
First Steps. Payne, Darwin
Reid. Southern Illinois
University Press, 1974,
Carbondale. LOCN: Pn 2091
S8 P35

3473   Design in the Russian
Theatre. Raffe, W.G.
Studio (The), Ja 1942, Vol.
123, P. 16-19.

3474   Design in the Theatre.
Sheringham, G. Blom, 1971,
New York. LOCN: Pn 2091 S8
S5 1971

3475   Design in the Theatre.
Marshall, Herbert. Studio
(The), F 1944, Vol. 127, P.
47-52.

3476   Design in the Works
Progress Administration's
Federal Theatre Project

(1935 to 1939). Billings, Alan G. Ph.D. Thesis, University of Illinois, 1967, Urbana-Champaign.

3477   Design Techniques of Gabor Forray, National Opera, Budapest, (The). Loney, Glenn. Theatre Design & Technology, O 1974, No. 38, P. 10-16.

3478   Design through Evolution: Michael Yeargan's Umbrellas of Cherbourg. McDowell, Michael S. Theatre Design & Technology, Wi, 1979, Vol. XV, No. 4, P. 23-25.

3479   Design With Computers? It's Whats Happening, Baby!. Stewart, Clifford Douglas. Progressive Architecture, Jl 1966, P. 157.

3480   Deus Ex Machina: Flying Effects on the Renaissance Stage. Mahler, Frank C. Theatre Survey No. 23, 1976/7.

3481   Developing the Undergraduate Designers Three-Dimensional Vision. Gordon, John. Theatre Crafts, S 1979, Vol. 13, No. 4, P. 95.

3482   Development of Adjustability in Platform Height (The). Parola, Gene. Aeta-Saa, 1966, Chicago, Illinois.

3483   Development of an Electrically Controlled Mobile Winch Fly System for the Theatre. Lusk, Carol Brooks. M.F.A. Thesis, Yale University, 1952.

3484   Development of Dramatic Art, (The). Stuart, Donald Clive. Dover Publications, Inc., 1960, New York.

3485   Development of Methods

of Flying Scenery on the English Stage 1860-1880 (The). Stockbridge, S. M.A. Thesis, Stamford University, 1961. LOCN: Pn 2091 S8 S75

3486   Development of Spectacle As Exemplified in the Ballet of Faust (The). Spielman, M. H. Magazine of Art, D 1895, P. 25-28.

3487   Development of Stage Rigging in the United States 1766-1893 (The). Green, John H. Ph.D. Thesis, University of Denver, 1955.

3488   Development of the English Playhouse (The). Leacroft, Richard. Cornell University Press, 1973, Ithaca, NY. LOCN: Na 6840 G7 L4

3489   Devices and Feintes of Medieval Religious Theatre in England and France. Young, Donald William. Ph.D. Thesis, Stanford, 1960. LOCN: 7381 S78y

3490   Device for Producing Stage Illusion. Popular Mechanics, N 1913, Vol. 20, P. 693.

3491   Device Operate Theatre Curtain Automatically. Popular Mechanics, S 1916, Vol. 26, P. 234.

3492   Devil Motorizes (The). Scientific American, Mr 1929, Vol. 140, P. 144, 145.

3493   De Cristoforo's Complete Book of Power Tools. De Cristoforo, R.J. Harper & Row, 1972, New York. LOCN: 72-90935 ISBN: 60-010999-8

3494   De Loutherbourg and Captain Cook. Allen, Ralph G. Theatre Notebook, 1962, Vol. IV, No. 3, P. 195.

3495   Diaghilev & Russian
Stage Designers.
International Exhibitions
Foundation. International
Exhibitions Foundation,
1972, Washington, D. C.

3496   Diagnosing the Physical
Stage. Drama, (The), F
1929, P. 149.

3497   Diary of a Designer:
Setting the Stage for
"Quadrille". Beaton, Cecil.
Theatre Arts, N, 1954, Vol.
XXXVIII, No. 11 , P. 21.

3498   Digital Device for
Telementry and Control in
the Theatre and Television
Applications. Read, James
L. M.F.A. Thesis, 1962,
Yale University.

3499   Dioramic Panorama of the
Exposition of 1900 (The).
Scientific American
Supplement, Ja 1900, Vol.
49, P. 20086, 20087.

3500   Directory of American
College Theatre (1976).
White, Allen S. American
Theatre Association
Publication, 1976.

3501   Directory of Bicentenial
Resources for Designers.
Theatre Crafts, O 1975.

3502   Directory of Canadian
Theatre Schools (A). Rubin,
Don and Cranmer-Bying,
Alison. Canadian Theatre
Review Publications
(Ontario) 1979. ISBN:
0-920644-71-6

3503   Directory of Costume
Related Supplies and
Equipment. USITT Costume
Commission. No Date.

3504   Directory of Graduate
Programs in Theatre Design
and Technology. Smith,
R.L. USITT Education
Commission, 1978.

3505   Directory of Technical
Literature. Lucier, Mary.
Theatgre Crafts, F 1978,
Vol. 12, No. 2, P. 4.

3506   Directory of Technical
Literature. Theatre Crafts,
Ja 1977.

3507   Discovering the Art of
Arena Musical Design.
Kimmel, Alan. Theatre
Crafts, S/O 1968, Vol. 2,
No. 5, P. 15.

3508   Discussion of Scene
Shops. Theatre Crafts, S
1970, P.28.

3509   Disegni Teatrali Di
Inigo Jones. Jones, Inigo.
N. Pozza 1969.

3510   Disneyland and
Disneyworld. Theatre
Crafts, S 1977, Vol. 11 No.
4, P. 33.

3511   Dissertation on the
Pageants or Dramatic
Mysteries Anciently
Performed at Coventry (A).
Sharp, Thomas. Rowman &
Littlefield, 1973, Totawa,
N.J.. LOCN: Pr644 C7 S5
1973 Folio

3512   Distance-Does It Lend
Enchantment?. Theatre
Crafts, My/Je 1971, Vol. 5,
No. 3, P. 26.

3513   Divertissements,
January, 1941; This
Festival Has Been Arranged
by Georges De Batz. Johns
Hopkins University, 1941.

3514   Do-It-Yourself Roofing
and Siding. Alth, Max.
Hawthorn Books, Inc., 1977,
New York. LOCN: 76-56515
ISBN: 0-8015-2150-5

3515   Dobson's Theatre Year
Book, 1948-49. Dennis
Dobson, 1948, London.

3516   Documents Relating to

the Office of the Revels in the Time Of Queen Elizabeth. Feuillerat, Albert (Ed). A. Uystpruyst, 1908, Louvain.

3517   Documents Relating to the Revels at Court in the Time of King Edward VI and Queen Mary. Feuillerat, Albert (Ed). A Uystpruyst, 1914, Louvain.

3518   Don't Rake the Stage. Tabs, Ap 1948, Vol. 6, No. 1, P. 21.

3519   Donald M. Oenslager: in Memorium. Carrington, Frank. Theatre Design & Technology, Fa 1975, No. 42, P. 9.

3520   Donald Oenslager: Stage Designer and Teacher. Detroit Institute of Arts, 1956.

3521   Don Juan Goes to Hell Electro Mechanically at Carnegie Mellon Univ. Theatre Design & Technology D 1965.

3522   Doors and Curtains in Restoration Theatres. Nicoll, Allardyce. Modern Language Review, 1920, Vol. 15, P. 137-142.

3523   Double Gothic: the Scenography of Michael Kirby. McNamara, Brooks. Theatre Design & Technology, Wi 1979, Vol. XV, No. 4, P. 20-23.

3524   Double Wall Cardboard Scenery. Hobgood, B.M. Players Magazine, Ja 1957, Vol 33, No 4, P. 86.

3525   Dover Stage Lift Helps Create a Theatre for All Seasons. Architectural Record, Ag 1971, P.34.

3526   Down to the Cellar. Simonson, Lee. Theatre Arts

Magazine, Ap 1922, Vol. VI, No. 2, P. 119.

3527   Do You Know the Exploration Gap?. Davidson, Gordon. Theatre Design & Technology, Su 1975, No. 41, P. 7.

3528   Drama: Its Costume and Decor. Laver, James. Studio, 1951, London.

3530   Dramatic Documents from the Elizabethan Playhouses. Greg, W. W. (Ed.). Oxford, 1931.

3531   Dramatic Festivals of Athens (The). Pickard-Cambridge, A. W. Oxford, 1953, London.

3532   Dramatic Imagination (The). Jones, Robert Edmond. Duell, Sloan & Pearce, 1941, New York.

3533   Dramatic Museum. Columbia University. Dramatic Museum of Columbia University, 1916.

3534   Dramatic Records of Sir Henry Herbert, Master of Revels, 1623-1673. Adams, Joseph Quincy, Editor. B. Blom, 1964, New York. LOCN: Pn2592 A5 1964

3535   Dramatizing the Theatre. Carter, Huntly. Forum, Jl 1914, Vol. 52, P. 60.

3536   Drama in a Supermarket Basement: the Roundabout Theatre Company. Theatre Crafts, Mr/Ap 1974, Vol. 8, No. 2, P. 12.

3537   Drawing, Design and Craftwork. Nagler, A.M. Scribner, 1934, New York, 262 P., Also, Batsford, London, 1920.

3538   Drawings for Film Sets, the Work of Antongrot. London Studio (The), D 1938, Vol. 16, P. 302-303.

3539   Drawings for the
Theatre. Jones, Robert
Edmond. Theatre Arts, Inc.,
1925.

3540   Drawing Distortion.
Conway, John A. Players
Magazine, O 1953.

3541   Drottingholm
Theatre--Past and Present
(The). Hillestrom, Gustaf.
Natur Och Kultur, 1956,
Stockholm.

3542   Drottingholm Theatre
Museum (The). Beijer, Agne.
Theatre Arts Magazine, Mr
1934, Vol. XVIII, No. 3.

3543   Drury Lane Stage, Its
Machinery and Mechanical
Equipment. Stage Year Book,
1910, P. 20-23.

3544   Dual Control. Loney,
Glenn. Opera News, D 1969,
Vol. 37, P. 25.

3545   Dual Role for the Safety
Curtain. Tabs D 1970.

3546   Duties of Stage Hands.
Shaw, Mary. Strand Magazine
(N.Y.), D 1912, Vol. 44, P.
605.

3547   Early American Scene
Painters. Lawrence, William
John. New York Dramatic
Mirror, Ja 13, 1917, Vol.
LXXVII, P. 7.

3548   Early American Scene
Painters. White, Carl. M.A.
Thesis, University of Utah,
1954.

3549   Early English Stages.
Wickham, Glynne W.
Columbia University Press
1959 New York. LOCN:
Pn2587. W53

3550   Early Multiple Settings
in England. Byrne, Muriel
St. Clare. Theatre
Notebook, 1953, Vol. 8, P.
81.

3551   Early Scene Design of
Mordecai Gorelik. Brasmer,
William. OSU Theatre
Collection Bulletin, 1965,
Vol. 12, P. 44-54.

3552   Early Scene Painting.
Cook, D. Builder (The),
1859, Vol. XVII, P. 354.

3553   Early Stage Decoration
in the American Theatre
1772-1872. Duerr, E. M.A.
Thesis Cornell Univ. 1931.

3554   Early 16th Centurey
Scenic Design in the
National Museum, Stockholm,
and Its Historical
Background. Beijer, Agne.
Theatre Notebook, 1962,
Vol. IV, No. 2, P. 85-155.

3555   Earth to Earth.
Simonson, Lee and Young,
Stark. New Republic, N 16,
1932, Vol. 73, P. 19-20.

3556   Easements of Light;
Modern Methods of Computing
Compensation. Swarbrick,
John. B.T. Batsford, 1931,
London.

3557   East and West Germany.
Riddell, Richard. Theatre
Design & Technology, Sp
1980, Vol. XVI, No. 1, P.
15-20.

3558   Easy Entrikin Hand
Puppet Booth. Entrikin,
Paul P. Players Magazine,
Mr, 1949, Vol. 25, No. 6,
P. 138.

3559   Edinburgh Festival: on
and Off the Fringe (The).
Loney, Glenn. Theatre
Crafts, My/Je 1979, Vol.
13, No. 3, P. 13.

3560   Education of Theatre
Technicians. Jewell, James
Earl. M.F.A. Thesis, Yale
University, 1958.

3561   Edward Gorden Craig &
Scenography. Bablet, Denis.

Theatre Research, 1971,
Vol. XI, No. 1, P. 7.

3562   Edward Gordon Craig and
Scenography. Fletcher, Ifan
Kyrle and Rood, Arnold.
Society for Theatre
Research, 1967, London.

3563   Edward Gordon Craig: a
New Stage Genius. Norman,
Gertrude. Theatre, Je 1905,
Vol. 5, P. 147.

3564   Edward Gordon Craig's
Theory of the Art of the
Theatre of the Future.
Herstand, Theodore. Ph.D.
Thesis, University of
Illinois, 1963.

3565   Edward Gordon Craig and
Macbeth. Sheren, Paul.
Ph.D. Thesis, Yale
University, 1974.

3566   Edward Gordon Craig
Designs for the Theatre.
Leeper, Janet. Penguin
Books, 1948, Harmondsworth,
England.

3567   Edward Gordon Craig.
Harsbarger, Karl. Plays and
Players, Ja 1956, Vol. 41,
P. 103.

3568   Edward Gordon Craig.
Nash, George. Her Majesty's
Stationary Office, 1967,
London.

3569   Edward Gordon Craig.
Bablet, Denis. Heinemann,
1966, New York.

3570   Edward Gordon Craig.
Bablet, Denis. Theatre Arts
Books, 1966, New York.

3571   Edward Gordon Graig: a
Check-List. Fletcher, Ifan
Kyrle. Theatre Arts
Monthly, Ap 1935, Vol. XIX,
No. 4, P. 293.

3572   Effects of Architectual
Training With Frank Lloyd
Wright on The Scene Designs

of Sean Kenny (The).
Hunter, Harold. Ph.D.
Thesis, University of Ohio,
1978.

3573   Effects of New Materials
and Techniques in Stage
Scenery on The Theater
Director and Designer.
Seay, Donald W. Ph.D.
Thesis, University of
Minnesota, 1969.

3574   Effects on the Stage.
Pomeroy, W. H. Home and
Country Magazine, N 1893,
Vol. 9, P. 1743-1754.

3575   Effect and the Cause:
Stage Illusions, The.
Illustrated London News, Je
1909, Vol. 134, P. 819.

3576   Egmont. Gouche Original
Drawing, 1949. located at
the Harvard Theatre
Collection.

3577   Egress from Theatres on
Alarm of Fire. Builder,
(The), F 20, 1864, Vol
Xxii, P. 138, See Also 115.

3578   Eidophusikon, (The).
Allen, Ralph G. Theatre
Design & Technology, D
1966, No. 7, P. 12-16.

3579   Eighteenth Century
Theatrical Illusions in
Light of Contemporary
Documents. Burnim, Kalman
A. Theatre Notebook, Wi
1959, Vol. XIV, No. 2, P.
45.

3580   Eldon Eldert Designs for
the Theatre. Drama Book
Specialists, 1979, New
York, New York, 10019.

3581   Electrical Aids to the
Drama. Scientific American
D 22 1888.

3582   Electrical and
Mechanical Equipment of a
Modern European Theatre,
the. Koester, Franz.

Electrical Review, My 1904,
Vol. 44, P. 729-732.

3583   Electrical Equipment of
the Modern Theatre (The).
Hume, D.C.M. Electrician,
(The), My 19, 1911, Vol.
LXVII, P. 253. See Also P.
206.

3584   Electrical Equipment of
the World's Largest Stage;
New Al Malaika Temple Civic
Auditorium in Los Angeles.
Sanborn, C.A. Journal of
Electricity, 1926, Vol. 57,
P. 80-85.

3585   Electrical Manipulation
of Theatrical Machinery
(The). Scientific American
Supplement, O 1899, Vol.
48, P. 19873.

3586   Electrical Safety.
Dahlquist, Ron. Lighting
Dimensions, O 1979, Vol. 3,
No. 10, P. 36-37.

3587   Electricity and the
School Entertainment.
Journal of Electricity,
1920, Vol. 44, P. 614-616.

3588   Electricity Behind the
Stage. Scientific American
Supplement, My 1890, Vol.
29, P. 11954.

3589   Electricity in the
Theater. Scientific
American Supplement, O
1896, Vol. 42, P. 17331,
17332.

3590   Electric Brakes Put
Quiet Stop and Hold
Performance Backstage at
the Met. Theatre Design &
Technology Wi 1976.

3591   Electric Cartooning:
Projections Simplify Set
Painting. Sporre, Dennis
J. Theatre Crafts, N/D
1971, Vol. 5, No. 6, P. 17.

3592   Electric Curtain of the
Comedie Francaise (The).

Scientific American
Supplement, Mr 1893, Vol.
35, P. 14367.

3593   Electric Drive Applied
to Movable Theatre Stages.
Holmes, J.T., Et Al.
Electrical World, 1926,
Vol. 87, P. 598-600.

3594   Electric Stage Lights.
Scientific American
Supplement, Jl 1911, Vol.
72, P. 53.

3595   Electric Stage Mechanism
at the Covent Garden Opera
House. Electrician, My
1901, Vol. 47, P. 85-88.

3596   Electronic Aid to a
Magical Act (The). ABTT
News, Je 1980, P. 22.

3597   Elegant Minimal
Settings. Theatre Crafts, O
1971, Vol. 5, No. 5, P. 6.

3598   Elements of a Work of
Living Art (The). Appia,
Adolphe. Theatre Arts
Monthly, Ag, 1932, Vol.
XVI, No. 8, P. 667.

3599   Elements of Stagecraft.
Baker, James W. Alfred
Publishing Co., 1978,
Sherman Oaks, Ca. LOCN:
Pn2086.B3 ISBN:
0-88284-053-3

3600   Elements of Stage
Design. Amberg, George.
Interiors, F 1948, Vol.
107, P. 86-89; Ap 1948, P.
105-112; Je 1948, P.
109-115.

3601   Elements on the Stage:
Thunder, Lightning, Wind,
Rain and Fire (The).
Scientific American, Ap
1913, Vol. 108, P. 369,
373, 374.

3602   Elephant Man, Anatomy of
a Design (The). MacKay,
Patricia. Theatre Crafts,
Ja/F 1980, Vol. 14, No. 1,
P. 24-25, 80-81.

3603   Eleven Designers Answer.
Plays and Players, N 1962,
Vol. 10, P. 21.

3604   Elizabethan Interior and
Aloft Scenes: a Speculative
Essay. Weiner, Albert B.
Theatre Survey, 1961, Vol.
II.

3605   Elizabethan Legerdemain
and Its Employment in the
Drama 1576-1642.
Schneidman, Robert. Ph.D.
Thesis, Northwestern
University, 1956. LOCN:
Pr658 M27 S25

3606   Elizabethan Playhouse
and Other Studies.
Lawrence, William John. J.
B. Lippincott Company,
1912, Philadelphia;
Shakespeare Head Press,
1912, Stratford-Upon-Avon.

3607   Empty Space, (The).
Brook, Peter. Atheneum
Press, 1968, New York.

3608   Encyclopaedia of
Superstitions. Radford, E.
and Radford, M.A.
(Editors). Philosophical
Library, 1949, New York.

3609   Encyclopedia of American
Scenographers: 1900-1960
(An). Hippely, E.C. Ph.D.
Thesis, University of
Denver, 1966.

3610   Encyclopedia of
Household Plumbing
Installation and Repair
(The). Clifford, Martin.
Bonanza Books, 1975, New
York. LOCN: 75-10777

3611   Encyclopedia of
Scenographers 534bc-1900
(An). Lacy, Robin. Ph.D.
Thesis, University of
Denver, 1959.

3612   Energy-Saving Home
Improvements. Drake, 1977,
New York. LOCN: 77-6208
ISBN: 0-8473-1567-3

3613   Engineering Concepts in
Stage Equipment. Soot, O.
Theatre Design & Technology
O 1966.

3615   Engineering on the
Stage. Fuerst, Artur.
Engineering Progress, 1920,
Vol. 1, P. 345-350.

3616   English Scene Painter in
America, An. Speaight,
George. Theatre Notebook,
Jl/S 1956, Vol. 10, P.
122-124.

3617   Ensemble Design.
Spector, Susan. Theatre
Crafts, Mr/Ap 1979, Vol.
12, No. 3, P. 24.

3618   Enter the Scenic Artist:
Robert Edmond Jones. Brown,
John Mason. Upstage: the
American Theatre in
Performance, 1930, P. 158.

3619   Epic Scene Design.
Gorelik, Mordecai. Theatre
Arts Magazine, O 1959, Vol.
XLII, No. 10, P. 75.

3620   Episode With Gas (An).
Applebee, L.G. Tabs, Ap,
1957. Vol. 15, No. 1, P.
31.

3621   Epoch, the Life of
Steele MacKaye. MacKaye,
Percy. Boni & Liveright,
1927, New York.

3622   Equipment for Stage
Production; a Manual of
Scene Building. Krows,
Arthur Edwin. D. Appleton &
Co., 1928, New York. LOCN:
Pn 2091 S8k7

3623   Equipment of the School
Theater (The). Smith,
Milton Myers. Bureau of
Publications, Teachers
College, Columbia
University, 1930, New York,
Ams Press, 1972, New York.
LOCN: Pn3178.S8 S6 1972
ISBN: 0404554210

3624   Equipment of the School
Theatre. Smith, Milton
Myers. Ph.D. Thesis,
Columbia University, 1930.

3625   Equipping the D. E.
(Dramatic Education) Room.
Tabs Mr 1966.

3626   Era of the Box Set
(The). Lawrence, William
John. New York Dramatic
Mirror, F 1917, Vol.
LXXVII, P. 7.

3627   Ernest Albert, Twenty
Years after. Krows, Arthur
Edwin. New York Dramatic
Mirror, N 19, 1913, P. 3.

3628   Romain de Tirtoff.
Spencer, Charles. C. N.
Potter, 1970, New York.

3629   Erwin Piscator's
Political Theatre. Innes,
C. D. Cambridge University
Press, 1972, Cambridge.

3630   Erwin Piscator and His
'Total Theatre'. Pugh,
Anthony. Cue Technical
Theatre Review, Ja/F 1980,
P. 8-9.

3631   Essays on Nineteenth
Century British Theatre.
Merchant, W. Moelwyn.
Methuen, 1971, P. 171.

3632   Essentials of Stage
Planning. Bell, Stanley and
Marshall, Norman and
Southern, Richard.' Muller,
1949, London. ISBN: 812
8413es

3633   Essentials of Stage
Scenery. Selden, Samuel and
Rezzuto, Tom.
Appleton-Century-Crofts,
1972, New York. LOCN:
Pn2091.S8 S44 ISBN:
0390793515

3634   Eton College: New Hall.
Reid, Francis. Tabs Mr
1969.

3635   Eugene Berman. Levy,
Julien. American Studio, C.
1940, New York.

3636   Eugene O'Neill and
Robert Edmond Jones: Text
into Scene. Sweet, Harvey.
Ph.D. Thesis, 1974,
University of Wisconsin,
Madison.

3637   Europe in the Seventies.
Loney, Glenn. Theatre
Crafts, Ja/F 1980, Vol. 14,
No. 1, P. 23.

3638   Evaluation of the
Employment of Panoramic
Scenery in the
Nineteenth-Century Theatre
(An). Wickman, Richard
Carl. Ph.D. Thesis, Ohio
State University, 1961.

3639   Evita: Staging on a
Grand Opera Scale. MacKay,
Patricia. Theatre Crafts,
N/D 1979, Vol. 13, No. 6,
P. 15-19.

3640   Evolution of a Play.
Theatre Magazine(The), ,
1902, Vol. II, No. 21, p.
14.

3641   Evolution of Baroque
Theatre Design in Italy
(The). Niemeyer, Charles.
Theatre Annual, 1942, P.
36-42.

3642   Evolution of Scene
Painting (The). Matthews,
Brander. Unlabeled
Clipping. Located at Forbes
Library, Northampton, MA.
LOCN: Vuf M43

3643   Evolution of Scenic
Spectacles in France
(1600-1673): National and
Italian Origins of the
Machines Play (The).
Langlois, Walter Gordon,
Jr. Ph.D. Thesis, Yale
University, 1955.

3644   Evolution of the Methods
of Shifting Scenery As

Practiced in European and American Theatres (The). Green, Norman Worcester. M.A. Thesis, Miami University, 1952.

3645   Exempt Organizations and the Arts. Lidstone, Herrick K. and Ruble, R.J. Volunteer Lawyers for the Arts, 36 West 44 St., Suite 1110, Ny, N.Y. 10036. No Date.

3646   Exhibition of Stage Architecture and Lighting at the Museum of Modern Art. Art Digest, S 1946, Vol. XX, P. 11.

3647   Exhibition of Theatrical Designs and Historical Materials from the Suny-Binghamton Theater Collections. University Art Gallery, 1970, Binghamton, New York.

3648   Experimenting With New Materials for Masks and Props. Skow, M. and Ackler, B. Theatre Crafts, S 1976.

3649   Experiments in Moving Scenery With Low-Friction Plastics. Glerum, Jay. Theatre Design & Technology, Su 1980, Vol. XVI, No. 2, P. 17-18.

3650   Experiments in the Use of Corrugated Cardboard for Stage Scenery. Bennett, Gordon. M.A. Thesis, University of Denver, 1961.

3651   Experiment in Ballet Design (An). Williams, Peter. Dance and Dancers, Ap 1959, P. 15-17.

3652   Experiment in Chemical Architecture (An). Drury, Ralph. Yale School of Art and Architecture, 1968, New Haven, Ct.

3653   Experiment in Response by Different Temperament

Types to Different Styles of Set Design. Pickett, Warren Wheeler. Ph.D. Dissertation, 1969, University of Michigan.

3654   Experiment in the Extension of the Opera Stage: Integration of Theatre and Film. Ford, Stephen. Theatre Design & Technology, D 1966.

3655   Explanation of Lumber Standards. Department of Agriculture, 1931, Washington, D. C.. Miscellaneous Publication No. 107.

3656   Explosives Add Realism to the Movies. Wharton, Mel. Explosives Engineer (The), Mr, 1930, Vol. 8, P. 103.

3657   Expo 70: Some Interesting Effects at Osaka. Ogawa, T. Theatre Design & Technology, D 1970.

3658   Expressionism in Twentieth Century Stage Design. Smith, Marjorie Marie. Unpublished Ph.D. Thesis, University of Michigan 1960.

3659   Expressionistic Scenography Without Complex Machinery: Georg Kaiser's Morn Till Midnight at the University of Vermont. Collett, Jerry and Robbins, Kathleen M. Theatre Crafts, S 1978, Vol. 12, No. 5, P. 48.

3660   Expression in Stage Scenery. Hewitt, Barnard. Studies in Speech and Drama in Honor of Alexander M. Drummond, Russell & Russell Publishers, 1944, P. 54.

3661   Fabrication of Dow Foam Plastics. Midland: the Dow Chemical Company, C. 1967.

3662   Fairwell to Scene
Architecture. Kernodle,
George R. Quarterly
Journal of Speech, 1939,
Vol. 25, P. 649.

3663   Falling Leaves in a
Nature Scene. Jocelyn, S.
E. Popular Mechanics, N
1913, Vol. 20, P. 762.

3665   Far Beyond Reality.
Schickel, Richard. New York
Times Magazine, M 18, 1980,
P. 40.

3666   Fatal Firearm Accidents
in the United States.
Statistical Bulletin
Metropolitan Life Insurance
C Company, S 1966, Vol.
XXXXVI, P. 1.

3667   Fear of Filing.
Volunteer Lawyers for the
Arts, 36 West 44 St., Suite
1110, Ny, Ny, 10036. No
Date.

3668   Federal Gun Laws. Henry
Schlesinger, 1963, New
York.

3669   Federal Theatre Project
Blueprints. Federal Theatre
Project-Research Centre at
George Mason University.

3670   Federal Theatre Project
Plates on Scenic
Construction, Painting.
Federal Theatre
Project-Research Centre at
George Mason University.

3671   Federal Theatre Project
Script Collection (By
Title). Federal Theatre
Project-Research Centre at
George Mason University.

3672   Federal Theatre Project
Technical Purchases Card
File. Federal Theatre
Project-Research Centre at
George Mason University.

3673   Feeling and Form.
Langer, Susanne. Charles

Scribner's Sons, 1953, New
York.

3674   Feller's Scenic Studio.
New Yorker, Je 2, 1975,
Vol. 51, P. 29-32.

3675   Festival Designs. Jones,
Inigo. Meridan Co., 1967.
LOCN: Nc 1115 J57 568

3676   Festive Face: Opera,
Theatre and Dance in
Celibration (The). Theatre
Crafts, Mr/Ap 1977, Vol.
II, No. 2, P. 8.

3677   Fiberglass for the
Theatre. White, R. K.
Theatre Design &
Technology, O 1969, No. 18,
P. 28.

3678   Fiberglass Layup and
Sprayup, Good Practices for
Employees. Government
Printing Office
017-033-00139-1. No Date.

3679   Fiberglass Reinforced
Plastics. Sonneborn, Ralph
H. Reinhold Publishing
Corp., 1954, New York.

3680   Fiber Glass Projects and
Procedures. Steele, Gerald
L. Mcknight & Mcknight
Publishing Co., 1962,
Bloomington, Ill.

3681   Field Constructed Long
Radius Tubing Bender.
Silberstein, F. Theatre
Design & Technology D 1972.

3682   Fifth-Century Skene: a
New Model (The). Kernodle,
George R. Educational
Theatre Journal, 1968, Vol.
20, P. 502-505.

3683   Fifty Years Backstage,
Being the Life Story of a
Theatrical Stage Mechanic.
Quinn, Germain. Stage
Publishing Co., 1926,
Minneapolis.

3684   Fifty Years in the Magic

Circle. Blitz, Antonio. Belknap & Bliss, 1871, Hartford.

3685   Fifty Years of Scene-Painting. Tabs, D 1954, Vol. 12, No. 3, P. 5.

3686   Files and Filing. Fremont, Charles. Pitman, 1920, London.

3687   Filling a Space With Expandofoam- Technical Report. Armstrong Cork Co., Lancaster, Penn. No Date.

3688   Film and Radio in Your Play. Skelly, Madge. Players Magazine, My, 1948, Vol. 24, No. 8, P. 178.

3689   Film Applications in Legitimate Theatre Production. Embler, Jeffrey. Ph.D. Thesis, Pittsburgh University, 1970.

3690   Film As Environment: an Examination of Multi-Screen Film and Film Techniques. Chew, Bill. Architectural Association Quartely, 1974, No. 3-4, P. 97-116.

3691   Film Figures Appearing As Actors on an Ordinary Stage. Illustrated London News, My 1913, Vol. 142, P. 601.

3692   Film Figures Seem Real through Illusion. Popular Mechanics, Ag 1913, Vol. 20, P. 246-247.

3693   Final Report: a Survey of the Status of Theatre in United States High Schools. Peluso, Joseph L. United States Department of Health Education and Welfare, 1970, Washington, D. C.

3694   Fine Art of Variation in the Scene Designs of Donald Mitchell Oenslager (The). Tollini, Frederick Paul.

Ph.D. Thesis, Yale University, 1971.

3695   Fiorentino Adds New Light to a Sparkling Diamond. Kalikow, Rosemary. Lighting Dimensions Je 1977.

3696   Fire-Making at Olympia; Steam Smoke and Silk Flames. Sketch, Ja 1912, Vol. 76, P. 289.

3697   Fire-Proofing Stage Scenery. Scientific American Supplement, Ja 1916, Vol. LXXXI, P. 51:.

3698   Firearm Accidents Costly in Lives. Statistical Bulletin Metropolitan Life Insurance Company, S 1959, Vol. XXXX, P. 8.

3699   Firearm Safety in the Theatre. Archer, Stephen. News, Secondary School Theatre Conference, 1966, P.5-9.

3700   Fireproofing Stage Scenery. Scientific American Supplement, Ja 1915, Vol. 81, P. 51.

3701   Fireproof Curtain in Theatres (The). Builder, (The), F 25, 1882, P. 214, 297.

3702   Fireproof Curtain. Scientific American Supplement, Je 1877, Vol. 2, P. 1213.

3703   Fires for Fireplaces. Chavez, Edmond M. Players Magazine, N 1955, Vol 32 No 2, P. 42.

3704   Fireworks As an Adjunct to Dramatic Entertainment. Scientific American, Jl 1896, Vol. 75, P. 25,26.

3705   Fireworks in Court Festivals of Germany, Austria, and Italy During

the Baroque Era. Schaub,
Owen W. Ph.D. Thesis, Kent
State University, 1976.

3706   Fireworks. Tabs, D,
1957, Vol. 15, No. 3, P.
29.

3707   Firework
Formulae--Colored Lights.
Scientific American
Supplement, Ja 1882, Vol.
13, P. 5055.

3708   Fire at Sea on the
Stage; Secrets of an
Illusion, A. Sketch, 1923,
Vol. 121, P. 13.

3709   Fire at the Theatre:
Theatre Conflagrations in
the United States from 1798
to 1950. Willis, Richard
A. Ph.D. Thesis,
Northwestern University,
1967. LOCN: Th9445 T3 W5
1976

3710   Fire Hazards of Cured
Sprayed Urethane Foams.
Technical Information
Bulletin, PPG Company, S 2,
1969, Pittsburgh, P. 1.

3711   Fire Places, Arches
Paint Bins. Players
Magazine, N 1939, Vol. 16,
No. 2, P. 20.

3712   Fire Protection for
Scenery. Martindell, Pamela
Ann. M.F.A. Thesis, Yale
University, 1978.

3713   Fire Protection for
Theatre Stages. Builder
(The), Mr 12, 1904, Vol.
LXXXVI, P. 272.

3714   Fire Protection in the
Chemical Industry.
Manufacturing Chemists
Association, Inc., 1964,
Washington D.C.,.

3715   Fitting the Theatre into
the Cultural Centre.
Raison, Francis. World
Theatre, 1967, Vol. XVI, P.
461.

3716   Five Centuries of Ballet
Design. Beaumont, Cyril
William. Studio
Publications, (The), 1939,
New York; Studio, Ltd,
(The), London.

3717   Five Stage Designers of
West Germany. Rothe, Hans.
Theatre Annual, 1945, Vol.
XII, P. 62-76.

3718   Flame Retardants.
Holderried, J.A. Modern
Plastics Encyclopedia,
1969, Vol. 46, No. 10A, P.
276.

3719   Flame Texturing Raw
Wood. Losby, John D.
Theatre Crafts, My/Je 1977,
Vol. 11, No. 3, P. 56.

3720   Flame Texturing Wood,
Follow Up. Arnett, Keith.
Theatre Crafts, Mr/Ap 1978,
Vol. 12, No. 3, P. 86.

3721   Flat Black Solution.
Koue, Scott. Theatre
Crafts, S 1979, Vol. 13,
No. 4, P. 4.

3722   Flexible Permanent Stage
for Contest Plays.
Winbigler, H. Donald.
Players Magazine, Mr 1940,
Vol. 16, No. 6, P. 11.

3723   Flexible Stock Platform
System (A). Stell, W.
Joseph. Theatre Design &
Technology Wi 1976.

3724   Flexible System of
Levels Producing Stage
Elevators. Wilson, Gene A.
M.F.A. Thesis, 1950, Yale
University.

3725   Flight of Steps Which
Gives Thrills. Popular
Electricity, D 1913, Vol.
6, P. 883.

3726   Floating the
Rhine-Maidens 1869-1913.
Johnson, W.H. Theatre
Survey My 1966.

3727   Fluid Power Systems in the Theatre. Cruse, William. Theatre Design & Technology, O 1970, No. 22, P. 17.

3728   Flying Machinery. Voss, Lawrence. Players Magazine, F, 1953, Vol. 29, No. 5, P. 114.

3729   Foamed Plastics Applications in the Pattern Shop. Young, M.K. United States Gypsum Co., Chicago. No Date.

3730   Fog Maker. American Cinematographer, O, 1959, Vol. 40, P. 606, P. 632.

3731   Foibles and Fallacies of Science. Hering, Daniel W. D. Van Nostrand Co., Inc., 1924, New York.

3732   Folding Jitney Bus New Stage Feature. Popular Mechanics, Jl 1915, Vol. 24, P. 15.

3733   Foolproof Corner Block (The). Ward, Michael G. Theatre Crafts, O 1978, Vol. 12, No. 6, P. 86.

3734   Footlights and Spotlights. Skinner, Otis. Blue Ribbon Books, 1924, New York.

3735   Form Casting With Flexible Foam. Billings, Alan G. Theatre Crafts O 1969.

3736   For Ways Out of Limbo. Dewey, Walter S. Players, D/J, 1970, Vol. 45, No. 2, P. 52.

3737   Four Centuries of Scenic Invention. Simpson, Shirley S. Theatre Design & Technology, D 1974, No. 39, P. 13.

3738   Four Centuries of Theater Design: Drawings for the Donald Oenslager Collection. Yale University, Art Gallery. Yale University Art Gallery, 1964, New Haven. LOCN: Pn 2019 1964 Y3

3739   Four Lectures Given at Harvard. Jones, Robert Edmond. Original Rendering, 1952. located at the Harvard Theatre Collection.

3740   Four Yale Designers: a Portfolio. Yale/Theatre, Fall 1970, Vol. 3, P. 19-25.

3741   Framed Houses of Massachusetts Bay, 1625-1725 (The). Cummings, Abbott Lowell. Harvard University Press, 1979.

3742   Franciska Themerson's Stage Designs. Studio International, Ag, 1966, P. 104.

3743   Franco Zeffirelli. Weaver, William. High Fidelity, Mr 1964, Vol. 14, P. 30.

3744   French's Catalogue of Scenery. Samuel French, Date Uncertain, New York. located at the Harvard Theatre Collection.

3745   French Baroque Theatre Technology: the Second Palais Royal Theatre, 1770. Hippely, E.C. Ph.D Thesis, University of Denver, 1972.

3746   French Theatrical Production in the Nineteenth Century. Moynet, J. American Theatre Association, Books of the Theatre Series, 1976, Vol. 10. LOCN: Pn 2087 F5 M613

3747   Frohman Forestalled: the Buskin and the Barge. Graphic, D 1910, Vol. 81, P. 249.

3748   From Art to Theatre;
Form and Convention in the
Renaissance. Kernodle,
George R. University of
Chicago Press, 1914.

3749   From a Wagnerian
Rockpile. Simonson, Lee.
Theatre Arts Monthly, Ja
1948, Vol. XXXII, No. 1, P.
39-42.

3750   From Neo-Realism to
Neo-Classic Art Deco
Musicals: John Lee Beatty
Simplyifying His Setting.
Jenner, C. Lee. Theatre
Crafts, O 1978, Vol. 12,
No. 6, P. 19.

3751   From Pencil Points to
Computer Graphics. Milne,
Murray. Progressive
Architecture, Je 1970, P.
169.

3752   From Stage Design to the
Organization of Scenic
Space. Lerminier, Georges.
World Theatre, Fall, 1961,
Vol. X, No. 3, P. 251.

3753   From the Attic of
Bam/Chelsea Theatre Center.
Theatre Crafts, Mr/Ap 1974,
Vol. 8, No. 2, P. 16.

3754   From the Cat-Bird Seat.
Downing, Robert. Theatre
Annual, 1956, Vol. 14, P.
46-50.

3755   Function of a Building
Code. American Architect, D
1913, Vol. CIV, P. 283.

3756   Function of the Setting.
Simonson, Lee. Arts, Ja,
1923, Vol. 3, P. 50.

3757   Fundamentals of
Carpentry. Durbahn, Walter
E. American Technical
Society, 1967, Chicago.

3758   Fundamentals of
Plastics. Richardson, H.M.
and Wilson, J. W. McGraw
Hill Book Company Limited,
1946, New York.

3759   Furniture and Lights at
Carnegie Tech. Weninger,
Lloyd. Theatre Arts
Magazine, Jl 1936, Vol. XX,
No.7, P. 551.

3760   Furttenbach Theatre in
Ulm (The). Nagler, A.M.
Theatre Annual, 1953, Vol.
11, P. 45-65.

3761   Future Decorative Art of
the Theatre. Jones, Robert
Edmond. Theatre, My 1917,
Vol. 25, P. 266.

3762   Future of Building
Control. ABTT News, F 1980,
P. 5-10.

3763   Future of Production
(The). Appia, Adolphe.
Theatre Arts Monthly, Ag
1932, P.649-66, Vol. XVI.

3764   Future of Stage Art
(The). Carr, Michael
Carmichael. Theatre Arts,
Ap, 1919, Vol. III, No. 2,
P. 116.

3765   G., W. P. the Revolving
Stage at the Munich Royal
Re sidential and Court
Theatre. American Architect
and Building News, S 1896,
Vol. 53, P. 83-84.

3766   Garbage to Grandeur:
Found Object Transformation
and Textural Solutions With
Flexible Urethane Foam.
Bakkom, James R. Theatre
Crafts, S 1978, Vol. 12,
No. 5, P. 30-35, 66-70.

3767   Gas and Air Compression
Machinery. Scheel, Lyman
F. McGraw-Hill Book
Company, 1961, New York.

3768   Geddes' Production of
Hamlet. Skinner, R. D.
Commonweal, N 18, 1931, P.
76.

3769   Gelled Stains for Wood
Grain Reproduction.
Matthews, William. Theatre

Crafts, O 1975, Vol. 9, No. 5, P. 46.

3770   General Metals. Feirer, John L. McGraw-Hill, 1967, New York.

3771   General Metal. Fraser, Roland R. and Bedell, Earl L. Prentice-Hall, 1962, Englewood Cliffs, New Jersey.

3772   General Plastics: Projects and Procedures. Cherry, Raymond. Mcknight, 1967, New York.

3773   General Principles of Play Production. Brown, Gilmor and Garwood, Alice. Samuel French, 1936, New York.

3774   General Wood Working. Groneman, Chris H. McGraw-Hill 1955, New York.

3775   Gentleman of the Decoration, the. New York Times, F 14, 1915, Section 7, P. 4.

3776   Gentleman of Verona: Beni Montresor. Stevenson, Florence. Opera News, F 1964, Vol. 28, P. 26.

3777   George Jenkins: a Pragmatic Designer. Salzer, Beeb. Theatre Design & Technology, My 1971, No. 25, P. 11.

3778   Deleted.

3779   Georgian Playhouse (The). Southern, Richard. Pleiades Books Limited 1948 London. LOCN: Na6840 G7 S6

3780   Germany's New Stagecraft. Bie, Oscar. International Studio, Ag 1922, Vol. 75, P. 425.

3781   Germany's Theatertreffen. Riddell, Richard. Theatre Crafts, Mr/Ap 1977, Vol. II, No. 2, P. 26.

3782   German Repertory Theatre System (The). Grosser, Helmut. Tabs Sp 1976.

3783   Getting the Most Our of Your Shaper. A.S Barnes, 1954, Cranbury, New Jersey.

3784   Getting the Most Out of Your Band Saw and Scroll Saw. A. S. Barnes, 1954, Cranbury, New Jersey.

3785   Getting the Most Out of Your Drill Press. A. S. Barnes, 1954, Cranbury, New Jersey.

3786   Getting Your Foot in the Door. Vornberger, Cal. Theatre Craft, Mr/Ap 1980, Vol. 14, No. 2, P. 90-91.

3787   Ghost, (The). Dircks, Henry. Spon, 1863 London.

3788   Gifts and Entertainment. Hanlon, R. Brendan. Theatre Crafts, Mr/ap 1979, Vol. 13, No. 2, P. 87.

3789   Gilbert & Sullivan in a Church Basement: Light Opera of Manhattan. Theatre Crafts, Mr/Ap 1974, Vol. 8, No. 2, P. 18.

3790   Giovan Battista Andreini As a Theatrical Innovator. Smith, Winifred. Modern Language Review, 1922, Vol. 17, P. 31-41.

3791   Give Us the Job, and We'll Finish the Tools. Dasilva, Ray. Cue, Technical Theatre Review, Mr/Ap 1980, P. 18-20.

3792   Glance Behind the Scenes (A). Appleton's Journal, Ap 1876, Vol. 15, P. 433.

3793   Glimpse of a Scenic Painter's Studio: a Profession That Calls for

an Intimate Acquaintance
With Historic Conditions
(A). Gradenwitz, Alfred.
Scientific American, O 26,
1912, P.348-49, 355.

3794   Glossary of Technical
Stage Terms. Loundsbury,
Warren C. M.A. Thesis,
University of Washington,
1952.

3795   Glue and Glue Testing.
Rideal, Samuel. Scott,
Greenwood, 1900, London.

3796   Glyndeborne Opera
Festival: a Dream of
Perfection (The). Loney,
Glenn. Theatre Crafts,
My/Je 1979, Vol. 13, No.3,
P. 19.

3797   Goethe's Faust: Notes
from a Project for the
Production. Appia, Adolphe.
Theatre Arts Monthly, Ag,
1932, Vol. XVI, No. 8, P,
683.

3798   Golden Gate an Islandic
Legend Meets the Aircore
transformer (The). Loreman,
R.L. Theatre Design &
Technology D 1974.

3799   Golden Horse Shoe: the
Life and Times of the
Metropolitan Opera House
(The). Merring, Frank and
freeman, John W. and
fitzgerald, Gerald and
Solin, Arthur. Viking
Press, 1956, New York.

3800   Good Common Senses.
Dewey, Walter S. Players,
D/J, 1971, Vol. 46, No. 2,
P. 50.

3801   Gordon Craig: the Story
of His Life. Craig, Edward
Anthony. Alfred A. Knoph,
1968, New York.

3802   Gordon Craig's Ghost
Walks at Bayreuth: Wagner's
Grandsons Fulfill Some
Prophecies. Rood, Arnold

and Loney, Glenn. Theatre
Design & Technology, My
1972, No. 29, P.5.

3803   Gordon Craig's
Production of Hamlet at the
Moscow Art Theatre. Osanai,
Kaoru. Educational Theatre
Journal, 1968, Vol. 20, P.
586.

3804   Gordon Craig, the Imp of
Fame. Trewin, J.C.
Birmingham Post (The), Ag
6, 1966.

3805   Gordon Craig,
Ueber-Director: Major
Influences on Craig's
Theory and Practice.
Kramer, William Case. Ph.D.
Thesis, Ohio State
University, 1974.

3806   Gordon Craig and the
Dance. Windham, Donald.
Dance Index, Ag 1943, Vol.
2, P. 97.

3807   Gordon Craig and the
Theatre - a Record and an
Interpretation. Rase, Enid.
Sampson Low, Marston and
Company, Ltd., London, No
Date.

3808   Gordon Craig and the
Theatre of the Future.
Corornos, John. Poetry and
Drama, S 1913, Vol. 1, P.
334.

3809   Gordon Craig Comes to
America. De Casseres,
Benjamin. Theatre Magazine,
1928, P. 22.

3810   Gordon Craig in His
Setting. Leeper, Janet.
Apollo, Ag 1967, P.
155-157.

3811   Gordon Craig Remembers
Stanislavsky: a Great
Nurse. Tutaev, David.
Theatre Arts, Ap 1962, Vol.
46, P. 17.

3812   Gordon Craig : Gollancz,

1968. Craig, Edward Gordon. Knopf, 1968, New York.

3813   Gorelik's Metaphor in Design. Leitner, Margaret. Players, Ja 1962, Vol. 38, P. 129.

3814   Government Regulation of the Elizabethan Drama. Gildersleeve, Virginia Crocheron. B. Franklin, 1961, New York. LOCN: Pn2590 L3 G5

3815   Grand Opera at Paris (The). Illustrated London News, O 1, 1853, Vol. 23, P. 280.

3816   Grand Opera Beyond the Curtain Line. Gorham, Mercy. Theatre, Ja 1915, Vol. 21, P. 21.

3817   Great Chariot Race: Scenic Effects at the Turn of the Century, (The). Arnold, Richard. Theatre Design & Technology, D 1970, No. 23, P. 12-15.

3818   Great Stage and a Great Curtain; in Front and Behind The Scenes at the Coliseum, London, (A). Sphere, My 1914, Vol. 57, P. 170-171.

3819   Greek Theatre Production. Webster, Thomas B. L. Methuen, 1970, London.

3820   Green Pastures. Jones, Robert Edmond. 2 Ink Original Drawings. located at the Harvard Theatre Collection.

3821   Grooves and Doors on the Seventeenth and Eighteenth Century Dutch Stage. Wren, Robert M. Theatre Research, 1965, Vol. VII, No. 1,2, P. 56.

3822   Growth and Development of Scenic Design for the

Professional Musical Comedy Stage in New York from 1866 to 1920 (The). Lerche, Frank Martin. Ph. D. Thesis, 1969, New York University.

3823   Guidelines for Organization of Production Elements for the Community Theatre Director. Herman, Elane. M.A. Thesis, California State University, Long Beach.

3824   Guide to Federal Programs of Possible Assistance to the Solar Energy Community. United States Government Printing Office, 1977, Washington, D. C.. LOCN: Tj 810 V614 1977

3825   Gummi; a Scenic Medium Based on Liquid Latex. Dunham, Richard. Theatre Design & Technology O 1968.

3826   Gun Which Shoots Sounds Only. Scientific American, 1919, Vol. 121, P. 192.

3827   Guthrie Theatre(The). Theatre Crafts, Ja 1975.

3828   Hail Don Giovanni, Farewell Theatre. Berman, Eugene. Saturday Review, O 26, 1957, Vol. 40, P. 45.

3829   Hamlet. Jones, Robert Edmond. Original Blueprint Drawings and Photo. located at the Harvard Theatre Collection.

3830   Handbook of American Mountaineering. Henderson, Kenneth A. Houghton Mifflin, 1942, Boston.

3831   Handbook of Foamed Plastics. Bender, Rene J. Lake Publishing Co., 1965, Libertyville, Ill..

3832   Handbook of Stress and Strength. Lipson, Charles

and Juvinall, Robert C.
Macmillian, 1963, New York.

3833   Handbook of Technical
Practice for the Performing
Arts. Bowman, Ned A.
Scenographic Media, 1972,
Wilkinsburg, Pa. LOCN:
Pn2091.S8 B65 ISBN:
0913868027

3834   Handbook of the Theatre,
(A). Crampton, E. Drama
Book Specialists, New York.
No Date.

3835   Handbuch Der Architektur
Part Iv. Semper, Manfred.
Arnold Bergstrasser
Verlagsbuchhandlung,
Stuttgart, 1904. located at
the Harvard Theatre
Collection.

3837   Handlist of Dictionaries
on Technical Theatre (A).
Trapido, Joel. Theatre
Design and Technology, My
1968 & O 1968, No. 13,
&14,.

3838   Hanley's Twentieth
Century Book of Formulas,
Processes and Trade
Secrets. Hiscox, Gardner
D. Books, Inc., 1962, New
York.

3839   Harlequin in His
Element: the English
Pantomime, 1806-1836.
Mayer, David, III. Harvard
University Press, 1969,
Cambridge, Massachusetts.

3840   Have a P.E.P.S. Tour.
Lighting Dimensions, Mr
1980, P. 6.

3841   Have You Tried Fiber
Glass?. Loundsbury, Warren
C. Educational Theatre
Journal, O 1964, Vol. XVI,
No. 3, P. 240.

3842   Haymarket Theatre,
Boston (The). Stoddard,
Richard. Educational
Theatre Journal, Mr 1975,
Vol. 27, P. 63-69.

3843   Hazardous to Your
Health: Toxic Substances in
the Entertainment Industry.
Davidson, Randall. Theatre
Crafts, Mr/ap 1978, Vol.
12, No. 3, P. 77.

3844   Hazard of Sudden
Darkness (The). Ellis,
F.H. Electrical
Engineering, Ja 1955, Vol.
LXXIV, P. 33-8.

3845   He, Also, Was a Scene
Painter. Southern, Richard.
Life & Letters To-Day, D
1939, Vol. 23, P. 294-300.

3846   Health and Safety at
Work Etc. Act 1974. ABTT
Pub. No. 123 1978.

3847   Health Hazards
Association With
Polyurethane Foams.
Dernehl, Carl V. Journal
of Occupational Medicine, F
1966, P. 59.

3848   Health Hazards of
Working With Polyurethane
Foam Materials and
Processing. Motion Picture
& Television Research
Center (The). No Date.

3849   Helen Goes to Troy.
Jones, Robert Edmond.
Original Technical
Drawings. located at the
Harvard Theatre Collection.

3850   Helps and Hints.
Mortensen, A.L. Players
Magazine, Ja 1950, Vol. 26,
No. 4, P. 86.

3851   Help the Underprivileged
Flyman. Dewey, Walter S.
Players, Ap/My, 1970, Vol.
45, No. 4, P. 152.

3853   Here's How: a Guide to
Economy in Stagecraft.
Hake, Herbert V. Row,
Peterson & Co., 1942, New
York. LOCN: Pn2091. S8 H25

3854   Herkomer on Scenic Art.

Building News, D 1895, Pp.
844-845.

3855   Hermann Rosse's Stage
Designs. Cheney, Sheldon.
Theatre Arts Magazine, Ap
1921, Vol. V, No. 2, P.
148.

3856   Hexcel Honycomb Panels.
Priest, John and Cayard,
Pierre. Theatre Crafts N
1977.

3857   Hidden Orchestra Feature
of Modern Theatres. Popular
Mechanics, Ag 1914, Vol.
22, P. 172-173.

3858   Highlights of New
Building Code for New York
City As Related to
Theatres. Justin, J. Karl.
Journal of the Society of
Motion Picture and
Television Engineers, F
1969, Vol. 78, P. 96.

3859   High School Stagecraft.
Smalley, Ralph E. Theatre
Arts Monthly, S, 1927, Vol.
XI, No. 9, P. 705.

3860   High Speed Electric
Screw Shooter. Stair, Mike.
Theatre Crafts, N/d 1978,
Vol. 12, No. 7, P. 85.

3861   Hippodrome and Its
Electrical Stage Effects,
(The). Voegtlin, Arthur.
Popular Electricity
Magazine, Ja 1913, Vol. 5,
P. 900-905.

3862   Hippodrome Mystery
Unveiled (The). Scientific
American, Ap 1907, Vol. 96,
P. 325, 322, 333.

3863   Historical and
Descriptive Accounts of the
Theatres of London.
Brayley, Edward Westlake.
J. Taylor, 1826, London.

3864   Historical Development
of the Box Set. McDowell,
John H. Theatre Annual
(The), 1945, P.74,76.

3865   Historical Study of
Jacques Copeau and the
Vieux-Colombier Company at
the Garrick Teatre in New
York City (1917-1919).
Katz, Albert M. Ph.D.
Thesis, University of
Michigan, 1966.

3866   Historical Study of
Stage Scenery in American
Theatre from 1900 to 1950
(A). Battle, E. M.A.
Thesis, Tenn. Agricultural
and Industrial College,
1953.

3867   Historical Study of the
Use of Film to Provide
Additional Content To
Theatrical Productions of
the Legitimate Stage.
Embler, Jeffrey. Ph.D.
Thesis, University of
Pittsburgh.

3868   Historic Theatres As a
Festival Focus. Theatre
Crafts, Mr/Ap 1977, Vol.
II, No. 2, P. 24.

3869   History and Arrangement
of Theatres. Phipps, J. C.
Builder, (The), Ap 25,
1863, P. 291.

3870   History and Development
of Simultaneous Scenery in
the West From the Middle
Ages to Modern United
States, (The). Peet, Alice
Lida. Ph.D. Thesis,
Wisconsin, 1961.

3871   History of American
Stage Scenery Until 1875.
Swanson, John. M.A. Thesis
Northwestern Univ. 1927.

3872   History of Conjuring.
Evans, Henry Ridgely.
International Brotherhood
of Magicians, 1928, Kenton,
Ohio.

3873   History of Fireworks
(A). Brock, Alan S.T.
1948, London.

3874   History of Magic (The).
Seligmann, Kurt. Pantheon
Books, 1948, New York.

3875   History of Magic and
Experimental Science.
Thorndike, Lynn. Columbia,
1958, 1923, New York.

3876   History of the
Armbruster Scenic Studios
of Columbus Ohio. Joyce,
Robert S. Ph.D. Thesis,
Ohio State University,
1970.

3877   History of the English
Puppet Theatre (The).
Speaight, George. John De
Graff, 1955, New York.

3878   History of the Institute
of Sceneography. Veber,
Vaclav. Interscaena-Acta
Scaenographica, Sum 1972,
Vol. 2, P. 5-18.

3879   History of the Milling
Machine. Woodbury, Robert
S. M.I.T. Press (The),
1960, Cambridge,
Massachusetts.

3880   History of the Theatre
Section of the New York
Times As a Record Of the
New York Commercial Theatre
(A). Hensley, Jack. Ph.D.
Thesis, University of
Wisconsin, 1965.

3881   History of the United
Scenic Artists Union.
Habecker, Thomas James.
Ph.D. Thesis, University of
Illinois (Urbana), 1974.

3882   His World's a Stage.
Barnes, Djuna. Theatre
Guild Magazine, Je 1931,
Vol. 8, P. 25-29.

3883   Hofstra's Mechanized
Stagehand. Loney, Glenn.
Theatre Arts, Je 1963, Vol
Xlvii, No 6, P. 67.

3884   Hollow Wooden Roller for
Stage Curtain. Work, Ja 17,
1903, Vol. 24, P. 442.

3885   Home Energy How-To.
Hand, A.J. Harper & Row,
1977, New York. LOCN:
76-053195 ISBN:
0-06-011774-5

3886   Home Workshop and Tool
Handy Book. Anderson, Edwin
P. Theodore Audel and
Company, 1964,
Indianapolis, Indiana.

3887   Horse Race on the Stage
(The). Scientific American,
Ap 25, 1891, Vol. 64, P.
263-64.

3889   Hoskins Chromel- a
Resistance Wire and Ribbon.
Hoskins Manufacturing Co.
Detroit: the Hoskins
Manufacturing Company, C.
1967.

3890   Hours of Leisure With
Cardboard and Glue; the
Model Theatre. Hembrow,
Victor and Robins, W.P.
Hours of Leisure Series,
No. 1, London & New York.
No Date.

3891   Housebuilding
Illustrated. De Cristoforo,
R.J. Harper & Row, 1977,
New York. LOCN: 77-6559
ISBN: 0-06-010987-4

3892   Houses That Jack Built.
Theatre Crafts, Mr/Ap 1971,
Vol. 5, No. 2, P. 10.

3893   House of Ideas: Creative
Interior Designs. Baker,
Bill. Macmillan, 1974, New
York. LOCN: 73-11734 ISBN:
0-02-506280-8

3894   How's Your Light Bridge
I and II. Dewey, Walter S.
Players, F/Mr and Ap/My,
1972, Vol. 47, No. 3 and 4
p. 98 and 156.

3895   How-To-Do-It
Encyclopedia. Fawcett, W.
H., Jr. Golden Press,
1961, New York, Vols. 1, 2,
5, 9.

3896   Howard Bay. Isaacs, Hermine Rich. Theatre Arts Magazine, Je 1943, Vol. XXVII, No. 6, P. 344.

3897   How a Stage Ship Is Made to Roll on a Stage Sea. Sketch, D 1913, Vol. 84, P. 402.

3898   How Barker Puts Plays On. Schmidt, Karl. Harper's Weekly, Ja 30, 1915, P. 115.

3899   How Different Can One Be?. Trilling, Ossia. World Theatre, Wi, 1963/4, Vol. XIII, No. 1/}, P. 95.

3900   How Fatal Accidents Occur in the Home. Statistical Bulletin, Metropolitan Life Insurance Company, S 1956, Vol. XXXVII, P. 6-8.

3901   How Firearm Accidents Occur. Statistical Bulletin, Metorpolitan Life Insurance Co 1956, Vol. XXXVII, P. 6-8.

3902   How It Was Done: an Exploding Adding Machine. Parry, Chris. A.B.T.T. News, Mr 1979, P. 22.

3903   How It Was Done. Cartwright, A. ABTT News, N 1978, P. 22.

3904   How Mechanical Progress Influences Drama. Popular Mechanics, N 1914, P.733-735, Vol. 22.

3905   How Modern Science Aids the Artistic Drama. Belasco, David. New York World, F 17, 1901.

3906   How Motion Picture Sets Are Decorated. Roberts, Casey. Theatre Magazine, O 1927, P 4.

3907   How Relevant Are the Unions? Do They Hurt More Than Help?. Carson, Howard. Theatre Crafts, N/d 1978, Vol. 12, No. 7, P. 82.

3908   How Stage Sounds and Storms Are Made. Popular Mechanics, Ag 1908, Vol. 10, P. 522-523.

3909   How Theatre Happens. Archer, Stephen. Macmillan, 1978, New York. No Date. ISBN: 0-02-303830-6

3910   How the Audience at the Shubert Is Taken Nightly to The Top of the Jugfrau. Evening Sun, Ja 1916, New York, P. 11.

3911   How the Rhine Maidens Are Able to Swim. Sphere, My 1907, Vol. 29, P. 133.

3912   How to Build a Wood Frame House. Anderson, L. O. Dover Publications, 1973, New York. LOCN: Th 4818 A52 1973 ISBN: 0-486-22954-8

3913   How to Build Your Own Home. Reschke, Robert C. Structures Publishing Co., 1976, Farmington, Mi. LOCN: Th4815.R48 ISBN: 0-912336-18-8

3914   How to Choose and Use Power Tools. Decristoforo, R. J. Arco, 1961, New York.

3915   How to Create a Stucco Wall. Mortensen, A.L. Players Magazine, F 1951, Vol. 27, No. 5, P. 108.

3916   How to Lower a Cloud With Persons in It. Amery, Colin. Architectural Review (The), D 1972, Vol. 152, P. 354-356.

3917   How to Make a Simple Stage, and the Scenery for It, With Diagrams. Fay, William George. French, 1931, London and New York, 56 P.

3918   How to Make Flexible
Model Moulds. Ferrari, E.
Modern Plastics, 1954, Vol.
31, No. 11, P. 93.

3919   How to Produce Amateur
Plays. Clark, Barrett H.
Little, Brown & Co., 1930,
Boston.

3920   How to Use Hand and
Power Tools. Daniels,
George. Harper and Row,
1964, New York.

3921   How to Work With Tools
and Wood; for the Home
Craftsman. Stanley Works,
1942, New Britain, Ct.

3922   Huga Baruch & Co: 126
West 46th Street, New York.
Original Watercolors, 8
Boxes, 12 X 18 With Photos
in Box. located at the
Harvard Theatre Collection.

3923   Hugh Stevenson Designer
for the Theater. Beaumont,
Cyril William. Studio,
(The), Ap 1944, Vol. 127,
P. 122-126.

3924   Human Engineering in the
Theatre. Howard, Donald.
M.F.A. Thesis, 1956, Yale
University.

3925   Hydraulic Air Casters.
Saterne, Terry. Theatre
Crafts, My/je 1975, Vol.
9, No. 3, P. 48.

3926   Hydraulic and Pneumatic
Power for Production.
Stewart, Harry L.
Industrial Press (The),
1963, New York.

3927   Hydraulic Bridges at
Drury Lane Theatre.
Engineering, Je 1898, Vol.
65, P. 754.

3928   Hydraulic Power for
Working the Stage. Emden,
Walter. Institution of
Civil Engineers, 1887, Vol.
94, P. 66.

3929   Hydraulic Rigging.
Theatre Crafts Mr 1970.

3930   I've Always Suffered
from Sirens. Barnes, Djuna.
Theatre Guild Magazine, Mr
1931, Vol. 8, P. 23-25.

3931   I.A.T.S.E. a Report.
Snowden, George W. M.F.A.
Thesis, 1954, Yale
University.

3932   Identification of
Plastics and Rubbers,
(The). Saunders, K. J.
Chapman and Hall, 1966,
London.

3933   If It Burns Forget It.
Koltai, Ralph. Theatre
Crafts Ja 1977.

3934   Illinois Circuit Court
Reports. Matthews, Francis
E. and Bangs, H al
Crumpton. Vol. I & II,
1907, Chicago.

3935   Illusions in
Cinematography. Waller,
Fred. Transactions of the
Society of Motion Picture
Engineers, Jl, 1927, Vol.
2, P. 61.

3936   Illusions of the Stage.
Scientific American
Supplement, F 1881, Vol.
11, P. 4265.

3937   Illusion and Background
in the Arena. Hetler,
Louis. Players Magazine, Ap
1959, Vol. 30, No. 7, P.
155.

3938   Illusion Factory. Wade,
Robert J. Players
Magazine, Mr 1940, Vol. 16,
No. 6, P 7..

3939   Illustrated Magic.
Fischer, Ottokar.
Macmillan, 1931, New York.

3940   Imitating Arctic Ice and
Snow. Operti, Albert.
Popular Mechanics, Mr 1913,
Vol. 19, P. 448-449.

3941   Imitation Arms and
Armor. Popular Mechanics, D
1909, Vol. 12.

3942   Imitation Guns Need a
Licence, Court Rules. The
Guardian, Sat. Ap 7, 1979.

3943   Impressionistic Settings
for Modern Opera.
Moderwell, Hiram Kelly.
Harvard Musical Review, O
1915, Vol. 4, P. 1.

3944   Improved Procedure for
the Development of Stage
Equipment and A Specific
Application. Hale, David.
M.F.A. Thesis, Yale
University, 1961.

3945   Improved Stage
Appliances at Drury Lane.
Builder, Mr 1897, Vol. 72,
P. 245.

3946   Improved Theatre (An).
Building News, Ja 1882,
Vol. 42, P. 8.

3947   Improved Wagon Platform
(The). Smith, R.L. Theatre
Crafts Ja 1969.

3948   Improved Wallpaper Peel
Paste. Meyer, Herbert and
Huntington, Dexter. Motion
Picture Research Council
Bulletin No 224, 1953,
Hollywood.

3949   Improvements in
Apparatus to Be Used in the
Exhibition of Dramatic and
Other Like Performances.
Sylvester, Alfred. Newton's
London Journal of Arts, Mr
1864, Vol. 19, P. 154.

3950   Index of Patents
Concerning Theatre
Illusions and Appliances.
Alexander, R.E. Thesis
U.C.L.A. 1964. LOCN: Ld
791.8 T3a377

3951   Index To: Photographs of
Scene Designs Theatre Arts
1916-1964 (An). Hammack,

Alan. Theatre
Documentation, Fall 1970,
Sp 1971, Vol. 3, No. 1 & 2,
P. 29.

3952   Index to the Story of My
Days. Craig, Edward Gordon.
Hulton Press, 1957, London.

3953   Indigo Jones and the
Revival of Chivalry.
Strong, Roy. Apollo, Ag
1967, P. 102-107.

3954   Indoor Fountains. Edison
Monthly, F 1916, Vol. 8, P.
358-359.

3955   Industrial Arts Teacher
As Technical Director
(The). Young, D. Palmer.
Players Magazine, Ap, 1949,
Vol. 25, No. 7, P. 160.

3956   Industry Speaks Out On:
Inovations of the 70's.
Theatre Crafts, Ja/F 1980,
Vol. 14, No. 1, P. 20.

3957   Inexpensive Inter- Com
System. Batcheller, David
R. Players Magazine, O,
1958, Vol. 35, No. 1, P.
19.

3958   Inexpensive System for
Shifting Scenery. Payne,
Darwin Reid. Players
Magazine, Ja 1959, Vol. 35,
No. 4, P. 78.

3959   Inigo Jones's Scenery
for the Cid. Freehafer,
John. Theatre Notebook,
1970-71, Vol. 25, P. 84-92.

3960   Inigo Jones and
Florimene. Southern,
Richard. Theatre Notebook,
Ja 1953, Vol. 7, No. 2, P.
37.

3961   Inigo Jones and the New
English Stagecraft. Hawley,
James. Ph.D. Thesis, Ohio
State University, 1967.

3962   Inigo Jones. Gotch, J.
Alfred. Benjamin Blom,

1968, New York. 1928, Reprint.

3963   Inigo Jones. Theatre Arts Monthly, My, 1928, Vol. XII, No. 5, P. 353.

3964   Innovations of Steele MacKaye in Scenic Design and Stage Practice As Contributions to the American Theatre (The). Guthrie, David G. Ph.D. Thesis, New York University, 1974.

3965   Inspection into Fire Safety; an Inspector from the Office of the Fire Marshal Gives a Theatre the Once-Over. Wikle, George R. The Exhibitor, New York State Edition, Je 5, 1946, P. 17-20.

3966   Inspection of Theatres. Builder (The), F 5, 1859, Vol. XVII, P. 87, See Also P. 200.

3967   Instructor's Notes & Lecture Plan for a Course in Structural Design. Silvestro, Richard. M.F.A. Thesis, Yale University, 1976. LOCN: S139 1976

3968   Interactive Computer Graphics. Ackler, Bryan H. and Baumann, Theresa G. Theatre Craft, Mr/Ap 1980, Vol. 14, No. 2, P. 29-33.

3969   Interesting Matter Relating to the Scenery, Decoration, Etc, of the Theatre Royal of Ipswich. Southern, Richard. Architectural Review, Ag 1946, Vol. 100, P. 41-44.

3970   Interior of Submarine Vividly Portrayed. Popular Mechanics, D 1917, Vol. 28, P. 904-905.

3971   Interior Settings of the Stage. Phillips, J.H. Architectural Review (The), 1919, Vol. 8, P. 33-44.

3972   International Exhibition in Amsterdam (The). Cheney, Sheldon. Theatre Arts Magazine, Ap 1922, Vol. VI, No. 2, P. 140.

3973   International Organization of Scenographers and Technicians (The). Rubin, Joel E. Theatre Design & Technology, Fall 1976.

3974   Interview With Four Leading American Designers. Drapalova, Iva. Theatre Design & Technology, Fall 1976, Vol. XII, No. 3, P. 45.

3975   Interview With Ming Cho Lee (An). Lee, Ming Cho. Yale/Theatre, Fall 1970, Vol. 3, P. 26-31.

3976   Introduction to Architectural Drawing. Field, Wooster Bard. McGraw, 1932, New York.

3977   Introduction to Plastics. Arnold, Lionel K. Iowa State University Press, 1968.

3978   Introduction to Plastic Stage Properties. Pecker, Sumner C. M.F.A. Thesis, 1957, Yale University.

3979   Introduction to Scenic Design (An). Gillette, A.S. Harper & Row, 1967, New York.

3980   Introduction to Specifications for the Theatre Technician (An). Long, Robert. Theatre Design & Technology Fall 1977.

3981   Introduction to the Stage Devices in the Siglio De Oro Drama (An). Weaver, William. Ph.D. Thesis, North Carolina University, 1937.

3982   Inventor Tells the
Secret of Amazing Stage
Effects. Carter, Lincoln
J. New York Times, N 9,
1913, Sec. 5, P. 12.

3983   Investigation of
Selected Contemporary
American Scene Designers
(An). Kuemmerle, Clyde
Victor, Jr. Ph.D. Thesis,
University of Minnesota,
1970.

3984   Investigation of the
Possible Adaptation of
Common Pipe and Angle to
Stage Settings (An). Cobes,
John Paul. M.A. Thesis,
Ohio State University,
1961.

3985   Investigation of the
Principles of Structural
Design As an Aid in
Creating the Stage Setting
(An). Francis, Paul J.
M.A. Thesis, Catholic
University, 1957.

3986   Invisible and Visible.
Young, Stark. New Republic,
Mr 8, 1932, Vol. 74, P.
102.

3987   Invisible Film Craft Art
Director Gene Rudolf's
Recent Film and Television
Work. Taylor, Clarke.
Theatre Crafts, My/Je 1978,
Vol. 12, No. 4, P. 24.

3988   In Production.
Bernstein, Aline. Atlantic,
S 1940, Vol. 166, P.
323-332.

3989   In Search of a Metaphor.
Gorelik, Mordecai. Players,
Ag/S, 1969, Vol. 44, No. 6,
P. 259.

3990   In Search of Design.
Ter-Arutunian, Rouben.
Dance Perspectives, Wi
1966, Vol. 28, P. 6.

3991   Ironic Prologue and
Epilogue to the Iroquois

Fire. Dryden, Wilma J.
Quarterly Journal of
Speech, Ap, 1968, P. 147.

3992   Irving's Scene Painters:
Principal Scenic Artists at
the Lyceum 1878-1898.
Gardner, John. Ph.D.
Thesis, Florida State
University, 1975.

3993   Is There a Scene Painter
in the House?. Hirst, C.
Tabs, S 1954, Vol. 12, No.
2, P. 21.

3994   Is the Realism of the
Stage Running to Seed?.
Current Literature, Ja
1912, P. 88-89.

3995   It's Done With Mirrors.
Horn, R. C. American
Cinematographer, D 1956,
Vol. 37, P. 728, 755.

3996   It's That Time of Year.
Dewey, Walter S. Players,
O/N, 1969, Vol. 45, No. 1,
P. 4.

3997   Italian Baroque
Theatre-Scenic Influences
(The). Hatfield, James.
Ph.D. Thesis, Wayne State,
1980.

3998   Italian Comedy (The).
Duchartre, Pierre Louis.
Dover, 1966, New York.
LOCN: Pq 4155 D82 1966

3999   Italian Stage Designs
from the Museo Theatrale
Alla Scala, Milan.
Monteverdi, Mario. HMSC,
1968, London. LOCN: Pn 2091
S8 M65

4000   Italian Stage Machinery,
1400 - 1800. Carrick,
Edward. Architectural
Review, 1931, Vol. LXX, P.
14 and P. 34.

4001   Italian Stage Machinery
1500-1700. Larson, Orville
K. Ph.D. Thesis,
University of Illinois,
1956.

4002   Italian Theatre Regulations. Builder (The), F 1888, Vol. VIL, P. 118 :10.

4003   It Is Better Upsidedown. Wehlburg, Albert F. C. Players Magazine, Sp, 1974, Vol. 49, No. 3-4, P. 60.

4004   I Took a Hammer in My Hand: the Woman's Build-It and Fix-It Handbook. Adams, Florence. Morrow & Co. (William), 1973, New York. LOCN: Tt151.A3 ISBN: 0-688-00165-3

4005   Jack-Knife Stage (The). Grantier, B.F. Theatre Arts Monthly, Jl 1939, Vol. XXIII, No. 7, P. 539.

4006   Jacques Copeau and This Theatre. Theatre, D 1917, Vol. 26, P. 342.

4007   Japanese Theatre Exibition. Theatre Notebook, 1952, Vol. 6, P. 83.

4008   Jeannerra Cochrane Theatre (The). Trangmar, Michael. Tabs Je 1965.

4009   Jean Nicolas Servandoni: His Scenography and His Influence. States, Bert Olen. Ph.D. Thesis, Yale University, 1960.

4010   John Conklin: Designer of Theatrical Gesture. MacKay, Patricia. Theatre Craft, My/Je 1980, Vol. 14, No. 3, P. 21, 46.

4011   John Craig's Notable Undertaking. Stearns, H. E. New York Dramatic Mirror, My 28, 1910, P. 4, 9.

4012   John Wenger. De Fornaro, Carlo. Joseph Lawren, 1925, New York.

4013   Jones at Radio City.

Young, Stark. New Republic, My 18, 1932, Vol. 71, P. 17.

4014   Josef Svoboda: Theatre Artist in the Age of Science. Burian, Jarka M. Educational Theatre Journal, My 1970, Vol. XX11, No. 2, P. 123.

4015   Josef Svoboda's American University Tour. Burian, Jarka M. Theatre Design & Technology, My 1973.

4016   Josef Svoboda Retires. Loney, Glenn. Theatre Crafts, Ja 1971.

4017   Josef Svoboda. Observer, My 11, 1967, P. 17.

4018   Joseph Andrews: Design Resources for 18th Century England. Theatre Crafts, Mr/Ap 1979, Vol. 12, No. 3, P. 32.

4019   Joseph Svoboda, Technician and Artist. Bablet, Denis. Encore, Jl/Ag 1964, Vol. 11, P. 37-41.

4020   Joseph Svoboda and His Czech Scenographic Millieu. Heymann, Henry. Theatre Design & Technology, F 1970.

4021   Joseph Svoboda Portfolio (A). Svoboda, Josef. Theatre Design & Technology, D 1966.

4023   Joseph Urban, Scenic Artist. Washburn-Freund, Frank E. International Studio, Ja 1923, Vol. 76, P. 357-359.

4024   Joseph Urban and His Work. Freund, F. E. W. International Studio, Ja, 1923, Vol. 76, P. 257.

4025   Joseph Urban. Dictionary of American Biography, Vol. XIX, P. 132. No Date.

4026   Jo Mielziner and Arena
Theatre Scene Design.
Larson, Orville K. Players
Magazine, Jq, 1961, Vol.
37, No. 4, P. 80.

4027   Jo Mielziner Approaches
Fifty Years in the Theatre.
Theatre Crafts My 1970.

4028   Jo Mielziner. Isaacs,
Hermine Rich. World
Theatre, 1951, Vol. II, No.
2, P. 41.

4029   Jo Mielzinger's
Contribution to the
American Theatre. Weiss,
David W. Ph.D. Thesis,
University of Indiana,
1965.

4030   Julliard's Movable
Ceiling. Progressive
Architecture, D 1970, P.
69.

4031   Kabuki Theatre (The),
Part 3: the Revolving Stage
and the Trap Door.
Kawatake, Toshio. Japan
Architect, N 1962, P.94-98.

4032   Kandinsky and Kokschka:
Two Episodes in the
Genesis. Swoope, Charles.
Yale Theatre, Fall 1970,
Vol. 3, P. 10.

4033   Karl Franz Akacs(Aktas)
Called Gruner. Dietrich,
Margret. Theatre Research,
1968, Vol. IX, No. 3, P.
147.

4034   Karl Lautenschlaeger:
Reformer of Stage Scenery.
Schoene, Guenter. In:
Innovations in Stage and
Theatre Design; Papers of
the Sixth Congress,
International Federation
for.

4035   Keeping Up With the New
Stagecraft. Sowers, William
Leigh. Drama V, N 1918,
Vol. 8, P. 515-523.

4036   Keep the Receipts!
Record Keeping for the
Performing Arts Taxpayer.
Hanlon, R. Brendan. Theatre
Crafts, N/D 1978, P.80,
Vol.12, No.7.

4037   Kemble's Production of
Macbeth (1794): Some Notes
on Scene Painters Scenery
Special Effects and
Costumes. Donohue, Joseph
W. Theatre Notebook, N
1966/7, Vol. XXI, No. 2,
P. 63.

4038   Kenny's First Tape.
Kenny, Sean. Encore, N/D
1960, P. 19-25.

4039   Keren: Spectacle and
Trickery in Kabuki Acting.
Leiter, Samuel L.
Educational Theatre
Journal, My 1976, Vol. 28,
No. 2, P. 175.

4040   King Richard III. Jones,
Robert Edmond. Original Ink
and Watercolor. located at
the Harvard Theatre
Collection.

4041   Kirby's Flying Ballet.
Myerson, Jeremy. ABTT News,
Ja/F 1979, P.16.

4042   Knots and How to Tie
Them. Babson, Walter B.
Frederick Fell, 1961, New
York.

4043   Kochergin Designs for
Leningrad's Gorky Theatre.
Levy, Micky. Theatre
Crafts, O 1977, Vol. 11,
No. 5, P. 39.

4044   L'envers Du Theatre:
Machines Et Decorations.
Moynet, M.J. Benjamin
Blom, Inc., 1972, New York.
LOCN: Pn2087. F5 M6 1972

4045   Lancaster, Nuffield
Studio (1969) Shepheard and
Epstein. New Theatres in
Britain, Strand Electric,
1970, P.91; S.A. Tabs,

P.36-43, Vol. 27 No.3.
Tabs, Vol. 27, No. 3, P.
36-43.

4046   Landscape on the
Seventeenth and Eighteenth
Century Italian Stage.
Eddelman, William S. Ph.D.
Thesis, Stanford
University, 1972.

4047   Landscape Theater in
America. Parry, Lee. Art in
America, N/D 1971, Vol. 59,
P. 52-61.

4048   Large-Scale Foam Core
Construction. Moore,
Richard. Theatre Crafts,
N/D 1979, Vol. 13, No. 6,
P. 30-31.

4049   Large Asbestos Theatre
Curtain and Steel Work,
(A). Engineering Record, Mr
1905, Vol. 51, P. 336.

4050   Large Scale Hot Knife
Sculpting Linear Styrofoam
Forms. Silberstein, F.
Theatre Design &
Technology, D 1973.

4051   Large Scale Scenic
Thermoforming in Film
Production: Hello Dolly.
Theatre Design &
Technology, O 1969.

4052   Laser Regulations: This
Time It's for Real.
Sandhaus, Dick. Lighting
Dimensions, Mr 1978, Vol.
2, No. 3, P. 21.

4053   Laser Safety Update.
Weiner, Robert. Lighting
Dimensions, S,1979, P. 43.

4054   Laser Theatre
Technology. O'Brien, Dr.
Brian B. Lighting
Dimensions, My 1980, P. 28.

4055   Las Vegas Spectacular.
Theatre Crafts, Mr/Ap 1976,
Vol. 10, No. 2, P. 6.

4057   Later Magic. Lewis,

A.J. E.P. Dutton & Co.,
1904, New York.

4058   Latest Stage Realism,
(The). Farwell, E. L.
Technical World, Je 1913,
Vol. 19, P. 512-591, 620.

4059   Lautenschlaeger's New
Revolving Stage. Scientific
American Supplement, Ag
1896, Vol. 42, P. 17230,
17231.

4060   Laws and Ordinances
Governing the City of
Chicago, As in Force April
2, 1890. Hutchinson, Jonas
and Robinson, M.W. 1890,
Chicago.

4061   Laws Relating to
Buildings in the City of
New York. Fryer, William
J., Editor. 1892, New York.

4062   Law Looks at the Theatre
(The). Ferrar, Eleanor B.
Theatre Design & Technology
D 1974.

4063   La Gioconda. Jones,
Robert Edmond. Original
Inkdrawing at Harvard
Theatre Collection.

4064   La Scala: 400 Years of
Stage Design from the
Musteatrale Alla Scala,
Milan. Monteverdi, Mario.
International Exhibitions
Foundation, 1971,
Washington. LOCN: Art: Pn
2091 S8 M67

4065   La Scena Per
Angolo-Magic by the
Bibienas?. Burnim, Kalman
A. Theatre Survey, 1961,
Vol. 2, P. 67.

4066   Leaves from Conjurers'
Scrap Books. Burlingame,
Hardin J. Donohue,
Henneberry & Co., 1891,
Chicago.

4067   Lediard and Early 18th
Century Scene Design.

Theatre Notebook, Ap, 1948, Vol. 2, No. 3, P. 49.

4068   Lee Simonson, Artist-Craftsman of the Theatre. York, Zack L. Ph.D. Thesis, University of Wisconsin, 1951.

4069   Lee Simonson. Current Biographies, 1948, P. 574.

4070   Leokerz's Design for Richard III. Larson, Orville K. Players Magazine, F, 1959, Vol. 35, No. 5, P. 100.

4071   Leonardo of Our Theatre (The). Macgowan, Kenneth. Theatre Arts, Ja 1961, Vol. 45, P. 63.

4072   Leon Bakst. Spencer, Charles. St. Martin's Press, 1973, New York.

4073   Leslie Hurry: Settings and Costumes for Sadler's Wells Ballets. Browse, Lillian. Faber and Faber, 1946, London.

4074   Lesson in Stagecraft (A). Simonson, Lee. Drama, Ja 1924, Vol. 14, P. 133.

4075   Let There Be Light. Matz, Mary Jane. Opera News, Ap 3, 1971, Vol. 35, P. 8-11.

4076   Lewis & Bartholomew's Mechanical Panorama of the Battle of Bunker Hill. Arrington, Joseph Earl. Old-Time New England, Fall 1961, Vol. 52, Winter 1962, P. 50-58, 81-89.

4077   Life Safety Code. National Fire Protection Association, 1970, Boston,.

4078   Life With Bobby: an Appreciation of Robert Edmund Jones, The Artist and the Man. Gorelik, Mordecai. Theatre Arts, Ap,

1955, Vol. XXXIX, No. 4, P. 30.

4079   Lighting at Yale and Lighting at Talladega. Theatre Arts Monthly, Jl, 1940, Vol. XXIV, No. 7, P. 533.

4080   Lighting by Logic. Anderson, Bob. Tabs Mr 1973.

4081   Limitations of Scenery (The). Archer, William. Magazine of Art, O 1896, Pp. 432-436.

4082   Limits of Scenic Effect, (The). Graphic, D 4, 1869, Vol. 1, P. 11.

4083   Limits of Stage Illusion (The). Living Age, D 3, 1910, Vol. 167, P. 587.

4084   Liquid Color Fires. Scientific American Supplement, Jl 1896, Vol. 42, P. 17133.

4085   List of Catalogs by Subject. Theatre Crafts Ja 1975.

4086   Literal Acceptance of Stage Illustion, (The). Graves, Thornton Shirley. South Atlantic Quarterly, Jl 1921, Vol. XX, P. 201-212.

4087   Lithuanian Scenography. Lithuania, 1968, Vilna.

4088   Lives of the Conjurors (The). Frost, Thomas. Chatto & Windus, 1881, London.

4089   Living Art or Still Life?. Appia, Adolphe. Theatre Annual (The), Vol. 1943, P. 38-46.

4090   Living on Hope. Fraser, Anne. Theatre Australia, D 1977, Vol. 2, No. 6, P. 48.

4091   Living Scene (The).
Macgowan, Kenneth. Theatre
Arts Monthly, Je, 1927,
Vol. XI, No. 6, P. 444.

4092   Lobero Theatre. Theatre
Arts Monthly, S, 1925, Vol.
IX, No. 9, P. 626.

4093   Location Transformation
for TV Public Affairs.
Hoffman, Paul S. Original
Inkdrawing at Harvard
Theatre Collection.

4094   London County Council
(The). Builder, the 1900
and after Continuing Short
Notes on Decisions.

4095   London Theatre: from the
Globe to the National.
Roose-Evans, James. Phaidon
Press, 1977. LOCN: Pn2596
L6 R59

4096   Long-Forgotten Magic
Lantern, from the Old-
Fashioned Slide Projector,
(The). Interiors, D 1948,
Vol. 108, P. 84-95.

4097   Lord Chamberlain's
Theatre Rules. Builder
(The), S 17, 1904, Vol.
LXXXVII, P. 288.

4098   Lost Panoramas of the
Mississippi (The).
Mcdermott, John Francis.
University of Chicago
Press, 1958, Chicago.

4099   Los Angeles and the
Legitimate Theatre. Baume,
Elson. Interiors, Ap 1945,
Vol. 104, P. 64-65.

4100   Louis Hartman:
Electrician, Inventor and
Stage Lighting Designer.
Weidner, R.W. Thesis, Penn
State University, 1973.
LOCN: 080 Po1973m

4101   Loutherbourg: Mystagogue
of the Sublime. Gage, John.
History Today, My 1963,
Vol. 13, P. 332-339.

4102   Lure of the Tanagra
Theatre, (The). Scientific
American, Je 1926, Vol.
134, P. 411.

4103   Lyceum Staff: a
Victorian Theatrical
Organization. Hughes, Alan.
Theatre Notebook, 1974,
Vol. XXVIII, No. 1, P. 11.

4104   Machinery Handbook.
Oberg and Jones. Industrial
Press, 1964, New York.

4105   Machinery in Theatrical
Representations. Scientific
American, Jl 1867, Vol 17
P. 9.

4106   Machinery of Grand
Opera, (The). Schlesinger,
Kathleen. World Work, 1903,
Vol. 2, P. 25-33.

4107   Machine Stage: Machine
Stage Mechanics As
Represented by Five Extant
Eighteenth Century European
Theatres (The). Ault, Cecil
Thomas. Ph.D. Thesis,
University of Michigan,
1974.

4108   Machining of Metals,
(The). Armarego, E. M. A.
and Brown, R. H.
Prentice-Hall, 1969,
Englewood Cliffs, New
Jersey.

4109   MacKaye Spectatorium
(The). Engineering News, Ag
1893, Vol. 30, P. 158.

4110   Macready's Richelieu
Prompt Books: Evolution of
the Enclosed Setting.
Huston, Hollis W. Theatre
Studies, 1974-75, No. 21,
P. 41.

4111   Magic. Stage Illusions,
Special Effects and Trick
Photography. Hopkins,
Albert A. Dover
Publications, Inc., 1976,
New York.

4112   Magic/Magic
Lantern/Lantern. Deshong,
Andrew. Yale/   Theatre 3,
Fall 1970, P.38-50.

4113   Magic, Stage Illusions,
Special Effects and Trick
Photography. Hopkins,
Albert A. Constable, 1976,
P. 556.

4114   Magic, Stage Illusions
and Scientific Diversions.
Hopkins, Albert A. Munn &
Co., 1898, New York,
Reissued Benjamin Bloom.

4116   Magic into Science.
Pachter, Henry M. Henry
Schuman, 1951, New York.

4117   Magic Theatre (The).
Corbett, Tom. Theatre
Crafts, S 1980, Vol. 14,
No. 4, P. 22.

4118   Magic Without Apparatus.
Gaultier, Camille. Fleming
Book Co., 1945, Berkeley
Heights, N.J.

4120   Maharam Awards: Broadway
and Off Broadway Design
Awards. Theatre Crafts,
Ja/F 1979, Vol. 13, No. 1,
P. 32.

4121   Making a Hanging Front
Stage Curtain. Work, D
1904, Vol. 28, P. 433.

4122   Making a Miniature
Theatre. Williams, Guyr.
Plays, Inc., 1976, Boston.
LOCN: Pn2091. M6w5

4123   Making a Stage Ocean
With Green Silk and an
Electric Fan. Popular
Science Monthly, Mr 1917,
Vol. 90, P. 372.

4124   Making of the Theatre
(The). Manson, George J.
New York Dramatic Mirror,
Je 27, 1896, P. 14.

4125   Making Originals for
Photographic Slides.

Conway, John A. Players
Magazine, My 1953.

4126   Making Switzerland on
Sixth Avenue. Theatre, New
York, Ja 1916, Vol. 23, P.
15.

4127   Making the Rhinegold's
Guardians Natural.
Illustrated London News, Ap
26, 1913, Vol. 142, P. 557.

4128   Making Varicolored Flash
Papers for Stage Effects.
Popular Mechanics, 1922,
Vol. 38, P. 803.

4129   Making Your Own Gobos by
Photofabrication. Pollock,
S.P. Theatre Crafts, S
1976.

4130   Malvern Festival.
Malvern Festival Exhibition
Committee, London, 1931.
LOCN: Pn 2091 S8m25

4131   Managers and ABTT Clash
Over Training. ABTT News, O
1979, P. 6. The Stage and
Television Today, S 1979.

4132   Manchester University
(1965) the Building
Partnership; Consultant:
Richard Southern. New
Theatres in Britain, Strand
Electric, 1869, P. 100-101.

4133   Manoeuvering the
Guardians of the Rhinegold.
Illustrated London News, F
23, 1907, Vol. 130, P. 285.

4134   Manual of Engineering
Drawing,(A). Franch, Thomas
E. McGraw-Hill Book Co.,
1929, New York.

4135   Manual of Engineering
Drawing for Students and
Draftsmen (A). French,
Thomas E. and Vierck,
Charles J. McGraw-Hill,
1960, New York.

4136   Manual of Explosives,
Military Pyrotechnics and

Chemical Warfare Agents. Bebie, Jules. Mcamillan Co., 1943, New York.

4137   Manual of Lathe Operation and Machinists Tables. Atlas Press Co., 1978, Kalamazoo, Michigan.

4138   Manual of Rope U.S.A.GE, How to Put Rope to Work in Industry; and Useful Knots and How to Use Them. Plymouth Cordage Company. Plymouth Cordage Co., 1948, Plymouth, Mass..

4139   Manual of Safety Requirements in Theatres and Places of Public Entertainment. Home Office. H.M. Stationery Office, 1935, London.

4140   Manual of Steel Construction. American Institute of Steel Construction, 1964, New York.

4141   Man of La Mancha at the Piccadilly Theatre. Albery, Ian B. Tabs Mr 1969.

4142   Marble Surface. Modern Plastics, 1954, Vol. 31, No. 9, P. 183.

4143   Marc Chagall: Drawings and Water Colors for the Ballet. Lassaigne, Jacques. Tudor Publishing Company, 1969, New York.

4144   Marc Chagall: His Lessons for the Theatre. Zimmerman, L. I. Educational Theatre Journal, 1962, Vol. 14, P. 203.

4145   Marc Chagall's Designs for Aleko and the Firebird. Amberg, George. Dance Index, N 1945, Vol. 4, P. 185-204.

4146   Mareorama, (The). Scientific American, Mr 1899, Vol. 80, P. 150.

4147   Mareorama at the Paris Exposition (The). Scientific American, S 1900, Vol. 83, P. 192, 198.

4148   Mark Taper Forum. Theatre Crafts, S 1980, Vol. 14, No. 4, P. 41.

4149   Marvels of Modern Mechanics. Wilkins, Harold T. 1926, London.

4150   Marvels of Sleight of Hand. Grainger, Hector. Everybody's Magazine, 1899, Vol. 1, P. 321-326.

4151   Masks, Mimes, and Miracles, Studies in the Popular Theatre. Nicoll, Allardyce. Harcourt, Brace & Co., 1931, New York.

4152   Mask of Reality; an Approach to Design for Theatre, (The). Corey, Irene. Anchorage Press, 1968, Anchorage, Kentucky. LOCN: Pn 2091 S8 C627

4153   Masonite Over Layered Plywood: a Stage Floor That Works. Glerum, Jay. Theatre Design & Technology Sp 1977.

4154   Masque of Queens. Jonson, Ben. Viking Press, 1930.

4155   Mass Audience Entertainment Events. Wills, Robert. Theatre Design & Technology, Sp 1977, Vol. XIII, No. 1, P. 9.

4156   Masters of Design 2-Norman Bel Geddes. Reid, Kenneth. Pencil Points Vol. XVIII, Ja 1937, P. 3.

4157   Master of Stage Illusion-Mr. Simonson. Vandamm. Theatre Magazine, F, 1931, P. 42.

4158   Materials and Crafts of

the Scenic Model. Payne,
Darwin Reid. Southern
Illinois University Press,
1976. LOCN: 2901 M6 P37

4159   Materials and Methods of
Sculpture (The). Rich,
J.C. New York Oxford
University Press, 1947, New
York.

4160   Materials Approach to
the Study of Stage Design
(A). Bruder, Karl C. Ed.D.
Thesis, Columbia
University, 1951.

4161   Materials of the Scene:
an Introduction to
Technical Theatre. Wolfe,
Welby B. Harper & Row,
1977, New York. LOCN:
2085.W6 ISBN: 0-06-047184-0

4162   Materials Presently Used
for Snow Effects. Meyer,
Herbert. Motion Picture
Research Council Bulletin
No. 279, 1957, Hollywood.

4163   Material for Cobwebbing.
Meyer, Herbert. Motion
Picture Research Council
Bulletin No. 307,
Hollywood, 1959.

4164   Mattress on a Postage
Stamp. Stell, W. Joseph.
Theatre Crafts, N/D 1967,
P. 13-17.

4165   Max Reinhardt and His
Theatre. Sayler, Oliver M.
Brentano's, 1924, New York.

4166   Max Reinhardt and I in
Austria, Berlin, England,
France, & the United
States. Theatre Notebook,
1963, Vol. V, No. 3.

4167   Mechanical Aids to
Production. Burris-Meyer,
Harold. Theatre Arts
Magazine, Ap 1932, Vol.
XVI, No. 4, P. 323.

4168   Mechanical Development
of the Modern German Stage

(The). Pridmore, J.E.O.
Architectural Review, N
1913, P.263:-68, No.2.

4169   Mechanical Engineer's
Handbook. Marks, Lionel S.
(Ed). McGraw-Hill Book Co.,
1930, New York. Repreinted
in 1951.

4170   Mechanical Fastening
Methods for Aluminum.
Reynolds Metals Company,
1951, Louisville, Kentucky.

4171   Mechanical Forces:
Improvements in Stage
Equipment, The. Moderwell,
Hiram Kelly. Theatre of
Today, The, 1914, P. 38-58.

4172   Mechanical in Grand
Opera, the. Popular
Mechanics, Ap 1910, Vol.
13, P. 530-531.

4173   Mechanical Joys of Coney
Island. Symons, Stephen W.
Popular Science Monthly, S
1916, Vol. 89, P. 394.

4174   Mechanical Plant of the
New York Hippodrome.
Engineering Record, Ag 26,
1905, Vol. 52, P. 229-234.

4175   Mechanics of Grand
Opera, The. McCafferty,
Grattan. Popular Mechanics,
D 1913, Vol. 20, P.
885-889.

4176   Mechanics of Sabbatini
(The). South, I. Jay.
M.F.A. Thesis, Carnegie
Institute of Technology,
1959.

4177   Mechanism of
Amphitheaters II (The).
Scientific American
Supplement, Ja 1901, Vol.
51, P. 20938, 20939.

4178   Mechanism of Grand
Opera, the Scenery from
Behind, (The). Illustrated
London News, My 7, 1904,
Vol. 124, P. 4.

4179   Mechanism of Grand Opera
(The). Forlow, L.S.
Theatre Magazine (The), D
1907, Vol. VII, No. 82, P.
332.

4180   Mechanized Multi-Form.
Progressive Architecture, F
1962, P. 116.

4181   Mechanized Theatre
(The). Poulson, David. New
Theatre Magazine, Vol. V,
No. 1, P. 10. No Date.

4182   Mechanized Theatre for
the Twentieth Century
(The). Poulson, David.
Stage, O 24, 1963, P. 20.

4183   Media. Jones, Robert
Edmond. Original Drawing.
located at the Harvard
Theatre Collection.

4184   Medieval Drama in
Chester. Salter, Frederick
M. University of Toronto
Press, 1955, Toronto.

4185   Medieval French Drama
(The). Frank, Grace. Oxford
University Press, 1954,
Oxford.

4186   Medieval Pageant Wagons
of Louvain (The). Kernodle,
George R. Theatre Annual,
1943, Vol. 2, P. 58-62.

4187   Medieval Theatre (The).
Wickham, Glynne W. St.
Martin's Press, 1974, New
York.

4188   Meetings With Gordon
Craig. Raeburn, Henzie.
Drama, Fall 1966, P. 42-43.

4189   Memoirs of Bartholomew
Fair. Morley, Henry. 1880,
London.

4190   Men As Stage Scenery
Walking. Simonson, Lee. New
York Times Magazine, My 25,
1924, P. 8 and 15.

4191   Men Behind the Scenes.
New York Dramatic Mirror, O
30, 1912, P. 5, Vol. 68.

4192   Met's Amazing Stage
(The). Architectural
Record, S 1966, Vol. 140,
P. 156-160.

4193   Met's Turntable (The).
Theatre Design &
Technology, F 1971,
P. 16-19.

4194   Metal, Student Manual,
Preparation Level. G.P.O.
017-080-01456-4 1.55. No
Date.

4195   Metalizing Process -
Research Council Formula
701-A. Meyer, Herbert and
Huntington, Dexter. Motion
Picture Research Council
Bulletin No 226, Hollywood,
1954.

4196   Metallurgy of Welding
and Brazing and Soldering,
(The). Lancaster, J. F.
American Elsevier, 1965,
New York.

4197   Metalsmithing for the
Artist-Craftsman. Thomas,
Richard. Chilton, 1960, New
York.

4198   Metalworking for the
Designer and the
Technician. Taylor, Douglas
C. Drama Book Specialists,
1979, New York.

4199   Metalworking. Boyd, T.
Gardner. Goodheart-Willcox,
1968, Illinois.

4200   Metal Sculpture. Lynch,
John. Viking Press, 1957,
New York.

4201   Metal Working for the
Technician. Taylor, Douglas
C. M.F.A. Thesis, 1966,
Yale University.

4202   Metempsychosis.
Scientific American, S
1897, Vol. 77, P. 187.

4203   Methods of Production in the English Theatre from 1550 to 1598. Rothwell, William. Ph.D. Thesis, Yale University, 1951.

4204   Methods of Staging in London Theatre in the Last Half Of the 19th Century. Abegglen, Homer N. Ph.D. Thesis, Western Reserve University, 1945.

4205   Method of Solar Air Conditioning (A). Dunkle, R.V. Mech. Chem. Engrg. Trans. Inst. Engr. (Australia), 1965, P.73, Vol. MC-1.

4206   Methyl Chloride in the Fabrication of Styrofoam (No. 157-221-62). Dow Chemical Co. Dow Chemical Co., Midland. No Date.

4207   Metropolitan Board of Works and London Theatres (The). Builder (The), F 1887, Vol. LII, P. 280.

4208   Mexican National Theatre (The). Architecture and Building, My 1911, Vol. 43, P. 328-329.

4209   Meyerhold on Theatre. Meyerhold, Vsevolod. Hill & Wang, 1969, New York.

4210   Michel Parent and Theatrical Experiments in Simultaneity. Knowles, Dorothy. Theatre Research, 1971, Vol. XI, Nci, P. 23.

4211   Midsummer Night's Dream: the English and American Popular Traditions and Harley Granville-Barker's "World Arbitrarily Made". Williams, Gary Jay. Theatre Studies, 1976-77, No. 23, P. 40.

4212   Mielziner. New Yorker, Mr 19, 1966, Vol. 42, P. 44-45.

4213   Mighty Hippodrome (The). Clarke, Norman. A.S. Barnes and Company, 1968, South Brunswick and New York.

4214   Million-Piece Theatre Curtain. Popular Mechanics, Jy 1911, Vol. 16, P. 24-25.

4215   Million Dollar Musicals. MacKay, Patricia. Theatre Crafts, My/Je 1978, Vol. 12, No. 4, P. 13.

4216   Ming Cho Lee, Designer. Flaten, David. Ph.D. Thesis, University of California, Santa Barbara, 1978.

4217   Ming Cho Lee on Six of His Sets. Theatre Design & Technology, F 1971, No. 24, P. 4-9.

4218   Ming Dynasty. Eaton, Quaintance. Opera News, O 12, 1968, Vol. 33, P. 15.

4219   Miniature Vs. Large Camera. Stainton, Walter H. Players Magazine, N 1941, Vol. 18, No. 2, P. 7.

4220   Minimum Standards for the Accredatation of Theatre Degree Programs in Colleges and Universities. Theatre News, (The), Mr 1978.

4221   Miracle-A Collaboration (The). Theatre Arts Monthly, Mr, 1924, Vol. VIII, No. 3, P. 171.

4222   Miracle in the Evening. Bel Geddes, Norman. Doubleday and Company, 1960, Garden City.

4223   Miracle Mongers and Their Methods. Houdini, Harry. E.P. Dutton & Co., 1920, New York.

4224   Mirror Curtains. Bligh, N.M. Theatre Notebook Fa 1960, Vol. XV, No. 1, P. 56.

4225   Mission of the Stage
Setting (The). Wenger,
John. Theatre Arts, Ap,
1919, Vol. III, No. 2, P.
93.

4226   Mixed Media Film and
Opera. Leacock, E. Theatre
Crafts Mr 1968.

4227   MLL - a New Base for
Scene Paint. Stock, William
H. Educational Theatre
Journal, O 1964, Vol. XVI,
No. 3, P. 237.

4228   Mobility of Theatrical
Sign, (The). Honzl,
Kindrich. Interscaena, Wi
1969, Vol. 3.

4229   Model-Theatre Craft;
Scenery, Actors and Plays.
Holmes, Ruth Vickery.
Stokes, 1940, New York, 186
P.; Mcclelland, Toronto.

4230   Model Making Shops in
the Offices of Norman Bel
Geddes. Pencil Points Vol.
XX No. 7, Jl 1939 P. 447.

4231   Model of the Globe
Playhouse 1599-1613 With
Plans. Hodges, G. Walter.
Harvard Theatre Collection
1980.

4232   Model Stage and Set
(The). Wade, Robert J.
Players Magazine, N/D 1938,
Vol. 15, No. 2, P. 7, No.
3, P. 9.

4233   Model Stage Lighting
Equipment. Tabs, Ap 1949,
Vol. 7, No. 1, P. 14.

4234   Model Stage Lighting.
Tabs, S 1938, Vol. 2, No.
1.

4235   Model Stage. Tabs, D
1947, Vol. 5, No. 3, P. 17.

4236   Modernism in Stage
Designing. Bergman, Gosta
M. American Scandanivian
Reivew, 1932, Vol. 20, P.
204-211.

4237   Modernizing the Scene
Shop. Arnold, Richard.
Players, Ag/S, 1968, Vol.
43, No. 6, P. 188.

4238   Modern Art and the
Ballet. Genauer, Emily.
Theatre Arts, O 1951, Vol.
35, P. 16.

4239   Modern Ballet Design.
Buckle, Richard. Macmillan,
1955, New York.

4240   Modern Building Codes
Promote Fire Safety. Wood,
B. L. American City, Jl
1946, Vol. LXI, P. 106.

4241   Modern Conjurer (The).
Neil, C. Lang. C. Arthur
Pearson, Ltd., 1903,
London.

4242   Modern Decorative Stage
Craft. Urban, Joseph.
Century Opera Weekly Vol.1
No.10 N 6,1913 P.6.

4243   Modern Opera Houses and
Theaters. Sachs, Edwin O.
and Woodrow, Ernest A.
B.T. Batsford, 1898,
London, Reissued by
Benjamin Blom, 1968. LOCN:
Na6821. S22 1968

4244   Modern Plastics
Encylcopedia 1955. Breskin
Publications, 1955,
Bristol, Connecticut.

4245   Modern Stage Effects.
Davids, Edith. Munsey, Jl
1901, Vol. XXV, P. 524-532.

4246   Modern Stage Mechanism.
Scientific American, O
1899, Vol. 81, P. 232, 233.

4247   Modern Stage Mounting in
Germany. Singer, Hans
Wolfgang. International
Studio, (The), 1906-1907,
Vol. 30, P. 244-247; Vol.
32, P. 219-223.

4248   Modern Stage Production.
Vernon, Frank. Stage, The,
1923.

4249   Modern Stage Settings, Shakespearian and Otherwise. Brown, Frank Chouteau. Harvard Engineering Journal, Ja 1907, Vol. 5, P. 158-74; Ap 1907, P. 16-34; Je 1907, P. 11-30.

4250   Modern Stage Settings. Lewis, Kate. Illinois Libraries, Ap 1920, Pp. 33-35.

4251   Modern Stage Settings. Atlantic Monthly, Ag 1900, P. 286.

4252   Modern Stage Setting. Spiers, A. G. H. Nation, D 27, 1917, P. 726-727.

4253   Modern Stage Trick (A). Scientific American, My 1890, Vol. 62, P. 329.

4254   Modern Steels and Their Properties. Bethlehem Steel Company, 1964, Bethlehem, Pennsylvania.

4255   Modern Theatre Practice. Heffner, Hubert C. and Selden, Samuel and Sellman, Hunton D. and Walkup, Fairfax P. Prentice-Hall, 1973, Englewood Cliffs, N.J. LOCN: 72-89404 ISBN: 0-13-598805-5

4256   Modern Theatre. Bussell, John Garrett. Dobson, 1948, London.

4257   Modifications to a Synchronous Winch System at Ucla. Crocken, W.E. Theatre Design & Technology O 1969.

4258   Modified Hand Guns for Stage Use. Ackler, Bryan H. Theatre Crafts J 1977.

4259   Modular Platform System for the Stage. Bowman, Ned A. and Eck, Philip R. Theater Design and Technology, D 1965, No. 3.

4260   Modular Scenic System (A). Kramer, Wayne. Theatre Crafts, N/D 1979, Vol. 13, No. 6, P. 31.

4261   Monster Motor Truck to Carry Scenery. Popular Mechanics, Ja 1912, Vol. 17, P. 22-23.

4262   Moral of Stage Machinery. Shanks, Edward. Living Age, 1923, Vol. 317, P. 490-491.

4263   Mordecai Gorelik. Barnes, Djuna. Theatre Guild Magazine, F 1931, Vol. 8, 42-45.

4264   More Than Interior Design. Smith, Oliver. Theatre Arts Magazine, Je 1958, Vol. XLII, No. 6, P. 19.

4265   Most Ingenious Act in the Lyceum Pantomime; the Rolling Cabin of the "Roley-Poley Good Ship Alice.", (The). Sketch, Ja 10, 1912, Vol. 77, P. 5, Supplement.

4266   Motion and Time Study. Barnes, Ralph M. John Wiley and Sons, Inc., 1946, New York.

4267   Motion Picture Operation, Stage Electrics and Illusions. Horstmann, Henry Charles. F.J. Drake & Co., 1914, Chicago. LOCN: Pn 1994.H7

4268   Motor-Car and Train Accident on the Stage, A. Sketch, D 31, 1913, Vol. 84, P. 402.

4269   Motorized Rigging for Theatres. Brennan, R. Theatre Crafts Ja 1969.

4270   Movable Sectional Theatre Stage, A. Engineering Record, O 29, 1904, Vol. 50, P. 523.

4271   Movable Structures for
Stages. Soot, O.
Progressive Architecture, S
1964, P. 196.

4272   Movable Theater Stages.
Scientific American, Ap
1884, Vol. 50, P. 207-208.

4273   Movable Theatre (A).
Theatre Arts Magazine,
1920, Vol. 4, P. 169.

4274   Movable Theatre Stages.
Scientific American
Supplement, Ag 1884, Vol.
18, P. 7210-7211.

4275   Moving (Dioramic)
Experiences. All the Year
Round, 1867, Vol. 17, P.
304-307.

4276   Moving Panorama (The).
Marsh, John L. Players,
Ag/S, 1970, Vol. 45, No. 6,
P. 272.

4277   Moving Panorama Gives
Effect of Real Life.
Popular Mechanics, S 1914,
Vol. 22, P. 378-379.

4278   Mr. Hammerstein's New
London Opera House: a View
Behind the Stage Showing
the Working of the Stage.
Graphic, N 11, 1911, Vol.
84, P. 705.

4279   Mr. Reinhardt's
Discovery. Stephenson,
Nathaniel Wright. Drama, My
1913, P. 225-233.

4280   Mr. Simonson's Big Idea.
Moderwell, Hiram Kelly. New
York Times, Je 18, 1916.

4281   Multi-Media Projected
Scenery at NYC Opera 3
Productions by Frank
Grisara. Guttman, Gilda.
Ph.D. Thesis, New York
University, 1980.

4282   Multi-Purpose Pylons.
Ackler, Bryan H. Theatre
Crafts, O 1978, P.88, Vol.
12, No.6.

4283   Multiple Stage in Spain
During the Fifteenth and
Sixteenth Centuries.
Shoemaker, William H.
Princeton University Press,
1935, Princeton, New
Jersey.

4284   Multiple Stage in Spain
and Catalonis During the
15th and 16th Century
(The). Shoemaker, William
H. Ph.D. Thesis,
Princeton, 1934. Also
Published by Greenwood,
1973, Princeton. LOCN: Pn
2087 S7

4285   Multi Media and the
Theatre. Theatre Crafts Ja
1970.

4286   Multum in Parvo. Cole,
Edward C. Theatre Arts
Magazine, Jl 1943, Vol.
XXVII, No. 7, P. 447.

4287   Munich Festival (The).
Theatre Crafts, Mr/Ap 1977,
Vol. II, No. 2, P. 18.

4288   Murderous Special
Effects: Something's Afoot
at Penn State. Holamon,
Ken. Theatre Crafts, S
1978, Vol. 12, No. 5, P.
41.

4289   Murray Laufer and the
Art of Scenic Design. Hood,
Hugh. Arts-Canada, D 1972,
Vol. 29, P. 59-64.

4290   Music and Scene by Appia
in Translation. Moore,
Ulric. Ph.D. Thesis,
Cornell University, 1929.
LOCN: Pn 1624 1929 M821

4291   Must Scenery Go?. Kenny,
Sean. Plays and Players, Ap
1961, P. 6-7.

4292   Mysteries End: an
Investigation of the Last
Days of the Medieval Stage.
Gardiner, Harold C. New
Haven, 1946.

4293   Mysterious Cage, The.
Hines, G. C. Modern
Mechanics, F 1915, Vol. 30,
P. 251-252.

4294   Mysterious Levitation
Act Explained, The. Popular
Electricity, Ja 1914, Vol.
6, P. 974-975.

4295   Mysterious Skeleton,
The. Bunnell, H. O.
Popular Electricity
Magazine, Ap 1913, Vol. 5,
P. 1374.

4296   Mystery and Magic.
Jaros, Smauel. Home and
Country Magazine, Ja 1893,
Vol. 8, P. 489-503.

4297   Mystery of the Chamber
Death, the. Popular
Electricity, Ag 1913, Vol.
6, P. 372-374.

4298   My Life, My Stage.
Stern, Ernst. Gollancz,
1951, London.

4299   National Electric Code
(The). Theatre Design &
Technology O 1970.

4300   National Stage Hands
Strike Fades Out. Jongh,
Nicholas De. ABTT News, Jl
1979, P. 8.

4301   National Theatre May
Close Down. Jongh, Nicholas
De. The Guardian, Mr 22,
1979.

4302   Native Son - Backstage.
Rosenthal, Jean. Theatre
Arts Monthly, Je, 1941,
Vol. XXV, No. 6, P. 467.

4303   Nature of the Scenic
Practices in Augustin
Daly's New York Productions
1869-1899 (The). Reed,
Ronald Michael. Ph.D.
Thesis, University of
Oregon, 1968.

4304   Naval Battle and a
Vocanic Eruption on the
Stage (A). Theatre
Magazine (The), F 1912,
Vol. XV, No. 132, P. 53.

4305   Necessary Illusion
(The). Simonson, Lee.
Theatre Arts, Ap, 1919,
Vol. III, No. 2, P. 91.

4306   Need Behind the Scenes:
(Wall Units;
Materials-Flats). Davis,
William Morris. M.F.A.
Thesis, 1948, Yale
University.

4307   Neglected Virtuoso (A).
Sutton, Denys. Apollo, F
1966, P. 138-147.

4308   Neher and Brecht.
Melchinger, Siegfried.
Drama Review, Wi 1968, Vol.
12, P. 134.

4309   Nineteenth Century
Theatrical Machinery in the
Theatre Royal. Leacroft,
Richard. Theatre Notebook,
1976, Vol. 30, No. 1, P.
21.

4310   Neo-Classic and Romantic
Destruction: Scene
Designers of Ruins from
1700-1850. Hall, Roger
Allan. Theatre Studies,
1972-73, No. 19, P. 7.

4311   Newly-Identified Drawing
of Brunelleschi's Stage
Machinery (A). Blumenthal,
Arthur R. Marsyas,
1966-67, Vol. 13, P. 20-31.

4312   News Views: Approaching
a TV News Setting. Hoffman,
Paul S. Theatre Crafts,
N/D 1979, Vol. 13, No. 6,
P. 26.

4313   New and Novel Use for
Aluminum. Scientific
American, O 1923, Vol. 129,
P. 254.

4314   New and Recycled: Robert
Yodice Designs for Opera
and Dance at The Julliard.

Theatre Crafts, My/Je 1976, Vol. 10, No. 3, P. 7.

4315   New Art of Model-Making. Jevons, Henry R. Technical World Magazine, Je 1911, Vol. 15, P. 438-449.

4316   New Art of Scenic Illusion. Literary Digest, Je 18, 1910, Vol. 40, P. 1224.

4317   New Building Code for Theatre Structures in the City of New York. Theatre Design & Technology O 1969.

4318   New Curtain at the Old Vic, (The). Sellman, H.D. New Statesman S 24, 1938, Vol. 16, P. 458.

4319   New Design Problem: Multi-Media Effects (The). Weiss, David W. Players, Ag/s 1970, Vol. 45, P. 264-67.

4320   New Development in Flying Systems. Holden, Michael. Theatre Quarterly, Jl 1971, Vol. 1, No. 3, P. 73.

4321   New Device for Scene Shifting (A). Krows, Arthur Edwin. New York Times, D 1, 1918, Sec. 7, P. 6.

4322   New Directions (Scenographic Quests) in Soviet Theatre. Gankovske, V. Theatre Design & Technology My 1973.

4323   New Elevations for Technical Theatre. Meisenholder, F. Theatre Design & Technology Sum 1977.

4324   New Elevations for Technical Theatre. Meisenholder, David. Players, My, 1964, Vol. XL, No. 8, P. 247.

4325   New Equipment With the

Fairy Play (A). De Foe, Louis V. Green Book Magazine, F 1915, Vol. 13, P. 267-278.

4326   New File and Loan System for Technical Data (A). Educational Theatre Journal, Mr 1952, Vol. IV, No. I, P. 48.

4327   New Form of Theatre Space (A). Hazucha, Vlado. Interscena, Acta Scaenographica Internationalia, Su 1967, Vol. 3, P. 35-41.

4328   New Genius of Stage Production, Isaac Grunewald (A). Arts and Decoration, Je 1923, Vol. 19, P. 24-25, 56.

4329   New H.Q. for the Welsh National Opera Company. Reid, Francis. Tabs Je 1969.

4330   New Macbeth: Gordon Craig Designs a Production for George Tyler. Theatre Arts Monthly, N, 1929, Vol, Xii, No. 11, P. 804.

4331   New Magician of the Stage: Russian Inventor Makes Startling Scenic Transformations Without the Aid of Settings. Bird, Carol. Theatre Magazine, F 1922, P. 80.

4332   New Medium for Modern Art. Dupont Magazine, N/D 1964, P.1.

4333   New Medium for Sculpture (A). Mortellito, Domenico. American Artsist, 1965 (Excerpt from Artfoam, Strux Corp., Lindenhurst, New York).

4334   New Methods and Materials in Stage Design. Yves-Bonnat. World Theatre, Sp, 1963, Vol. XII, No. 1, P. 5.

4335   New Method of Constructing Scaffolding, (A). Builder (The), N 30, 1889, Vol. LVII, P. 389.

4336   New Model Casting Materials. Scientific American, S 1933, Vol. 149, P. 123.

4337   New Movement in Theatre. Cheney, Sheldon. Mitchell Kinnerley, 1914, New York.

4338   New Optical Illustion, a. Scientific American, N 1858, Vol. 14, P. 80.

4339   New Pattern for Building Legislation (A). Vermiya, Howard. Architectural Record, Mr 1946, Vol. XCIX, P. 68.

4340   New Pigment Binder (A). Bladow, Elmer L. Educational Theatre Journal, Mr 1960, Vol. XII, No. 1, P. 24.

4341   New Plastic Effects and the Revival of Perspective. Nagy, Elmer. Players Magazine, Ja 1942, Vol. 18, No. 4, P. 6.

4342   New Production and Scenography. Poleiri, Jacques. World Theatre, 1966, Vol. XV, No. 1, P. 10.

4343   New Products: Automatic Safety Rope Brake Equipment. Theatre Design & Technolgoy, 1973, No. 35, P. 29.

4344   New Products: Flooring Mig Welder. Thompson, Richard. Theatre Design & Technology, Wi 1975, No. 43, P. 33.

4345   New Products and Processes. Newsweek Inc. 1979 Box 424 Livingston, Nj 07039.

4346   New Russian Stage, a Blaze of Color. Roberts, Mary Fanton. Craftsman, D 1915, Vol. 29, P. 257.

4347   New Scene Paint (A). Mitchell, Lee. Theatre Arts Monthly, Jl, 1937, Vol. XXI, No. 7, P. 581.

4348   New Scenic Art in the American Theatre. Current Opinion, My, 1919, Vol. 66, P. 301.

4349   New Sensation at the Hippodrome; How the Elephants Came Down the Slide, (A). Sphere, Ja 9, 1904, Vol. 16, P. 45.

4350   New Series of Stage Settings for Shakespeare's Romeo and Juliet. Brown, Frank Chouteau. Architectural Record, S 1905, P. 175-191.

4351   New Spirit in Drama and Art. Carter, Huntly. Mitchell Kennery, 1913, New York.

4352   New Stage-Craft in America (The). Macgowan, Kenneth. Century, Ja 1914, Vol. 87, P. 416-421.

4353   New Stagecraft: Developments in Scenery and Lighting on the New York Stage Bewteen 1900 and 1915, (The). Arnold, Richard. Ph.D. Thesis, Northwestern University, 1962.

4354   New Stagecraft: Illustrated by Josef Urban's Imaginative Settings for Shakespeare, (The). Mann, Dorothea Lawrence. Crafts Man My, 1916, Vol. 30, P. 168.

4355   New Stagecraft: Its Relation to Easel Painting. Taylor, Mildred A. K. Ph.D. Thesis, Stanford University, 1953.

4356   New Stagecraft: Robert
Edmond Jones, Norman Bel
Geddes, Lee Simonson (The).
Mcevoy, Owen. Ph.D. Thesis,
New York (School of the
Arts), 1980.

4358   New Stage Designing
(The). Johnson, Craymond.
Theatre Arts, Ap, 1919,
Vol. III, No. 2, P. 121.

4359   New Stage Effect, (A).
Scientific American, Mr
1922, Vol. 126, P. 211.

4360   New Stage Mechanics
Exibited in London. Musical
Courier, Ap 29, 1914, Vol.
68, P. 5.

4361   New Stage of the
Metropolitan Opera House,
The. Scientific American, F
6, 1904, P. 113, 117-118.

4362   New Stage Settings in
Germany. Pirchan, E.
Studio, Mr 1931, Vol. 101,
P 216.

4363   New Staging, The.
Barney, Charles Gorham.
Colonnade, Ap 1915, P. 125.

4364   New Standard Theatre
(The). Illustrated London
News, My 1845, Vol. 6, P.
320.

4366   New Theatre's Turn-Table
Stage. Dodge, Wendell
Phillips. Technical World,
F 1911, Vol. 14, P. 677.

4367   New Theatre; F. L.
Wright Sees His
Long-Planned Theatre
Nearing Construction in
Hartford, Connecticut.
Lewis, L. Theatre Arts, Jl
1949, Vol H. Xxxiii, P H.
33-34.

4368   New Theatres for Old.
Gorelik, Mordecai. Samuel
French 1955 New York.

4369   New Theatres for Old.

Eustis, Morton and Morton,
Frederick. Theatre Arts
Monthly, D 1935, Vol. XIX,
No. 12, P. 910.

4370   New Theories and Methods
of American Staging As
Developed in The Period
During 1910-1920. Whited,
Norstrom. M.A. Thesis,
University of California
Los Angeles, 1951.

4371   New Theory of Stage
Production. Bulloch, J. M.
Lamp, Ag 1903, Vol. 27, P.
23.

4372   New Triumph in the Art
of the Theatre (A). Arts
and Decoration, Je 1919,
Vol. 11, P. 80-81.

4373   New Triumph in the Art
of the Theatre (A).
Scientific American, F 6,
1904, Vol. 90, P. 113,
117-118.

4374   New Version of the
Revolving Stage Idea (A).
Scientific American, Ap
1923, Vol. 128, P. 224-25.

4375   New Visions in Opera
Design: Rudolph Heinrich in
Retrospect. Loney, Glenn.
Theatre Crafts, N/D 1976,
Vol. 10, No. 6, P. 13.

4376   New Wagon Stage (A).
Throckmorton, Cleon.
Theatre Arts Monthly, 1927,
Vol. 11, P. 130-132.

4377   New Ways in
Czechoslovakia. Svoboda,
Josef. World Theatre, Sp,
1963, Vol. XII, No. 1, P.
32.

4378   New Way of Outlining
Theatre Scenery (A).
Scientific American
Supplement, Ap 1877, Vol.
2, P. 1083.

4379   New Way of Outlining
Theatre Scenery. American

Architect, Mr 1877, Vol. II, P. 72.

4380   New York City Booth's Theatre Stage Plans and Settings, 18 73-1884; Fifth Avenue Theatre 1878-1884. Yale University Collection. No Date. LOCN: Film B851 1

4381   New York City Building Control 1800-1941. Comer, John P. 1942, New York.

4382   New York Moving Picture Theatre Law. Blackall, Clarence H. Brickbuilder, 1914, Vol. 23, P. 46-50.

4383   New York Public Library Theatre Collection (The). Freedley, George. OSU Theatre Collection Bulletin, Fall 1956, Vol. 3, No. 1, P. 4.

4384   Niagara of Bubbles, (A). Science and Invention, 1921, Vol. 8, P. 1065.

4385   Nicola Sabbattini's Description of Stage Machinery from Practica Di Fabricar Scene E Machine Ne'teatri: an Explanation & Commentary. Larson, Orville K. Players, O 1962, P.13-20, Vol. 39; Also N 1962, P.47, Vol. 39.

4386   Nijinsky and Til Eulenspiegl. Jones, Robert Edmond. Dance Index, Ap 1945, Vol. 4, P. 44-54.

4387   Nineteenth-Century Timber Stage Machinery at the Theatre Royal. Kilburn, Michael. Architectural Review, F 1973, Vol. 153, P. 131.

4388   Nineteenth Century Century Stage Machines. Elleman, Joseph. M.A. Thesis, Ohio State University, 1951.

4389   Nineteenth Century

Machinery File. Harvard Theatre Collection. No Date.

4390   Nineteenth Century Theatrical Machinery in the Theatre Royal, Bath. Leacroft, Richard. Theatre Notebook, 1976, Vol. XXX, No. 1, P.21.

4391   Norman Bel Geddes: Artist-Craftsman of the Theatre. Bickley, Charles E. M.A. Thesis, University of Wisconsin, 1951.

4392   Norman Bel Geddes: Theatre Artist. Hunter, Frederick J. Texas Quarterly, Wi 1962, Vol. 5, P. 164-189.

4393   Norman Bel Geddes' Notes on Art in the Theatre. Hunter, Frederick J. Theatre Survey, 1962, Vol. 3, P. 32-40.

4394   Norman Bel Geddes Artistic Lighting Designer. Mecham, E.J. M. F. A. Thesis, University of Texas, Austin, 1966.

4395   Norman Bel Geddes on Scene Design. Larson, Orville K. Players, O, 1963, Vol. XL, No. 1, P. 8.

4396   Norman Wilkinson's Decoration of a Midsummer Night's Dream at The Savoy Theatre. Wood, T. Martin. International Studio, Je 1914, P. 301-307.

4397   Notable Stage Elevator Installation. Engineering and Contracting, 1923, Vol. 70, P. 1354.

4398   Notes & Queries 14375. Scientific American, D 1921, Vol. 125, P. 155.

4399   Notes & Queries 16. Scientific American, Mr 1877, Vol. 36, P. 171.

4400   Notes & Queries   18.
Scientific American, Ap
1877, Vol. 36, P. 267.

4401   Notes & Queries   26.
Scientific American, Ag
1878, Vol. 38, P. 139.

4402   Notes and Queries   31.
Scientific American, Ja
1875, Vol. 32, P. 75.

4403   Notes for Technicians.
Cole, Wendell. Educational
Theatre Journal, D 1951,
Vol. 111, No. 4, P. 349.

4404   Notes from Reuth.
Dunham, Richard B. Theatre
Design & Technology, D
1968, No. 15, P. 29.

4405   Notes on Little-Known
Materials for the History
of the Theatre. Rapp,
Franz. Theatre Annual 3
1944 P. 60.

4406   Notes on Scene Painting.
Ashworth, Bradford.
Whitlock, 1952, New Haven.

4407   Notes on the
Construction of the Globe
Model. Smith, Irwin.
Shakespeare Quarterly, Ja
1951, Vol. 2, P. 12-18.

4408   Notes on the History of
the Revels Office Under the
Tudors. Chambers, Sir
Edmund Kerchever. A.H.
Bullen, 1906, London. LOCN:
Pn2590 R4 C4

4409   Notes on Two
Pre-Restoration Stage
Curtains. Mcmanaway, James
G. Philological Quarterly,
1962, Vol. 41, P. 270-274.

4410   Notes Towards a
Reconstruction of Le
Mystere Des Actes Des
Apotres As Presented at
Bourges, 1536. Hasim,
James. Theatre
Research/Recherches
Theatrales, 1972, Vol. 12,
P. 29-73.

4411   Note About Lee Simonson
(A). Moderwell, Hiram
Kelly. Theatre Arts, D,
1917, Vol. II, No. 1, P.
12.

4412   Note on Ellen Terry,
Gordon Craig, and Screens.
Sheren, Paul. Yale Theatre,
Fall 1970, Vol. 3, P. 4.

4413   Note on Japanese
Marionettes (A). Craig,
Edward Gordon. Mask (The),
My, 1915, Vol. 7, NO. 2, P.
104.

4414   Note on the Theatre.
Jones, Robert Edmond.
Provincetown Playbill, J 4,
1924, No. 1, P. 3. located
at the Harvard Theatre
Collection.

4415   Note on the Use of
Scenery at the Cockpit-In
Court, (A). Star, L. R.
Theatre Notebook, 1972,
Vol. XXVI, No. 3, P. 89.

4416   Novel Effects Used by
Beerbohm Tree. Theatre
Magazine (The), Ap, 1906,
Vol. VI, P. 94.

4417   Novel Way to Sculpt. Dow
Diamond (Dow Chemical Co.,
Midland), 1966, Vol. XXIX,
No. 1, P. 16.

4418   Now Is the Time for All
Good Men. Gould, Mervyn.
Cue Technical Theatre
Review, S/O 1979, P. 29.

4419   No Wings No Flies.
Jager, D.V. Theatre Design
& Technology F 1973.

4420   NRA Home Firearm Safety.
National Rifle Association,
1962, Washington, D.C.

4421   NRA Hunter Safety
Handbook. National Rifle
Association, 1957,
Washington, D.C.

4422   Obscure Pioneer of the

Newest Art in the Theatre. Current Opinion, Ag 1916, P. 101-102.

4423   Observations on Lansdowne Ms. No. 1171. Theatre Notebook, O, 1947, Vol. 2, No. 1, P. 6.

4424   Off Off Broadway: Circle Repertort Theatre Company. Theatre Crafts, Mr/Ap 1974, Vol. 8, No. 2, P. 8.

4425   Of Things Theatrical in Germany and England. Kingston, Gertrude. Nineteenth Century, D 1909, Vol. 66, P. 990-1007.

4426   OISTT Reports on Theatre Training. Theatre Design & Technology Fall 1976.

4427   Old and the New Magic (The). Evans, Henry Ridgely. Open Court Publishing Co., 1906, Chicago.

4428   Old Bristol Theatre: the Puzzle of the Sloat (An). Southern, Richard. Life & Letters To-Day, S 1939, P.426-33, Vol. 22.

4429   Old Drury at War; ENSA Headquarters and Workshop. Theatre Arts Magazine, My 1944, Vol. XXVIII, No. 5, P. 285.

4430   Old French Ironwork: the Craftsman and His Art. Frank, Edgar B. Harvard University Press, 1950, Cambridge, Massachusetts.

4431   Old Stage Effects. Scientific American, Mr 1900, Vol. 82, P. 187.

4432   Old Vic & New: Theatre Royal , Bristol. Architectural Review, F 1973, Vol. 153, P. 123-131.

4433   Olivier Flying System (The). Brett, Richard.

Sightline, Sp 1979, Vol. 13, No. 1, P. 49.

4434   Olympian Theatre, Vicenza (The). Builder, (The), D 12, 1863, P. 881.

4435   Once Again--The Raked Stage. Tabs, Ap 1956, Vol. 14, No. 1, P. 20.

4436   One Man Show: Retrospective Exhibition at New York Museum of Modern Art. Brown, John Mason. Saturday Review of Literature, My 12, 1945, Vol. 28, P. 18.

4437   One Set for Four Faces: Michael Yeargan's Scenic Solutions for Sganarelle. MacKay, Patricia. Theatre Crafts, S 1978, Vol. 12, No. 5, P. 26.

4438   On Architecture. Vitruvius Pollio. William Heinemann, 1931, London; G P. Putnam's Sons, 1931-1934, New York.

4439   On Being Upstaged by Scenery. Hatch, Robert. Horizon, S 1962, Vol. 5, P. 110-112.

4440   On Bellman's Scenography. Arnold, Richard. Lighting Dimensions, Ag 1979, P. 50.

4441   On Cosmoramas, Dioramas, and Panoramas. Penny Magazine, 1842, Vol. 11, P. 363-364.

4442   On Scenic Illusion and Stage Appliances. Fitzgerald, Percy. Journal of the Royal Society of Arts, Mr 18, 1887, Vol. 35, P. 456-66.

4443   On Stage. Modern Plastics, 1952, Vol. 30, No. 1, P. 94.

4444   On the Art of the

Theatre. Craig, Edward
Gordon. Small Maynard,
1925.

4445   On the Safeguarding of
Life in Theatres. Freeman,
John R. American Society
of Mechanical Engineers,
1906, New York.

4446   On the Scenery and Stage
Decorations of Theatres.
Builder (The), Ap 24, 1846,
Vol. 6, P. 191.

4447   Open Air Theatre in
America. Row, Arthur.
Harper's Weekly, O 4, 1913,
P. 21.

4448   Open Stage and the
Modern Theatre in Research
and Practice (The).
Southern, Richard. Faber
and Faber, 1953, London.

4449   Opera on Television:
David Myersgouch-Jones
Designs for the Camera.
Loney, Glenn. Theatre
Crafts, N/D 1977, Vol. 11,
No.6, P. 33.

4450   Opera Scenery Can Be
Built on a Shoestring.
Molyneux, William. Musical
American, F 15, 1954, Vol.
74, No. 28, P. 166-167.

4451   Opera Urbanized. Eaton,
Quaintance. Opera News, F
27, 1965, Vol. 29, P.
26-30.

4452   Opinions on the Relation
of Decor to Choreography.
Chagall, Marc. Dance
Magazine, My 1946, Vol. 20,
P. 26-27.

4453   Orchestra Lift at the
Colony Theatre, New York
(The). Architecture and
Building, 1925, Vol. 57, P.
27.

4454   Ordinance Relating to
the Department of Buildings
(An). Moorman and Geller
1905 Chicago.

4455   Orestia at Stanford,
(The). Haag, A. Evan.
Theatre Crafts, My/Je 1977,
Vol. 11, No. 3, P. 20.

4456   Organizing the Property
Crew. Tolch, John. Players
Magazine, Mr 1961, Vol. 37,
No. 6, P. 131.

4457   Origins of the Box Set
in the Late 18th Century.
Lee, B.H. Theatre Survey N
1977.

4458   Orphan Annie Goes from a
Hard-Knock Life to Easy
Street. MacKay, Patricia.
Theatre Crafts, N/D 1977,
Vol. 11, No. 6, P. 29.

4459   OSHA and the
Entertainment Code: the
Short, Stormy Road to
Acceptance of Safety
Standards. Eastman, James
Earl. Ph.D. Thesis, Bowling
Green University, 1977.

4460   Othello. Jones, Robert
Edmond. Original Pencil
Drawing. located at the
Harvard Theatre Collection.

4461   Other Places, Other
Times Patrizia Von
Brandenstein Designs for
Film. Napoleon, Davi.
Theatre Crafts, N/D 1979,
Vol. 13, No. 6, P. 21.

4462   Our Magic. Maskelyne,
Nevil and Devant, David.
E.P. Dutton & Co., 1911,
New York.

4463   Our Navy on the Stage.
Electrical Experimenter, S
1917, Vol. 5, P. 294.

4464   Our Poisoned Scene
Shops. Adducci, Alexander
F. Educational Theatre
Journal, My 1971, Vol.
XXIII, No. 2, P. 109.

4465   Our Theatre Today.
Bricker, Herschel (Editor).
French, 1936, New York.

4466   Outdated Building Codes.
American City, Je 1943,
Vol. LVIII, P. 123.

4467   Outline of Theatre Law.
Jacobs, M C. Jacobs, M.C.,
1949, New York.

4468   Out of Dust. Jones,
Robert Edmond. 23 Original
Drawings & Photographs.
located at the Harvard
Theatre Collection.

4469   Overhead-Handling,
Universal-Positioning
Device. Lighting
Dimensions, Ap 1978, Vol.
2, No. 4, P. 34.

4470   Over a Second Avenue
Shop: the Negro Ensemble
Company. Theatre Crafts,
Mr/Ap 1974, Vol. 8, No. 2,
P. 10.

4471   Oxford As Scenic
Pioneer. Lawrence, William
John. New York Dramatic
Mirror, Mr 23, 1907, P. 13.

4472   Oxford Companion to the
Theatre (The). Hartnoll,
Phyllis (Editor). 1957
London, New York, Ontario.

4473   Oxy-Acetylene Welder's
Handbook (The) Sixth
Edition. Jefferson, T. B.
Welding Engineer
Publications, 1960, Morton
Groves, Illinois.

4474   Oxyacetylene Welding.
Potter, Morgan H. American
Technical Society 1942,
Chicago.

4475   O Showes, Showes, Mighty
Showes: The Jones-Jason
Controversy and Illusionistic
Staging in 17th Century
British Drama. Presley,
Horton Edward. Ph.D Thesis,
University of Kansas, 1966.

4476   Pacific Overtures:
Veteran Designer Boris
Aronson Creates a Personal

View of 19th Century Japan.
Theatre Crafts, Ja/F 1976,
Vol. 10, No. 1, P. 8.

4477   Pageant Stage Screened
by Curtain of Steam.
Popular Mechanics, S 1915,
Vol. 24, P. 342-343.

4478   Pagent Era (The).
McNamara, Brooks. Theatre
Crafts, S 1975, Vol. 9, No.
4, P. 10.

4479   Painted Scenery Versus
Built Scenery. Bergman,
Robert W. Almanac,
1940-41, United Scenic
Artists, 1941, P.37-41.

4480   Painter and the Stage
(The). Simonson, Lee.
Theatre Arts, D 1917, Vol.
II, No. 1, P. 3.

4481   Painter in the Theatre
(The). Cheney, Sheldon.
Theatre Arts Magazine Jl
1922, Vol. 1, No.3, P.191.

4482   Painter on Stage. Show,
Mr 1962, Vol. 2, P. 76.

4483   Painting Acres of
Scenery for Opera. Popular
Mechanics, N 1924, Vol. 42,
P. 744-746.

4484   Painting a Yosemite
Panorama. Robinson, C. D.
Overland, S 1893, Vol. 22,
P. 243-256.

4485   Painting of Panoramas
(The). Magazine, of Art,
1900, Vol. 24, P. 555-558.

4486   Painting of Scenery,
(The). Telbin, William.
Magazine of Art, 1889, P.
92-97, 195-201.

4487   Painting Scenery: a
Handbook for Amateur
Productions. Jones, Leslie
Allen. Walter H. Baker,
1935, Boston. LOCN: Pn2091
S8j57 (Mwep)

4488   Paint and Painting. Peck, Clemen M. Players Magazine, N/D 1946, Vol. 23, No. 2, P. 39.

4489   Paint Frame (A). Hake, Herbert V. Theatre Arts Monthly, Jl, 1938, Vol. XXII, No. 7, P. 531.

4490   Panaromic Scenery at Sadler's Wells. Phillabaum, Corliss E. OSU Theatre Collection, Bulletin 6, 1959, P. 20.

4491   Panel: National Electric Code. Theatre Design and Technology, O 1970, P.29-33.

4492   Panoramas of the Exposition of 1900 (The). Scientific American Supplement, Ag 1900, Vol. 50, P. 20602, 20603.

4493   Panoramas of the Paris Exposition (The). Scientific American Supplement, S 1900, Vol. 50, P. 20602, 20603.

4494   Paper Honeycomb Sandwich Panels As Lightweight Structural Components. Reichard, Thonias W. National Bureau of Standards; Washington, 1972; for Sale By Us Government Printing Office.

4495   Paper Honeycomb Sandwitch Pannels As Material for Construction of Stage Scenery. Lampman, Michael. M.A. Thesis Univ. of Wisconson 1974. LOCN: Awd L2385 M525

4496   Parade: Cubism As Theatre. Aysom, Richard Hayden. Ph.D. Thesis, University of Michigan, 1974.

4497   Paradox of Multi-Dimensional Scenographic Presentations or Why Models Are No Damn Good (The). Salzer, Beeb. Lighting Dimensions, D 1978, Vol. 12, No. 10, P. 20.

4498   Parallele De Plans Des Plus Belles Salles De Spectacles D'italie Avec Des Details De Machines Theatrales. Dumont, Gabriel Pierre Martin. Paris, 1763,. LOCN: Na 6820 D8 1968

4499   Parisian Boulevard Theatres from 1779 to 1791: the Development Of Stage Spectacle. Jenkins, Charles A. Ph.D. Thesis, Indiana University, 1974.

4500   Paris Stage (The). All the Year Round, Je 1868, Vol. 20, P. 33-35.

4501   Part of a Lifetime; Drawings and Designs, 1919-1940. Simonson, Lee. Duell, Sloan and Pearce, 1943.

4502   Path of Decoration in the English Theatre (The). Shipp, H. Apollo, My 1926, Vol. 3, P. 282.

4503   Paying for Stage Equipment. Burrows, Robert B. Players Magazine, Ap 1940, Vol. 16, No. 7, P. 6.

4504   Pedal Power in Work Leisure, and Transportation. Mccullaugh, James C. (Ed.). Rodale Press, 1977, Emmaus, Pennsylvania. ISBN: 0-87857-178-7

4505   Pelleas and Meusande. Jones, Robert Edmond. 6 Original Ink Drawings. located at the Harvard Theatre Collection.

4506   Pellon: New Material for Designers. Stillwell, L. H. Theatre Design & Technology, My 1967.

4507   Pentathlon. Bentham, Frederick. Sightline; ABTT Journal, 1978, Vol. 12, No. 1, P. 17-25.

4508   Perfection Stage Lighting. Lawrence, William John. Dramatic Mirror, F 24, 1917, Vol. 77.

4509   Perfect Scarf Joints Every Time. Chambers, R.C. Theatre Design & Technology, O 1974.

4510   Perforated Structural Square Steel Tubing in the Theatre. Hunt, Derek. Theatre Design & Technology, F 1968.

4511   Performing Arts Library Lincoln Center Original Designs. Origional Artwork in N.Y.C.P.L. Collection. No Date.

4512   Performing Arts Library Lincoln Center Original Designs. Origional Artwork in N.Y.C.P.L. Collection. No Date.

4513   Performing Arts Management and Law Forms, Vol. 5: Sound and Sound Copyright. Taubman, Joseph. Law-Arts Publishers, Inc., F 1978, N.Y.

4514   Performing Arts Management and Law Forms, Vol. 6: Music Publishing. Taubman, Joseph. Law-Arts Publishers, Inc., F 1978, New York.

4515   Periaktoi at the Medici Court?. Nagler, A.M. Theatre Annual, 1956, Vol. 14, P. 28-36.

4516   Periaktoi for Modern Use. Lewis, Colby. Players Magazine, N 1941, Vol. 18, No. 2, P. 7.

4517   Periaktoi in the Old Blackfriars. Miller, William. Modern Language Notes, 1959, Vol. 74, P. 1-3.

4518   Period Costumes & Settings for the Small Stage. Green, Joyce Mary Conyngham. G. G. Harrap, 1936, London. LOCN: Pn 2067 G66

4519   Permanent Set in Theatrical Design. Southern, Richard. Atelier, Ap 1931, Vol. 1, P. 248.

4521   Personal Code Is Better. Dewey, Walter S. Players, D/J, 1972, Vol. 47, No. 2, P. 50.

4522   Perspective in the Renaissance Theatre. the Pictorial Sources and the Development of Scenic Forms. Kernodle, George R. Ph.D. Thesis, Yale University, 1937.

4523   Perspective Landscape in the English Theatre 1660-1682 (The). Jackson, Allan S. Ph.D. Thesis, Ohio State University, 1962.

4524   Perspective Rendering by Hand-Held Calculator. Hoffman, Paul S. Theatre Design & Technology, Winter 1978, Vol. XIV, No. 4, P. 5.

4525   Perspective Scenery: Science and Symbol. Kernodle, George R. Theatre Studies, 1975-76, No. 22, P. 5.

4526   Perspective Scenery and the Caroline Playhouses. Freehafer, John. Theatre Notebook, 1973, Vol. XXVII, No. 3, P. 98.

4527   Peter Behrens and the Theatre. Leeper, Janet. Architectural Review, Ag 1968, Vol. 144, P. 138.

4528   Peter Goffin. Laver, James. Studio, Jl 1961, P. 16-19.

4529   Peter Nichol Son and the Scenographic Art. Armstrong, William A. Theatre Notebook, 1954, Vol. 8, P. 91.

4530   Art of Scenic Design and Staging for Children's Theatre. Davis, Jed H. Ph.D. Thesis, University of Minnesota, 1959.

4531   Phillippe Jacques De Loutherbourg Eighteenth Century Artist and Scene Designer. Preston, Lilian E. Thesis, University of Florida, 1957.

4532   Philosophy in a New Key. Langer, Susanne. Harvard University Press, 1951, Cambridge; New American Library, 1948, New York.

4533   Photgraphic Sources of Productions of Vsevolod Emiliovich Meyerhold. Kezler, William. Theatre Documentation, 1971, Vol. 4, No. 1, P. 31.

4534   Photographic Techniques for Creating Projected Effects. Lessley, Merrill. Lighting Dimensions, O 1978, Vol. 2, No. 10, P. 26-44.

4535   Photographing Your Play at Small Cost: Valuable Suggestions for Amateur Groups. Duthie, Hermione. Players Magazine, N/D 1931, Vol. VII, No. 2, P. 5.

4536   Photographing Your Play. Miller, James H. Players Magazine, My, 1949, Vol. 25, No. 8, P. 181.

4537   Photography for the Theatre Some How To's for Photo Call. Smith, Winifred. Theatre Crafts N 1975.

4538   Photograpy: Its Materials and Processes. Neblette, C. B. and Others. D. Van Norstand Co., Inc., 1962, New York.

4539   Photo Murals for the Stage. Weldin, Scott. Theatre Crafts, My/Je 1977, Vol. 11, No. 3, P. 26.

4540   Physical and Chemical Examination of Paints, Varnishes, Lacquers and Colors. Gardner, Henry A. Institute of Paint and Varnish Research, 1935, Washington, D. C.

4541   Picasso: Theatre. Cooper, Douglas. Henry N. Abrams, 1968, New York. ISBN: 0-8109-0396-2

4542   Pickets Face NT Writ. ABTT News May 1979. The Guardian April 30, 1979.

4543   Pictorial Composition in American Stage Design. Crepeau, George Paul. Ph.D. Thesis, 1962, Cornell University.

4544   Pictorial History of the American Theatre, 1900-1950, A. Blum, Daniel. Greenberg, 1950, New York.

4545   Pictorial History of the Russian Theatre (The). Marshall, Herbert. Crown Publishers, Inc., 1977, New York.

4546   Pictorial in English Theatrical Staging, 1773-1833 (The). Watters, Don Albert. Ph.D. Thesis, Ohio State University, 1954.

4547   Places of Public Entertainment Technical Regulations. London County Council, 1952, London.

4548   Place of Stage Decoration: a Secondary

Theatre Art, Never As
Important As Acting, (The).
Crafton, Allen. Players,
Magazine, Mr/Ap 1931, Vol.
VII, No. 3, P. 5.

4549   Plane Geometry. Hawkes,
Herbert E. Ginn and
Company, 1920, Boston.

4550   Planning for Dramatic
Education. Corry, Percy.
Tabs, Mr 1966.

4551   Planning of the "Oliver"
National Tour. Albery, Ian
B. Tabs Mr 1966.

4552   Planning of the Motion
Picture Theater (The).
Architectural Forum, Je
1925, Vol. 42, P. 385-388.

4553   Planning Settings in
Summer Stock Theatres.
Lodge, Nancy. Players
Magazine, O 1941, Vol. 18,
No. 1, P. 9.

4554   Planning the Small
Stage. Corry, Percy. Tabs,
D 1953, Vol. 11, No. 3,.

4555   Plans. Theatre Arts
Magazine, D 1922, Vol. VI,
No. 4, P. 297 & P. 345.

4556   Plan and Working
Drawings for a Multiple-Use
Stage Setting Suitable for
a Touring Theatre. Pannett,
Murrell. M.A. Thesis,
University of Washington,
1948.

4557   Plan for a Folding Stage
Adaptable for Puppets,
Marionettes, and Shadows
(A). McPharlin, Paul.
McPharlin, 1934,
Birmingham, Mich., 3 P.

4559   Plan for the Use of
Prefabricated Aluminum
Sectional Units As a Means
of Rendering More Effective
the Construction and Use of
Frame d Scenery for the
Stage. Baron, Robert H.

M.A. Thesis, 1949, Smith
College.

4560   Plaster Casting for the
Student Sculptor. Wager,
Victor, H. Manual Arts
Press, 1944, Peoria,
Illinois.

4561   Plastico Masks. Players
Magazine, D, 1951, Vol. 28,
No. 3, P. 68.

4562   Plastics and the
Building Codes. Rarig,
F.J. Progressive
Architecture, O 1970, P.
97.

4563   Plastics As an Art Form.
Newman, Thelma R. Chilton
Book Co., 1969, New York.

4564   Plastics at the Guthrie.
Scales, Robert and Bakkom,
J. Theatre Design &
Technology D 1970.

4565   Plastics Foams- Storage,
Handling, and Fabrication.
Manufacturing Chemists
Association, 1960,
Washington, D.C.

4566   Plastics from Farm and
Forest. Lougee, E. F.
Plastic I. T. Institute,
1943, New York.

4567   Plastics in
Architecture. Progressive
Architecture, Je 1960,
Whole Issue.

4568   Plastics in the
Do-It-Yourself Market.
Modern Plastics, 1954, Vol.
31, No. 12, P. 87.

4569   Plastics in the Theatre.
Theatre Crafts O 1970.

4570   Plastics Primer (A).
Chastain, Charles E.
Modern Plastics
Encyclopedia, 1969, Vol.
46, No. 10, P. 25.

4571   Plastics Research and

Technology at the National Bureau of Standards. Kline, Gordon M. U.S. Government Printing Office, Je 1950, Washington, D.C

4572   Plastics Scientific and Technological. Fleck, H. R. Chemical Publishing Company, Inc., 1945, New York.

4573   Plastics. Kay F. George. Roy, 1969, New York.

4574   Plastics. Cope, Dwight W. and Conaway, John O. Goodheart-Wilcox, 1966, Homewood, Illinois.

4575   Plastic Foams. Benning, Calvin J. John Wiley and Sons, 1969, New York.

4576   Plastic Foam for Arts & Crafts. Yates, Brock. Sterling Publishing Co., Inc. 1965, New York.

4577   Plastic Lighting. Mason, Jero. Players Magazine, Ap 1957, Vol. 33, No. 7, P. 163.

4578   Plastic Molding Technique. Dearle, D. A. Chemical Publishing Compnay, 1970, New York.

4579   Plastic People: Extras for Milwaukee Repertory Theatre. Baun, J.T. and Foster, E. Theatre Crafts N 1975.

4580   Plastic Production. Hake, Herbert V. Players Magazine, D 1940, Vol. 17, No. 3, P. 7.

4581   Plastic Sheet Forming. Butzko, Robert L. Reinhold Publishing Corp., 1958, New York.

4582   Platform Clamps. Howard, John T. Jr. Theatre Crafts, O 1978, Vol. 12, No. 6, P. 89.

4583   Plays Produced Under the Stage Direction of David Belasco. Belasco, David. David Belasco Publisher, 1925, New York.

4584   Play Production for Amateurs and Schools. Jeffreys, Montagu, V.C. and Stopford, R.W. Methuen, 1945, London. LOCN: Pn3155.J4 1945

4585   Play Production for Amateurs. Koch, F. H. 1921.

4586   Play Production for Little Theatres, Schools, and Colleges. D. Appleton-Century, 1948, New York.

4587   Play Production in America. Krows, Arthur Edwin. Henry Holt & Co., 1916, New York.

4588   Play Production. Hewitt, Barnard. J.B. Lippincott Co., 1940, Philadelphia.

4589   Play Production. Nelms, Henning. Barnes & Noble, Inc., 1950, New York.

4590   Plywood's Future Has Just Begun. Ottinger, Lawrence. Pencil Points, My 1944, P. 79.

4591   Pneumatic Cylinders at the Guthrie. Asteren, Terry. Theatre Crafts, O 1977.

4592   Pneumatic Scenery Built for the German Stage. Popular Mechanics, O 1914, Vol. 22, P. 483.

4593   Pneumatic Tools for the Theatre. Leuking, Arthur Lance. M.F.A. Thesis, 1966, Yale University.

4594   Pocket Welding Guide. Hobart Bros., Troy, Ohio. No Date.

4595   Polish Exhibition (The).
Eddelman, William S.
Theatre Design &
Technology, Sp 1980, Vol.
XVI, No. 1, P. 21.

4596   Polythene. Tabs, S,
1958, Vol. 16, No. 2, P.
23.

4597   Polyurethanes. Dombrow,
Bernard A. Reinhold
Publishing Corp., 1965, New
York.

4598   Polyurethane and
Polyester Molding Compounds
for Furniture Applications.
Levy, Marshall M. PPG
Industries, 1969,
Pittsburgh.

4599   Polyurethane Foam.
Crandell, K. Clarke.
Theatre Crafts, Ja/F 1980,
Vol. 14, No. 1, P. 6.

4600   Popular Triumph of the
New School of Scene
Painting. Current Opinion,
Ag 1915, P.103.

4601   Portable Accumulators
for Stage Effects.
Scientific American
Supplement, N 1892, Vol.
34, P. 14044.

4602   Portable Woodworking
Power Tools. Haines, Ray
E. Van Nostrand, 1954, New
York.

4603   Portal - a Partial
Answer (The). Davis, Jed
H. Players Magazine, Ja,
1958, Vol. 34, No. 4, P.
79.

4604   Portfolio of Work of
Polish Scenographer Zofia
Wierchowicz. Wierchowicz,
Zofia. Theatre Design and
Technology, D 1967, No. 11,
P. 24-29.

4605   Portrait of a Theatre.
Adams, Mildred. Theatre
Arts Monthly, O, 1934, Vol.
VIII, No. 10 , P. 759.

4606   Power Caster Unit
Applicable to Stage Wagons
and Turntables. Glen, Todd
V. M.F.A. Thesis, 1965,
Yale University.

4607   PQ '75: a Critical
Report. Theatre Design &
Technology, Fall 1976, Vol.
XII, No. 3, P. 29.

4608   PQ 67, PQ 71, PQ 75.
O.I.S.T.T. Publications,
1967, 1971, 1975.

4609   PQ 79. Society of
British Theatre Designers.
USITT, Je 1979, London.

4610   Practical and Industrial
Formulary. Freeman,
Mitchell. Chemical
Publishing, 1962.

4611   Practical Carpentry and
Joinery (Second Edition).
Kay, N.W. (Ed.).
Transatlantic, 1961, New
York.

4612   Practical Carpentry.
Mix, Floyd.
Goodheart-Wilcox Co., 1963,
Homewood, Ill., 448 P..

4613   Practical Guide to Scene
Painting and Painting in
Distemper. Lloyds, F.
Excelsior Publishing House,
1883, New York.

4614   Practical Instructions
for Private Theatricals.
Emerson, W.D. Dramatic
Pub. Co., 1899, Chicago.

4615   Practical Problems of
Accomplishing Theatre
Designs. Powers W. G.
Theatre Design & Technology
O 1966.

4616   Practical Scenery
Inventory. Yeaton, Kelly.
Players Magazine, Ap. 1950,
Vol. 26, No. 7, P. 156.

4617   Practical Scene Painting
for Amateurs. Benwell,

Henry N. Amateur Work, D
1884, Vol. 4, P. 7.

4618   Practical Stage-Craft, a
Manual for Little Theatre
Work and Directors of
School Dramatics. Hynes,
Mary Helen. Walter H. Baker
Co., 1930, Boston.

4619   Practical Stage-Craft
for Amateurs.
Brandon-Thomas, Jevan.
Bridgman, New York,. No
Date.

4620   Prague Quadrennial '79:
Theatre Architecture and
Design on Display.
Fielding, Eric. Theatre
Crafts, N/D 1979, Vol. 13,
No. 6, P. 24.

4622   Prague Quadrennial 1979
(The). Burian, Jarka M.
Theatre Design &
Technology, Sp 1980, Vol
Xvi, No. 1, P. 4-12.

4623   Prague Scenographic
Institute (The). Kouril,
Miroslav. World Theatre,
1965, Vol. 14, P. 303-306.

4624   Praise of Paris (The).
Child, Theodore. Harper &
Brothers, 1893, Vol. VIII,.

4625   Pre-Restoration Stage
Studies. Lawrence, William
John. Harvard University
Press, 1927, Cambridge.

4626   Precautions and Safe
Practices. Linde Air
Products Company, 1960, New
York.

4627   Prefabrication of Wooden
Doors and Windows (The).
Bel Geddes, Norman. United
Nations, 1973, New York.
LOCN: Th 2261 R74

4628   Preparing Ben Hur for
the Stage. Henderson, W.
J. Harpers's Weekly, N
1899, Vol. 43, P.
1167-1168.

4629   Preparing for the
Pantomimes. Illustrated
London News, D 1868, Vol.
53, P. 641.

4630   Preparing for the
Pantomime. Illustrated
London News, Ja 1881, Vol.
78, P. 6.

4631   Preparing the
Professional Designer.
Elder, E. Theatre Crafts
My 1969.

4632   Present-Day Decoration
in the Moscow Art Theatre.
Carter, H. Creative Art,
Ag, 1929, Vol. 5, P. 579.

4633   Pirate Ship That Rolls
and Pitches on the Stage.
Popular Mechanics, Jl 1916,
Vol. 26, P. 21.

4634   Primer of Special
Effects for Low Budget
Theatre. Williams, Jan.
M.A. Thesis, California
State University, Long
Beach, 1976.

4635   Primer of Stagecraft
(A). Nelms, Henning.
Dramatists Play Service,
1941, New York.

4636   Primitive Stage Setting.
Austin, Mary. Theatre Arts
Monthly, Ja, 1928, Vol.
XII, No. 1, P. 49.

4637   Principles of Fluid
Dynamics. Eskinazi,
Salamon. Allyn and Bacon,
Incorporated, 1962, Boston,
Massachusetts.

4638   Principles of
Perspective Drawing. Shah,
M.G. and Kale, C. Asia
Publishing House, 1965,
India.

4639   Principles of Physics,
III, Optics. Sears, Francis
W. Addison-Wesley Press,
1948, Cambridge,
Massachusetts. Third
Edition.

4640   Prinzrengenten Theatre, Munich. Electrical Review, My 14, 1904, Vol. 44, P. 729.

4641   Problems in Design. Moiseiwitsch, Tanya. Drama Survey, My 1963, Vol. 3, P. 113.

4642   Problems of a Scene Designer. Simonson, Lee. New York Times, N 17, 1929.

4643   Problems of Design: Shakespeare's Plays. Russell, Douglas A. Players, F/Mr 1975, Vol. 50, P. 70.

4644   Problem Exit the Castle. Rockey, L. Theatre Crafts N 1972.

4645   Problem of Setting in Early Humanist Comedy in Italy, (The). Sabatini, Mary Hieber. Ph.D. Thesis, Columbia University, 1973.

4646   Problem Solving in Las Vegas. Foy, P. Theatre Crafts Mr 1976.

4647   Process of Play Production (The). Crofton, Allen and Royer, Jessica. Crofts, 1928, New York.

4648   Producing in Little Theaters. Stratton, Clarence. Henry Holt and Co., 1921, New York.

4649   Producing on Broadway: a Comprehensive Guide. Faber, Donald C. DBS Pub., 1969, New York. LOCN: Pn2291. F33

4650   Producing Plays; a Handbook for Producers and Players. Purdom, C.B. E.P. Dutton & Co., 1930, New York.

4652   Producing Shakespeare. Bragdon, Claude. Architectural Record (The), Mr 1925, Vol. 57, P. 266-275.

4653   Producing the Play (Contains New Scene Technician's Handbook). Gassner, John and Barber, Philip. Dryden Press, 1941, New York. Holt, Rinehart & Wilson, 1953, New York. LOCN: Pn2037 G3 1953 ISBN: 0-03-005565-2

4654   Producing Your Own Plays. Russell, Mary M. Smith, Inc., 1931, New York.

4655   Production; Being Thirty Two Collotype Projected or Realised for the Pretenders Produced at the Royal Theatre, Copenhagen. Craig, Edward Gordon. H. Milford, Oxford University, 1930.

4656   Production, 1926 (A). Oxford Univ. Press, 1930, London.

4657   Production and Imagination in Euripides: Form and Function of The Scenic Space. Hourmouziades, Nicolaos C. Greek Society for Humanistic Studies, 1965, Athens.

4658   Production and Stage Management at the Blackfriars Theatre. Isaacs, Jacob. Oxford University Press, 1933, London.

4659   Production and Staging of Plays (The). Carter, C. and Bradbury, A.J. and Howard, W.R.B. Arc Books, 1953, New York.

4660   Production Concepts Exemplified in Selected Presentations Directed by Robert Edmond Jones. Waldo, Paul Robert. Ph.D. Thesis, University of Oregon, 1970.

4661   Production Handbook. Alford, L. P. and Bangs, J. R. (Eds). Ronald Press Company, 1953, New York.

4662   Production of Grand
        Opera (The). Scientific
        American, Mr 29, 1897, Vol.
        LXXVI, P. 346.

4663   Production of Later
        Nineteenth Century American
        Drama, a Basis for
        Teaching. Leverton, Garrett
        H. Columbia University,
        1936, New York.

4664   Production of
        Shakespeare's Plays at the
        Globe 1599-1609. Beckerman,
        Bernard. Ph.D. Thesis,
        Colorado, 1965.

4665   Production Staffing in
        College and University
        Theatre a 1974 Sampling.
        Symons, James M. Players
        Magazine, Sum, 1975, Vol.
        50, No. 5, P. 142.

4666   Professional Movie
        Tricks for Amateurs. Lane
        Tamar. Amateur Movie
        Publishing Co., 1928,
        Hollywood.

4667   Professional Scenery
        Construction. Fitzkee, D.
        Banner Play Bureau, 1930,
        San Francisco. LOCN: Vun
        F57

4668   Professor Pepper's
        Phantasmagoria. Tabs S
        1971.

4669   Profile Staging: Designs
        for Found Theatre Spaces.
        Britch, Carol. Theatre
        Crafts, O 1975, Vol. 9, No.
        5, P. 16.

4670   Progress of the New
        Stagecraft in America
        (The). Sowers, William
        Leigh. Drama, N 1917, Vol.
        7, P. 570-589.

4671   Projection Towards Stage
        Architecture, (A). Kurth,
        Henry. Theatre Annual,
        1963, Vol. 20, P. 72-88.

4672   Project for a Theatrical

Presentation of the Divine
Comedy Of Dante Alighieri.
Bel Geddes, Norman. Theatre
Arts, Inc., 1924, New York.

4673   Project for the Ring.
        Oenslager, Donald. Theatre
        Arts Monthly, Ja, 1927,
        Vol. XI, No. 1, P. 35.

4674   Project in Scenic and
        Lighting Design for a
        Production of Tobacco Road,
        Utilizing Polyurethane Foam
        As a Construction Material
        (A). Steil, William B.
        Mankato State College,
        1970, Mankato, Minn.

4675   Prompters Boxes for
        Theatres. Scientific
        American Supplment, O 1916,
        Vol. 82, P. 279.

4676   Properities and
        Mechanics of Materials.
        Laurson, Philip and Cox
        Gustave and Junkin,
        William. John Wiley & Sons,
        1931, New York.

4677   Proposed Theatre
        Building Code, New York.
        Pawley, Frederic Arden.
        American Architect and
        Architecture New York, Ap
        1936, P. 63-68.

4678   Propping Up the American
        Conservatory Theatre: an
        Interview With San
        Francisco's A.C.T. Prop and
        Set Departments. Theatre
        Crafts, O 1972, Vol. 6, No.
        5, P. 12.

4679   Proscenium and
        Sight-Lines. Southern,
        Richard. Theatre Arts,
        1964, Faber and Faber,
        1964, London. LOCN: Pn 2091
        S8 S63 1964

4680   Psychological Stage
        Scenery. Literary Digest,
        Ja 25, 1913, P. 183.

4681   Psychology of
        Prestidigitation (The).

Binet, Alfred. Smithsonian
Institute Annual Report for
1894, Washington, P.555.

4682   Psychology of the
Medieval Stage Scene (The).
Fruth, Mary Ann. Thesis
(M.A.), Smith College,
1957.

4683   Puppet Anatomy. Bufano,
Remo. Theatre Arts Monthly,
Jl 1928, Vol. XII, No. 7,
P. 497.

4684   Puppet Theatre in
America (The). McPharlin,
Paul. Harper & Bros., 1949,
New York.

4685   Putting on a Play.
Moulton, Robert H.
Technical World, Ja 1912,
Vol. 16, P. 571-579.

4686   Put "Theatre" in Your
World's Fair Thinking.
United Scenic Artists of
America (Local 829). 1963,
New York.

4687   Pyrotechnics. Tabs, D
1949, Vol. 7, No. 3, P. 28.

4688   Quantitative
Investigation of Audience
Response to Theatrical
Settings. Caldwell, George
Rollin. Ph.D. Thesis,
Bowling Green State
University, 1974.

4689   Queen of Spades.
Original Rendering, 1971.
located at the Harvard
Theatre Collection.

4690   Question of Design (The
Broken Heart)(A). Taylor,
Mark. Plays and Players, Jl
1972, P. 15.

4691   Question of Scenery
(The). Eaton, Walter
Prichard. American
Magazine, Jl 1911, Vol. 72,
P. 374.

4692   Quick Change Scene

Device (A). Conway, John
A. Players Magazine, Ja,
1955, Vol. 31, No. 4, P.
93.

4693   Radical Technology at
the National. Pilbrow,
Richard. ABTT News, O 1979,
P. 15.

4694   Radio City Music Hall,
Stage Settings. Jones,
Robert Edmond and Young,
S. New Republic, Ja 25,
1933, Vol. 73, P. 294. See
Also Collier's, D 30, 1933,
Vol. 92, P. 15.

4695   Radio Frequency Energy-A
Potential Harzard in the
Use of Transportation of
Electrical Blasting Caps.
Institute of Makers of
Explosives, 1962, New York.

4696   Rainmaker. Young, D.
Palmer. Players Magazine,
Mr 1960, Vol. 36, No. 6, P.
136.

4697   Rare Breed of Theatre in
the Golden West (A).
Theatre Crafts, J/F 1974,
Vol. 8, No. 1, P. 12.

4698   RCI Plastics for
Furniture Parts and Home
Furnishings. Reichhold
Chemicals, White Plains,
New York. No Date.

4699   Realism of Stage
Effects, The. Thomas, Frank
D. Green Book Album, My
1911, Vol. 5, P. 1006-1011.

4700   Realism on the Stage.
Notes and Queries, 1872,
Series 4, Vol. 10, P. 28.

4701   Realistic Marine Warfare
on the Stage. Mount, Harry
A. Popular Mechanics,
1921, Vol. 36, P. 43-44.

4702   Realistic Trees.
Blakely, Don. Players
Magazine, O, 1954, Vol. 31,
No. 1, P. 10.

4703   Reality in Stage Rooms.
New York Times, N 9, 1913,
Section 10, P. 10.

4704   Real Nautical Scene in
Opera Performance. Popular
Mechanics, S 1911, Vol. 16,
P. 316-317.

4705 · Recent Ballet Design.
Bland, Alexander. Ballet
Annual, 1963, P. 58:62; A.
& C. Black, 1963, London.

4706   Recent Building Code
Recommendations for Theatre
Building in New York City.
Architecture and Building,
My 1911, Vol. 43, P.
367-372.

4707   Recent Building Code
Recommendations for Theatre
Building. Architecture and
Building, My 1911, Vol. 43,
P. 367.

4708   Recent Developments:
Polysar Sb-407. Gaiser,
Gary. Theatre Design &
Technology, F 1968, No. 12,
P. 32.

4709   Recent Developments: Use
of Plastics. Gaiser, Gary.
Theatre Design &
Technology, O 1968, No. 14,
P. 31.

4710   Recent Trends in Scene
Design: History Does Repeat
Itself in the Scene Shop.
Philippi, Herbert. Players
Magazine, F, 1945, Vol. 25,
No. 5, P. 107.

4711   Recollections of a Scene
Painter. Harvey, E.T. W.A.
Sorin Co., 1916,
Cincinnati. Also Published
by E.T. Harvey, 1916,
Cincinnati.

4712   Recollections of the
Scenic Effects of Covent
Garden Theatre During the
Season 1838-1839. Scharf,
George. James, Pattie,
1839, London.

4713   Reconstruction of
Leonardo Da Vinci's
Revolving Stage (A).
Steinetz, Kate T. Art
Quarterly, 1949, Vol. 12,
P. 325-38.

4714   Reconstruction of
Theatrical and Musical
Practice in the Production
Of Italian Opera in the
Eighteenth-Century (A).
McClure, Theron Reading.
Ph.D. Thesis, Ohio State
University, 1956.

4715   Reconstruction of the
Settings for Three Operas
Designer by Filippo Juvara
in Rome 1710-1712 (A). Tew,
Thomas Charles. Ph.D.
Thesis, Louiisiana State
University & Argricultural
& Mechanical College, 1973.

4716   Records of the New York
Stage from 1750 to 1860.
Ireland, Joseph N. T.H.
Morrell, 1867, New York.

4717   Rediscovered Theatre
Drawings by Antonio
Bibiena. Collier, William.
Appollo, Ag 1967, Vol. 86,
P. 108.

4718   Reflections of a
Stagebuilder. Roth,
Wolfgang. Theatre Design &
Technology, Fa 1975, No.
42, P. 19.

4719   Regulations and Rules
for Electrical
Installations in Places.of
Public Entertainment.
London County Council. No
Date.

4720   Regulations and Rules
for Places of Public
Entertainment. Tabs, S
1947, Vol. 5, No. 2, P. 25.

4721   Regulation of Theatres
and Music Halls (The).
Builder (The), Ap 1884,
Vol. XLVI, P. 493, P. 837,
P. 459,.

4722   Regulation of Theatres and Other Places of Public Amusement (The). Builder, (The), Je 3, 1865, Vol Xxiii, P. 387, See Also P. 248.

4723   Relating to the Scenery, Decoration, Etc. of the Theatre Royal At Imperwich. Architectural Review, The, Ag 1946, Vol. 100, P. 41-44.

4724   Relief for the Amateur Stage Carpenter. Scientific American, Mr 1933, Vol. 148, P. 184-185.

4725   Remarks on the Scenery Introduced at the Drury Lane Theatre in The Comedy: a Bold Stroke for a Wife. Monthly Mirror, 1804, Vol. 17, P. 42-43.

4726   Remembering Reinhardt. Theatre Crafts, N/D 1973, Vol. 7, No. 6, P. 22.

4727   Remote Controlled Precision Crash. Tabs Ap 1974.

4728   Renaissance and Baroque Theatre in France; the Playhouses and the Mise En Scene 1550-1700 (The). Niemeyer, Charles. Ph.D. Thesis, Yale, 1942.

4729   Renaissance Stage in Italy: a Study of the Evolution of The Perspective Scene (The). Eckert, William. Ph.D. Thesis, University of Iowa, 1961.

4730   Renovation Concepts, Unique Product Resource: Architectural Catalogue. Renovation Concepts, P.O. Box 3720, Minneapolis, Minnesota 55403.

4731   Renzo Mongiardino. Corathiel, Elisabethe H. C. Theatre World, Ag 1964, Vol. 60, P. 28.

4732   Reports on Theatre Design As Theatre: a Delicate Balance. Smith, C. Ray. Theatre Design & Technology, O 1966, No. 6, P. 50.

4733   Reports on Theatre Design As Theatre: 69th Street Armory. Smith, C. Ray. Theatre Design & Technology, F 1967, No. 8, P. 30.

4734   Reports on Theatre Design As Theatre-Antony and Cleopatra. Smith, C. Ray. Theatre Design & Technology, D 1966, No. 7, P. 26.

4735   Reports on Theatre Design As Theatre-Marat-Sade 1 Man of La Mancha. Smith, C. Ray. Theatre Design & Technology, O 1966, No. 6, P. 22.

4736   Research in Prompt Books. McDowell, John H. OSU Theatre Collection Bulletin, Sp 1955, Vol. 1, No. 2, P. 5.

4737   Research in Theatre Architecture and Design. Educational Theatre Journal, Je 1967, Vol. XIX, No. 2a, P. 255.

4738   Research Possibilities in Scene Design. OSU Theatre Collection Bulletin 2, Fall 1955, P. 11.

4739   Restless Genius of Norman Bel Geddes. Pulos, Arthur J. Architectural Forum, Jl/Ag 1970, Vol. 133, P. 46.

4740   Restoration Court Stage, (The). Boswell, Eleanore. Harvard University Press, 1932, Cambridge, Massachusetts.

4741   Restoration Scenery,

1656-1680. Jackson, Allan
S. Restoration and
Eighteenth-Century Theatre
Research, N 1964, Vol. 3,
P. 25-38.

4742   Revival of the Whip at
Drury Lane; a Glimpse of
the Hunting Men from the
Flies, the. Graphic, Mr 26,
1910, Vol. 81, P. 432.

4743   Revolvers in
Czechoslovakia. Theatre
Design & Technology My
1966.

4744   Revolving Stage, The.
Theatre Arts Magazine, Jl
1932, Vol. XVI, No. 7, P.
589.

4745   Revolving Stages Long
Used in Japan. Vertical
File, Room 121, New York
Public Library. No Date.

4746   Revolving Stage (A).
Hedin, Richard H. Players
Magazine, D, 1954, Vol. 31,
No. 3, P. 64.

4747   Revolving Stage and
Impressions Held of It by
American Universities and
Colleges (The). Allred,
Robert Gordon. M.A. Thesis,
Brigham Young University,
1961.

4748   Revolving Stage of the
Variety Theater at Paris
(The). Scientific American
Supplement, My 1898, Vol.
45, P. 18713, 18714.

4749   Richard Foreman's
Scenography: Staging
Ontological-Hysteric
Theater in a Soho Loft.
Davy, Kate. Theatre Crafts,
My/Je 1978, Vol. 12, No. 4,
P. 31.

4750   Richard III. Jones,
Robert Edmond. Original
Drawings (1920 and 1946).
located at the Harvard
Theatre Collection.

4751   Rigid Foams Systems
Application Information.
Reichhold Chemicals, 1968,
White Plains, New York.

4752   Rigid Plastics Foams.
Ferrigno, T.H. Reinhold
Publishing Corp., 1967, New
York.

4753   Rigid Polylurethane Foam
for the Stage. Allen, Susan
V. M.A. Thesis, University
of Wisconsin, 1971.

4754   Rigid Urethane Foam,
Application Information.
Chemicals for Cellular
Products: Union Carbide
Corp., 1968, New York.

4755   Rigoletto. Amberg,
George. Interiors, D 1951,
Vol. III, P. 106.

4756   Rings, Riggings and
Highwires: Settings for
Circus Performers. Theatre
Crafts, S 1972, Vol. 6, No.
4, P. 19.

4757   Ripples and Rainbows.
Leon, Walter De. Saturday
Evening Post, Ap 11, 1925,
Vol. 197, P. 25.

4758   Rise of Realism on the
Eighteenth Century Stage
(The). Hunter, Jack W. OSU
Theatre Collection
Bulletin, Sp 1958, Vol. 5,
No. 1, P. 27.

4759   Rise of Spectacle in
America, (The). Lawrence,
William John. Theatre
Magazine (The), Ja 1917,
Vol. XXV, P. 44.

4760   Rise of the American
Professional Lighting
Designer to 1960. Murray,
Donald Louis. Ph.D. Thesis,
University of Michigan,
1970. LOCN: Pn2091 E4m8
1976

4761   Robertson's
Phantasmagoria in Madrid,

1821. Varey, J. Theatre Notebook, 1954, Vol. 9, P. 84.

4762   Robert Edmond Jones: Stage Director. Hicks, Lee Roy. Ph.D. Thesis, University of Colorado, 1969.

4763   Robert Edmond Jones: 1887-1954. Brown, John Mason. Saturday Review, Ja 1, 1955, Vol. 38, P. 60-62.

4764   Robert Edmond Jones' Henry VIII. Larson, Orville K. Players Magazine, D, 1966, Vol 37, No. 3, P. 53.

4765   Robert Edmond Jones, Artist of the Theatre. Sayler, Oliver M. New Republic, Je 23, 1920, Vol. 23, P. 122-124.

4766   Robert Edmond Jones, Designer for the Theater. American Artist, Je-Ag 1958, Vol. 22, P. 52-57, 85-87.

4767   Robert Edmond Jones, 1887-1954. Packard, Frederick C., Jr. Chrysalis, 1955, Vol. 8, Nos. 1-2, P. 4-12.

4768   Robert Edmond Jones and the Modern Movement: a Study of Related Elements in Art, Architecture, and Theatre. Miller, Thomas Charles. Ph.D Thesis, 1977, University of Colorado at Boulder.

4769   Robert Edmond Jones. Young, Stark. New Republic, Ap 23, 1945, Vol. 112, P. 556.

4770   Robert Edmond Jones. Oenslager, Donald. Yale/Theatre, Fall 1970, Vol. 3, P. 7-9.

4771   Robert Edmond Jones. Mannes, Marya. Theatre Guild Magazine, N 1930, Vol. 8, P. 14-19, 62-63.

4772   Robert Edmond Jones. Macgowan, Kenneth. Theatre Arts Monthly, N, 1925, Vol. IX, No. 11, P. 720.

4773   Robert Edmond Jones. Seldes, G. Creative Art, Ap, 1932, Vol. 10, P. 289.

4774   Rockwell Router (The). Rockwell Manufacturing Co., 1968.

4775   Rock Pile Thermal Storage for Comfort Air Conditioning. Close, D.J. Mech. Chem. Engrg. Trans. Inst. Engr. (Australia), 1965, Vol. MC-1, P. 11.

4776   Rock Tour Lighting: the Contract and Technical Riders. Moody, James L. Theatre Crafts, N/D 1978, P.69, Vol. 12, No. 7.

4777   Roger Furse. Tabs, S 1952, Vol. 10, No. 2, P. 5.

4778   Role of Contemporary Scene Building Houses for Broadway Theatre(The). Collom, Jeffrey Robert. Ph.D. Thesis, Michigan State University, 1975. LOCN: Pn 2091 S8c6 1979

4779   Roller Extensions. Mortensen, A. L. Players Magazine, N, 1950, Vol. 27, No. 2, P. 44.

4780   Rolling Stone in Parsifal; How It Worked, the. Sphere, Ja 31, 1914, Vol. 56, P. 131.

4781   Romance Restored: the League of Historic American Theatres. Chesley, G. Theatre News (Ths) Ja 1978.

4782   Romantic Realism and the Cosmic: Gunther Schneider-Siemssen Designs the Literal and the

Symbolic. Loney, Glenn.
Theatre Crafts, O 1978,
Vol. 12, No. 6, P. 29.

4784   Roman Perspective
Painting and the Ancient
Stage. Little. Star Press
but Distributed by Author,
P. O. Box 1554 , Wheaton,
Md 20902. No Date. LOCN: Nd
2885 L54

4785   Roof Over Your Head (A):
a Problem-Solving Casebook
in Drafting, Designing, and
Constructing a Hanging
Trapezium Ceiling.
Williams, John. Theatre
Crafts, Mr/ap 1978, Vol.
12, No. 3, P. 34.

4786   Royal Festival Hall.
Tabs Je 1965.

4787   Tabs, Summer 1978, Vol.
36, No. 2, P. 3.
Mackintosh, Iain. Tabs,
Summer 1978, P. 3, Vol. 36,
No. 2.

4788   Rules and Examples of
Perspective. Pozzo, Andrea.
Benjamin Blom, 1971, New
York.

4789   Rumanian Set and Costume
Designs on Tour. Noris,
Stefan. Rumania Today,
1963, No. 6 P. 4.

4790   Runnin' the Show; a
Practical Handbook. Whorf,
Richard B. and Wheeler,
Roger. W.H. Baker, 1930,
Boston.

4791   Running the World's
Largest Rep: Artistic and
Business Decision Making at
the Metropolitan Opera.
Theatre Crafts, O 1976,
Vol. 10, No. 5, P. 15.

4792   Russell Smith, Romantic
Realist. Lewis, Virginia
E. University of
Pittsburgh Press, 1956,
Pittsburgh.

4793   Russian Theatre of the
Thirties (The). Hill,
Derek. Apollo, Ag 1967,
Vol. 86, P. 142.

4794   Saddler's Wells Scene
Book (A). Rosenfeld, Sybil.
Theatre Notebook, Fa 1960,
Vol. XV, No. 1, P. 57.

4795   Saddler's Wells at the
London Coliseum. Bentham,
Frederick. Tabs, D 1968,
Vol. 26, No. 4, P. 10.

4796   Safety and Health in
Building and Civil
Engineering Work.
International Labor Office,
Geneva, 1972.

4797   Safety at Work: the Law
That Will Brook No Excuses.
ABTT News, D/Ja 1980, P.
15.

4798   Safety by Manual,
Regulation and Code. Adams,
David and Others.
Sightline, Sp 1979, Vol.
13, No. 1, P. 19.

4799   Safety Checklists for
Theatre Managements.
A.B.T.T. Information Sheet
No. 5. No Date.

4800   Safety Facts: Fire
Safety Precautions Urged
for Hot Work Around Plastic
Foams. Theatre Design &
Technology, Sp 1976, Vol.
XII, No. 1, P. 33.

4801   Safety Guide Sg-15
Training of Process
Operators. Manufacturing
Chemists Association, 1963,
Washington, D.C.

4802   Safety Precautions Urged
for Hot Work Around Plastic
Forms. Theatre Design &
Technology Sp 1976.

4803   Safety Regulations.
Tabs, Ap 1949, Vol. 7, No.
1, P. 26.

4804   Safety Sources and Resources. Lucier, Mary. Theatre Craft, My/Je 1980, Vol. 14, No. 3, P. 86-87.

4805   Safety With Firearms. American Rifleman (The), Reprint R13, National Rifle Association, 1965, Washington, D.C.

4806   Safe Practices in the Arts & Crafts: a Studio Guide. Barazani, Gail Coningsby. College Art Association of America (The), 1978, New York.

4807   Safe Sound. Signtline, Sp 1979, Vol. 13,no. 1.

4808   Saga of Special Effects (The). Fry, Ron and Fourzon, Pamela. Society of Motion Picture and Television Engineers, Inc., 1963. Distributed by Scenographic Media, Norwalk, Connecticut.

4809   Sagging Stage Doors. Voss, Lawrence. Players Magazine, Mr, 1952, Vol. 28, No. 6, P. 144.

4810   Salzburg Festival (The). Theatre Crafts, Mr/Ap 1977, Vol. II, No. 2, P. 20.

4811   Samuel Hume: Artist and Exponent of American Art Theatre. Bolin, John S. Ph.D. Thesis, University of Michigan, 1970.

4812   Samuel Pepys and the World He Lived in. Wheatley, Henry Benjamin. Bickers & Son 1895 London.

4813   Samuel Phelps: Producer of Shakespeare at Sadler's Wells. Bangham, P. Jerald. OSU Theatre Collection Bulletin, 1959, Vol. 6, P. 9-20.

4814   Sand, Smoke, and Rag Pictures. Goldston, Will. Magician, The, Ltd., 1913,.

4815   Sandboxes of Dilettantism. Dodge, Gordon. Theatre Crafts, S/O 1967, P. 24-27.

4816   Sandwich Panel Design Criteria. Building Research Institute. BRI Fall Conferences, N 1959, Washington, D.C.; 1960, National Academy of Sciences National Research.

4817   Sanity and Stage Settings. New York Times, Ap 20, 1919, Section 4, P. 2.

4818   Sante Fe Opera's Apprentice Technician Training Program (The). Ohl, Theodore G. Lighting Dimensions, Jy/ag 1978, Vol. 2, No. 6, P. 33.

4819   San Francisco Opera Company Scene Design, 1932-1955. Bower, Homer Thomas. Ph.D. Thesis, Stanford University, 1963.

4820   Saratoga. Beaton, Cecil. Pencil & Ink Original, 1959. located at the Harvard Theatre Collection.

4821   Scaenographia; the Ancient Stage and Painting. Little, A.M.G. Art Bulletin, The, S 1956, Vol. 18, P. 407-418.

4823   Scene-Changing at the Palais Royal 1770-1781. Hawley, James and Jackson, Allan S. OSU Theatre Collection Bulletin, 1961, Vol. 8, P. 9-23.

4824   Scene-Designing in the American Theatre. Stage (The), Ja, 1934, Vol. 11, P. 23.

4825   Scene-Painting As a Fine Art. Ritter, John P. Cosmopolitan, N 1889, Vol. 8, P. 43-49.

4826   Scene Design at the
Commedie-Francaise
1901-1920. Bielenberg, John
E. Ph.D. Thesis, Osu,
1970.

4827   Scenery: a Manual of
Scene Design. Helvenston,
Harold Finley. Stanford
University Press, 1931,
Vol. XVI, P. 95.

4828   Scenery, Dresses and
Decoration. Turner,
Godfrey. Theatre, Mr 1884,
Vol. 3, P. 126, Published
in London.

4829   Scenery and Design:
Documentation. New York
Public Library. New York
Publich Library, 1974, New
York.

4830   Scenery and Drama.
Simson, Lee. Atlantic, My
1929, Vol. 143, P. 639.

4831   Scenery and Furniture.
Brown, Frank Chouteau.
House Beautiful, N 1914, P.
180-183.

4832   Scenery and Machines on
the English Stage During
the Renaissance. Campbell,
Lilly Bess. Cambridge
University Press,1923.

4833   Scenery and Panoramic
Views. Builder (The), Ap
13, 1850, Vol. VIII, No.
375.

4834   Scenery and Scenic
Artists. Lawrence, William
John. Gentleman's Magazine,
Je 1889, Vol. 266, P.
608-614.

4835   Scenery and Special
Effects in Satirical
Prints. McDowell, John H.
OSU Theatre Collection
Bulletin, Fall 1956, Vol.
3, P. 9-25.

4836   Scenery and Stage
Decorations; Color - Light

- the New Art. Hewlett,
J.M. American Architect
(The), Ap 1918, Vol. 113,
Pt. 2, P. 425-430.

4837   Scenery and Stage
Decoration. Hewlett, J.M.
American Architect, Jl
1917, P. 41-47.

4838   Scenery and Stage
Decoration. Hewlett, J.M.
Brooklyn Museum Quaterly
(The), 1917, Vol. 4, P.
115-123.

4839   Scenery and Staging of
Uncle Tom's Cabin: Allegory
and Ohio River Scenes.
Fruth, Mary Ann. Ohio State
University Theatre
Collection Bulletin, 1963,
No. 10, P. 31-39.

4840   Scenery and the Drama.
Simonson, Lee. Atlantic, My
1929, Vol. 143, P. 639-645.

4841   Scenery at the Book
Leagur. Theatre Notebook,
1950, Vol. 5, P. 35.

4842   Scenery Design for the
Amateur Stage. Friederich,
Willard J. and Fraser, John
H. Macmillan Co., 1950,
New York.

4843   Scenery for Salzbergs
Super Stage. Loney, Glenn.
Theatre Design & Technology
D 1971.

4844   Scenery for the Dance.
Laban, Juana De. Dance
Observer, Ap 1942, P.
48-49; My 1942, P. 62.

4845   Scenery for the High
School Stage. Borrows,
Robert B. Players
Magazine, D 1939, Vol. 16,
No. 3, P. 7.

4846   Scenery for the Theatre.
Burris-Meyer, Harold and
Cole, Edward C. Little,
Brown and Company 1971
Boston Toronto. LOCN:
Pn2091. S8b8 1971

4847 Scenery General Comments Nineteenth Century File. Harvard Theatre Collection. No Date.

4848 Scenery General Comments Twentieth Century File. Harvard Theatre Collection. No Date.

4849 Scenery History File. Harvard Theatre Collection. No Date.

4850 Scenery in Restoration Theatres. Nicoll, Allardyce. Anglia, 1920, Vol. 44, P. 217-225.

4851 Scenery on the Building Block Principle. Scientific American, F, 1924, Vol. 130, P. 95.

4852 Scenery on the Early American Stage. Hamar, Clifford E. Theatre Annual, 1948-49, Vol. 7, P. 84-103.

4853 Scenery on the New York Stage, 1900-1920. Cole, Wendell. Ph.D. Thesis, Stanford University, 1951.

4854 Scenery on Tour. Lawrence, William John. Magazine of Art, 1896, Vol. 19, P. 476-479.

4855 Scenery or No Scenery? a Symposium. Theatre Workshop, Ap-Je 1938, Vol. 2, P. 5-21.

4856 Scenery Scene Painting File. Harvard Theatre Collection. No Date.

4857 Scenery Simplified. Webster, G.R. Eldridge Entertainment House, Inc., 1934, Denver, Colorado.

4858 Scenery That Helps the Actor. Moderwell, Hiram Kelly. Theatre Magazine (The), S 1916, Vol. XXIV, No. 187, P. 128.

4859 Scenery Then and Now. Oenslager, Donald. Russell & Russell, 1966, New York. LOCN: Pn2091. S804 1966

4860 Scenery Twentieth Century File. Harvard Theatre Collection. No Date.

4861 Scenery. Stell, W. Joseph. Rosen, 1970, New York. LOCN: Pn 2091 S8 S73

4862 Scenes and Machines on the English Stage During the Renaissance. Campbell, Lilly Bess. Ph.D. Thesis, University of Chicago, 1921/University Press, 1923, Cambridge/Barns & Noble, 1960, New York. LOCN: Pn2590.S7 C3 ISBN: 0-389-01756-6

4863 Scenes for Scene-Painters. Rose, A. Routledge, 1925, New York. located at the Harvard Theatre Collection.

4864 Scenewright; the Making of Stage Models and Settings (The). Smith, Andre. Macmillan, 1926, New York.

4865 Scene Design; a Guide to the Stage. Nelms, Henning. Sterling Pub. Co. 1970 New York. LOCN: Pn2091.S8 N36 ISBN: 0806970146

4866 Scene Designer's Requirements in Planning Small Stages for Play-Acting (The). Southern, Richard. Royal Institute of British Architects Journal, D 1937, Third Series Vol. 45, P. 180-187.

4867 Scene Designs of William Capon. Rosenfeld, Sybil. Theatre Notebook, 1956, Vol. 10, P. 118.

4868 Scene Design and Stage

Lighting. Parker, W. Oren
and Smith, Harvey K. Holt,
Rinehart & Winston, 1963,
1968, 1974, New York, 597
P. LOCN: Pn2091.S8p3 1974
ISBN: 0-03-089446-8

4869   Scene Design at the
Court Theatres of
Seventeenth Century Spain.
Wilkinson, Eileen. Ph.D.
Thesis, University of
Michigan, 1977.

4870   Scene Design for Stage
and Screen. Larson, Orville
K. Michigan State
University Press, 1961,
East Lansing, Michigan.
LOCN: Pn 2091 S8 L29

4871   Scene Design in England.
Sheringham, G. Theatre
Guild Magazine,my, 1931,
Vol. 8, P. 12.

4872   Scene Design in the
Theatre. Macgowan, Kenneth.
Creative Art, Jl 1928.

4873   Scene Painter's Progress
(The). Tweddell, George.
Era, Ja 1913, Vol. 76, P.
13.

4874   Scene Painters and Their
Work in America before
1800. Wolcott, John R.
Theatre Survey, My 1977.

4875   Scene Painting and
Bulletin Art. Atkinson,
Frank H. Drake & Co. 1916
New York.

4876   Scene Painting and
Design. Tabs, S 1955, Vol.
13, No. 2, P. 19.

4877   Scene Painting and
Design. Joseph, Stephen.
Pitman Publishers, 1964,
New York. LOCN: Nd2885.J6

4878   Scene Painting at the
Norwich Theatre, 1758-1799.
Fawcett, Trevor. Theatre
Notebook, 1971, Vol. XXVI,
No. 1, P. 15.

4879   Scene Painting Course
Outline. Forrester,
William. Theatre Crafts,
N/D 1979, Vol. 13, No. 6,
P. 78-81.

4880   Scene Painting in the
Greek Theatre. Builder
(The), Je 3, 1899, Vol.
LXXVI, P. 537.

4881   Scene Painting or Stage
Design. Borgen, Johan.
World Theatre, Wi, 1963/4,
Vol. XII, No. 4, P. 327.

4882   Scene Painting. New York
Daily Tribune , Ap 21,1895,
P. 25.

4883   Scene Painting.
Johnstone, Alick. Artist,
N/D 1952, Vol. 44, P.
65-67, 77-79.

4884   Scene Painting. Forman,
Robert. Pitman, 1950, Vol.
VIII, P. 40.

4885   Scene Shops from Design
to Reality. Theatre Crafts
S 1970.

4886   Scene Shop on Wheels
(A). Lyndrup, Allen and
Grayson, Phil. Dramatics,
Mr 1978, No. 4.

4887   Scene Shop (The). Dewey,
Walter S. Players, Ag/s,
1970, Vol. 45, No. 6, P.
254.

4888   Scene Technician's
Handbook (The). Barber,
Philip W. Whitlock's Book
Store, 1928, New Haven,
Ct., 93 P.

4889   Scene Types in Action.
Cole, Wendell. Players, O
1948, Vol. 25, P. 6.

4890   Scene. Craig, Edward
Gordon. Oxford, University
Press, 1923, London.

4891   Scenic and Dramatic
Form. Gorelik, Mordecai.

Arts, N, 1923, Vol. 4, P.
285.

4892   Scenic Arrangements of
the Philoktetes of
Sophocles (The). Woodhouse,
W. Journal of Hellenic
Studies, 1912, Vol. 32, P.
239-249.

4893   Scenic Art, 1872-1901
(The). James, Henry.
Rutgers, Univ. Press, 1948,
New Brunswick.

4894   Scenic Art in Mr.
Irving's Faust. Weers,
Lyman H. Dramatic Year:
1887-1888, Ticknor and Co.,
1889.

4895   Scenic Art of David
Balasco a Reappraisal
(The). Marker, Lise-Lone.
Ph.D. Thesis, 1969, Yale
University.

4896   Scenic Art of J.
Blanding Sloan (The). Carr,
Michael Carmichael. Theatre
Arts Monthly, 1918, Vol.
II, No. 3, P. 159.

4897   Scenic Art of Joseph
Urban (The). Taylor, Deems.
Architecture, N.Y. My 1954,
Vol. 69, P. 275-290.

4898   Scenic Art of Leon Bakst
(The). Theatre Magazine
(The), Ja 1914, Vol. XIX,
No. 155, P. 11.

4899   Scenic Art. Albert,
Ernest. Inland Architect
and News Record, My 1891,
Vol. 17, No. 4, P. 44-47.

4900   Scenic Design:
Rhinoceros. Kerz, Leo.
Theatre Arts, Jl 1961, Vol.
45, P. 20.

4901   Scenic Designs of Isaac
Gruenewald, (The).
Blomquist, Allen Palmer.
Ph.D. Thesis, University of
Minnesota, 1967.

4902   Scenic Design and
Lighting. Eckart, Jean and
Eckart, William. Theatre
Arts Magazine, Jl 1960,
Vol. XLIV, No. 7, P. 55.

4903   Scenic Design and Model
Building; a Handybook for
Amateur Producers. Jones,
Leslie Allen. Walter H.
Baker Company, 1939.

4904   Scenic Design for
Amateurs. Etheridge, Ken.
Albyn Press, Edinburgh,
1947; Ravin, Universal
Distributors, New York,
1949.

4905   Scenic Design for the
Musical Stage. Bay, Howard.
Theatre Arts, Ap, 1959,
Vol. XLIII, No. 4, P. 56.

4906   Scenic Design in the
U.S.A. Simonson, Lee.
Studio, (The), Je 1944,
Vol. 127, P. 196-200.

4907   Scenic Design of the
Central City Opera Company
1946-1970. Eide, Joel
Sylvester. Ed.D. Thesis,
University of Northern
Colorado, 1972.

4908   Scenic Equipment for the
Small Stage. Wilson, R.A.
G. Allen and Unwin, 1933,
London.

4909   Scenic Hints for Amateur
Producers. Yellenti,
Nicholas. Theatre Magazine,
Au 1925, P. 47.

4910   Scenic Imagination:
Still Evolving, (The).
Gorelik, Mordecai. Players,
O/n, 1967, Vol. 34, No. 1,
P. 22.

4911   Scenic Imagination
Seminar (The). Gorelik,
Mordecai. Theatre Crafts, S
1978, Vol. 12, No. 5, P.
98.

4912   Scenic Modeling. Hobbs,

Edward W. Cassell, 1930,
London, Toronto, 154 P.;
Blandford, London.

4913   Scenic Options at the
Comedie Francaise
1901-1920. Bielenberg, John
E. Theatre Studies,
1971-72, No. 18, P. 34.

4914   Scenic Panel Solutions:
Photo Mural Panels for
29.00. Mccarry, Charles.
Theatre Crafts, Vol. 13,
No. 3, My 1979, P. 30.

4915   Scenic Panel Solutions:
Screenwire Panels. Glenn,
David. Theatre Crafts, My
1979, Vol. 13, No. 3, P.
31.

4916   Scenic Settings in
America. Hamilton, Clayton.
Bookman, Mr 1916, Vol. 43,
P. 20.

4917   Scenic Showonders of the
Stage. Popular Mechanics,
Ap 1928, Vol. 29, P.
627-632.

4918   Scenic Solutions With
Fibers: Curtains, Columns,
and Forests With Rope
Fibers. Wong, Carey.
Theatre Crafts, S 1978,
Vol. 12, No. 5, P. 37-40.

4919   Scenic Studio. Factories
of Illusion (The). Stage
(The), Jl, 1934, Vol. 11,
P. 17.

4921   Scenic Styles in the
Modern American Theatre.
Douty, John. Ph.D. Thesis,
University of Denver, 1953.

4922   Scenic Styles. Cole,
Wendell. Players Magazine,
Ap, 1953, Vol. 29, No. 7,
P. 163.

4923   Scenic Wagon Restraint
Systems. Silberstein, F.
Theatre Design & Technology
Sum 1977.

4924   Sceno-Graphic
Techniques. Parker, W.
Oren. Carnegie-Mellon
University, 1969,
Pittsburgh. LOCN: Pn 2091
S8 P34 1969

4925   Scenografia Italiana.
Mariani, V. Rinascimento
Del Libro, 1930, Firenze.

4926   Scenographer's Work:
Josef Svoboda's Designs,
1971-1975. Burian, Jarka
M. Theatre Design &
Technology Sum 1976.

4927   Scenographer As an
Artist, Part III. Salzer,
Beeb. Theatre Design &
Technology, Fall 1977, Vol.
XIII, No. 3, P. 25.

4928   Scenographer As an
Artist, Part II (The).
Salzer, Beeb. Theatre
Design & Technology, Su
1977, Vol. XII, No. 2, P.
21.

4929   Scenographer As an
Artist, Part I (The).
Salzer, Beeb. Theatre
Design & Technology, Sp
1977, Vol. XII, No. 1, P.
15.

4930   Scenographic Expression
of Nature (1545-1845)
(The). Rothgeb, John R.
Ph.D Thesis, Case-Western
Reserve University, 1971.

4931   Scenography and Stage
Technology; an
Introduction. Bellman,
Willard F. Crowell, 1977,
New York. LOCN: Pn2085. B43
ISBN: 0690008724

4932   Scenography of Jose F
Svoboda (The). Burian,
Jarka M. Wesleyan
University Press, 1971,
Middletown, Connecticut.

4933   Scenography of Kabuki
Theatre (The).
Mitsubayashi, Ryotaro.

Interscaena-Acta Scaenographica, Sum 1967, Vol. 1, P. 42-46.

4934 Scenography of Ladislav Vychodil. Burian, Jarka M. Theatre Design & Technology, Su 1979, Vol. XV, No. 2, P. 8.

4935 Schools: Movable Platform Steps. Progressive Architecture, Je 1951, P. 111.

4936 School of Scene Design: Sketch of Drama School at Carnegie Institute. Clements, C.C. Drama (The), F, 1918, Vol. 8, P. 135.

4937 School Theatre; a Handbook of Theory and Practice (The). Mitchell, Roy. Brentano's, 1925, New York.

4938 Science & Technology in the Arts. Kranz, Stewart. Van Nostrand Reinhold, 1974, New York. LOCN: Nx180.S3k72 709.04 ISBN: 0-442-24532-7

4939 Science and Practice of Welding, (The). Davies, A. C. Cambridge University Press, 1963, Cambridge, England.

4940 Science and the Contemporary Theatre (In Ten Talents in The American Theatre David H. Stevens Ed.). Izenour, George C. University of Oklahoma Press, 1957, Norman Oklahoma.

4941 Science at the Theatre,. Scientific American Supplement, Ja 1880, Vol. 9, P. 3331.

4942 Science in the Theater. Scientific American Supplement, Mr 1902, Vol. 53, P. 21924, 21925.

4943 Science in the Theater. Scientific American Supplement, D 1890, Vol. 30, P. 12475.

4944 Science in the Theatre. Scientific American Supplement, My 1902, Vol. 53, P. 22068, 22069.

4945 Scientific American and Its Supplement As Sources for Information About Theatre Technology. Hubbell, Douglas Kent. Ph.D. Thesis, Indiana University, 1978.

4946 Scored for All Operas; the Marked Boards of Covent Garden. Illustrated London News, Ap 29, 1911, Vol. 138, P. 617.

4947 Scotchlite Process, (The). Fielding, Raymond E. American Cinematographer, Ap, 1962, Vol. 43, P. 228 Andp. 242.

4948 Screen on Stage (Gulliver's Travels). Kenny, Sean. View, Jl 1970, P. 2-5.

4949 Screen Sets. Payne, Darwin Reid. Players Magazine, Ja 1954, Vol. 30,n No. 4, P. 92.

4950 Scrim Curtains: Mielziner and Ingegnieri. Larson, Orville K. Educational Theatre Journal, O 1962, Vol. XIV, No. 3, P. 229.

4951 Sculptor's Manual (A). Clarke, Geoffrey and Cornock, Stroud. Reinhold Book Corp., 1968, New York.

4952 Sculpture in Plastics. Roukes, Nicholas. Watson-Guptill, 1978, New York. ISBN: 0 8230-4701-6

4953 Sean Kenny and His Philosophy of Anti-Theatre.

Studio, Ja, 1963, Vol. 165, P. 2.

4954   Sean Kenny Sets the Stage. Eichelbaum, Stanley. Theatre Arts Magazine, D 1962, Vol. XLVI,NO. 12, P. 19.

4955   Seasonable Scenes at the Hippodrome: Performances and Mechanical Devices. Illustrated London News, Ja 2, 1904, Vol. 124, P. 10.

4956   Season in Federal Street: J.B. Williamson and the Boston Theatre, 1796-1797 (A). Alden, John. Proceedings of the American Antiquarian Society, 1955, Vol. 65, P. 9-74.

4957   Sea and the Sky: a Home-Made Cyclorama (The). Pennymore, A.F. and Brodie, F. Drama (The) Jl-S, 1938, Vol. 16, P. 152.

4958   Secrets of Scene Painting and Stage Effects. Browne, Van Dyke. Routledge & Sons, 1913, London, E.P. Dutton, 1913, New York.

4959   Secrets of the Revolving Stage Revealed, (The). O. M. Sayler, Max Reinhardt and His Theatre, 1924, New York.

4960   Secrets of the Stage. Belasco, David. Leslie's Weekly, My 1899, Pp. 406-407.

4961   Secret of How to Startle (The). Beaton, Cecil. Theatre Arts, My, 1957, Vol. XLI, No. 5, P. 72.

4962   Secret Regions of the Stage (The). Logan, Olive. Harper's New Monthly Magazine, Ap 1874, No. 287, P. 628.

4963   Sectional Stages Long before "Angelo" Was

Produced at Drury Lane: Continuous Drama in Shakespeare's Day. Illustrated London News, 1923, Vol. 162, P. 746-747.

4964   Secular Dramatics in the Royal Palace, Paris, 1378, 1389, And Chaucer's Tregetoures. Loomis, Laura H. Speculum, 1958, Vol. 33, P. 242-255.

4965   Security Is More Than a Blanket. Dewey, Walter S. Players Magazine, Je/Jl, 1972, Vol. 47, No. 5, P. 218.

4966   Seen on the Stage. Vogue, Ja L, 1915, P. 110, Jl 1, 1915, P. 84.

4967   Selected Drawing Systems Appropriate for the Scene Designer. Palkovic, Timothy J. Ph.D. Thesis, University of Minnesota, 1978.

4968   Selected Formulae--Pyrotechnic Papers. Scientific American Supplement, S 1903, Vol. 56, P. 23180.

4969   Selected Set-Construction Techniques. Meyer, Herbert. Journal of the Society of Motion Picture and Television Engineers, S 1955, Vol. 64, P. 1473.

4970   Selected Sources and a Bibliography for a History of Scenery to 1660. Nacarow, David A. M.F.A. Thesis, 1963, Yale University.

4971   Selective Bibliography of Handbooks and Textbooks on Metal Working and Plastic Working for the Theatre Scene Shop. Brunt, T.V. Theatre Design & Technology S 1975.

4972   Semi-Automatic Tools.
Work, William. Players
Magazine, 0, 1955, Vol. 32,
No. 1,p. 18.

4973   Semantic Approach to the
Problem of the Duality of
Stage Design As A Spatial
and Temporal Art. Josal,
Wendell John. Ph.D. Thesis,
Northwestern University,
1961.

4974   Sensational Magical
Illustions; the Most
Complete. Strand, D 1902,
Vol. 24, P. 754-762, Jc
1903, Vol 25, P. 63-66.

4975   Service Bulletin Gc-36,
Carbopol Water-Soluble
Resins. B.F. Goodrich
Chemical Co., Cleveland,
Ohio. No Date.

4976   Sets: Painted Drops and
Fabulous Props. Theatre
Crafts, S 1973, Vol. 7, No.
4, P. 21.

4977   Sets and Lights for
"Sherry". Randolph, Robert.
Theatre Crafts, Mr/Ap 1967,
Vol. 1, No. 1, P. 13-15.

4978   Sets in the Workshop
(The). Theatre Arts
Magazine, My 1940, Vol.
XXIV, No. 5, P. 374.

4979   Settings/Cabins, Tents
and the Govenor's Mansion.
Theatre Crafts, S 1975,
Vol. 9, No. 4, P. 20.

4980   Settings/See Moscow
Burn! Witness the Great
Flood!. Theatre Crafts,
Mr/Ap 1976, Vol. 10, No. 2,
P. 18.

4981   Settings and Costumes by
Lee Simonson. Larson,
Orville K. Theatre Design
& Technology, F 1973, No.
32, P. 7.

4982   Settings and Costumes of
the Modern Stage.

Komisarjevsky, Theodore and
Simonson, Lee. Studio
Publications (The), 1933.

4983   Settings by Joseph
Urban: an Evaluation of His
Stage Craft. Marks, Samuel,
M. Ph.D. Thesis,
University of Wisconsin,
1955.

4984   Settings for a New Shape
Stage. Theatre Crafts Ja
1971.

4985   Settings for
Shakespearean Productions.
Hammack, Alan. Players, J
1956, Vol. 41, P. 96.

4986   Settings. Bay, Howard.
Theatre Arts, F, 1953, Vol.
XXXVII, No. 2, P. 66.

4987   Setting a Touch of the
Poet. Edwards, Ben. Theatre
Crafts, Jl/ag 1967, P. 24.

4988   Setting by Donald
Oenslager. Theatre Annual,
1951, Vol. 9, P. 70-71.

4989   Setting for the Albert
Hall (A). Builder (The), Ap
1943, Vol. 101, P. 307-308.

4990   Setting Sail for Yet
Another Part of the Forest.
Don, Robin. Cue Technical
Theatre Review, My/Ju 1980,
P. 7.

4991   Setting Up a Technical
Department. Evans, C.
Theatre Crafts, 0 1969.

4992   Set Designs and Costumes
for Television. Theatre
Quarterly, Ap, 1972, Vol.
II, No. 6, P. 35.

4993   Set to Go. Ardoin, John.
Opera News, Mr 18, 1967,
Vol. 31, P. 6-7.

4994   Seventeenth Century
Design for Theatre
Mechanism (A). Mask (The),
Ap, 1928, Vol. 14, No. 2,
P. 68.

4995   Shadow Puppet Primer
(A). Malkin, Michael R. and
Drake, William J.
Dramatics, My 1978, No. 5,
P. 31.

4996   Shakespeare's First
Globe Theatre. Harvard
Theatre Collection. Harvard
Theatre Collection, 1980,
Cambridge.

4997   Shakespeare's Globe
Playhouse: a Modern
Reconstruction in Text and
Scale Drawings. Smith,
Irwin. Charles Scribner,
1956, New York.

4998   Shakespeare's
Legerdemain. Mitchell, Lee.
Speech Monographs, 1949,
Vol. XVI, No. 1, Pp.
144-161.

4999   Shakespeare's Stage.
Nagler, A.M. Yale
University Press, 1958, New
Haven, Connecticut.

5000   Shakespearean
Representations, Their Laws
and Limits. Fitzgerald,
Percy. Gentleman's
Magazine, Ap 1903, Vol.
294, P. 323-45.

5001   Shakespearean Stage
1574-1642. Gurr, Andrew.
University Press, 1970,
Cambridge (England).
located at the Harvard
Theatre Collection.

5002   Shakespearean Staging,
1599-1642. King, Thomas
James. Harvard University
Press, 1971, Cambridge, Ma.
LOCN: Pn2590.S7 K5 ISBN:
0674804902

5003   Shakespeare's Workshop.
Lawrence, William John.
Basil Blackwell, 1928,
Oxford.

5004   Shakespeare and Gordon
Craig. Laver, James.
Apollo, Ap 1964, P.
326:327.

5005   Shakespeare at the
Globe. Beckerman, Bernard.
Macmillan, 1962, New York.

5006   Shakespeare Memorial
Library Stratford-Upon-Avon
(The). Fox, Levi. OSU
Theatre Collection
Bulletin, Sp 1959, Vol. 6,
P. 5.

5007   Shakespeare With Movies.
Andrus, T.O. Players
Magazine, D 1950, Vol. 27,
No. 3, P. 62.

5008   Shakesperian Stage
(The). Albright, Victor
Emanuel. Columbia
University Press (The),
1909, New York.

5009   Shaking Canvas. Voss,
Lawrence. Players Magazine,
O,1952, Vol. 29, No. 1, P.
20.

5010   Shall We Realize
Wagner's Ideals?. Van
Vechen, Carl. Musical
Quarterly, Jl 1916, Vol.2 ,
P. 387.

5011   Shear Impact and Shear
Tensile Properties of
Adhesives. Silver, I.
Modern Plastics, My 1949,
Vol. XXVI, P. 95.

5012   Sheet Metal Shop
Practice. Bruce, Leroy F.
and Meyer, Leo A. American
Technical Society, 1965,
Chicago.

5013   Sheet Metal Technology.
Budzik, Richard S. Howard
W. Sams, 1971,
Indianapolis.

5014   Shipping. Schoelzel,
Stephanie. Theatre Crafts,
S 1979, Vol. 13, No. 4, P.
4.

5015   Ship in the New French
Ballet of the Tempest
(The). Scientific American
Supplement, S 1889, Vol.
28, P. 11450.

5016   Ship Is More Than the
Crew (The). Tenham,
Dorothy. Cue Technical
Theatre Review, S/O 1979,
P. 30.

5017   Shopping for the Best
Price. Enoch, Howard. New
England Entertainment
Digest, S 12, 1979,vol. 1,
No. 3,p. 11.

5018   Shop Built Fog Machine.
Gillette, F. M. Theatre
Crafts O 1976.

5019   Shop Designed for a
Coastal Repertory Theatre.
Baily, Albert Lang. M.A.
Thesis, University of
Denver, 1952. LOCN: Micro
Film M 1952 Reel 1 Item 8

5020   Shop Tools. Hunt,
Dewitt. Van Nostrand, 1958,
Princeton, New Jersey.

5021   Short Course in
Scenography-University of
California, Santa Barbara.
Vychodil, Ladislav. Theatre
Design & Technology, O
1974, No. 38, P. 23.

5022   Short History of Armor
and a Method of
Constructing Armor for The
Stage (A). Zirke, Larry
Edwin. M.A. Thesis,
University of Washington,
1958.

5023   Short History of Scene
Design in Great Britain
(A). Rosenfeld, Sybil.
Basil Blackwell, 1973,
Oxford.

5024   Short History of the
Building Crafts. Briggs,
Martin S. Clarendon, 1925,
Oxford.

5025   Showcase for the New
Stagecraft: the Scenic
Designs of The Washington
Square Players and the
Theatre Guild. Nordvold,
Robert O. Ph.D. Thesis,
Indiana University, 1973.

5026   Shows That Didn't Come
Off. Kernodle, Portia.
Players Magazine, Mr 1943,
Vol. 19, No. 6, P. 11.

5027   Show Business and the
Occupational Safety and
Health Act. Davidson, R.
Theatre Crafts My 1975.

5028   Shubert Archive (The): a
Future Dream for Scholars.
Ndini, William. Theatre
Design & Technology, Fall
1978, Vol. XIV, No. 3, P.
23.

5029   Shuffling the Schouwburg
Scenes. Gascoigne, Bamber.
Theatre Research, 1968,
Vol. IX, No. 2, P. 88.

5030   Siegfried Buemann,
Spanish Scene Painter.
Schalcher, Traugott.
International Advertising
Art, Je 1937, Vol. 14, P.
18-23.

5031   Siegfried Performance in
Paris. Scientific American
Supplement, Mr 29, 1902,
Vol. 53, P. 21941.

5032   Sign Painting Up to Now.
Atkinson, Frank H. F. J.
Drake, 1937. Originally
Published, F. J. Drake,
1909.

5033   Silencers. Sterett,
Larry S. Gun Digest, 1964,
18th Ed., P. 135-138.

5034   Simple Modules
Signifying Much: Staging 16
Plays a Summer at The
O'neill. Jenner, C. Lee.
Theatre Crafts, My/Je 1979,
Vol. 13, No. 3, P. 32.

5035   Simplicity in Settings.
Hake, Herbert V. Players
Magazine, F 1940, Vol 16,
No. 5, P. 7.

5036   Simplification of Stage
Scenery. Matthews, Brander.
Unpopular Reviews, Ap 1919,
Pp. 350-362.

5037   Simplified Engineering for Architects and Builders Third Edition. Parker, Harry. John Wiley and Sons, 1961, New York.

5038   Simplified Scenery. Adix, Vern. Players Magazine, Ap, 1961, Vol. 37, No. 7, P. 156.

5039   Simplified Stagecraft Manual (The). Stahl, Leroy. T.S. Dennison, 1962, New York.

5040   Simplified Stage Scenery. Cole, Wendell. Church Property Administration, S 1953, Vol. 17, P. 54-56, 134-138.

5041   Sir James Thornhill and the Theatre Royal, Drury Lane, 1705. Barlow, Graham. In Essays on the Eighteenth-Century English Stage, Methuen & Co., 1972, London.

5042   Sixteenth & Seventeenth Century Theatre Design in Paris. Arts Council of Great Britain. Arts Council of Great Britain, 1956, London. LOCN: Pn 2091 S8 A75

5043   Sixteen Designs for the Theatre. Rutherston, Albert Daniel. Oxford University, 1928, London.

5044   Six Drawings for the Cenci. Jones, Robert Edmond. Theatre Arts Monthly, Je, 1924, Vol. VIII, No. 6, P. 408.

5045   Six Medieval Theatres in One Social Structure. Kernodle, George R. Theatre Research, 1960, Vol. II.

5046   Six Stages in One. Scientific American, Mr 1923, Vol. 128, P. 154,155.

5047   Six Stages Within One Stage: a Revolution in Theatrical Mechanics. Illustrated London News, 1923, Vol. 162, P. 544-545.

5048   Six Vital Stage Sets. Atkinson, Brooks. New York Times Magazine, Ap 11, 1954, P. 24.

5049   Size-Water. Voss, Lawrence. Players Magazine, Ja, 1952, Vol. 28, No. 4, P. 95.

5050   Sketch Beneath the Stage During a Performance of the Opera of Hamlet (A). Graphic, Ja 1880, Vol. 12, P. 100.

5051   Sketch of the History of Scene Painting. Builder, 1859, Vol. 17, P. 353-354.

5052   Sloping Acting Area on a Flat Stage Floor. Tabs, S 1956, Vol. 14, No. 2, P. 16.

5053   Slovak National Theatre Shops (The). Islava, Bratislava. Theatre Design & Technology F 1970.

5054   Small Barn Theatre With Curved Curtains. Holmes, R.R. Drama, Mr, 1937, Vol. 15, P. 96.

5055   Small Business or Luxury Item?. Lee, Ming Cho. Theatre 4 the American Theatre, 1970-1971, Scribner's ' Sons, 1972, New York.

5056   Small Stage and Its Equipment (The). Wilson, R.A. Allen & Unwin, 1930, London.

5057   Small Studio Set Construction: How to Build and Use Flats for Erection of Interior Sets. American Cinematographer, Je 1956, Vol. 37, No. 6, P. 360-361, 383-384.

5058   Smoother Scene Change at the Nt. ABTT News, O 1979, P. 14.

5059   Solar Electricity: an Economic Approach to Solar Energy. Palz, Wolfgang. Bottersworth, 1978, Boston. LOCN: Tk 1056 P34 ISBN: Isbn 0:408-70910-3

5060   Solar Energy: Fundamentals in Building Design. Anderson, Bruce. McGraw-Hill, 1977, New York. LOCN: 76-45467 ISBN: 0-07-001751-4

5061   Solar Energy and Building. Szokalay, Sv. Architectural Press, 1977, London/John Wiley & Sons, 1977, N.Y. LOCN: Th7413 S96 1977 ISBN: 0-470-99235-2

5062   Solar Energy. Messel, H. and Butler, S. T. Pergamon Press, 1975, New York. LOCN: Tj 810 147 1974 ISBN: Isbn 0-08-619817-1

5063   Solar Heating and Cooling: Engineering, Practical Design, And Economics. Kreider, Jan F. and Kreith, Frank. Hemisphere Publishing Corp., 1975, Washington. LOCN: 75-6646 ISBN: 0-07-035473-1

5064   Solar Home Book; Heating, Cooling and Designing With the Sun (The). Anderson, Bruce and Riordan, Michael. Cheshire Books, 1976, Harrisville, Nh. LOCN: 76-29494 ISBN: 0-917352-01-7

5065   Solutions for Painting and Plumbing. Grayson, Phillip. Theatre Craft, My/Je 1980, Vol. 14, No. 3, P. 42.

5066   Something New. Voss, Lawrence. Players Magazine,

Ap, 1953, Vol. 29, No. 7, P. 163.

5067   Some American Stage Settings. Mannes, Marya. Creative Art, D, 1930, Vol. 7, P. 449.

5068   Some Architectural Designs of Padrepozzo (1649-1709 for the Theatre of the Seventeenth Century). Semar, John (Introduction). Mask (The), Jl 1914, Vol. 7, No. 1, P. 39.

5069   Some Extracts from the Practice of Making Scenes and Machines in Theatres. Sabbattini. Mask (The), Ap, 1926, Vol. 12, No.2, P. 78.

5070   Some Extracts from the Practice of Making Scenes and Machines in Theatre. Sabbattini. Mask (The), Ja, 1929, Vol. 15, No. 1, P. 13.

5071   Some Extracts from the Practice of Making Scenes and Machines in Theatres. Sabbattini. Mask (The) O, 1928, Vol. 14, No. 4, P. 162.

5072   Some Ideas on Stage Decoration. Terry, Ellen. McClure's Magazine, Ja 1911, P. 289-294.

5073   Some Illusions of the Theatre. Mannering, Mary. New York Dramatic Mirror, Ja 31, 1912, Vol. 67, P. 8.

5074   Some New Scenic Materials and Techniques. Crabs, Donald. Theatre Design and Technology, D 1968, No. 15, P. 7.

5075   Some Notes on Aaron Hill and Stage Scenery. Burnim, Kalman A. Century, 1920, New York.

5076   Some Notes on Stage

Design. Lauterer, Arch.
Theatre Arts Monthly, O,
1945, Vol. XXIX, No. 10, P.
596.

5077   Some Practical
Suggestions for the Design
and Equipment Of Theatre
and School Stages. Flagg,
Edwin H. Architect and
Engineer of California, Ja
1917, Vol. 48, No. 1, P.
79.

5078   Some Principles of
Elizabethan Staging.
Reynolds, George Fullmer.
AMS Press, 1970. LOCN: Pn
2590 S7 R4 1970

5079   Some Realistic
Stage-Effects. Chamber's
(Edinburgh) Journal, 1896,
Vol. LXXIII.

5080   Some Scenic Directions.
Daspinlamberto, Giulio
Trolila. Mask (The) Ap,
1927, Vol. 12, No. 2, P.
59.

5081   Some Stage-Trades.
Chamber's (Edinburgh)
Journal, 1888, Vol. LXV.

5082   Some Stage Effects:
Their Growth and History.
Lawrence, William John.
Gentleman' Magazine, Jl
1888, Vol. 265, P. 83-95.

5083   Some Stage Effects in
Ben Hur. Scientific
American, Ag 1900, Vol. 83,
P. 187.

5084   Some Stage Effects.
Robertson, W. B. Cassell's
Magazine, 1899, Vol. 29, P.
94-99.

5085   Some Superfluous
Requirements of Our Theatre
Laws. Blackall, Clarence
H. American Architect,
1915, Vol. 107, Part 1, P.
105-211.

5086   Sonderheft. Sightline

(ABTT Journal), Autumn
1978, Vol. 12, No. 2, P.
66.

5087   Sounding the Depths:
Harry Horner. Lingg, Ann
M. Opera News, Ja 25,
1964, Vol. 28, P. 33.

5088   Sources of Theatrical
History. Nagler, A.M.
Theatre Annual, Inc., 1952,
New York, P.113-164.

5089   Source Book in
Theatrical History (A).
Nagler, A.M. Dover
Publications, Inc. 1952,
New York.

5090   South Coast Repertory.
Gray, Beverly. Theatre
Crafts, S 1980, Vol. 14,
No. 4, P. 36.

5091   South Italian Vases and
Attic Drama. Weshbster, T.
B. L. Classical Quarterly,
1948, Xlii.

5092   Soviet Scene Design.
Gorelik, Mordecai. New
Theatre and Film, Ap 1937,
Vol. 4, P. 22.

5093   Soviet Stage Design in
the 20th Century.
Pojarskia, Militza. World
Theatre, Fall, 1961, Vol.
X, No. 3, P. 223.

5094   Space Doesn't Count.
Leberman, Joseph. Theatre
Arts, S, 1952, Vol. XXXVI,
No. 9, P. 78.

5095   Space Stage (The).
Cheney, Sheldon. Theatre
Arts Monthly, O 1927, Vol.
XI, No. 10, P. 762-775.

5096   Spatial Problems of the
Theatre. Honzl, Kindrich.
Interscaena, Sp 1970, Vol.
4, P. 1-10.

5097   Special Effects-A
Segment of Motion-Picture
and TV Production. Ponedel,

Frederic L. Journal of the Society of Motion Picture and Television Engineers, O 1962, Vol. 71, P. 760-761.

5098   Special Effects/ Flash Pots and Fire Works. Theatre Crafts, S 1975, Vol. 9 No. 4, P. 24.

5099   Special Effects Cinematography: a Bibliography. Fielding, Raymond E. Journal of the Society of Motion Picture and Television Engineers, Je, 1960, Vol. 69, P. 421.

5100   Special Effects File. Harvard Theatre Collection. No Date.

5101   Special Effects for the Amateur Theatre Organization. Hoh, Lavahn G. M.F.A. Thesis, University of Wisconsin, 1973. LOCN: Awo H717 L393

5102   Special Effects in Cinematography. Bullied, Henry A.V. Fountain Press, 1954, London.

5103   Special Effects in Motion Pictures. Clark, Frank P. Society of Motion Picture and Television Engineers 1966 New York. LOCN: Tr 858 C56

5104   Special Effects. Poe, Harold W. Players Magazine, D, 1958, Vol.35, No. 3, P. 59.

5105   Specifications Booklet: Lightweight, Glassless Mirrors. Kamar Products, Inc., 2 South Buckhout, Irvington-On-Hudson, New York, 10533. No Date.

5106   Spectacles of the House of Savoy During the Eighteenth Century. Kozelka, Edwin P. Ph.D. Thesis, Yale, 1945. Second Source - 1970 As Date.

5107   Spectacle and Drama. Bookman, Ja 1915, P. 547-552.

5108   Spectacle in the Theatres of London 1767-1802. Thomas, Russell, B. Ph.D. Thesis, Chicago, 1942.

5109   Spectacular Effects in the Tempest. McDowell, John H. Theatre Studies 18 1971 P. 65.

5110   Spectacular Effects on the Seventeenth Century Continental Stage. Mohler, Franklin Calvin II. Ph.D. Thesis, Ohio State University, 1976.

5111   Spectacular Scenic Effects of the Eighteenth-Century Pantomime. Wells, Mitchell. Philological Quarterly, 1938, Vol. 17, P. 67-81.

5112   Spectacular Stage Lighting at the Circus Schumann, Berlin. Electrical World Vol. 55 F 10,1910 P. 361.

5113   Spin Your Own Cobwebs. Henry, Joseph. American Cinematographer, Je 1959, Vol. 40, P. 352, 17378.

5114   Spiral Stair Design and Construction. Sultan, J. Theatre Crafts N 1974.

5115   Spirit Shadow, The. World's Advance, Jl 1915, Vol. 31, P. 77.

5116   Splendid Time Is Guaranteed for All. Wagner, Robin. Theatre Crafts, N/D 1973, Vol. 7, No. 6, P. 6.

5117   Spot Dimmers. Ackler, Bryan H. Theatre Crafts, Mr/ap 1979, Vol. 13, No. 2, P. 89.

5118   Spray for Clearing

Stages of Smoke and Haze. Meyer, Herbert. Motion Picture Research Council Bulletin No. 253, Hollywood, 1955.

5119   Springtime Design for an Orchestra. Wexler, Peter. Theatre Crafts, S 1969, Vol. 3, No. 4, P. 7-11.

5120   SR Survey of Stage Design. Saturday Review of Literature, D 12, 1964.

5121   St. Louis Municipal Opera (The). Voss, Lawrence. Players Magazine, N, 1954, Vol. 31, No. 2, P. 38.

5122   Stage-Setting for Amateurs and Professionals. Southern, Richard. Theatre Arts Books, 1964, New York. Faber, 1938, London. LOCN: Josten: Pn 2091 S8 S64 1964

5123   Stage, (The). White, Matthew, Jr. Munsey's Magazine, Ja 1911, P. 564.

5124   Stagecraft, Your Introduction to Backstage Work. Lord, William H. William H. Lord, 9210 North College Ave, Indianapolis, In., 46240. No Date.

5125   Stagecraft and Scene Design. Philippi, Herbert. Houghton Mifflin Co., 1953, Boston. LOCN: Pn2091. S8 P48

5126   Stagecraft Forum (The). Frost, Eugene. Drama (The), Mr 1929, Vol. V, P. 182.

5127   Stagecraft for Nonprofessionals. Buerki, F.A. University of Wisconsin Press 1972 Madison. Alos Published in 1955. LOCN: Pn2091.S8 B74 1972 ISBN: 0299062341

5128   Stagecraft from the Director's Point of View. Stewart, Hal D. Pitman, 1949, London.

5129   Stagecraft of the Medieval English Drama (The). Shull, Virginia. Ph.D. Thesis, Yale University, 1941.

5130   Stagecraft. Bradbury, A. J. and Howard, W.R.B. H. Jenkins, 1953, London. LOCN: Pn2091.S8b7

5131   Stagecraft. Pausback, Nicholas J. Pausback Scenery Co., 1928, Chicago.

5132   Stages, Scenery, and Props. Yerian, Cameron John and Yerian, Margaret. Childrens Press, 1975, Chicago. LOCN: Pn2091.S8 Y4 1975 ISBN: 0516013138

5133   Stages and Scenery. Pilbrow, Richard. Twentieth Century, 1961, Vol. 169, P. 118-28.

5134   Stage Accident at Drury Lane, (The). Builder, O 1897, Vol. 73, P. 255.

5135   Stage Alterations at Covent Garden. Engineering, My 24, 1901, Vol. 71, P. 659-660, 674, 724.

5137   Stage and Ballet Designs of Eugene Berman (The). Delarue, Allison. Dance Index, Ja 1946, Vol. 5, P. 4-23.

5138   Stage and Film Decor. Myerscough-Walker, Raymond. Pitman & Sons, 1940, London. LOCN: Pn 2091 S8 M9

5139   Stage and Stage Settings. Jossic, Yvonne Francoise. H. C. Perleberg, 1933.

5140   Stage Art - New and Old. Belasco, David. Saturday Evening Post, Mr 20, 1920, Vol. CXCII, P. 22-23.

5141   Stage Bridges at the
Covent Garden Opera House,
London, England. Scientific
American Supplement, S 21,
1901, Vol. 52, P. 21511-12.

5142   Stage Carpentry. Work,
1891, Vol. P. 561-562,
632-634, 712-713, 792-794.

5143   Stage Construction for
School Plays. Jones, Eric.
Batsford, 1969, London, 388
P.. LOCN: Pn2091.S8 P3
1974 ISBN: 0030894468

5144   Stage Craft for
Non-Professionals. Buerki,
F.A. University of
Wisconsin, 1945, Madison.
LOCN: Pn2091 S8 B74 1972

5145   Stage Craft for Small
Drama Groups. Carey, Grace.
Ravin, 1948, New York;
Albyn, London.

5146   Stage Craft. Hoggett,
Christ. A and C Black,
1975, London. LOCN: Pn2085.
H6 ISBN: 0713615575

5147   Stage Crews Handbook for
Children's Theatre
Directors (The). Lewis,
George. Ph.D. Thesis,
University of Denver, 1952.

5148   Stage Crew Handbook (A).
Cornberg, Sol and Gebaur,
Emanuel L. Emanuel L.
Harper, 1957, New York.
LOCN: Pn2091.S8 C63 1957

5149   Stage Curtain. Jonas,
Maurice. Notes and Queries,
1899, Series 9, Vol. 4, P.
45.

5150   Stage Decoration in
France in the Middle Ages.
Stuart, Donald Clive. Ph.D.
Thesis, Columbia
University, 1910.

5151   Stage Decoration in
France in the Middle Ages.
Stuart, Donald Clive. New
York, Columbia University
Press, 1910, P. 230.

5152   Stage Decoration in
Japan. Kitamara, Kihachi.
World Theatre, Fall,1954,
Vol. III, No. 4, P. 11.

5153   Stage Decoration.
Cheney, Sheldon. B. Blom
1966 New York. John Day
Co., 1928, New York,
138p.. LOCN: Pn2091.S8 C5
1966

5154   Stage Deluge, (A).
Literary Digest, Mr 1918,
Vol. 56, No. 9, P. 25.

5155   Stage Design: New
Directions or Dead End?.
Benslager, Donald. Theatre
Arts, O, 1956, Vol. XL, No.
10, P. 26.

5156   Stage Designers--I:
Francesco Santurini.
Seligman, Janet. Ballet, My
1948, Vol. 5, P. 17.

5157   Stage Designers--Iv:
Edward Burra. Crossley,
Dorothy. Ballet, Ja 1949,
Vol. 7, P. 18.

5158   Stage Designers--Vi:
Pierre Ciceri. Guest, Ivor.
Ballet, Jl 1949, Vol. 8, P.
20.

5159   Stage Designers--VII:
Eugene Berman. Gomez,
Simonetta. Ballet, D 1949,
Vol. 8, P. 25-32.

5160   Stage Designers--VIII:
Giacomo Torelli. Fletcher,
Ifan Kyrle. Ballet, F 1950,
Vol. 9, P. 28.

5161   Stage Designers--X:
Theodor Jachimowicz.
Seligman, Janet. Ballet, Je
1951, Vol. II, P. 24.

5162   Stage Designers--Xi:
Andre Beaurepaire. Buckle,
Richard. Ballet, Jl/Ag
1950, Vol. 10, P. 19.

5163   Stage Designer (The).
Rosse, Herman. Theatre Arts

Monthly, My, 1924, Vol.
III, No. 5, P. 321.

5164   Stage Designer (The).
Otto, Teo. World Theatre,
1953, Vol. II, No. 4, P.
35.

5165   Stage Designer Theatre's
Step-Child. Whittaker,
Herbert. Canadian Art,
My-Je 1965, Vol. 22, P.
41-47.

5166   Stage Designs and
Costumes. Messel, Oliver
Hilary Sambourne. Lane,
1933, London.

5167   Stage Designs for the
Florentine Intermezzi of
1589. Laver, James.
Burlington Magazine (The),
1932, Vol. LX, P. 294.

5168   Stage Designs of Herman
Rosse (The). Dorr, Charles.
Theatre Magazine, S 1921,
P. 162.

5169   Stage Designs of the
Cooper Union Museum. (In
Cooper Union for the
Advancement of Science and
Art, New York). Berliner,
Rudolf. Museum for the Arts
of Decoration Chronicle, Ag
1941, Vol. 1, No. 8 P.
184-320.

5171   Stage Designs of
Yesteryear in Old Prints
and Drawings. Hobbies, Ag
1951, Vol. 56, P. 36.

5172   Stage Designs. Jeudwine,
Wynne. Feltham, Country
Life Books, 1968. LOCN: Pn
2091 S8j4

5173   Stage Design in
Australia. Ashbolt, Allan.
World Theatre, Fall, 1954,
Vol. III, No. 4, P. 64.

5174   Stage Design in Italy.
Povocedo, Elena. World
Theatre, Sum, 1962, Vol.
XI, No. 2, P. 1839,.

5175   Stage Design in Italy.
Pacuvio, Guilio. World
Theatre, Wi, 1966, Vol. V,
No. 4, P. 169.

5176   Stage Design in Rumania.
Arta Grafica, 1965,
Bucharest.

5177   Stage Design of
Rumania--Prague
Quadrennial--1971.
Published by Rumanian
Center of the International
Organization of
Sceneo-Traphers and
Theatre.

5178   Stage Design Throughout
the World Since 1935.
International Theatre
Institute. Harrap, 1956,
London.

5179   Stage Design Throughout
the World Since 1950.
International Theatre
Institute. Theatre Arts
Books, 1964.

5180   Stage Design Throughout
the World Since 1960.
Hainaux, Rene. Theatre Arts
Books, 1973, New York.
LOCN: Pn 2091 S8 H23

5181   Stage Design Throughout
the World: 1970-1975.
Hainaux, Rene. Theatre Arts
Books, 1976, New York.

5182   Stage Design. Rowell,
Kenneth. Reinhold Book,
Corp., New York; Studio
Vista, 1968, London. LOCN:
Pn 2901 S8 R63

5183   Stage Design. Bay,
Howard. Drama Book
Specialists, 1974, New
York.

5184   Stage Design. Simonson,
Lee. Encyclopaedia
Britannica, 1929, 14th Ed.
Vol. XX, P. 281-285.

5185   Stage Design. Mielziner,
Jo. Interiors, O 1941, Vol.
101, P. 28-29.

5186   Stage Design. Interiors, F 1942, Vol. 101, P. 50-51.

5187   Stage Design. Interiors, N 1941, Vol. 101, P. 40-41.

5188   Stage Design. Interiors, F 1946, Vol. 105, P. 82-83.

5189   Stage Devices; Development of Theatrical Effects from the Time of the Greeks to the Present Day. Matthews, Brander. Theatre Magazine, F 1914, Vol. 24, No. 2, P. 82.

5191   Stage Draperies. Work, 1892, Vol. 4, P. 390-391.

5192   Stage Effects: How to Make and Work Them. Rose, A. George Routledge & Sons, 1926, London.

5193   Stage Effects and How to Get Them. Theatre Magazine, Jl 1924, P. 12.

5194   Stage Effects in Ben-Hur. Werner's Magazine, O 1900, Vol. 26, P. 161-164, D 1900, P. 311-327.

5195   Stage Equipment: Data and Details. Architectural Forum, S, 1932, Vol. 57, P. 275.

5196   Stage Equipment for the Drama Theatre, University of New Mexico Fine Arts Center. Mcmullan, Bruce. M.F.A. Thesis, Yale University, 1961.

5197   Stage Equipment. Theatre Management, D 1931, P. 14.

5198   Stage Equipment. Architectural Forum, S 1932, P. 275.

5199   Stage Fire Illusion. Popular Electricity, O 1911, Vol. 4, P. 525.

5200   Stage Floor Structure

and Surfaces for Dance. Calva, L.F. Theatre Design & Technology Fall 1975.

5201   Stage Goes "Air Minded" Airplane Set for Dancing Partner. Scientific American, N, 1930, Vol. 143, P. 355.

5202   Stage Greenery Solutions: Fiberglass Trees. Sullivan, William. Theatre Crafts, Vol. 13., No. 3 My 1979, P.28.

5203   Stage Groove and the Thunder Run (The). Southern, Richard. Architectural Review, My 1944, Vol. 95, P. 135-36.

5204   Stage Hands Seek Official Backing. The News Line, Ap 12, 1979.

5205   Stage Hand Ethics. the Overalls Deus Ex Machina Behind the Curtain. Jenks, George, C. Theatre Magazine, 1921, Vol. 33, P. 334, 370.

5206   Stage Illusions and Entertainments. Jones, Bernard E. (Ed). Funk, 1923.

5207   Stage Illusion in Levitation. Radcliffe, W. H. Theatre Magazine (The), Ag 1913, Vol. XVIII, No. 150, P. 62.

5208   Stage in Aristophanes (The). White, J. W. Harvard Studies in Classical Philology, 1891, II.

5209   Stage Is Set (The). Simonson, Lee. Theatre Arts Books, 1964, New York. Also Published by Harcourt, 1932 and Dover 1946. LOCN: Pn2037. S5 1964

5210   Stage Layout and Equipment. Kearney, Edward

H. Architectural Forum, 1925, Vol. 42, P. 409-410.

5211   Stage Lift Complex: MGM Grand Hotel Las Vegas. Cummings, R.J. Theatre Design & Technology Sp 1976.

5212   Stage Lighting, 1966. Corry, Percy. Drama, Wi, 1966, P. 42.

5213   Stage Lighting. Architectural Forum, S 1932, P. 274.

5214   Stage Lighting. Athenaeum, My 2, 1919, P. 278.

5215   Stage Lights of Theatres. Builder, (The), F 7, 1863, P. 105.

5216   Stage Machinery and Lighting Equipment for Small Theatres and Community Buildings. Pichel, Irving. Theatre Arts Magazine, Ap 1920, Vol. IV, P. 137-52.

5217   Stage Machinery at the Drottningholm Theatre. Sizer, Theodore. Ph.D. Thesis, University of Michigan, 1953.

5218   Stage Machinery at Wiesbaden. Builder, N 1893, Vol. 65, P. 388.

5219   Stage Management for the Amateur Theatre. Halstead, William Perdue. F.S. Crofts & Co., 1937, New York.

5220   Stage Mechanism. Sachs, Edwin O. Journal of the Society of Arts, Ap 22, 1898, Vol. 46, P. 5231.

5221   Stage Noises and Effects. Green, Michael. Herbert Jenkins, 1958, London.

5222   Stage Photography.

Wendland, Charles W. Players Magazine, Ap 1945, Vol. 21, No. 7, P. 15.

5223   Stage Photography. Maurer, John. Players Magazine, My/Je 1929, Vol. V, No. 4, P. 3.

5224   Stage Realism Begins With a Cheese-Grater and a Jar of "Gunk". Field, June. Daily Telegraph, Ag 26, 1970, P. 13.

5225   Stage Realism. Andrews, Charlton. New York Dramatic Mirror, My 29, 1912, P. 5, 12.

5226   Stage Scenery: Its Construction and Rigging. Gillette, A.S. Harper and Row, 1972, New York. LOCN: Pn2091. S8 G5 1972 ISBN: Pn2091 S8 G5

5227   Stage Scenery and Lighting; a Handbook for Non-Professionals. Selden, Samuel. F.S. Crofts & Co., 1930, New York. LOCN: Pn 2091 S8s45

5228   Stage Scenery and the Men Who Paint It. Theatre Magazine (The), Au 1908, Vol. VIII, No. 90, P. 203.

5229   Stage Scenery and the Vitascope. Lathrop, George Parsons. North American Review, Vol. CLXIII, S 1896, P. 377-381.

5230   Stage Scenery As an Art. Hamilton, Clayton. Art and Progress, Je 1910, Vol. 1, P. 213-218.

5231   Stage Scenery in the Eighteenth Century. Lawrence, William John. Magazine of Art, 1895, Vol. XVIII, P. 387.

5232   Stage Scenery on the Building Block Principle. Scientific American, F 1921, Vol. 130, P. 95.

5233   Stage Scenery. Wyatt, Jenifer. Barrie & Jenkins, 1957.

5234   Stage Scenery. Scientific American, Jl 1864, Vol. 11, P. 54.

5235   Stage Scenes Reversed. New York Time, N 11, 1883, P. 5.

5236   Stage Sets. Morin, Roi L. American Architect, Ap 1923, Vol. 123, No. 2418, P. 350-353 Illustrations, No. 2419; My 1923, P. 405-408.

5237   Stage Setting: Realistic and Impressionistic. Howe, Samuel. International Studio, O 1912, Vol. 47, P. Xlix-Liv.

5238   Stage Settings and Sceneries. Holt, C.H.G. Architects Journal (The), 1922, Vol. 56, P. 39-41.

5239   Stage Settings by American Architects. American Institute of Architects Journal, 1921, Vol. 9, P. 77-84, 128-134, 240-243.

5240   Stage Settings for Amateurs and Professionals. Southern, Richard. Theatre Arts, 1960, New York.

5241   Stage Settings for Operas. Grain, Amelia. Philadelphia, No Date.

5242   Stage Setting of Hell and the Iconography of the Middle Ages (The). Stuart, Donald Clive. Romanic Review, 1913, Vol. 4, P. 330-342.

5243   Stage Setting Since 1945. Reinking, Wilhelm. World Theatre, Fall, 1960, Vol. IX, No. 3, P. 249.

5244   Stage Spectacles of

Philip James De Loutherbourg (The). Allen, Ralph G. D.F.A. Thesis, Yale University, 1960.

5245   Stage Spectacle and Victorian Society. Kernodle, George R. Quarterly Journal of Speech, 1954, Vol. 40, P. 31.

5246   Stage Storms. All the Year Round, Ag 1872, Vol. 8, P. 304-308.

5247   Stage Thunder. Cook, D. Once a Week, Vol. XIV, P. 685. No Date.

5248   Stage to Screen: Theatrical Method from Garrick to Griffith. Vardac, A. Nicholas. Harvard Univ. Press 1949 Cambridge, Mass..

5249   Stage Warfare. Cassell's Magazine, London, 1901, Vol. 31, P. 227-231.

5250   Stage Wonders Work of Hidden Toilers. Popular Mechanics, Mr, 1924, Vol. 41, P. 384.

5251   Stage World of Charlie Brown (The). Kimmel, Alan. Theatre Crafts, S/O 1967, P. 28-31.

5252   Staging and Scenery in the Ancient Greek Theatre. Webster, Thomas B. L. Bulletin of the John Rylands Library, 1959-1960, Vol. 42, P. 493-509.

5253   Staging at Shiraz. Merin, Jennifer. Theatre Crafts, Mr/Ap 1977, Vol. II, No. 2, P. 28.

5254   Staging a Popular Restaurant. Dodge, Wendell Phillips. Theatre, O 1912, Vol. 16, P. 104, X-Xi.

5255   Staging in the French

and English Theatre.
Bourdon, Georges.
Fortnightly Review 77, Ja
1902, P. 154-69.

5256   Staging Made Easy.
Withey, J. A. Players
Magazine, N, 1958, Vol. 35,
No. 2, P. 34.

5257   Staging of Eighteenth
Century Designs for Scenery
(The). Southern, Richard.
Royal Institute of British
Architects Journal, Ag
1935, Vol. 42, P.
1021-1037.

5258   Staging of Elizabethan
Plays in Private Theatres
1632-1642. Hammer, Gael
Warren. Ph.D. Thesis,
University of Iowa, 1972.

5259   Staging of English
Mystery Plays(The). Weary,
Erica H. Ph.D. Eng.
Thesis, Southern
California, 1939.

5260   Staging of Grand Opera,
The. Lowrey, Edward W. New
England Magazine, D 1913,
P. 415-418, 423-427.

5261   Staging of Lope De
Vega's Comedias, The. Revue
Hispanique, 1906, Vol. 15,
P. 453-485.

5262   Staging of Pantomime at
Sadler's Wells Theatre
1828-1860. Morrow, John
Charles. Ph.D. Thesis, Ohio
State University, 1963.

5263   Staging of Pantomime
Entertainments on the
London Stage 1715-1808
(The). Miesle, Frank
Leland. Ph.D. Thesis, Ohio
State University, 1955.

5264   Staging of Plays at the
Salisbury Court Theatre,
1630-1642. Stevens, David.
Theatre Journal, D 1979,
Vol. 31, No. 4, P. 511.

5265   Staging of Shakespeare,
a Defence of the Public
Taste. Tree, Herbert
Beerbohm. Living Age, Ag
11, 1900, P. 352-363.

5266   Staging of Shakespeare,
(The). Dillon, Arthur.
Westminster Review, O 1900,
P. 427-431.

5267   Staging of the "Creacion
of the World" (The). Neuss,
Paula. Theatre Notebook,
1979, Vol. XXXIII, No. 3,
P. 116-125.

5268   Staging of the "Miracles
De Nostre Dame Par
Personnages". Penn,
Dorothy. Institute of
French Studies, Columbia
University, 1933, New York.

5269   Staging of the
Comedia. The Curtain,
Scenery, Stage
Machinery.. Rennert, Hugo
Albert. 1909.

5270   Staging of the
Donaueschingen Passion
Play. Modern Language
Review, 1920, Vol. 15, P.
65:76, 279-297.

5271   Staging Practices in the
Restoration Theatres
1660-1682. Langhans, Edward
A. Ph.D. Thesis, Yale,
1955.

5272   Staging the Dance.
Melcer, Fannie Helen. W.C.
Brown, 1955, Dubuque, Iowa.

5273   Staging TV Programs and
Commercials: How to Plan
and Execute Sets, Props and
Production Facilities.
Wade, Robert J. Hastings
House, 1954.

5274   Stained Glass.
Gambacorta, Leo. Theatre
Craft, My/Je 1980, Vol. 14,
No. 3, P. 40.

5275   Standard American

Encyclopedia of Formulas
(The). Hopkins, Albert A.
Grosset & Dunlap, 1953.

5276   Standing Places Licensed
for Public Entertainments.
Builder (The), F 13, 1909,
Vol. XCVI, P. 183.

5277   Stanislaw Sliwinski:
Stage Designer and Man of
the Theater. Winkler,
Konrad. Studio, N 1935,
Vol. 110, P. 294-295.

5278   Stanley Tool Guide.
Stanley Tools, Inc., 1942,
New Britain, Ct.

5279   Stan White on Designing
for the Theatre. Canadian
Art, Jl/Ag 1963, Vol. 20,
P. 232-237.

5280   State Anti-Sound Piracy
Laws and a Proposed Model
Statute: a Time to
Consolidate the Victories
Against Sound Pirates.
Pesserilo, Ira M.
Performing Arts Review,
1978, Vol. 8, No. 1, P. 1.

5281   State Pistol Laws. Henry
Schlesinger, 1962, New
York.

5282   Status of the Designer
T.D. in American
Educational Theatre,
1961-1971. Batcheller,
David R. Educational
Theatre Journal, D 1973,
Vol. 25, No. 4, P. 473.

5283   Status of the Technical
Director in American
Educational Theatre: a
Survey (The). Batcheller,
David R. Quarterly Journal
of Speech, D 1964, Vol.
XLVIII, No. 4, P. 388.

5284   Status of the Technical
Director in American
Educational Theatre.
Batcheller, David R. Ph.D.
Thesis, Ohio State
University, 1961.

5285   Steam Shovel. Jones,
Rupel J. and Gillete, A.S.
Players Magazine, My/Je
1939 H, Vol. 15, No. 5, P.
20.

5286   Steele Mackey: Producer
and Director. Curry, Wade
C. Ph.D. Thesis,
University of Illinois at
Urbana, 1958.

5287   Steel Construction, a
Manual for Architects,
Engineers and Fabricators
of Buildings and Other
Steel Structures. American
Institute of Steel
Construction. American
Institute of Steel
Construction, 1961, New
York.

5288   Steel Tubing
Construction. Durst,
Richard W. Theatre Crafts,
N/D 1979, Vol. 13, No. 6,
P. 32.

5289   Stenciling With
Photographs. Janesick,
Gerald. Theatre Crafts S
1976.

5290   Stephenson's Patent
Theatre Machinery.
Stephenson, R.M. 1845
Located at the New York
Public Library Theatre
Collection.

5291   Stockholm Symposium
(Continued). Theatre
Notebook, 1961, Vol. III,
No. 2 & No. 3, P. 77 & 157.

5292   Stockholm Symposium on
the Birth and Artistic
Functions of the
Perspective Stage in the
Renaissance and Baroque
Periods and its Relation to
Dramatic Repertory. Theatre
Research, 1961, Vol. III,
O. 1, P. 6.

5293   Stock Platforms.
Trumpler, Allan. Theatre
Crafts, Vol. 13, Number 3,
My 1979, P. 33.

5294   Stock Scenery in 1798.
Stoddard, Richard. Theatre
Survey, 1972, Vol. 13, P.
102-3.

5295   Story of Stockwell's
Panorama. Arrington, Joseph
Earl. Minnesota Historical
Society, 1953, St. Paul
(Also Minnesota History,
Autumn, 1959, Vol. 33, No.
7).

5296   Stratford Revisted.
Bentham, Frederick. Tabs Mr
1972.

5297   Stravinsky and the
Theatre: a Catalogue of
Decor and Costume Designs
for Stage Productions of
His Works. New York Public
Library, 1963.

5298   Stream-Line in the
Theatre. Caparn, Anne. Arts
and Decoration, Mr 1936,
Vol. 44, P. 16-18.

5299   Streetcar Named Desire
(A). Original Watercollor,
1947. located at the
Harvard Theatre Collection.

5300   Stressed-Skin Scenery
for the Theatre. Jackson,
Robert C. Theatre Crafts,
Ja/f 1978, Vol. 12, No. 1,
P. 24.

5301   Stress Skin Panel
Design. Heller, Robert C.
M.F.A. Thesis, Yale
University, 1978.

5302   Stuart Masques and the
Renaissance Stage. Nicoll,
Allardyce. B. Blom 1963 New
York. G. G. Harrap & Co.,
1937, London/Harcourt
Brace, 1938, New. LOCN:
Pr658.M3 N5 1963

5303   Stuart Masque at the
Asolo Theatre (A). Moffett,
Sandy. Theatre Crafts, N/D
1969, Vol. 3, No. 6, P.
26-30.

5304   Stuart Walker's
Portmanteau Theatre, The
Most Compact Playhouse in
the World. Current Opinion,
S 1915, P. 175.

5305   Stuart Wurtzel: Working
on Stage and in Films.
Napoleon, Davi. Theatre
Crafts, Ja/F 1980, Vol. 14,
No. 1, P. 34-39.

5306   Student Design
Awards/actf XI. Theatre
Crafts, My/Je 1979, Vol.
13, No. 3, P. 38.

5307   Studies in Stagecraft.
Hamilton, Clayton. Henry
Holt and Co., 1914, New
York.

5308   Studio and Stage.
Harker, Joseph. Nisbet &
Co, 1924, London. located
at the Harvard Theatre
Collection.

5309   Study of Ancient Greek,
Roman and Medieval Theatre
Conventions and Devices
(A). Butler, James H.
Ph.D. Thesis, Southern
California, 1948.

5310   Study of Cleon
Throckmorton's Career As a
Designer. Paparone, Joseph
C. Ph.D. Thesis, Indiana
University, 1976.

5311   Study of Plastics
Available for Theatrical
Design (A). Burr, Charles.
University Microfilm Order
Number M-3735 Xi/¦/1. No
Date.

5312   Study of Some of the
Renaissance and Baroque
Factors in the Theatre
Style of Inigo Jones.
Mccalmon, George. Ph.D.
Thesis, Case-Western
Reserve University, 1946.

5313   Study of the Educational
Scene Shop and Its
Equipment (A). Dorck, Ralph

Wellington. M.A. Thesis,
1956, State University of
Iowa.

5314   Study of the History and
Methods of Production for
Theatre:In-The-Round (A).
Hutchinson, William C.
M.A. Thesis, West Texas
State College, 1958.

5315   Study of the I.A.T.S.E.
(A). Cauble, J.R. M.A.
Thesis, U.C.L.A., 1964.
LOCN: Ld 791.8 T3031

5316   Study of the Nineteenth
Century Innovations in
Scenic Design and Stage
Practice of Steel MacKaye
As These Contributed to the
American Theatre (A).
Guthrie, David G. Ph.D.
Thesis, New York
University, 1973.

5317   Stunts of the Stage.
Mount, Harry A. Scientific
American, F 1921, Vol. 124,
P. 105, 118.

5318   Stylizing Slide Images
Photography through
Patterned Glass to Modify
Source Material. Dehm, G.
Theatre Design & Technology
Sum 1975.

5319   Deleted.

5320   Styrofoam - Fabrication,
Adhesives and Coatings. The
Dow Chemical Company, 1955,
Midland, Michigan.

5321   Styrofoam and Canvas.
Rubenstein, Marc L.
Theatre Crafts, S 1979,
Vol. 13, No. 4, P. 4.

5322   Styrofoam Expanded
Polystyrene (No.
171-262-10m-665). Dow
Chemical Co. Dow Chemical
Co., Midland, Michigan. No
Date.

5323   Styrofoam for the Stage.
Sweet, Harvey. M.S. Thesis,

University of Wisconson,
1967. LOCN: Awo S9744 H341

5324   Styrofoam. Dow Diamond
(Dow Chemical Co., Midland,
Michigan), 1964, Vol.
XXVII, No. 4, P. 25-27.

5325   Submarine Setting on the
Stage, A. Popular
Mechanics, D 1911, Vol. 16.

5326   Success on a
Shoe-String. Jackson,
Peter. Plays and Players,
Ja 1961, Vol. 8, P. 9.

5327   Suit and Countersuit.
Theatre Crafts, Mr/Ap 1975,
Vol. 10, No. 2, P. 2.

5328   Summer, 1976:
Scenography Plays a Large
Role in European Opera.
Loney, Glenn. Theatre
Design & Technology, Sp
1976, Vol. XII, No. 1, P.
26.

5329   Summer Repertory
Solutions: Scene Design and
Building for the Pacific
Conservatory of the
Performing Arts. Davis,
Peter. Theatre Crafts, Vol.
13, No. 3 My 1979, P. 36.

5330   Summer Theatre Supply
List. Howard, John T. Jr.
Theatre Craft, My/Je 1980,
Vol. 14, No. 3, P. 88.

5331   Sumptuous Revival:
Bakst's Designs for
Diaghilel's Slepping
Princess (A). Howard,
Deborah. Apollo, Ap 1970,
Vol. 91, P. 301.

5332   Super Graphing Sets and
Costumes for the Life of
Orestes. Wong, C.G.
Theatre Crafts S 1976.

5333   Supply, Demand and the
Performing Arts.A Critical
Look at The Business of
Supplying Show Business.
Thompson, Richard and

Jones, Ted and Tawil, Joseph and Davis, James. Theatre Design & Technology, Winter 1975, No. 43, P. 27.

5334   Support Grows for Theatre Strikers. The News Line, Mr 20, 1979.

5335   Survey of Solar Energy Products and Service-- May, 1975. United States Government Printing Office, 1975, Washington, D. C. LOCN: Tj 810 V6 1975

5336   Survey of Theatre Engineering. Kupferschmid, M. Theatre Design & Technology S 1975.

5337   Survey of Theatrical Machines and Stage Devices Used in The Production of Melodrama in the Nineteenth Century. Ricks, Clyde. M.A. Thesis, Brigham Young University, 1956.

5338   Survey of the Teaching Load of Educational Workers Engaged In Actual Theatre Production. West, E.J. Educational Theatre Journal, D 1950, Vol. 11, No. 4, P. 343.

5339   Suspension Structures in Scenic Design. Stone, James Merrill. Theatre Design & Technology, Wi 1979, Vol. XV, No. 4, P. 10-16.

5340   Swift's Fire-Tard 7228 Adhesive: Product Data. Product Data, S 16, 1965, (Swift & Co., Chicago).

5341   Symposium on Structural Sandwich Constructions. American Society for Testing Materials. Astm, Second Pacific Area National Meeting, S 20, 1956. American Society for Testing Materials, 1956,.

5342   Synthesized Systems for

the Performing Arts. Polansky, Jonell and Slutske, Robert A. Theatre Design & Technology, F 1974, No. 36, P. 11.

5343   Tale of the Vienna Workshops. Loney, Glenn. Theatre Crafts, O, 1979, Vol. 13, No. 5, P. 39.

5344   Talking About Design. Williams, Peter. Dance and Dancers, Ap 1963, P. 26-72.

5345   Teaching First Aid and Fire Safety for the Theatre. Kirk, W.A. Theatre Crafts S 1976.

5346   Teaching of Technical Production on the Undergraduate Level (The). Daubenspeck, Robert. M.F.A. Thesis, 1956, Yale University.

5347   Teaching Stage Design in the United States, Canada an d Czechoslovakia, 1967: a Discussion at Pq '75. Theatre Design & Technology, Fall 1976, Vol. XII, No. 3, P. 21.

5348   Technical Advancements for the American Theatre. Weaver, Clark. Players Magazine, Mr 1959, Vol. 35, No. 5, P. 134.

5349   Technical Advancements in American Theatre. Weaver, Clark. Players Magazine, My, 1959, Vol. 35, No. 6, P. 134.

5350   Technical Aspects of Rural Area Theatres. Pullinger, Albert J. H. M.F.A. Thesis, 1949, Yale University.

5351   Technical Assistance Group (The). Lucier, Mary. Theatre Craft, Mr/Ap 1980, Vol. 14, No. 2, P. 43, 68-70.

5352   Technical Assistance Is
Plain "How". Vogel,
Frederic B. Theatre
Crafts, S 1979, Vol. 13,
No. 4, P. 10.

5353   Technical Information on
Upson Boards (Bulletin No.
92). Upson Company (The)
and Gremler, H. (Prepared
By). Upson Company (The), D
5, 1962, Lockport.

5354   Technical Internship
Program: LATA Strikes CETA
Gold. Theatre Crafts, S
1980, Vol. 14, No. 4, P.
49.

5355   Technical Organization
of the Karlsruhe State
Theatre. Hunke, Walter.
Theatre Design & Technology
Fall 1977.

5356   Technical Possibilities
(The). Flanagan, Arena
Hallie. Federal One, D
1977, Vol. 2,no. 3,
Published Occasionally by
the Research Center for the
Federal Theatre Project,.

5357   Technical Problems 1.
Staging of Don Giovanni.
Thomas, Rene. World
Theatre, 1950, Vol. I, No.
2, P. 6.

5358   Technical Production in
the Classical Greek
Theatre. Mccaw, B. Robert.
M.F.A. Thesis, 1966, Yale
University.

5359   Technical Theatre
Requirements for Puppetry.
Theatre Crafts, Mr 1975.

5360   Technical Training at
Carnegie Mellon Univ..
Theatre Crafts O 1973.

5361   Technicians Are Seldom
Between Engagements. Dewey,
Walter S. Players, F/M,
1969, Vol. 44, No. 3, P.
86.

5362   Technicians Roundtable
(The). Gillette, A.S.
Dramatics, My 1945, Vol
Xvi, No 8, P. 17.

5363   Technician As Engineer
(The). Rabbitt, Michael.
Theatre Design &
Technology, O 1970, No. 22,
P. 16.

5364   Techniques of Set
Photography. Watson, Lee.
Theatre Design &
Technology, F or My, 1974.

5365   Techniques of Television
Production. Bretz, Rudy.
McGraw Hill Book Co., Inc.,
1953, New York.

5366   Technique of Casting for
Sculpture (The). Mills,
John W. Reinhold
Publishing Co., 1967, New
York.

5367   Technique of Special
Effects Cinematography
(The). Fielding, Raymond E.
Hastings House, 1965, New
York. ISBN: 8038-7031-0

5368   Technique of Stage
Design in Its Relation to
Theatre Architecture (The).
Gregor, Joseph. Theatre
Arts Monthly, Mr 1933, Vol.
XVII, No. 3, P. 215.

5369   Technique of Theatrical
Production As Illustrated
by Walter Hampden's the
Light of Asia.
Architectural Record, Ag,
1929, Vol. 66, P. 109.

5370   Technology As Art: the
American Contemporaty
Theatre. Kirby, E. T.
Theatre Design & Technology
Sum 1978 Vol.Xiv.

5371   Telemeters, Aids to
Efficient Stage Technology.
Hoffmann, R. and Becker,
H. Theatre Design &
Technology F 1967.

5372   Template Spun Polystyrene Foam for Stage Furniture. Chapman, Richard H. Theatre Crafts N 1977.

5373   Temple, a Forest, and a Palace in One Room Created by Reflection in the Palace of Mirages, (A). Illustrated London News, Ap 24, 1909, Vol. 134, P. 596-597.

5374   Tenderhooks of Temptation (The). Brown, John Mason. Theatre Arts Monthly, 1925, Vol. 9, P. 429-443.

5375   Ten Commandments of Safety (The). Gun Digest 1964 P.336.

5376   Ten Thousand Scenes in One Scene. Craig, Edward Gordon. Interscena, Acta Scaenographica Internationalia, Sp 1967, Vol. 2, P. 42-45.

5377   Ten Years of American Scene Design-A Project Report. Shesley, Gene. Theatre Design & Technology, D 1974, No. 39, P. 17.

5378   Terrible to the Eye Alone. Popular Science Monthly, Mr 1917, Vol. 90, P. 379.

5379   Tests of Theatre Proscenium Curtains. Mitchell, Nolan Dickson. United States Government Printing Office, 1933.

5380   Test of Poly-Vinyl Flooring; for Facilities Utilized by Dance and Theatre (A). Sporre, Dennis J. Theatre Design & Technology, Spring 1979, Vol. XV, No. 1, P. 12.

5381   Textile Fabrics and Their Selection. Wingate, Isabel. Prentice-Hall, 1935, New York.

5382   Thank You, Fred. Tabs Ap 1974.

5383   That's Live Entertainment: on Stage in the Parks. Theatre Crafts, S 1977, Vol. 11, No. 4, P. 47.

5384   Theaters-Stage-Setting and Scenery. Aujourd'hui, Art Et Architecture, Whole Issue, O 1963, Vol. 8, No. 4.

5385   Theater Drawings from the Donald Oenslager Collection. Mayor, A. Minneapolis Institute of Arts Bulletin (Whole Issue) Mr 1963, Vol. 52 No. 1.

5386   Theater of Marvels (The). Winter, Marian Hannah. Oliver Perrin, 1962, Paris, Also Benjamin Blom, 1964, New York.

5387   Theater of the Bauhaus, (The). Wesleyan University Press, 1961, Middletown, Connecticut.

5388   Theater Secrets. Scientific American Supplement, Ja 1886, Vol. 21, P. 8336, 8352.

5389   Theatre's Most Formidable Job: Stage-Managing a Broadway Musical. Linden, Robert. Theatre Crafts, N/D 1968, P. 21-29.

5391   Theatres: the Law and the Lord Chamberlain. Builder, (The), Ja 27, 1877, P. 74.

5392   Theatres (Part) Xxii. Woodrow, Ernest A.E. Building News, Je 23, 1893, Vol. 64, P. 830.

5393   Theatres and Motion Picture Houses. Meloy, Arthur S. Architects Supply & Publishing Co., 1916, New York City.

5394   Theatres and the
Metropolitan Board of
Works. Builder, (The), My
10, 1879, Vol Xxvii, P.
524, 552, 698, 785, 1212.

5395   Theatres Must Be
Theatrical. Corry, Percy.
Tabs Fall 1975.

5396   Theatres Must Be
Theatrical. Corry, Percy.
Theatre Design & Technology
Wi 1976.

5397   Theatres. Building News,
O 26, 1894, Vol. 67, P.
566-569.

5398   Theatre (The). Jones,
Robert Edmond. Theatre Arts
Monthly, S, 1927, Vol. XI,
No. 9, P. 661.

5399   Theatre Advancing, The.
Craig, Edward Gordon.
Little Brown, Inc., 1919,
New York.

5400   Theatre and Industrial
Education. Andrus, T.O.
Players Magazine, My, 1952,
Vol. 28, No. 8, P. 186.

5401   Theatre and Stage: an
Encyclopedia Guide to the
Performance of All Amateur,
Dramatic, Operatic, and
Theatrical Work. Downs,
Harold (Editor). Sir Isaac
Pitman & Sons, 1951,
London.

5402   Theatre and Stage, Vols,
I & II. Downs, Harold
(Editor). Greenwood Press,
Inc., Westport, Ct., 1978.
LOCN: Pn2035.D6 1978 ISBN:
0-313-20222-2

5403   Theatre and the Graphic
Arts, (The). Hewitt,
Barnard. Ph.D. Thesis,
Cornell University, 1935.

5404   Theatre Archaeology:
Drury Lane. Marshall, E.
R. ABTT News, N 1979, P.
20.

5406   Theatre Architecture and
Stage Machines. Diderot,
Denis and Alembert, Jean
Lerond D'. B. Blom 1969 New
York. LOCN: Na6820. E5 1969
Fol.

5407   Theatre Arts Prints.
John Day, 1929, New York.

5408   Theatre Art. Simonson,
Lee. Cooper Square
Publishers, 1969, New York.
LOCN: Pn 2091 S8s54 1934a

5409   Theatre Art. D'Amico,
Victor Edmond. Manual Arts
Press, 1931, Peoria, Il.

5410   Theatre at the Kacina
Chateau (The). Vadlejchova,
Ivana. Interscaena-Acta
Scaenographica Sum 1973,
Vol. 3, P. 20-26.

5411   Theatre Automatique.
Architectural Forum Vol.113
No.4 O 1960 P.90, 182.

5412   Theatre Backstage from A
to Z. Loundsbury, Warren
C. University of
Washington Press, 1967,
Seattle.

5413   Theatre Collection in
the Folger Shakespeare
Library (The). Mason,
Dorothy E. OSU Theatre
Collection Bulletin, Sp
1955, Vol. 1, No. 1, P. 3.

5414   Theatre Construction and
Maintenance. Buckle, James
G. The Stage" Office,
1888.

5415   Theatre Consultant
(The). Risser, Arthur C.
Players, D/J, 1969, Vol.
44, No. 2, P. 60.

5416   Theatre Consulting.
Long, Robert. M.F.A.
Thesis, 1976, Yale
University.

5417   Theatre Craft: the A to
Z of Show Business.

Melvill, Herald. Rocklife, 1954, London.

5418   Theatre Delays Shortened. Sayler, Oliver M. Scientific American, Mr 1923, Vol. 138, P. 249, 250.

5419   Theatre Designs by Normal Bel-Geddes. Creative Art, F, 1933, Vol. 12, P. 128.

5420   Theatre Design in Germany. Muller, Ingvelde. World Theatre, Wi, 1953, Vol. III, No. 3, P. 38.

5421   Theatre Design. Izenour, George C. McGraw-Hill Book Company 1977 New York. LOCN: Na6821 I94 Folio ISBN: 0070320861

5422   Theatre Education in California: the Golden Paradox. Earle, James R. Jr. Theatre Crafts, S 1980, Vol. 14, No. 4, P. 127.

5423   Theatre Employment Contracts. Nuckolls, James L. Theatre Design & Technology D 1965.

5424   Theatre Fire Prevention Laws in Model Building Codes. Warfel, William B. M.A. Thesis, Yale University, 1957.

5425   Theatre Hygiene; a Scheme for the Study of a Somewhat Neglected Department of Public Health. Roth, W. E. Bailliere, 1888, London.

5426   Theatre Inventory of the First Empire (A). Carlson, Marvin. Theatre Survey, 1970, Vol. 11, P. 36-49. My, 1970.

5427   Theatre in Action. Whitworth, Geoffrey Arundel. Studio Publications, 1938.

5428   Theatre in Parma (The). Carrick, Edward. Theatre Arts Monthly, 1931, Vol. XV, P. 201.

5429   Theatre in Poland (The). Szydlowski, Roman. Interpress, 1972, Warsaw.

5430   Theatre in the Age of Grarrick. Price, Cecil. Rowman & Littlefield, 1973, Totowa, New Jersey.

5431   Theatre in the Round: Scenery and Sound. Sightline (ABTT Journal), 1978, Vol. 12, No. 1, P. 5-12.

5432   Theatre Machinery, Nineteenth Century Relics at the Theatre Royal. Leacroft, Richard. Architectural Review (The), Ag 1954, Vol. 116, P. 113-114.

5433   Deleted.

5434   Theatre Machines and Other Projects by Normal Bel Geddes. Moore, P. L. Arts, F, 1931, Vol. 17, P. 324.

5435   Theatre Machines in Italy, 1400-1800. Garrick, Edward. Architectural Review, Jl 1931, Vol. 80, P. 9-14, Plates Iv-Vi; Ag 1931, P. 34-36, Plates II & III.

5436   Theatre Management Comes of Age. MacKay, Patricia. Theatre Crafts, Mr/Ap 1979, Vol. 13, No. 2, P. 19.

5437   Theatre Managers Worried About Technical Training. ABTT News, O 1979, P. 7. NATTKE News Letter, O 1979.

5438   Theatre of a Thousand Souls, The. Thompson, Paul. Burr Mcintosh Monthly, (The) , D 1908, Vol. 18, No. 69, P. 61-65.

5439   Theatre of Beauty (The).
Yeats, William Butler.
Harper's Weekly, N 1911,
Vol. 55, P. 11.

5440   Theatre of Dionysius in
Athens (The).
Pickard-Cambridge, A. W.
Clarendon Press, 1946,
Oxford.

5441   Theatre of Donald
Oenslager, (The).
Oenslager, Donald. Wesleyan
University Press, 1978,
Middletown, Connecticut.
LOCN: Pn 2096 04 A37 1978

5442   Theatre of Machines.
Keller, A. G. Macmillan,
1965, New York.

5443   Theatre of Meyerhold:
Revolution on the Modern
Stage (The). Braun, Edward.
Fletcher & Son, Ltd., 1979,
Norwich, England. Drama
Book Specialists, 1979, New
York. ISBN: 0-89676-003-0

5444   Theatre of Performing
Lights (The). Brill, Louis
M. Lighting Dimensions, S,
1979, P. 16.

5445   Theatre of Robert Edmond
Jones, (The). Pendleton,
Ralph. Wesleyan University
Press, 1958, Middletown,
Connecticut.

5446   Theatre of the Absurd
and the Art of Scene
Design. Krempel, Daniel.
Players, D, 1963, Vol. XL,
No. 3, P. 72.

5447   Theatre of the Future
(The). Bel Geddes, Norman.
Theatre Arts, Ap, 1919,
Vol. III, No. 2, P. 223.

5448   Theatre of the Stuart
Court (The). Jones, Inigo.
Univ. of California Press,
1973, Berkeley. LOCN: Nc
242 J65 073 1973

5449   Theatre of Today, (The).

Moderwell, Hiram Kelly.
John Lane, 1914, New York.
1926 Edition, John Lane,
London.

5450   Theatre of Tomorrow.
Macgowan, Kenneth.
Liverright, 1921. Harcourt,
Brace & Co., 1922, New
York.

5451   Theatre on the Stage, a.
Popular Mechanics, Mr 1910,
Vol. 13, P. 379.

5452   Theatre People: Tharon
Musser. Widem, Allen M.
Hartford Times, Jy 18,
1965, P.21.

5453   Theatre Photography.
Vickers, John. Tabs, D
1960, Vol. 18, No. 3, P.
23.

5454   Theatre Pictorial: a
History of World Theater As
Recorded In Drawings,
Paintings, Engravings, and
Photographs. Alman, George.
University of California
Press, 1953, Los Angeles.

5455   Theatre Planning. Ham,
Roderick (Editor).
University of Toronto
Press, 1972, Toronto. LOCN:
Na6821. T45 1972b ISBN:
0802019382/{802002781
(Microfliche)

5456   Theatre Plans in
Harsdoerffer's Frauenzimmer
- Gespraechspiel. Jordan,
Gilbert J. Journal of
English and Germanic
Philology, 1943, Vol. 42,
P. 475.

5457   Theatre Poster
Catalogue. Triton
International Theatre
Posters, 323 West 45
Street, New York 10036,
1979.

5458   Theatre Project by Inigo
Jones, (A). Keith, William
Grant. Burlington Magazine,
Ag 1917, Vol. 31, P. 61-70.

5459   Theatre Scenecraft: for the Backstage Technician and Artist. Adix, Vern. Children's Theatre Press, 1956, Anchorage, Ky.

5460   Theatre Student: Scenery (The). Stell, W. Joseph. Richards Rosen Press, 1970, New York. LOCN: Pn 2091 S8 S73 Folio ISBN: 0-823901521

5461   Theatre Technicians Associate. Corry, Percy. Tabs, Ap 1961, Vol. 19, No. 1 P. 14.

5462   Theatre Technology. Progressive Architecture, D 1970, P.65-71.

5463   Theatre Transformed, Being a Description of the Permanent Setting by Norman Bel Geddes for Max Reinhardt's Spectacle, the Miracle (A). Bragdon, Claude. Architectural Record, (The), 1924, Vol. 55, P. 388-397.

5464   Theatre Union: a History (The). Winsten, Lynne Robin. Ph.D. Thesis, University of California, Los Angeles, 1978.

5465   Theatre Union: a History 1933-1937 (The). Weisstuch, Mark. Ph.D. Thesis, CLUNY, 1978.

5466   Theatre Unions. Nuckolls, James L. Theatre Design & Technology My 1966.

5467   Theatre Without a Stage (A). Hopkins, Albert A. Scientific American, Ap 1924, Vol. 130, P. 228, 229.

5468   Theatre Workshops for the Old Vic, the Cut, London. Architects Journal, The, F 1959, Vol. 129, P. 309-316.

5469   Theatre Work of Paul Nash. Bottomly, Gordon. Theatre Arts Monthly, Ja, 1924, Vol. VIII, No. 1, P. 38.

5470   Theatrical Activity of Gianlorenzo Bernini. Fahrner, Robert and Kleb, William. Educational Theatre Journal, Mr 1973, Vol. 25, P. 5.

5471   Theatrical and Circus Life; Or, Secrets of the Stage, Greenroom and Sawdust Arena. Jennings, John J. Laird & Lee, 1893.

5472   Theatrical Architecture and Stage Mechanics. Athenaeum, 1871, Vol. 58, P. 440-441, 472-473.

5473   Theatrical Art of the Italian Renaissance: Interchangeable Conventions in Painting and Theatre in the Late Fifteenth and Early Sixteenth Centuries, (The). Rutledge, Barbara Louise Saenger. Ph.D. Thesis, University of Michigan, 1973.

5474   Theatrical Contributions of Norman Bel Geddes. Dresen, James William. Ph.D. Thesis, Northwestern University, 1968.

5475   Theatrical Counselor. Berezniak, Leon A. Chicago 1923.

5476   Theatrical Designs from the Baroque through Neoclassicism: Unpublished Material from American Private Collections. Freedley, George. Bittner, 1940, New York.

5478   Theatrical Designs of George Grosz (The). Deshong, Andrew. Ph.D. Thesis, 1971, Yale University.

5479   Theatrical Design in Sweden. Theatre Arts Magazine, 1922, Vol. 6, P. 320-325.

5480   Theatrical Engineering Past and Present. Lautenschlaeger, Carl. Scientific American Supplement, Jy 15, 22, 1905, Vol. 60, P. 24686-87, 24701.

5481   Theatrical Equipment of the Stage. Hagen, Claude L. Architecture and Building, N 1913, P.457-461. See Also Following Issues.

5482   Theatrical Firearms. Scientific American Supplement, My 1887, Vol. 23, P. 9477.

5483   Theatrical Illusions. Scientific American, Ap 1891, Vol. 64, P. 259.

5484   Theatrical Law; the Legal Rights of Anger: Artist, Author and Public. Brackett, J. Albert. Clark Publishing, 1907, Boston.

5486   Theatrical Lighting Practice. Rubin, Joel E. and Watson, Leland H. Theatre Arts Books, 1954, New York. LOCN: Pn2091.E4 R8

5487   Theatrical Machinery in the Paris Opera House. Engineer, F 1884, Vol. 57, P. 162-164.

5488   Theatrical Mechanism at the Lyceum Theatre. Engineer, Ap 1886, Vol. 61, P. 260.

5489   Theatrical Mechanism. Scientific American Supplement Xxi My 22 1886 P. 8648.

5490   Theatrical Meterology. Graphic, Ja 1875, Vol. 11, P. 78.

5491   Theatrical Night Scene With the Appearance of Fireflies. Popular Mechanics, O 1913, Vol. 20, P. 604.

5492   Theatrical Records of the London Guilds, 1655-1708. Morrissey, L. J. Theatre Notebook, 1975, Vol. XXIX, No. 3, P. 99.

5493   Theatrical Scenery: a Manual of Construction Designs Based On Showboat Theatre Practice. Johnson, L.E. M.A. Thesis, University of Washington, 1950. LOCN: 792 Th 6332

5494   Theatrical Scene Painting: a Thorough and Complete Work on How to Sketch Paint and Install Theatrical Scenery. Appleton Publishers, 1916, Omaha.

5495   Theatrical Set Design: the Basic Techniques. Welker, David. Allyn and Bacon, Inc., 1969, Boston. LOCN: Pn 2091 S8 W38

5496   Theatrical Set Design. Architecture, D, 1927, Vol. 5, P. 85.

5497   Theatrical Stage Arrangements and Machinery. Builder (The), Ap, 20, 1861, P. 261.

5498   Theatrical Trends and Production Techniques of the Art and Commercial Theatres of Chicago 1900-1920. Czechowski, Jan. Ph.D. Thesis, University of Michigan, 1978.

5499   Theatrical Tricks. Walker, Gladys R. Players Magazine, Mr/Ap 1933, Vol. IX, No. 4, P. 5.

5500   Theatrical Use of Air Flotation Systems. Crawford, J.C. Theatre

Design & Technology My
1970.

5501   Theatron. Stratton,
Clarence. Henry Holt, 1928,
New York.

5502   Theme Parks: USA.
MacKay, Patricia. Theatre
Crafts S 1977.

5503   Theories of Style in
Stage Production. Brockett,
Lenyth Spenker.
Interscaena-Acta
Scaenographica, Sp 1973,
Vol. 3, P. 1-7.

5504   Theory and History of
Environmental Scenography
(The). Aronson, Arnold P.
Ph.D. Thesis, New York
University, 1977.

5505   Theory of the Modern
Stage, (The). Bentley, Eric
(Ed.). Pengiun Books, 1968,
Middlesex.

5506   There Are No Emergency
Exits for Actors. Cocroft,
Thoda. Theatre Magazine, My
1927, P. 10.

5507   Thermoformed Plastics on
Your Stage. Dunton, R.G.
Theatre Design & Technology
O 1969.

5508   Thermoplastic Scenery
for Theatre. Bryson,
Nicholas. Drama Book
Specialists/Publishers 1972
New York. LOCN: Pn2091.S8
B69 ISBN: 0910482394

5509   Thesaurus of Technical
Stage Terms. Thorton,
Helen. Ph.D. Thesis,
University of Denver, 1951.

5510   Thirty-Second
Internationalen
Handwerksmesse, Munich,
1980. Cue Technical Theatre
Review, My/Ju 1980, P. 18.

5511   This Month's Products.
Progressive Architecture,
1948, Continuing Feature.

5512   Those Stage Settings.
Cram, Mildred. Theatre
Magazine, Ap 1918, P. 228.

5513   Three Award-Winning
Exhibitions. Fielding,
Eric. Theatre Design &
Technology, Sp 1980, Vol.
XVI, No. 1, P. 22-24.

5514   Three Model Theatres:
Elizabethan, Eighteenth
Century, Modern. Smith,
Roy. T. Nelson, 1960,
Edinburgh. LOCN: Pn2091.
M6s4

5515   Three Technical
Analyses. Wade, Robert J.
Players Magazine, Ja 1940,
Vol. 16, No. 4, P. 6.

5516   Throw Out the Mummy
Cases. Davis, W. Theatre
Crafts My 1968.

5517   Tidal Wave Making on the
Stage. Scientific American,
Ja 1909, Vol. 100, P. 1,8.

5518   Time and Motion Study
and Formulas for Wage
Incentives. Lowry, Stewart
M. McGraw-Hill Book Co.,
1940, New York.

5519   Tobacco Road. Bendevski,
Peter. Theatre Craft, My/Je
1980, Vol. 14, No. 3, P.
44.

5520   Togetherness. Dewey,
Walter S. Players, F/M,
1971, Vol. 16, No. 3, P.
90.

5521   Tolylene Diisocyanate.
Manufacturing Chemists
Association, 1959,
Washington D.C..

5522   Tom Walsh. Theatre
Crafts, S 1980, Vol. 14,
No. 4, P. 45.

5523   Tools and How to Use
Them. Jackson, Albert and
Day, David. Knopf, 1978,
New York. LOCN: 78-54896
ISBN: 0-394-73542-0

5524   Tools and Their Uses.
U.S. Navy, (The Bureau of
Naval Personnel). Dover
Publications, 1973, New
York.

5525   Tools for the Scene
Shop. Minter, Gordon.
Players Magazine, N/D 1945,
Vol. 22, No. 2, P. 8.

5526   Touring Dance Company
(The). Skelton, Tom. Dance
Magazine, Ag 1957, P.
80-81.

5527   Touring Equipment. Bock,
Frank. Players Magazine, F
1957, Vol 33 NO 5, P. 104.

5528   Towards a New Theatre;
Forty Designs for Stage
With Critical Notes by the
Inventor, Edward Gordon
Craig. Craig, Edward
Gordon. Dent & Sons, 1913,
Ontario.

5529   Toward an Alternative
Theatre Technology.
Wickinson, Darryl and
Mckenzie, Ian. Theatre
Australia, Ag 1976, Vol.1,
No.1, P.49.

5530   Town Hall Theatre at
Put-In-Bay, Ohio (The).
Barrow, Jack W. OSU
Theatre Collection
Bulletin, 1961, Vol. 8, P.
24-34.

5531   Toxic and Hazardous
Materials, Amptp Research
Center Report. Meyer,
Herbert and Holm, W. R.
Motion Picture and
Television Research Center,
(The), 1969, Hollywood.

5532   To House a New Order of
Entertainment:
Reconstructing Steele
MacKaye's Spectatorium.
Hannon, D. Theatre Crafts,
O 1976.

5533   To the Dawn of a Better
Decor at the Opera.

Lansdale, Nelson. Art News,
Mr 15, 1942, Vol. 41, P.
9-11, 33-34.

5534   Traditional Country
Craftsmen. Jenkins, J.
Geraint. Routledge and
Paul, 1965, London.

5535   Training of Process
Operators. Manufacturing
Chemists Association, 1963,
Washington D.C..

5536   Training Technicians
Theatre Engineers and
Scenographers (On).
Mielziner, Jo. Theatre
Design & Technology S 1976.

5537   Traite De Scenographie.
Sonrel, Pierre. O.
Lieutier, 1943, Paris.

5538   Transparency by Thomas
Greenwood the Elder (A).
Rosenfeld, Sybil. Theatre
Notebook, Fa 1964, Vol.
XIX, No. 1, P. 21.

5539   Transporation and Travel
Expenses. Hanlon, R.
Brendan. Theatre Crafts,
Ja/f 1979, Vol. 13, No. 1,
P. 75.

5540   Traps, Flaps and
Transformations. Walker,
Donald. ABTT News, O 1979,
P. 19.

5541   Traumas With Sets and
Costumes at New Haven's
Long Wharf Theatre. Theatre
Crafts O 1973.

5542   Treasure Island's
Realistic Ship. Scientific
American, F 1916, Vol. 114,
P. 201, 206.

5543   Treatise on the
Decorative Part of Civil
Architecture (A). Chambers,
William. Blom, 1968, New
York.

5544   Trial Stage for Lighting
Investigation (A). Winds,

Adolf. Buhne Und Welt Ap 1910.

5545   Trick-Work in the English Nineteenth Century Theatre. Southern, Richard. Life & Letters To-Day, My 1939, Vol. 21, P. 94-101.

5546   Tricks of the Trade. Sobel, Bernard. Theatre Arts, O, 1957, Vol. XLI, No. 10, P. 75.

5547   Trick Ventriloquism. Merton, H.R. Technical World, Ap 1913, Vol. 19, P. 226.

5548   Trojan Horse at the Paris Opera House (The). Scientific American, D 1899, Vol. 81, P. 392.

5549   Trunk Mystery, The. Popular Mechanics, O 1914, Vol. 22, P. 621-622.

5550   Tudor Interlude; Stage, Costume and Acting (The). Craik, Thomas W. Leicester, 1958.

5551   Turning Dreams into Reality. Prerauer, Maria. Elizabethan Trust News, Ju 1972, No. 3, P. 11.

5552   Turn of the Decade (The). Wills, Robert. Theatre Crafts, Ja/F 1980, Vol. L, No. 1, P. 19.

5553   Twelth Night. Original Watercolor, 1960. located at the Harvard Theatre Collection.

5554   Twentieth-Century Design: Its History and Stylistic Origins. Thompson, James Robert. Ph.D Thesis, University of Minnesota. No Date.

5555   Twentieth-Century Innovations in Stage Design, Stage Machinery, and Theatre Architecture in

Austria. Dietrich, Margret. In: Innovations in Stage & Theatre Design (Papers of the 6th Congress, Internat'l. Federation.

5556   Twentieth Century Machinery File. Harvard Theatre Collection. No Date.

5557   Twentieth Century Magic and the Construction of Modern Magical Apparatus. Hopkins, Nevil Monroe. Chatto & Windus, 1898, London.

5558   Twentieth Century Stage Decoration. Fuerst, Walter Rene and Hume, Samuel J. Alfred A. Knopf, 1928, London; Blom, 1967, 2 Vols.. LOCN: Pn 2091 S8 F8

5559   Twenty Years of French Theatrical Design. Laver, James. Studio, Ag 1955, Vol. 150, P. 40.

5560   Twenty Years of Scenography. Bablet, Denis. World Theatre, 1968, Vol. XVII, No. 1/, P. 35.

5561   Two Level Counterweight Arbor (A). Senie, Curtis Jay. Theatre Design & Technology, Spring 1978, Vol. XIV, No. 1, P. 25.

5562   Two Optical Illusions. Scientific American, N 1884, Vol. 51, P. 311,312.

5563   Two Solution from the Vassar Shop. Ackler, Bryan H. Theatre Crafts, My/Je 1976, Vol. 10, No. 3, P. 56.

5564   Types of Adaptable Forestage. Unruh, Walter. World Theatre, Fall 1954, Vol. III, P. 35.

5565   Tyrone Guthrie: the Artist As Man of the Theatre. Hatch, Robert. Horizon, N 1963, P. 25-41.

5566   Ubu in the New World.
Dennis, Wendell. Canadian
Theatre Review, Wi 1975,
No. 5, P. 129-135.

5567   Ultra-New in Stage
Decoration, The.
Upholsterer, The, Ap 1915,
P. 71-72.

5568   Ultraviolet Luminescent
Effects and Their Uses.
Strobl, Alexander and
Zahour, Robert L.
Transactions of the
Illuminating Engineering
Society, Jy 1933, Vol.
XXVIII, P. 612-618.

5569   Ultraviolet Radiation.
U. S. Government Printing
Office Washington, D.C..
No Date. ISBN:
017-033-00208-8

5570   Unconventional Uses of a
Conventional Theatre.
McNamara, Brooks. Theatre
Crafts, N/D 1968, P. 15-20.

5571   Underwriters Eye
Theatres Closely. National
Underwriter, S 1952, Vol.
LVI, P. 13.

5572   Uniform Platform-Wagon
Unit (A). Melo, R.F.
Theatre Design & Technology
S 1975.

5573   Unintensional Lighting.
Dewey, Walter S. Players,
D/J, 1969, Vol. 44, No. 2,
P. 42.

5574   Unions: Questions and
Answers. Webb, Elmon.
Theatre Crafts, My 1979,
Vol. 13, No. 3, P. 91.

5575   Unistrut Theatre
Architecture - a Use Study.
Locklin, David Hartt.
M.F.A. Thesis, Yale
University, 1957.

5576   Unistrut Used for House
Framing. Progressive
Architecture, O 1954, P.
100.

5577   United Artists
Association Almanac. 1960,
New York.

5578   United Scenic Artists
and Associates, Local 829.
Chassman, Arthur. M.F.A.
Thesis, Yale University,
1955.

5579   United Scenic Artists
Infomration to Applicants.
United Scenic Artists
Union, No Date, New York.

5580   United Scenic Artists
1940-1941 Almanac. United
Scenic Artists of America
(Local 829). New York,
1940.

5581   United States and
British Patents for Scenic
and Lighting Devices for
the Theatre from 1861 to
1915. Johnson, Raoul
Fenton. Ph.D. Thesis,
University of
Illinois-Urbana, Champaign,
1966. LOCN: Pn 2091 S8 J6
1976

5582   United States Patents
for Scenic and Lighting
Devices for the Theatre
from 1876 to 1975.
Boatright, Joel. Ph.D.
Thesis, Florida State
University, 1976.

5583   in the New Stagecraft: a
Study of Productions
Designed and Directed by
Norman Bel Geddes. Bogusch,
George. Ph.D. Thesis,
Indiana University, 1968.

5584   Unit Sets As Entire
Theatre. Theatre Crafts S
1971.

5585   Unknown Fairyland and
the Known; Jack and the
Beanstalk's Famous Home,
(The). Illustrated London
News, D31, 1910, Vol. 137,
P. 1042-1043.

5586   Unrecognized Document in

the History of French
Renaissance Staging (
(An). England, Sylvia
Lennie. The Library,
London, 1935, Vol. XVI, No.
2 P. 232-2 35.

5587   Unsinkable Molly Brown.
Original Rendering, 1966,
New York. located at the
Harvard Theatre Collection.

5588   Upholsterer's Bible
(The). Blandford, Percy W.
Tab Books, 1978, Blue Ridge
Summit, Pa.. LOCN:
Tt 198.B53 ISBN:
0-8306-1004-9

5589   Upside Down Airbearings.
Davis, Peter. Theatre
Crafts, Mr/Ap 1976, Vol.
10, No. 2, P. 64.

5590   Upstage. Brown, John
Mason. W.W. Norton, 1930,
New York.

5591   Urban Scenery and Some
Other Matters, (The). New
York Times, S 30, 1917,
Section 3, P. 8.

5592   Urethane Foams. Small,
F.H. Modern Plastics
Encyclopedia, 1969, Vol.
46, No. 10a, P. 248.

5593   Urethane Foam Facsimiles
Lighten Sets in Camelot.
Urethane Spectrum; Upjohn
Co. (No. B-1307), Torrance,
Calif.. No Date.

5595   Use of Light, Sound and
Mechanics (The). Little,
Theodore. Players Magazine,
N/D 1933, Vol. 4, No. 2, P.
9.

5596   Use of Plastic Film
(The). Billings, Alan G.
Players, D/J, 1971, Vol.
46, No. 2, P. 65.

5597   Use of Real Flame in
Theatres-Some Anomalies Are
Widespread. Harrison,
Sally. ABTT News, N 1978,
P. 16.

5598   Use of the Design
Elements in the Stage
Designs of Robert Edmond
Jones and Lee Simonson.
Middleton, Herman David.
Ph.D. Thesis, University of
Florida, 1964. LOCN:
709.025 M628u

5599   Use of the Linnebach
Projector for Scenic
Projection (The). Renolds,
L.L. M.A. Thesis Stamford
1950. LOCN: 3781 S78tr
ISBN: 0-06-031560-1

5600   Use Those Light Stands.
Bowman, Wayne. Players
Magazine, O, 1956, Vol. 33,
No. 1, P. 17.

5601   USITT Engineering
Commission Looks at the
Winch System in the New
Metropolitan Opera House.
Theatre Design &
Technology, My 1968.

5602   USITT Fourth Annual
Conference. Rose, Philip.
Tabs S 1964.

5603   USITT Vs. the Attorney
General. Theatre Design &
Technology, D 1971, No. 27,
P. 29.

5605   Vacuum Heat Forming
Equipment. Meyer, Herbert
and Huntington, Dexter.
Motion Picture Research
Council Bulletin, No. 235,
Hollywood, 1954.

5606   Value of the Painter's
Genius in Stage Productions
(The). Carter, Leslie. Burr
Mcintosh Monthly, My 1909,
P.46-50.

5607   Van Nostrand's Practical
Formulary. Minrath, William
R. Van Nostrand, 1957.

5608   Van Rosen, 1926: a Study
of His Life and Art,
Together With An Essay on
Style. Burlyuk, David D. E.
& J. Weiss, 1926, New York.

5609   Variable Geometry at
Stratford. Nunn, Bill. Tabs
Je 1972.

5610   Varied Suggestions.
Nelms, Henning. Players
Magazine, Ap 1941, Vol. 17,
No. 7, P. 20.

5611   Vasari's Description of
Stage Machinery. Larson,
Orville K. Educational
Theatre Journal, 1957, Vol.
9, P. 287.

5612   Vaulted Set. Mckinney,
George W. Players
Magazine, Mr 1957, Vol 33,
No 6p, P. 137.

5613   Versatile Cobweb Machine
for Special Effects.
Huggins, Richard C.
Theatre Crafts, Ja/f 1979,
Vol. 13, No. 1, P. 84.

5614   Versatile Cut Drop
Stages a Come Back (The).
Bailey, B.L. Theatre
Crafts N 1972.

5615   Victorian Theatre: a
Pictorial Survey (The).
Southern, Richard. Theatre
Arts Books, 1970, New York.

5616   Victoria and Albert
Museum. S. Phillips & Co.,
Ltd., 1922.

5617   Vienna: More Than a
Tourist Town. Salzer, Beeb.
Lighting Dimensions, O
1979, Vol. 3, No. 10, P.
41-42.

5618   Village Technology
Handbook. Communications
Resources Division.
Department of State, 1963,
Washington, D. C..

5619   Village Technology
Handbook. Communications
Resources Division.
Department of State, 1965,
Vol. 2, Washington, D. C..

5620   Vision of Appia. Apollo,
Ja 1971, Vol. 93, P. 2.

5621   Visual Interpretation of
Music. Fraser, Grace Lovat.
Studio, N 1941, Vol. 122,
P. 137.

5622   Visual Perception of
Depth on the Stage. Miller,
Harry B. M.A. Thesis,
1948, Smith College.

5623   Vivat Vivat Carl Toms.
Theatre Crafts, Ja/F 1972,
Vol. 6, No. 1, P. 12.

5624   Volcanic Erruptions on
the Stage. Popular
Mechanics, Mr 1912, Vol.
17, P. 415.

5625   Wadsworth Anthenaeum:
the Diaghilev Era
1909-1929. Leeper, Janet.
Apollo, D 1968, Vol, 88, P.
482.

5626   Wagner's Das Rheingold.
Krehbiel, Henry Edward.
Harper's Weekly, Ja 1889,
Vol. 33, P. 70-71.

5627   Wagner, Appia, and the
Idea of Musical Design.
Kernodle, George R.
Educational Theatre
Journal, 1954, Vol. 6, P.
223-30.

5628   Wagner and Scenic Art.
Apthorp, William F.
Scribner's, N 1887, Vol. 2,
P. 515-31.

5629   Wagon Stage (The).
Stevens, Richard. M.F.A.
Thesis, Carnegie Institute
of Technology, 1961.

5630   Walter Hampden's
Production of Cyrano De
Bergerac. Bragdon, Claude.
Architectural Record (The),
D 1923, Vol. 54, P.
553-564.

5631   Wandering Years:
Diaries, 1922-1939 (The).
Beaton, Cecil. Weidenfeld &
Nicholson, 1961.

5632   Wartime Settings in
Planned Economy. Wade,
Robert J. Players
Magazine, Ja 1943, Vol. 19,
No. 4, P. 7.

5633   Wartime Staging. Wade,
Robert F. Theatre Arts
Magazine, Jl 1943, Vol.
XXVII, No. 7, P. 451.

5634   War and Theatrical
Supplies. Rosenthal, Jean.
Players Magazine, Mr 1944,
Vol. 20, No. 6, P. 8.

5635   War Surplus. Adix, Vern.
Educational Theatre
Journal, O 1952, Vol. IV,
No. 2, P. 238.

5636   Washington Square. 13
Water Color, Original
Drawings, 1947. located at
the Harvard Theatre
Collection.

5637   Was There a Medieval
Theatre in the Round.
Schmitt, Natalie Crohn.
Theatre Notebook, 1968-69,
Vol. 23, P. 130-142;
1969-70, Vol. 24, P. 18-25.

5638   Water Effects. Hoult,
Robert L. British
Cinematographer, O 1953,
Vol. 23, P. 86.

5639   Water Soluble Contact
Cement. Gatzke, Larry C.
Theatre Crafts, O 1977,
Vol. 11, No. 5, P. 77.

5640   Ways to Stencil Walls.
Ventrone, Gen. Sampler of
Early American Craft
Projects, the Early
American Society, 1979,
Gettysburg, P. 5-8.

5641   Way in (A). Mezekiel.
Theatre Crafts O 1973.

5642   Weather on the Stage.
Mantle, Burns. Green Book
Album, Ja 1909, Vol. 1, P.
151-156.

5643   Webster College and the
Loretto Hilton Repertory
Two Projects One Building.
Theatre Crafts Ja 1975.

5644   Welding Basics for
Strength and Design
Flexibility. Sealey, D.
Theatre Crafts S 1976.

5645   Welding Engineer's
Handbook. Oates, J.A.
George Newness, Ltd., 1961,
London.

5646   Welding Safety. U.S.
Government Printing Office
Washington, D.C.. No Date.
ISBN: 017-033-00209-6

5647   Westward Look: an
English Designer on
Broadway. Ffolks, David.
Theatre Arts, Ja 1947, Vol.
31, P. 27.

5648   West Side Story: Rumble
Scene. Original Rendering,
1957. located at the
Harvard Theatre Collection.

5649   What Do You
Mean--Rayon?. Scientific
American, My 1929, Vol.
140, P. 476.

5650   What Is "The Scene".
Fitzgerald, Percy. Living
Age, O 1897, Vol. 215, P.
274.

5651   What It Costs to Put on
a Show - and Why. Shubert,
J.J. Theatre Magazine, S
1925, Vol. 42, P. 9, 54.

5652   What Modern Scene
Painters Are Doing for the
Stage. Moses, M. J.
McClure, O 1920, Vol. 52,
P. 22.

5653   What New Scenery?.
Loundsbury, Warren C.
Players, Mr, 1964, Vol. XL,
No. 6, P. 179.

5654   What Price Scenery?.
Macgowan, Kenneth. Theatre
Magazine, Jl 1927, P. 10.

5655   What Shall We Act?.
James, M.E. George Bell &
Sons, 1882, London.

5656   What the New York
Building Code Gives to
Theatres. Isaacs, Edith J.
R. Old West Publishing
Co., 1941, Denver.

5657   Where Conceptual and
Performance Art Meet: Mabou
Mines Creates
Multidimentional Theatre.
Goldman, H. Merton. Theatre
Crafts, Mr/Ap 1978, Vol.
12, No. 3, P. 20.

5658   Where Dream-Worlds
Become Pseudo Realities.
Theatre Magazine (The), F
1910, Vol. XI, No. 108, P.
49.

5659   Where Symbolism Matters:
a Stage Designer Discusses
the Essentials of His Art.
Sharpe, Robert Redington.
Theatre Magazine, Ap, 1931,
P. 30.

5660   Where the Fairies Roost
During the Christmas
Holidays. Sphere, Ja 4,
1913, Vol. 52, P. 30-31.

5661   Whip and Its Mechanism
(The). Scientific American,
Ja 1913, Vol. 108, P. 81,
89, 102.

5662   White Art and the
Automobile Leap at the
Hippodrome. Scientific
American, F 1914, Vol. 110,
P. 181.

5663   Whittington's Dictionary
of Plastics. Whittington,
Lloyd R. Technomic
Publishing Company, 1968,
Stanford, Connecticthut.

5664   Whole Is the Sum of Its
Parts (The). Dewey, Walter
S. Players Magazine, F/Mr,
1973, Vol. 48, No. 3, P.
94.

5665   Who Is Josef Svoboda.
Jindra, Vladimir. Orbis,
1968, Prague.

5666   Who Paints the Scenery?.
Bowers, Faubian. Opera
News, F 8, 1969, Vol. 33,
P. 26-29.

5667   Why New Building
Regulations Are Doomed to
Costly Failure. Allen,
John. ABTT News, Ap 1980,
P. 16. Guardian (The),
Friday, Mr 28, 1980.

5668   Wieland Wagner: the
Positive Sceptic. Skelton,
Geoffrey. St. Martins
Press, 1971, New York.

5669   Wife's Secret: History
of a Victorian Play.
Wilson, M. Glen. Theatre
Studies, 1973-74, No. 20.
P. 9.

5670   Wilfried Minks: the
Influential West German
Designer at Mid-Career.
Riddell, Richard. Theatre
Crafts, Ja/F 1978, Vol. 12,
No. 1, P. 27.

5671   Williamtown: 25 Summers
of Theatre in the
Berkshires. Levi Wallach,
Susan. Theatre Crafts,
My/Je 1980, Vol. 14, No. 3,
P. 17.

5672   William Bloch's the Wild
Duck. Waal, Carla.
Educational Theatre
Journal, D 1978, Vol. 30,
No. 4, P. 495.

5673   William Telbin's
Theories of Scene Painting:
the Aesthetic of Romantic
Realism. Berry, Douglas M.
Theatre Studies, 1974-75,
No. 21, P. 52.

5674   Wimbledon Theatre. Tabs,
Ap 1938, Vol. 1, No. 4, P.
3.

5675   Winged Victory in

Production. Horner, Harry
Aritist. Theatre Arts
Monthly, F 1944, Vol.
XXVIII, No. 2, P. 93.

5676   Wings and Backdrops: the
Story of American Stage
Scenery from The Beginnings
to 1875. Swanson, Wesley.
Drama, O 1927- Ja 1928,
P.5-7, 30, 41-42, 63-64,
78-80, 107, Vol. 18.

5677   Winkies Released (The):
Crafting Foam Heads for
Instant Transformation.
Theatre Crafts, N/d 1978,
Vol. 12, No. 7, P. 27.

5678   Winter and Summer
Theatre on a Limited
Budget. Gunnell, John.
Theatre Arts, My, 1951,
Vol. XXXVI, No. 5, P. 47.

5679   Winter Garden. Metcalfe,
J.S. Life, F 27, 1919,
Vol. 73, P. 330.

5680   Winter Theatres, As
Connected With the Fine
Arts, (The). Annals of the
Fine Arts, 1820, Vol. 4, P.
491-495.

5681   Wireless on Off
Switching. Nuckolls, James
L. Theatre Crafts Mr 1970.

5682   Witchcraft, Magic, and
Alchemy. De Givry, Grillot.
Frederick Publications,
1954, New York.

5683   Witchcraft. Hughes,
Pennethorne. Longmans,
Green & Co., 1952, London.

5684   Wiz Is a Wow Again
(The). MacKay, Patricia.
Theatre Crafts, N/D 1978,
Vol. 12, No. 7, P. 18.

5685   Women Behind Scenes of
Success. Rickards, J.
Times (The), Jl 19, 1967,
P. 7.

5686   Women Who Are Stage

Designers. Von Wien,
Florence. Independent
Woman, My 1946, Vol. 25, P.
134-136.

5687   Wonderful Revolving
Stage at the London
Coliseum, (The).
Illustrated London News, D
24, 1904, Vol. 125, P. 952.

5688   Wonderful Revolving
Stage. Popular Mechanics, F
1905, Vol. 7, P. 224-225.

5689   Wonderful World of the
Theatre (The). Priestley,
J.B. Doubleday & Co., 1969
New York.

5690   Wonder of Our Stage
(The). Waddington, M. and
Barnett, M. Theatre Design
& Technology, Spring 1979,
Vol. XV, No. 1, P. 8.

5691   Wood-Turning Lathe
(The). Haines, Ray E. Van
Nostrand, 1952, New York.

5692   Wood, Student Manual,
Preparation Level. G.P.O.
017-080-01422-0 1.15. No
Date.

5693   Woodburners Encyclopedia
(The). Shelton, Jay W.
Vermont Crossroads Press,
1976, Waitsfield, Vt. LOCN:
Tp324.S5 ISBN:
0-915248-08-5

5694   Woodshop Tool
Maintenance. Cunningham,
Beryl M. and Holtrop,
William F. Charles
Bennett, 1956, Peoria,
Illinois.

5695   Woodwork. Goodman, W.
L. Blackwell, 1962,
Oxford.

5696   Woodworking Technology.
Hammond, James J.
Mcknight, 1961, New York.

5697   Woodworking With
Machines. Douglass, James

H. Mcnight Publishing Co.,
1960, Skyforest,
California.

5698   Wood Energy: a Practical
Guide to Heating With Wood.
Twitchell, Mary. Garden Way
Publishing, 1978,
Charlotte, Vt. ISBN:
0-88266-145-0

5699   Wood Handbook: Wood As
an Engineering Material.
Forest Products Laboratory,
Forest Service, U. S.
Department of Argriculture.
U.S. Government Printing
Office, 1974, Washington,
D. C.

5700   Wood Words. Koetting,
Daniel. Theatre Crafts, O
1978, Vol. 12, No. 6, P.
79-85.

5701   Word to the Wise on
Stage Photography. Bender,
Eric. Players Magazine, D
1942, Vol. 19, No. 3, P.
18.

5702   Working Conditions in
the Theatre, Now & Then.
Tabs, D 1947, Vol. 5, No.
3, P. 8.

5703   Working Drawings from
Three Hundred Broadway
Shows: a Gift from Jo
Mielziner. Glerum, Jay.
Theatre Design &
Technology, Wi 1979, Vol.
XV, No. 4, P. 29-30.

5704   Working Stage Curtain.
Work, Ja 16, 1909, Vol. 36,
P. 396.

5705   Working With Appia. Van
Wyck, Jessica Davis.
Theatre Arts Monthly, D,
1924, Vol. VIII, No. 12, P.
817.

5706   Working With Plexiglas.
Rohm and Hass Company,
1947, Philadelphia,
Pennsylvania.

5707   Working With Wood.
Lawrence, Michael. Crowell,
1979, New York. ISBN:
0-690-01820-7

5708   Work of C. Raymond
Johnson (The). Tietjens,
Eunice. Theatre Arts
Magazine, Jl 1920, Vol. IV,
No. 3, P. 227.

5709   Work of Joseph Urban in
Stage Settings. Green Book
Magazine, F, 1915, Vol. 13,
P. 267.

5710   Work of Joseph Urban in
Stage Settings. Current
Opinion, Jl, 1915, Vol. 59,
P. 103.

5711   Work of Lee Simonson,
Designer. Studio, S, 1933,
Vol. 6, P. 145.

5712   World Behind the Scenes
(The). Fitzgerald, Percy.
Benjamin Blom 1972 New
York. LOCN: Pn2085 F5 1972

5713   World of Flo Ziegfeld
(The). Carter, Randolph.
Praeger Publisher, 1974,
New York and Washington
D.C..

5714   Youngest Among the
Moderns: James Reynolds As
an Artist in Settings and
Costumes. Bishop, John
Peale. Theatre Arts
Magazine, Ja 1921, Vol. V,
No. 1, P. 75.

5715   Youth, Art, and Mr.
Belasco. Peirce, Francis
Lamont. Drama, My 1917,
P. 176-183.

5716   You and the Stage.
Lissim, Simon. Design, N/D
1954, Vol. 56, P. 87.

5717   Ziller Profile. Cue
Technical Theatre Review,
Ja/F 1980, P. 23-25.

5718   1912 - the Stage Picks a
Symbol of Security. Chaney,

Stewart. Interiors, Mr
1945, Vol. 104, P. 76-77.

5719   3000 Years of Drama,
        Acting, and Stagecraft.
        Cheney, Sheldon. Longmann,
        1952, New York.

Subject Index

Research Materials and Collections

Acoustics and Sound

Lighting

Properties

Scenery

Author Index

Arrowsmith, John. 1340
Arts Council of Great Britain.
    5042
Ash, Lee. 65
Ashbery, John. 1682
Ashbolt, Allan. 5173
Ashbrook, Carolyn S. 1367
Ashby, C. 1512
Ashworth, Bradford. 4406
Asteren, Terry. 4591
Aston, Frank. 2225 2674
Aston, Tom A. 2089
Atkinson, Brooks. 5048
Atkinson, Frank H. 4875
    5032
Atkinson, J.A. 2793
Atkinson, Philip. 1101
Ault, Cecil Thomas. 4107
Austin, Mary. 4636
Austin, Roland. 2582
Aveline, Joe. 2735
Averyt, B. 83
Averyt, William Bennet. 1548
Aylward, J. D. 2797
Aysom, Richard Hayden. 4496
Bablet, Denis. 3561 3569
    3570 4019 5560
Babson, Walter B. 4042
Backus, John. 172
Badmaieff, Alexis. 304
Bagal, H. 217
Bagenal, Hope. 205 216
    382 471 476
Bagman, P. Jerald. 1790
Bagwell, Richard. 2601
Bailey, Allan. 1694
Bailey, Anthony. 1683
Bailey, B.L. 5614
Bailey, Ralph Sargent. 1908
    2546
Baily, Albert Lang. 5019
Bake, Geoffrey. 2726
Baker, Barbara. 3259
Baker, Bill. 3893
Baker, Blanch M. 137
Baker, David. 868
Baker, Douglas. 1649
Baker, James W. 1103 3599
Bakkom, J. 4564
Bakkom, James R. 3766
Bakshy, Alexander. 2971
Balance, John. 2873
Balbi, C. M. R. 469
Baldwin, Chris. 2490
Balleisen, Charles E. 2893
Band-Kuzmany, Karin. 62
Band, Edwin H. 1141
Banderbilt, Paul. 66

Bangham, P. Jerald. 2460
    4813
Bangs, Hal Crumpton. 3934
Bangs, J. R. 4661
Baranek. 360
Barazani, Gail Coningsby.
    4806
Barber, Philip. 387 2918
    2093 4653 4888
Barbrow. 707
Barlow, Anthony D. 1505
Barlow, Graham. 5041
Barnes, Djuna. 3882 3930
    4263
Barnes, Ralph M. 4266
Barnett, M. 509 5690
Barney, Charles Gorham. 4363
Barnsley, Alan. 3377
Baron, Robert H. 4559
Barrow, Jack W. 5530
Barsacq, Leon. 675 3247
Barsness, Lawrence. 2186
Bartholomew, Wilmer T. 198
Barton, Margaret. 1212
Barton, Mike Alan. 3027
Bartram, Reg. 418 3395
Bartusek, Antonin. 3262
Barua, D.S. 2759
Baston, Paul. 2778
Batcheller, David R. 311
    758 3461 3957
    5282 5283 5284
Batcheller, Joseph Donald.
    804 866
Bates, Ronald L. 2702
Bates, William. 2995
Battersby, Martin. 3303
Battle, E. 3866
Bauer, Mary V. 2259
Baugh, Christopher. 1632
Baumann, Theresa G. 3968
Baume, Elson. 4099
Baume, Michael. 467
Baun, J.T. 2887 4579
Baur-Heinhold, Marharet. 3156
Baxter, S.S. 577 1698
Bay, Howard. 1858 3471
    4905 4986 5183
Bayles, E.R. 3060
Beagle, T.A. 917
Bean, Arthur Robert. 1533
    2849
Bean, Louis Burke. 598
Bear, B. E. 655 2132
    2328
Beaton, Cecil. 3497 4820
    4961 5631

ABOUT THE AUTHOR

JOHN T, HOWARD, JR., is Assistant Professor of Theatre Studies at Mount Holyoke College in South Hadley, Massachusetts. His articles have appeared in such journals as *Theatre Crafts* and *Theatre Design and Technology*.